I Love the Illusion

The Life and Career of

Agnes Moorehead

by Charles Tranberg

I Love the Illusion
The Life and Career of Agnes Moorehead
© 2007 Charles Tranberg

Published in the USA by:

BearManor Media
PO Box 71426
Albany, GA 31708
www.BearManorMedia.com

Library of Congress Cataloging-in-Publication Data:

Tranberg, Charles.
   I love the illusion : the life and career of Agnes Moorehead / by
Charles Tranberg. -- 2nd ed.
      p. cm.
   Includes bibliographical references and index.
   ISBN 978-1-59393-095-0
   1. Moorehead, Agnes, 1906-1974. 2. Actors--United
States--Biography. I. Title.

   PN2287.M698T73 2007
   791.4302'8'092--dc22
   [B]
                                   2007023093

Printed in the United States.

Design and Layout by Valerie Thompson.

TABLE OF CONTENTS

Introduction & Acknowledgements

I stumbled upon the subject of this book by accident. While visiting the Wisconsin State Historical Society archives in Madison, Wisconsin, doing research on another subject, I discovered that the archives held the papers of Agnes Moorehead — in fact, 159 boxes of papers, scrapbooks, reviews, scripts, and other memorabilia. I almost immediately ordered some boxes to review, and I was hooked. I found the subject of the book I always wanted to write. And a fascinating subject she turned out to be.

Agnes Moorehead had a distinguished career in all medias of show business. She was in vaudeville with Phil Baker and other comics, often getting more laughs than the comics she supported. She became one of the most successful actors in radio and a true star in that medium. It was while working in radio that she met the young Orson Welles and soon joined his innovative and celebrated "Mercury Theatre." But if there is one role on radio she is best known for, it is her Mrs. Elbert Stevenson in "Sorry, Wrong Number," which she performed on the classic series *Suspense*. Her repeated appearances on that show earned her the title "The First Lady of Suspense."

Orson Welles brought her to Hollywood where her first two films are widely considered masterpieces: *Citizen Kane* and *The Magnificent Ambersons*. *Kane* is certainly one of the most influential films ever made and Agnes' five-minute appearance as Kane's mother was enough to convince Hollywood of her talent. She never looked back. Her second film, a mangled masterpiece, and in many ways superior to *Kane*, is her finest film performance. Her Aunt Fanny in *The Magnificent Ambersons* brought her her first Oscar nomination and the New York Film Critics Award. From there, she went on to make almost 60 more films, of varying quality, and ended up with three more Oscar nominations and a Golden Globe Award.

By the early 1950's her real passion as an actress was the stage. With

Charles Laughton, Charles Boyer and Sir Cedric Hardwicke, Agnes helped revolutionize the theatre with the First Drama Quartette's interpretation of *Don Juan in Hell*. By the middle of the decade she was selling out concert halls and college auditoriums doing her own justly acclaimed "one-woman" show. Over the next decade she would mount tours in four other stage shows on behalf of that human dynamo, producer Paul Gregory.

Financial security was always important to Agnes and by the early 1960's she was ready to accept doing a television series, in part because it would offer her a steady paycheck. She had by the mid-50's begun appearing regularly on television in guest shots. Out of the blue came the opportunity to play a witch who objects to her daughter marrying a mortal in a pilot titled *Bewitched*. She accepted the part and filmed the pilot, not expecting it would sell. It did, and how. It became the most popular new series of the 1964–65 season (only the long-running *Bonanza* was higher in the ratings). Agnes was now "stuck" — her words not mine. But the show propelled her from the ranks of well-known and respected character actress to cultural icon as Endora.

Despite all her accomplishments, it is probable that most people know her today as Endora. When friends and strangers asked me who I was doing my book on and I told them "Agnes Moorehead," I mostly got blank stares When I said, "Endora, on *Bewitched*," the blank looks were replaced by ones of instant recognition, *"Oh, yeah!!"*

Without diminishing "Endora," my hope is that this book will show or remind readers that Agnes was one of the most successful and well-known character actresses in show business, and that even if she never essayed the role of Endora, her place in show business history is secure. I also hope to bring out the human side of one of the most private of all Hollywood celebrities. A previous memoir, published shortly after her death by a friend, was titled *A Very Private Person*. Her friend honored her wishes and if you read that memoir you wouldn't know such things as Agnes' true age, that she had two husbands, and a foster child who eventually drifted away from her. According to fellow *Bewitched* actress Kasey Rogers, Agnes would flamboyantly say, "I love the illusion!" It is clear that she wasn't speaking only of the illusion of transforming herself into a character for an acting part, but also the illusion she presented to the public. The persona she wanted to be seen as was that of a glamorous Hollywood star and dedicated actress.

Georgia Johnstone, Agnes' secretary for many years, would state, after

Agnes died, "Agnes had a firm belief that in order to maintain her glamorous image as a star, it was essential to remain aloof." But, in that aloofness, she often showed great dedication and bravery — holding her own in what is often a man's world or profession, and bravery in maintaining a work schedule in the last two years of her life that would tire a healthy person, not to mention a 71-year-old woman battling cancer. But it worked — few people knew of her fight against cancer until the very end — and even then she requested that the reason for her death not be disclosed.

I am very much indebted to the following people for allowing me to interview them for this book: Arthur Anderson, Richard Anderson, William Asher, Quint Benedetti, Conrad Binyon, Himan Brown, Norman Corwin, Gordon Emery, Nanette Fabray, Bernard Fox, Paul Gregory, Dora Guerra, Orland Helgeson, Ted Key, Carol Lynley, James MacArthur, Laurie Main, Karl Malden, Rose Marie, Jeanne Marking, Herbie J Pilato, Elliott Reid, Debbie Reynolds, Kasey Rogers, Larry Russell, Charles Stumpf, William Windom, Jane Wyatt, Jane Wyman, Joey York.

I owe a big debt of gratitude to Derek Tague, who took extensive notes from the Georgia Johnstone collection re: Agnes Moorehead at the New York Public Library, Billy Rose Theatre Collection at Lincoln Center in New York City. Derek has done this kind of research for many other authors and his dedication and competence is well known. Wade Ballard provided most of the photographs which appear in this book — my sincere thanks to him. Julia Devlin is a fellow Agnes Moorehead historian and a huge fan who contributed photographs and her expertise to me. Francine McAsey, an Australian fan of Agnes' that I befriended, sent me some valuable articles. Carl Dickson, my longtime friend, contributed photographs for this book from a trip we took to Reedsburg, Wisconsin — the hometown of Agnes' mother, Mollie.

As a first time author, my gratitude goes out to those who have already published books and gave me their insight and, in many cases, guidance: Lynn Kear, whose book *Agnes Moorehead: A Bio-Bibliography,* is an essential reference book on Agnes' career; Martin Grams, Jr., who generously sent me copies of his books *The History of The Cavalcade of America* and *Suspense: Twenty Years of Thrills and Chills;* and James Robert Parish, whose book, *Good Dames,* contains a marvelous chapter on Agnes. I also must thank Jimmy Bangley, who sadly has passed away since the publication of this book, and Allen Ellenberger. Herbie J Pilato, whose book, *Bewitched Forever,* is the definitive biography of that classic television series. Sandra

Grabman, who published a wonderful book about the actor Albert Salmi, *Spotlights and Shadows,* for her support and advice. Claudia Kuehl, a writer and publisher of Dick York's memoirs, *The Seesaw Girl and Me,* also provided encouragement.

The staffs of the Wisconsin State Historical Society Archives in Madison, Wisconsin, The Billy Rose Library in New York City, The University of Wyoming American Heritage Center Archives in Laramie, Wyoming, The Lilly Library in Bloomington, Indiana, and Betty Lawson and her staff with the American Academy of Dramatic Arts, all deserve a great big Thank You for the important work they provide.

Additionally, I would like to thank Allison Mack, for her friendship and guidance throughout this journey; Melanie Parker and the good folks at the website Harpies Bizarre; Judy Jackson, for her patience and support when I read various chapters to her; my friends at Meriter Hospital for their encouragement; my sister, Deb Tranberg; and my friend, Nancy Markowitz.

Finally, I would like to thank Ben Ohmart and BearManor Media for taking a chance on a first time writer and the support they have given me. They are a fine publishing house and I'm proud to be associated with them.

CHARLES TRANBERG
MADISON, WISCONSIN
JANUARY 2005

1

RELIGION SOFTENS THE EDGES

Agnes was more than tired — she was exhausted. It was so unlike her. For years she had traveled the country with her justly acclaimed one-woman show, traveling from town to town for weeks, even months, only to come out of the experience rejuvenated in body and spirit. But now she couldn't shake her weariness.

Part of the weariness wasn't physical but mental. She had a genuine concern that her latest Broadway show, *Gigi*, wasn't up to par. Her own reviews were as good as ever; *The Nation* praised her performance as Aunt Alicia by stating that her "expertise gives her poise." But the show itself was described as, " . . . a gorgeous flower without fragrance." The New York critics seemed equally unimpressed. But it was more than the show that was bothering her and deep down she realized it. She was increasingly in pain. Not only from her worsening arthritis, but a pain she felt in the pit of her stomach and the stiffness she had in her neck and upper back, yet nothing, not even the pain drugs injected into her system by a sympathetic nurse/traveling companion relieved the pain for very long.

Gigi opened at the Uris Theatre in New York City on November 13, 1973. Prior to the New York opening Agnes had toured twenty-five weeks across country. That should have been nothing for her since she loved touring and was used to the rigors of taking a show on the road. But now as she was approaching her seventy-third birthday — perhaps she thought she was finally feeling her age. Perhaps she was feeling that the cross-country tour had been a mistake. Why hadn't they just previewed the show in a few select cities to work the bugs out — Boston, Pittsburgh and then on to New York? The most taxing part of the tour had come in her hometown of St. Louis where the cast performed outdoors in pouring rain. Agnes was a trouper, but the two hours in the rain did her arthritis no good.

Agnes as Aunt Alicia in *Gigi* (1973), with Maria Karnilova. This was Agnes' last stage role.

Gigi was her second theatrical production in two years. In 1972 she had toured in a revival of *Don Juan in Hell*, the very same show that had revolutionized the theatre with Charles Laughton, Charles Boyer, Sir Cedric Hardwicke and Agnes in the 1950's. Most of 1973 had been devoted to *Gigi*. She needed to work to help maintain the lifestyle she had become accustomed to as one of the most celebrated character stars in the industry. She was supporting a home in Beverly Hills, a farm in Ohio and her elderly mother in Wisconsin. She had a devoted staff whose salaries she was responsible for. She was building her dream house on the property in Ohio which had been in her family for 140 years. Yet, the residuals she was receiving for *Bewitched* and an occasional television or movie role, along with some select appearances in her one-woman show, should have been enough to keep her and her dependents financially solvent. The truth is that she needed to work to feel alive and challenged — and there is no greater challenge than taking a play to Broadway.

(Courtesy of Wade Ballard)

She was not the first choice to play Aunt Alicia. This was a pivotal role and the producers were looking for an actress who was "old enough to have Alicia's authority and yet glamorous enough to be believable as an aging courtesan." Some of the aging actresses considered "still saw themselves as younger leading women," no doubt ready to compete with young Karin Wolfe, who had the title role, for the attentions of her young suitor Gaston. Edwin Lester wrote to Agnes earlier in the year: "Our situation has not changed . . . I am in the unusual position of having a lot of people to please besides myself. Were I operating as I normally do, I would be busy wooing you to play Alicia in *Gigi*. At this point none of us are in agreement about anybody . . . You are still my first choice and I hope that if my associates come my way, you will still be available and interested." The producers finally, sensibly, approached Agnes.

The cast chosen to play with her was stellar. Along with Karin Wolfe, producers Arnold Saint-Subber and Edwin Lester had selected the venerable Broadway veteran Alfred Drake to play Honor Lachailles (the same role Maurice Chevalier had played in the famous 1958 film). Daniel Massey was cast as the romantic lead — Gaston Lachailles, Maria Karnilova as Inez Alvarez and Sandahl Bergman as Liane d'Exelmans. The cast was gathered when Agnes made her first rehearsal appearance:

". . . The principles are gathered, all but Miss Moorehead, who has been at Western Costume Company for fittings and will be making her first rehearsal appearance today. She enters. Acknowledges introductions cooly and sits down, her mind seemingly a thousand miles away. A few of the others wonder . . . is this lady not going to try to have fun in the show? That mystery is quickly settled. In a quick run through of both acts, she knows the whole script virtually cold and does a real Agnes Moorehead number with her lines: potato chip of the mouth, nostrils dilated with offended good taste, one eyebrow level with disdain, the other semi-circular with disbelief. She spits out Alicia's words as if they are objects of disgust. At the end the others burst into spontaneous applause for Miss Moorehead's rehearsal debut. Not to worry."

As always, she was a professional, and an example to the younger players.

Prior to leaving on tour, she had hip surgery. The procedure went well and her mobility was not affected in any noticeable way. She was recovering nicely, but her arthritis, along with being in a production which required thirteen set changes twenty-six times in the course of each performance, exasperated the pain. But she didn't grumble. To be a pro means to live with life's little difficulties and not advertise them. To a close friend, such as Cesar Romero, Agnes could let her guard down just a little. He asked her how she felt. "I'm tired into the future," was the surprising reply he received from his usually indefatigable friend.

Agnes was relieved to be in New York. She was staying in the comfortable and spacious Manhattan apartment of her good friend, Mary Roebling, the wealthy head of the Trenton Trust Company. Furthermore, another good friend, Debbie Reynolds, was also in New York appearing in *Irene*. Reynolds picked Agnes up at the Uris Theatre every Sunday after a matinee and together they would go to Debbie's townhouse for dinner. While Debbie would prepare a full-course meal, she noticed that Agnes would only eat mashed potatoes. When Debbie asked her why, Agnes would reveal nothing more than she had an upset stomach. Yet Debbie never fully suspected just how ill she was because Agnes continued to eat her favorite chocolates with great ferocity.

The holidays were always Agnes' favorite time of the year. For the second year in a row she would not be hosting her elegant and well-attended combination birthday and Christmas party at her home in Beverly Hills. Her holiday party was always one of the Hollywood community's perennial events and usually the lead off to the holiday season. She missed it. Instead Christmas, 1973 — her last — she took the train to the Trenton, New Jersey home of Mary Roebling and spent the day with Miss Roebling's family. Mary was concerned by how tired her friend was and how weak she appeared. Miss Roebling's grandchildren were visiting and no matter how weak Agnes was she put considerable energy toward entertaining the children. The children were fans of *Bewitched* and to their young minds she was Endora and they pleaded with her to perform magic as she did on the show. "I left my magic at home," she apologetically told them. But in true Moorehead style she won the children over and they ended up embracing her. At Christmas dinner Agnes ate little and retired early.

Her family farm in Ohio was cared for by a family named the Stovers. They were dedicated to Agnes and always looked forward to her visits. She usually visited three to four times per year or as her schedule allowed. While Agnes was in New York, Christmas packages from famous friends and fans were constantly delivered to the farm. Margery Stover asked Agnes what she wanted done with the packages. Agnes told her to keep them unopened until she was able to come herself. She loved opening up Christmas packages — with care — no tearing them open for her. She savored the moment.

As usual at the holidays, Agnes sent out and received many Christmas cards and letters. Telegrams came wishing her a "Merry Christmas and a Happy New Year." One greeting Agnes neither sent nor received was from her now twenty-four-year-old foster son, Sean. The divisions and hurt between the two were so great that even a Christmas greeting was sacrificed.

On New Year's Eve Agnes and Debbie Reynolds hosted a combined party for the cast and crews of *Gigi* and *Irene*. Debbie remembers the evening as "great fun" and Agnes having a "grand time." It would be the last party Agnes would ever attend. Shortly after the New Year, Debbie left the cast of *Irene* and returned to California where she stayed at Agnes' Beverly Hills home due to stress in her marriage to shoe tycoon, Harry Karl. Agnes felt for her friend, despite her fondness for Harry Karl, because it was clear that Debbie was under great stress. Debbie, for her part, was concerned about Agnes' health. Most of all Agnes was sad that Debbie was leaving New York.

Another old friend of Agnes' came to New York in early January. Paul Gregory was responsible (along with Charles Laughton) for *Don Juan in Hell* and later produced such Moorehead plays as *The Rivalry* and *Lord Pengo*. Gregory arranged to have dinner with Agnes at "21," her favorite restaurant in Manhattan. The evening was pleasant, but a bit subdued. Agnes, as always, enjoyed seeing her friend. Gregory noticed, too, how little Agnes ate. After dinner, Agnes suggested to Gregory that they take a stroll up Fifth Avenue rather than take a cab. It was a chilly evening and the request struck him as odd. Agnes needed to tell him something and it was best said in the open rather than inside a cab. As they strolled up Fifth Avenue, Agnes turned to Gregory and said, "Paul, I'm never going to see you again." Gregory asked what was wrong. Agnes shook her head indicating she didn't know. Gregory told her she had to live each day for itself and not worry about the future. He asked if she was in much pain. "Religion softens the edges," was Agnes' reply. As it turned out, Agnes was correct, she never did see Paul Gregory again.

A few days later, Debbie Reynolds received a call from a mutual friend, set designer Jerry Wunderlich. He called to say that he had just taken Agnes to the train station. She was leaving *Gigi* and going to the Mayo Clinic in Rochester, Minnesota for tests. Debbie told Wunderlich that maybe she should go and be with Agnes. "No, she didn't even want me to tell you," Wunderlich said.

Agnes made this last lonely journey alone.

2

"WHO ARE YOU TODAY, AGNES?"

Agnes Moorehead had a happy childhood. She never felt unloved or unwanted. She was never brought up to believe that children were to be "seen and not heard." She was blessed with two parents she adored, and, in the case of her father, idolized.

Agnes Robertson Moorehead was born on December 6, 1900. This is one detail she never alluded to. Like many actors of her era (and still true today) she "fudged" on her age. Agnes' friend and publicist, Peter Opp, Jr., was told Agnes' real age by her mother. "Mrs. John once told me A's correct age at a birthday party Madame held in Cheviot Hills. 'I don't know *why* Agnes twists the truth,' she said. Aye, pretzel has less twists than our departed friend possessed." She told the Academy of Dramatic Arts on her application that she was born in 1903. For many years her "official" birth year was 1906. When she died in 1974, every obituary listed her age as 67, rather than the 73 years she actually was.

Her father, John Henderson Moorehead, of Scottish descent, was born in December 1870, in Rich Hill Township, a part of Muskingum County in Southern Ohio where the Moorehead family farmed. Agnes' paternal grandparents were Hannah Maria Humphrey, born in 1841, and Robert H. Moorehead, born in 1839. Her Grandmother Hannah would live in Rich Hill Township all of her long life (she would die in 1927 at the age of 86 — well over the life expectancy of that time), and Agnes became especially close to her.

Her mother, Mary Mildred McCauley, born in Pittsburgh, Pennsylvania in 1883, and of Irish stock, was a vivacious girl who had a strong interest in music and dreamed of becoming an opera singer. She was talented enough to tour on the Chautauqua circuit. Her friends and family called her by her nickname, Mollie, which she went by all of her life. It was while

Mollie was studying voice at the Cincinnati Conservatory of Music in 1898 that she met John H. Moorehead, then a seminary student in nearby Xenia. Much to Mollie's parent's consternation, the two fell in love and made plans to marry. It wasn't that Mollie's parents didn't think that John Moorehead was a good and able man, who could provide a good home for their daughter, but they hesitated because he was nearly twice her age — 28 to her 15. After some prodding her parents gave in and John and Mollie were married on August 30, 1899, five days after Mollie's sixteenth birthday.

The couple soon left Ohio for Clinton, Massachusetts, some twenty miles to the west of Boston, where John was assigned his first parish. The choice to pursue the ministry was not a surprising one for John Moorehead to make, but early on he was conflicted between the ministry and an interest in archaeology. In the Moorehead family were two illustrious uncles, one a famous Bible scholar and the other a leading archaeologist. John's great-uncle, William Gallogly Moorehead, was a noted Bible scholar and prominent Presbyterian minister. Dr. W.G. Moorehead had been an editor of the *Scofield Reference Bible*. He was well-respected for the many papers he published on bible study including, "Outlines in Studies in the Old Testament," "Studies in the Mosaic Institutions," and "Studies in the Four Gospels." He also served as Professor of New Testament Language and Literature at Xenia Theological Seminary, as well as serving as president of the faculty.

No less impressive was another uncle, Warren King Moorehead, a noted archaeologist, who became known as the "Dean of American Archaeology." Warren Moorehead had spent three years studying under Dr. Thomas Wilson, the curator of prehistoric anthropology at the Smithsonian Institute. He was a member of the field staff at the Chicago World's Fair of 1883. He served as the first curator of the Ohio Historical Society and director of the Robert S. Peabody Museum of Archaeology at Philips Academy in Andover. He would later gain great acclaim for his excavations in and around Cahokia. The Cahokia Mounds Historical Site is the largest prehistoric mound center in North America covering fourteen square kilometers in Illinois. Young John Moorehead was always fascinated by the stories his Uncle Warren told and as a young boy dreamed of accompanying him on some excavation in a far off place.

John Moorehead's own father, Robert, was a farmer who worked the land on the family farm which had been deeded to the Moorehead family by two presidents: James Monroe and John Tyler. There was no man John

Moorehead admired more than his own father and his father believed that his son had the makings of a pastor. That decided the issue. John Moorehead attended Xenia Seminary at the time his Uncle William was a professor and president of the faculty. He felt overshadowed, but was remembered by his contemporaries as a serious young man and excellent student. John Moorehead, like his father and great-uncle, believed that the Bible should be taken literally. He became, in every way, a Scottish Presbyterian fundamentalist clergyman.

By the time he and Mollie arrived in Clinton, Massachusetts to begin work at his first parsonage, John Moorehead felt prepared both by education and life experience for his duties. John and Mollie impressed the community with their commitment and teamwork. John preached and offered spiritual guidance. Mollie, in addition to her role as choir director, also served as Sunday school teacher. "She was a tremendous teacher and youth leader," Gordon Emery would recall of Mollie, who also served in that capacity years later when she moved to Reedsburg, Wisconsin following the sudden death of her husband. Parishioners must have been struck by the contrast in their personalities. John was studious, reserved and low-key except when at the pulpit. At the pulpit John Moorehead was a spellbinder who could hold the congregation in the palm of his hand. Agnes would recall her father as a "great man with a magnificent voice and very handsome . . . he could quote great swatches from the Bible — and Shakespeare . . . he was quite a showman."

Dr. Moorehead always put his sermons on one 3x5 file card. He felt that if he wrote out the sermon from start to finish that he would "drive himself nuts" trying to stay on message. The only thing he might write out was a quotation, but otherwise he would only write cue words. The bottom line for John was that he had better know what he was talking about or else the parishioners would lose confidence in him.

Mollie was louder, opinionated and had a flair for dramatics. Tom Groeneweg, who later got to know the widowed and elderly Mollie, described her as "an imposing lady of strong opinions and very outspoken. In many respects, I had great admiration for her and held her in high esteem. However, like many fundamentalists . . . she on occasion (could) demonstrate a lack of sensitivity and love for others . . . despite some deep flaws . . . her life for the most part was lived for the glory of God."

Both John and Mollie were gracious and good-humored and became very popular in the community. Mollie's musical abilities were so admired that she was invited to give concerts away from church. Shortly after settling into the parsonage Mollie discovered she was pregnant. Mollie's pregnancy didn't stop her from carrying out her duties and when the blue-eyed, red-haired Agnes was born the baby was always with her mother in church, choir practices and Sunday school classrooms. Within a couple of years another baby girl, Margaret, named after John's paternal grandmother, blessed the Moorehead home.

It was shortly after Margaret was born that John was assigned to a new parish in Hamilton, Ohio. While John and Mollie would miss the many friends they made in Clinton, both were excited to be closer to family. It was while living in Hamilton that young Agnes made her first public appearance as a performer. She sang the hymn "The Lord is My Shepherd" as a soloist in church with her proud mother accompanying her on the organ. The congregation was captivated by the young girl and many would ask little Agnes, "Well, what will you sing for us today?" when they came into contact with her. For Agnes this was an introduction to a love of the limelight and the recognition which came with it. For such a intensely private person, she greatly enjoyed being recognized. Another love which lasted a lifetime was her love for the state of Ohio, in particular the southeastern portion of the state. She and Margaret spent summers at the Moorehead farm in the Muskingum Valley, a farm and life Agnes grew to love and appreciate.

The Muskingum Valley is a picturesque portion of southeastern Ohio. Nearly everything in the area at that time was dominated by the Muskingum River. This part of Ohio was always among the most economically depressed in the state, the major reason being the annual flooding which took place before the dams and locks were built. The flooding left population levels down and businesses out, but it also helped to bind the people in the region together. They could depend on one another for refuge and friendship. This sense of community deeply affected Agnes. Throughout her life Agnes would return to the Muskingum Valley and keep the family farm and build onto it. She would continually decline lucrative offers from strip-mining operators who wanted to buy the land — at a considerable profit to Agnes. Even after her death she would make sure the family farm, and the land surrounding it, remained safe from developers.

While growing up Agnes and Margaret would be teased by other kids because they were PK (preacher's kids). They spent a lot of time in church attending services and prayer meetings and helping their parents out. Agnes, who had an active imagination, began to mimic the congregation. "My sister and I used to come to the Sunday table filled with deviltry," Agnes recalled years later. "We loved to give impressions of peculiar people we'd picked on in church. It was a kind of silent game we played with father. I'd settle fussily into my chair and with a simpering look ask sister to pass the potatoes. She'd pass them, with much ado and self-consciousness. We'd keep it up — always with one eye on father. He'd know darn well that we were imitating the lady who led the choir with the young man who handed out the hymn books, but he'd sit there with a perfectly solemn face as if nothing unusual were going on at all. We'd get all the applause we needed from the look of amused recognition he couldn't keep out of his eyes, but pretty soon after that we'd also get a look that said act was over — and it always was."

While they were brought up in a home full of love, music, books and religion, Agnes and Margaret, like all children, got into mischief. When it came to discipline, her father's favorite method would be to sit the girls up on a shelf of books and give them a psalm to memorize which they would later have to recite back to him by memory. Agnes would later consider this the primary reason why she was a quick study at memorizing scripts and other material she would eventually use in her one-woman shows. To memorize a psalm Agnes would write it out in longhand and then read it over and over until it stuck. She would later learn her lines in a similar fashion — writing them out in longhand and studying them. When it came to discipline, however, her mother was less imaginative. Agnes would recall that Mollie's "tiny hand could smart."

Agnes developed a headstrong, lively personality and a sharp wit which reminded many people of Mollie, and, in fact, Agnes and Mollie would be remembered for being very similar in attitudes and behavior. Margaret was more like her father, low-key and shy. Agnes loved her mother, but idolized her father. He was the most important man in her life, probably the only one she really truly loved. She later had great affection for Orson Welles, Charles Laughton and Paul Gregory, but when it came to a deep and abiding love, John Henderson Moorehead had no rival — not even from the two men Agnes eventually married. In interview after interview throughout her life, Agnes would describe her father as: "great," "brilliant," "amazing," "spellbinding," "inspirational," and so on. In later years when asked about her childhood Agnes would always describe it as "very happy" and then invariably relate some anecdote related to her "wonderful and supportive" father.

Agnes was a voracious reader as a child and would continue to be throughout her life. As a youngster she was brought up on fairy tales. She enjoyed Mother Goose, but loved Grimm. Unlike many other children she didn't get frightened when she read Grimm Fairy Tales. She got caught up in the adventures without the side effects of nightmares. Agnes lost herself in the stories and could spend hours sitting alone reading and then, afterward, would spend hours acting out what she read. She would be in a fantasy world of her own and her best friend was her imagination. Her great joys as an adult were the same as a child — reading a good story and then acting it out — except as an adult she would be on a far larger stage than the one in her bedroom. The Mooreheads had a set of china with designs inspired from Charles Dickens stories and were used only on special occasions such as birthdays or holidays. But when they were used, "each person at the table was always required to weave a story about his or her plate."

Mollie once found Agnes huddled in a corner of her bedroom crying and shivering with a sweater on, despite it being a warm day.

"What's the matter?" a concerned Mollie asked.

"Nothing!" responded the still crying and shivering Agnes.

"Are you cold?"

"No"

"Unhappy?"

"No," Agnes replied through the tears streaming down her cheeks.

What Mollie found out later was that Agnes had just read *The Poor Little Match Girl* and was pretending that she too was alone, cold and hungry. Agnes continued to let her imagination rule her life. She would pretend to be a character out of a book, mimic a member of her father's congregation, or would just study the way a person walked and copy it. These things became such a common occurrence that Mollie began to ask Agnes, with an understanding smile on her face, "Who are you today, Agnes?"

II

The Mooreheads spent seven years living in Hamilton, six for Agnes since she developed whooping cough and the family doctor advised John and Mollie to send Agnes to a dry climate. She ended up spending a year with an aunt in Denver. Hamilton was perfect for the family since it was close to the Moorehead family farm and John's parents. Agnes became especially close to her Grandmother Moorehead. Agnes recalled that Grandma Hannah "taught me everything about the house — how to cook, make beds, everything — my sister and I used to make up all kinds of things in the kitchen." But Grandma Hannah also tried to steer Agnes away from her ambition to be an actress. She felt that such dreams were impractical and better for Agnes to concentrate on learning how to sew and keep house and find a husband to take care of her.

Agnes was also close to her maternal grandfather. He was a very religious man and used to speak to Agnes about God and the gospel. One Sunday afternoon it appeared he was asleep in the big comfortable easychair he often sat in when telling Agnes stories from the Bible. Agnes went up, as she sometimes did when he fell asleep in the chair, and tapped him on the shoulder. However, this time he didn't wake up. He was dead. Agnes would recall that she cried for days. Years later, as a struggling actress in New York City, she wasn't working and one night she was very lonely when a friend invited her to a party. "It will be a real wild party, why don't you come." Not having anything else to do, and to quench her loneliness, Agnes decided to accept the invitation. At the party she was shocked to find people drinking, in an age of prohibition, couples making out, and people so drunk they were passed out under tables. Agnes didn't consider herself a prude, but the scene was upsetting to her in large part due to her religious upbringing and beliefs. But she wanted to make friends and feel like she was one of the crowd, so she was about to begin to mingle when she heard a voice whispering in her ear, "Get up and leave, girl. Don't be afraid of offending anyone. They're not worth your friendship." She looked around and saw nobody. But the voice was as clear and distinct as could be. She decided to leave and, once outdoors, it occurred to her — the voice she heard so distinctly telling her to leave was that of her beloved grandfather. He was still looking out for her, she felt, from beyond the grave.

In 1912 John relocated to the First Presbyterian Church in St. Louis. To move from the security of friends and family in Ohio to the big city of St. Louis was not an easy one for Agnes. She later recalled crying herself to sleep the first two weeks after the family arrived. By 1912 St. Louis was one of the largest cities in the country with a metro area in excess of 500,000 and, due to its proximity to the Mississippi River, was a major port city. St. Louis had hosted the World's Fair only a few years earlier and, the same year the Mooreheads arrived, hosted the 1912 National Democratic

Convention, which nominated Woodrow Wilson, himself a son of a Scottish Presbyterian minister. The Mooreheads moved into a modest house located at 4531 McPherson Avenue.

The summer after her arrival, when she was twelve, Agnes tried out for the St. Louis Municipal Ballet. With her long legs and red hair tied tightly in a bun, Agnes tried to make it appear that she was older than she actually was, already assuming a role she would often essay on screen. She was chosen to perform in the ballet and, due to her fine soprano voice, in the choir. But she needed her father's permission, and was apprehensive about approaching him. To her great relief, he seemed genuinely pleased. "Well, isn't that wonderful? My little girl is good enough to make the ballet — why certainly you have my permission." But it came with the condition that she not neglect her education. Why was Dr. Moorehead such an easy touch in allowing Agnes to perform in a business many in that period thought was full of sin? Agnes believed her father was a frustrated showman in his own right and that it was "only a step from the pulpit to the stage."

Agnes later related that she was "always interested in theatre . . . it was always a goal, an ambition, a desire, to enter the theatre; I never had to find myself, the way so many people do. I always knew what I wanted and where I wanted to go. I had to go to school in the wintertime, of course, but even there I always managed to get involved in producing or directing or appearing in drama — not only drama, but anything being offered that involved a stage. Public speaking, oratory — all of it. I never had anything else in mind. So I can't say that there was a time when I made up my mind to be an actress; the determination was there from the very start."

Over the next four summers she performed with the Opera Company, as well as handling props and running errands for the other actors in exchange for acting advice. "I think my first professional appearance was in St. Louis as a Nubian slave in *Aida*. And I appeared in all the musical comedies — *Rio Rita*, the whole run of operettas so popular then, including Gilbert and Sullivan. We did a new show every week for years — Herbert, Friml, Lehar, etc." The experience with the Municipal Ballet only increased her determination of making a career out of acting, but she also had promised her father she would get a quality education to fall back on. When Agnes graduated from Central High School in 1919 she was ready to keep her end of the bargain by attending Muskingum College, a denominational (Presbyterian) school which one of her uncles had helped found, located in New Concord, Ohio; her major was Biology.

(Photo by Carl Dickson)

The church in Reedsburg, Wisconsin, where Agnes' father officiated from 1919–1924.

The same year Agnes enrolled at Muskingum, John, Mollie and Margaret packed up and moved to a new parish located in beautiful Reedsburg, Wisconsin. Its population only numbered a couple of thousand and was located about an hour east of the state capitol in Madison. The move from such a large city to a small town took some adjusting. But Mollie, in particular, took to Reedsburg and made many friends there, including Miss Grace Conkling, who became a lifelong friend; when the widowed Mollie returned to Reedsburg years later, the two friends moved in together to keep each other company. Agnes enjoyed visiting during her vacations from Muskingum, and off and on for the rest of her life, Agnes would often visit Reedsburg.

Agnes took to college life with gusto. She became involved with the Glee Club and the Girls Athletic Association — where she excelled at horseback riding, tennis and archery. She performed in such school plays as *The Aristocrat* in her junior year and the historical drama, Friend Hannah in her senior year. But the most fun she had was helping to write and perform in a revue titled *Kolossal Kampus Kapers* or, regrettably, KKK for short. She would later recall that she both shocked and delighted the audience by doing a spoof of a bump-and-grind routine which was routinely "banned in Boston." The dance won her a visit to the Dean's office. One of her professors, Charles R. Layton, would recall Agnes as a "popular campus personality . . . who could get away with things others couldn't," apparently due to her vivacious personality. While she enjoyed the campus social activities she didn't allow fun to interfere with her education and neglect her studies.

Up until she attended Muskingum, Agnes never went on a date without a chaperon, but this didn't bother her. She would later remember that this was a simpler time and that young people appreciated their elders more than the young people of the 60's and 70's did. "I never had a date by myself until I was in college. I was always chaperoned. There were parties, dances, and great sleigh rides but always there were older people with us, but not hampering us. Oh, we had a great time."

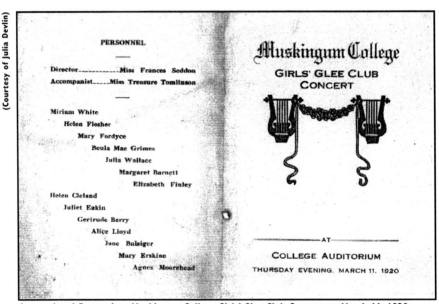

Agnes played Romeo in a Muskingum College Girls' Glee Club Concert on March 11, 1920.

While at Muskingum, Agnes read many brochures on acting schools and decided that she most wanted to attend the prestigious American Academy of Dramatic Arts (AADA) located in New York City. She wanted to attend this school not only for its fine reputation, many top stage actors came out of the AADA, but because they used actual Broadway directors to stage their shows, something she felt was a great way to make contacts in the theatre. But to attend such a prestigious institution took a good deal of money for those days — money she didn't have and that her parents couldn't afford on a pastor's salary. She knew she would have to earn the money herself.

Program

PART I

DRAMATIC BALLAD

The Lady of Shalott........................Bendall
Soprano Soloist, Juliet Eakin
Glee Club

Tone Poem—Song of the Sea.........Ware
Treasure Tomlinson

SONGS IN COSTUME

The Land of the Sky-Blue Water...Cadman
Beula Mae Grimes
The Jap Doll........................Gaynor
Mary Erskine
Duet—The Four-Leaf Clover.........Long
Elizabeth Finley, Helen Flesher

Cahouca—Caprice.............Joachim Raff
Treasure Tomlinson

Intermission

PART II

ROMEO AND JULIET
A Farce

DRAMATIS PERSONAE

Heads of Hostile Houses—
Montague.................Mary Erskine
Capulet.............Margaret Barnett

Romeo, son to Montague...Agnes Moorehead

Tybalt, nephew to Lady Capulet.......
....................Gertrude Berry

Lady Capulet, wife to Capulet..........
....................Mary Fordyce

Juliet, daughter to Capulet...Miriam White

Nurse to Juliet.............Jane Baisiger

Cast credits from Glee Club Concert program (inside).

Upon graduating from Muskingum in 1923, Agnes joined her family in Wisconsin. She attended the University of Wisconsin in Madison, working on her Masters in English and Speech. To earn the money she would need, not only for her living expenses but to put toward her goal of attending the AADA, she took on the job of school teacher at Centralized High School in tiny Soldiers Grove, Wisconsin, where she taught English, Speech and Ancient History. Agnes would look back on her years in Soldiers Grove with great affection and in many respects always considered herself a teacher as well as an actress. After she was established in Hollywood, she would become popular in the acting community for tutoring actors for roles; an example of this would be her stint as unofficial dialogue coach for Jeffrey Hunter, playing Christ, in the film *King of Kings* in 1961. She would also spend many years operating an acting school.

Agnes spent the next five years in Soldiers Grove and became very popular with the students and community. One student, Orland Helgeson, recalls Agnes as "nice and nice looking, but I didn't fully appreciate her because I was interested in other subjects at the time." He also recalled Agnes as having "a smile for her students — she was a good teacher and could be strict at times especially regarding manners." Agnes also coached the debate team to many championships, as well as directing school plays.

One such play was *Peter Pan* which, according to local historian John Sime, had begun as the senior class play, but, by the time Agnes had finished, she had involved practically the entire school, but "it was very well-done and received."

Agnes maintained fond memories of her teaching days throughout her life. "That was a heart-warming experience," she would recall, "being among those kindly Scandinavian people in that little Kickapoo valley community. Everyone was so kind to me, and I had great luck preparing my youngsters for the oratorical contests with other schools. We won time after time, and Soldiers Grove went right to the top."

As a teacher Agnes considered herself a role model for her young students and tried to instill in them the values of good citizenship and hard work. "I feel strong about them that to compromise any one of them would be, for me, an act of hypocrisy. As a teacher, who is not true to his or her own values, is not a teacher at all." In the turbulent 60's and 70's, Agnes would become quite outspoken about what she perceived as a lack of manners and respect among the young people of the day. She often longed for these earlier days.

She could have continued teaching had she wanted to. But she had not forgotten her true ambition — the stage. She was able to indulge herself by directing class plays and performing in stock during summers, but to become a legitimate stage actress would mean taking the major step and move to New York City. In the summer of 1926 she left the security of Soldiers Grove and traveled by train to New York City, where an audition was arranged for her at the American Academy of Dramatic Arts. It was now or never.

3

"There Goes the Straightest Back I've Ever Seen"

On August 14, 1926, Agnes Moorehead auditioned before Charles Jehlinger, the well-respected Director of Instruction at the American Academy of Dramatic Arts (AADA). She shaved two years off her age, according to her audition report; she said she was 23, rather than the 25 years she actually was. Her height is listed as 5'4"; weight, 116, and hair coloring is described as "brunette." The report rated Agnes in the following categories:

Proportions:	Good
Physical Condition:	Good
Personality:	Good
Stage Presence:	Good
Birthplace:	Mass.
Nationality:	Irish-Scotch-English
General Education:	B.A. Muskingum College – Post Grad. Univ. of Wisconsin.
Occupation:	Teacher of Eng. and math – High School
Stage Experience:	Amateur
Voice:	Good (somewhat nasal)
Pronunciation:	Midwest R
Memory:	(this was left blank)
Reading:	Very intelligent
Spontaneity:	Good
Versatility:	(also left blank)
Characterization:	Good

DISTINCTION:	(BLANK)
PANTOMIME:	GOOD
DRAMATIC INSTINCT:	YES
TEMPERAMENT:	MENTAL-NERVOUS-VITAL
INTELLIGENCE:	KEEN
IMITATION:	(BLANK)
RECITATION:	"ITALIAN DIALECT RECITATION" — "QUALITY OF MERCY" — "BARBARA"
IMAGINATION:	GOOD

Summing up her audition, Jehlinger wrote: "Individuality and promise of a positive personality. Has promise. Acceptable." Jehlinger was skeptical that with Agnes' already formidable background in stock, along with her extensive education, additional training was needed. He advised her to go out and audition for acting jobs. Agnes took in what Jehlinger told her and began to sob, "'Oh, I can't stand it, I'm not very good.' Tears began rolling down my cheeks, and he said, 'Well, if that's the way you feel, we'd love to have you, but you don't have to have us.'"

The AADA was founded in 1884 and was the first conservatory of its kind dedicated to the training of professional actors. Among its distinguished alumni were Spencer Tracy, Edward G. Robinson, Hume Cronyn, Walter Abel, and Betty Field, and, in the years following, included Kirk Douglas, Lauren Bacall, Elizabeth Montgomery and Lee Remick.

Lawrence Langner, for many years the head of the Theatre Guild, was once asked by an English producer, "Why is it that you have so many magnificent American actors and actresses who are trained both for dramatic and comedy roles and are able to play emotional scenes without the inhibitions which plague our English actors?" Langner replied that it was largely due to the existence of the American Academy of Dramatic Arts, "which, under the artistic direction of Charles Jehlinger, had developed a native method of teaching which particularly fits the actor for playing naturalistic, emotional roles."

"The Jehlinger Method," according to Langner, stressed "the exercise of the imagination," and his teaching method, above all, was aimed at "spontaneity of action and reaction on the part of the actor." Jehlinger, himself, explained, "If I were to be asked to state the most important contribution you can supply, you the student, it is listening. Hearing is simply making use of the ear. We listen with our minds. Hearing is merely sound. It penetrates the ears; in one and out the other usually. Listening, however, reaches the intellect and enriches the understanding and comprehension. In all my experiences I have not discovered anything that is so productive of intelligence as listening." The Jehlinger Method stressed "concentration, relaxation and follow through."

Agnes was accepted into the class of 1929 along with another would-be teacher with dreams of being an actress: Rosalind Russell. In fact, Russell had a five-year plan. "I'd serve my apprenticeship, play bit parts, maids, whatever I could latch on to, and try to work my way up, but if I hadn't made good in five years, I'd go back to the idea of teaching." Russell also recalled Jehlinger. "We referred to him as Jelly — who managed to communicate both method and magic to his students." Of the academy, Russell would sum up her two years positively. "I know some actors sneer at dramatic schools, say they're nonsense, but I feel a school gives you the kind of confidence it would take you years to acquire anywhere else."

Agnes recalled that the Academy taught her a great deal about technique but because she was older and more experienced than many of her fellow classmates she had a better understanding of many other aspects of acting. "I was more mature and I had the valid experiences of a university to help me. I was able to cope better with whatever I had to learn. For instance, I could understand my scripts better. I knew what to expect. I understood the purposes and intents of writers and so on. I wasn't just pulling things out of the air which a lot of actors and actresses do when their minds haven't been trained. Everything I worked with in college I've used in the theater."

While she attended the AADA, Agnes also took courses at Columbia University which she attended to get her PhD in Speech. She had a roommate while attending the AADA to help cut down on expenses. Her roommate, Elizabeth Council Crafts, later recalled: "We moved around quite a bit that year (1927–1928). We lived at Barbizon for Women, The Mayflower, Central Park West, and I recall one place up on Riverside Drive. In those days, Agnes was called 'Bobby.' I don't recall why, but that is what everybody called her." Agnes took on a variety of jobs to pay her living and educational expenses, including that traditional occupation of the struggling actor — waitressing. She also worked part-time as a drama instructor at the Dalton School, an exclusive private school for girls.

The AADA taught students many different things other than theories of acting, such as posture. "My stint at the Academy had equipped me,"

Rosalind Russell recalled, "how to stand, how to sit, how to fence, how to walk into a room without looking down at their feet, how to step over a doorsill without tripping." Notebooks from her AADA years indicate that Agnes studied voice, speech, theatrical history, costuming, makeup, stagecraft, dramatic analysis and pantomime.

Lectures delivered by Charles Jehlinger were always anticipated by the students, and one such lecture was on "The Process for Creative Work." According to Agnes' notes, the lecture emphasized the following:

1) Dramatic Art is not a system. A system never produced anything. An individual must give thorough attention to his art. A continuity of thought is required.

2) Characters are real human beings — there is no end to knowing characters — *acting is a human thing.*

3) How do you find the character of the individual in the play?
   a) The basic material comes from the author
   b) Follow Nature's laws
   c) The best lesson in acting is observing situations which occur in human life (which as we have seen Agnes had been doing since she was a young child).

Jehlinger stressed that absolute attention must be given to the author/playwright. The actor holds his audience by his powers of concentration. The play read the second time gives a better understanding of the theme. The mood does not change unless character changes it. Never be disrespectful to your audience. Even if the character in the play is to be hated — do not create that feeling of hatred for yourself.

Agnes wrote a paper titled "Analysis of a Character," which indicates that Agnes paid close attention to Jehlinger's lectures. "Careful examination of text of a play must take into account what the author says about the character.

What does character say about himself?
What are exact circumstances under which he speaks?
What do others say about him?
   a) Enemy opinion
   b) Friendly opinion. Judge him by what he does or does not do. Actions speak louder than words."

The paper went on to list a series of questions the actor should ask to determine his portrayal:

1) Who are you?
2) What is your nationality?
3) In what country do you live?
4) What is the period of the play?
5) What is your age? **a)** single **b)** married **c)** divorced
6) Have you children? How many? Gender?
7) Physical description — any unusual physical features or defects, even gestures?
8) Are you neat, or careless, in dress or manner?
9) Posture — constant? Changing? Habitual?
10) How do you walk? Rise? Sit?
11) Characteristic voice — tone, pitch, defects? (lisp or stutter), monotonous (maybe necessary for characterization)
12) Are you in good health? If not, what is the cause?
13) Character's distinction in society — distinguished or not in play?
14) Financial status? Poor, rich, white collar, etc.?
15) Education? Good English? Illiterate? Dialect? Regional?
16) Kind of home you live in? Elegant, poor, modern, etc.? How furnished — period or type.
17) What kind of life have you led?
18) Who are your ancestors?
19) What do you do in your spare time?
20) What is your religion?
21) What are your political views?
22) What are the things you are deeply interested in?
23) At the beginning of the play, what is your attitude toward each of the other characters?
24) Why do you feel this way?
25) How do they feel toward you?
26) Do your feelings change in the course of the play? If so, Why? In what way?

In addition to lectures and classes, the students were encouraged to see leading actors and plays on Broadway and write of their experiences. Agnes along with a fellow classmate, Vera Krug of New Jersey, went to see the noted stage actress Jane Cowl in a play called *Road to Rome*. In her report on the experience, Agnes notes that she and Vera first had lunch (they must have attended a matinee) at the Old English Tea Room. Of the play itself Agnes writes: "Most thrilling. Enjoyed every minute. Much impressed with Jane Cowl's voice and her excellent hand acting, characteristic gestures and poses. The play surprised me. A modern theme in a Roman atmosphere." She then went on to describe her reaction to each of the three acts. On November 21, 1927, Agnes again viewed a play with Miss Krug, *Porgy and Bess*, presented by the Theatre Guild and directed by Rouben Mamoulian (who would later become a prominent Hollywood director and direct Agnes in the 1948 film *Summer Holiday*). Her review of this effort was a bit less enthusiastic: "Very realistic — draggy in places — general atmosphere of the play was human. Would arouse sympathy toward the black race. Spirituals were good — the laughs and agonizing cries of the women were especially good."

As Mr. Jehlinger had lectured, lessons in acting can come from observing real situations in everyday life. Agnes attended a class at the AADA called "Life Study" taught by a Miss Wittington, where if the notes are correct, the students would go out of class and observe real people and write of their experiences. For instance, in Agnes' notebook are several examples observing people at the following locations:

5TH AVENUE 59TH STREET, 7:30-8:30 PM LOBBY OF PLAZA HOTEL
THE RITZ AT 46TH STREET
42ND STREET ON BROADWAY
THE BOWERY

She was to observe what took place, every movement, pantomime it, then write about the type of character traits the person processed, giving specific details by taking notes. Here are a few of her notes on what she observed from the Plaza observation: "Three women come in — look out of place. One woman seems very relaxed. One woman throws coat around her, proceeds to take gloves off. Looks at watch. Crosses legs — gets pocket book, looks for powder and proceeds to powder — looks around her — puts powder back in pocket book — hands folded in lap — very glamorous . . . One woman smoking — puffs long." Of course this was familiar territory for a girl who used to observe parishioners at her father's church and then mimic their various styles of praying.

One day as she was walking to her next class at the AADA, she heard a male voice behind her say, "There goes the straightest back I've ever seen on a girl." She spun around to face the man whom within three years would become her first husband, a fellow classmate who she had noticed once or twice before, primarily due to his dark good looks — John Griffith Lee, called Jack. Jack Lee was from a prominent northern California family. His father, John Lee, Sr., was a headliner in Vaudeville as a ventriloquist and his aunt, Harriet S. Lee, was apparently one of the originators of "Mother's Day." One newspaper, which did a profile on Lee, described his early career before the AADA: "He trouped with a 'humpty dumpy' stock company on the West Coast, played in the Little Theatres of San Francisco, his native city, and is a graduate of the Seargent's school of New York and numerous road companies." Lee was one of the top male students attending the Academy that term. Actor Elliott Reid, who befriended Agnes years later, would recall that Lee "was a handsome man who dressed well in pinstripe suits and was very charming — the perfect escort."

Jack Lee had auditioned before the AADA some time after Agnes' audition on March 27, 1928. His audition report describes him as 25 years of age, 6' and 168 pounds with dark hair. His proportions, physical condition, personality and stage presence are all described as "good." His voice is described as nasal but his pronunciation is good. He gave an "intelligent" reading with "enough" characterization. His temperament was described as "vital-sensitive" and his imagination is "good." Jehlinger summed up Jack's audition by writing: "should develop well — acceptable."

Jack Lee later recalled that the AADA "didn't favor young love. Whenever they noticed any twos-ing among the embryonic thespians, it was promptly nipped in the bud. Just what led them to encourage Aggie and me, we don't know. They really got behind the idea." Agnes recalls that the instructors at AADA seemed to believe that the pairing of her with Lee was 'inevitable.' There was one teacher who used to make a low bow and say, 'I've saved a seat for you, Sister Moorehead, right next to Brother Lee.' I used to get furious. It sounded like I was bribing the man."

In her second year at the AADA, the students presented a series of plays which were directed by prominent Broadway directors and presented at the Lyceum Theatre on West 45th Street near Broadway — actually a part of Carnegie Hall. On February 1, 1929, two plays were presented — a one-act play, in which Agnes played a character named Ah Mee, *Chinese Love*, and the other play was the three-acter, *Innocent Anne*, which featured

Rosalind Russell and Jack Lee in prominent roles. *Billboard* wrote up these presentations, stating, "Of the two plays given Friday afternoon by the American Academy of Dramatic Arts, the short curtain raiser *Chinese Love* by Clare Kummer, was of far more importance from the standpoint of individual performances than the three-acter, *Innocent Love*." Of Agnes, the reviewer wrote: "Agnes Moorehead is another who seems born for the stage and she made much of a small role, as was to be expected." Jack Lee, who was in the less well-received full-length play, was praised for his performance: "Jack Lee did some clever work and has enough personality to get him by in any part."

Two weeks later on Friday, February 15, 1929, Agnes appeared in *Gloria Mundi*, described as a macabre one-act play in which the characters are inmates of an insane asylum. It got good reviews and Agnes was one of several actors complimented as "competent in their small parts."

The biggest production presented by the senior AADA students was on March 1, 1929 of Frederick Lonsdale's comedy, *The Last of Mrs. Cheney*. As it turned out, it would be the role which helped launch Rosalind Russell, who was discovered by an agent who attended this performance. Russell played the lead role of Mrs. Cheney. Also in the cast was both Agnes, as Mrs. Wynton, and Jack Lee, as Charles. *Billboard* called this, the sixth production of the AADA season, "easily the best work of the season and showed just what these students can do once they get into their stride." Russell was lauded as "perfectly cast for the part and played brilliantly, creating as exquisite and appealing a Mrs. Cheney as ever graced the boards. Her work alone put the production well above the average." Jack, in a relatively big part as Charles, the gentlemanly crook, was also applauded for "a very good performance." Agnes along with two other young ingénues were singled out as "very good in the minor feminine roles."

Agnes' big AADA production occurred in January with the play *Captain Applejack*, which was the first production by the senior class of 1929. Agnes had the leading female role of Anna Valeska in the popular comedy of that era. *Billboard's* review maintains: "There was little fault to be found with the performances of any of the cast. It was played smoothly throughout, and in the boisterous second act the players manhandled each other with an almost dangerous enthusiasm." Agnes was applauded as "outstanding . . . She had a fine intuition and gave a polished, almost flawless performance." Like the other plays presented by the AADA students during the next week, *Captain Applejack* was given a week-long run at the Columbia University Theater.

In addition to these plays, Agnes also appeared in *The First Year, The Best People,* and *The Springboard* during her time at the AADA. As a result of her performances in these productions Agnes was offered an opportunity to join a stock company in New Orleans, which she declined because she believed that it would be of more value to finish up with the AADA, and the added opportunity of appearing on Broadway in the AADA productions was too great to pass up.

Agnes graduated from the AADA on March 18, 1929, in a ceremony which featured Edward G. Robinson as commencement speaker. Of some 350 students in her class only two would really make it — Agnes and Rosalind Russell. At first many thought that Jack would also be among those

(Courtesy American Academy of Dramatic Arts)

Agnes R. Moorehead

Agnes at The AADA, circa 1929.

who had an excellent opportunity to make the grade given his fine work at the Academy. In fact, he would soon be cast in a Broadway show in a role which would generate a great deal of publicity despite his only uttering at most three lines and being killed off early in the first act.

Shortly after graduation Agnes visited Columbus, Ohio, where her parents and sister moved to in 1925 as Dr. Moorehead took over yet another pastorate. She stayed for about a month and then it was back to New York and hitting the pavement in hopes of finding an agent. She was given a list of theatrical managers in New York City — some 66 of them including Jed Harris and George M. Cohen. It was shortly after she was back in New York that she received word from her mother that her sister, Margaret, had suffered a heart seizure. Margaret was taken to the Miami Valley Hospital in Dayton, one of the best heart hospitals in the country.

Telegram Agnes received from her mother regarding sister Margaret.

Shortly after learning the news, Agnes was told that the emergency had passed and that there was no reason for her to come at once. Mollie wrote to Agnes on Miami Valley Hospital stationery:

My Dear Agnes,

I didn't intend to . . . frighten you so last night . . . for I didn't want that word to go over the telephone but as you know what happened why you are prepared for the worst if things don't go on well. I came down early and Margaret is sleeping — had a fair night. They kept her doped and we have two good nurses . . . we will send for you if we think things are going against us. Mother came and is at the house, we dad and I can take turns being here. I in the morning and he in the afternoon. Peg realizes now what a mistake she made and says she was to blame and wants me to forget all the trouble which I told her I would and ask her to forgive me for being crass and unreasonable. I told her, she and you were the only things we had in the world and we couldn't lose her. She said she would fight and has been. She says she took care of a girl who was worse than she is and she pulled through. Agnes, I think Frank was cruel to her, for out of a clear sky he said they would quit and she fainted and he never called me. And if he had I could have watched her. I'll try to keep calm and keep your dad cheered up. Please think of us . . . He (her father) has been a peach and he directed things when we needed a cool head around. Let us hear from you.

We all send love.

Lovingly yours,

Mother

This letter raises some questions. For one, who is Frank? It doesn't appear from obituaries that Margaret was married, so Frank could have been a suitor. Mollie writes that Frank was "cruel" to Margaret and said they would "quit" — does that mean that he told her they would break up? It appears that after Margaret got this rejection, she fainted — or perhaps had her seizure — but there had been a delay in getting her help. Mollie also mentions that Margaret said she had "took care" of a girl "worse than she," which indicates that perhaps Margaret had been a nurse. Finally, what was Margaret asking forgiveness from Mollie for? Was there a family disagreement, along with a romantic rejection, which might have led to Margaret's attack?

According to the *Reedsburg Wisconsin Times* issue of July 19, 1929, Margaret died on Monday, July 15, from a severe heart attack which had struck on Wednesday, July 10. She was only 26. Agnes had been summoned by telegram to come to Dayton the day before her death and, leaving immediately, she arrived just before Margaret died.

Margaret's passing hit Agnes hard. She wrote of her feelings in her AADA notebook shortly after the funeral: "A week later — so many things have happened and my own dear sister — where are you? Where can you be? . . . How brave and courageous you are — to face death so young — how you know our maker — the secret of life and death — you know . . . How I wanted to see you — and yet the thought of seeing you . . . was beyond my strength . . . I loved you — I love you now — you asleep in a little cold bed in a tomb like the good father who created you. And you were beautiful . . . I only wish you could talk to me sometimes . . . I know you are alive and well and even so much better off than we. If you could only have come to us . . . Men are so heartless — so cruel . . . Poor dear little girl, how your words of last year ring in my ears, "you never loved a man like I have" — now you know I have . . . your spirit will know -now you know how I feel toward Jack . . . My little sister — I love you so — I have always loved you and prayed for your happiness . . . I dreamed of you last night . . . I love you." It is a sad and anguished letter — hard at times to decipher. But many of the sentences are clear as a drum, and the agony that Agnes feels engulfs the reader. In the years which followed, she rarely spoke of her sister. (Since the first edition of this book came out many sources have contacted me to say that the reason there was so much mystery behind Margaret's death, and the reason Agnes rarely spoke of it, was because Margaret did not suffer a heart attack but instead died from complications from a suicide attempt —

something rarely discussed back then.)

II

In the months after graduation both Agnes and Jack hit the pavement in search of work. Jack found employment in a Broadway play called *Subway Express*. It was not a big part, but he was on stage throughout and the focus of the story. It was a murder mystery, taking place in a subway car, with Jack portraying the murder victim. He wore a hat throughout and had only a few lines of dialogue before he sits down for a subway ride home. There is a shot which rings out and it isn't noticeably apparent that the victim is Jack because he is still seated in an upright position. Broadway columnist Walter Winchell was so intrigued by how Jack accomplished such a dead-eyed look that he investigated and found that Jack's dead-eye stare was accomplished by make-up. The make-up artist painted dark dead eyes on his upper eyelids, so as he is seated, he actually closed his eyes, but to the audience it is as if he has them open, with huge dead-eyes, unblinking. Jack is in this position for the first two acts of the play as the murder investigation progresses around him. In that time he had to remain motionless and, since he was still in full view of the audience, he could not so much as sneeze. The part got him some good notices. *Commonweal* wrote: "Jack Lee as the murdered man does some of the most sensational bit of acting seen in a long time — and for a reason you can appreciate only after seeing the play and knowing its strange secret." The *New York Post* wrote: "Without a single line to speak, Mr. Lee could hardly have found a part more important to the play. He is the pivot upon which the whole plot turns . . . Yet Mr. Lee is no more human and he may be seized some evening around 10 o'clock with a desire to sneeze, or yawn, or slap a mosquito, someone may step upon his toe causing him to shout, 'OW!'"

Jack received a good deal of publicity in the New York City press for his part and wrote of his experience in several of them. In the *New York Telegram* (October 27, 1929) he says: "They call me in and they hire me as an actor and they tell me I'm to play the part of a dignified stock broker and I'm all excited about the only Broadway role I've played outside of Chinese O'Neill last year and then what does it turn out to be . . . I look at my part and it has exactly three lines and all during the rest of the show I just sit and sit and sit." He told another paper: "That any wax figure replaces me on the stage I want to deny. When I'm dead, I'm dead and it's my job to stay good and dead until I am carried off stage. Then I come to life and after I stretch and get the kinks out of myself I am alive again. As a corpse I am just as inactive as any other corpse. That I am on view for a matter of two hours every time 'Subway express' is played, proves that I am a pretty good corpse. Audiences think so anyway for they always give me a hand. That applause always brings me back to life and makes me feel like a real live human being again." The show was a hit, but unfortunately for Jack it would prove to be the highpoint of his career. He did some other parts in the theatre, mainly in summer stock or on the road, and he did go to Hollywood briefly where he did some bits for Paramount — but Jack Lee would never again generate the kind of excitement and notices he did in his first production after leaving the AADA — playing a corpse on stage for two hours.

The profiles of Jack do give some background: "Lee is in his twenties, is engaged to be married (that is all the mention Agnes gets), and is an unassuming and likeable chap. His favorite sport is football . . . to watch baseball . . . he is 'a good hand' with a knife and fork . . . likes chicken fricassee . . . believes that the stage has unlimited possibilities . . . hopes to become a fine actor . . . has played dead for over a hundred performances . . . hopes to play a hundred more. Was he choosing his own part he would like to play a role similar to that of Hannibal's brother Margo in *The Road to Rome*."

For her part, Agnes was not generating as much publicity, but she did find work. Agnes recalled years later: "After I was graduated from the Academy I started working on Broadway. I

Agnes, probably in the late 1920s.

understudied in *Courage* and *All the King's Horses* and actually got on stage in *The Scarlet Pages* with Elsie Feguson. I did *Soldiers and Women* with an all-English cast (she was again an understudy but did get on stage to replace an actress named Sarat Lahiri and the play, set in an obscure military outpost in Northern, India, allowed Agnes to play a local), and *Candlelight* with Gertrude Lawrence (as well as Leslie Howard and Reginald Owen — the play was an adaptation of a P.G. Wodehouse story, about a maid and valet who pretend to be rich royalty)." In most of these productions Agnes worked as either an understudy or a bit player. These bit roles gave her experience but did little to create an impression for her in the industry. It would take another medium to do that.

Agnes was the classic struggling actress during this period and later wrote in *Guidepost* magazine of her sparse existence during these salad days during the early months of the Great Depression: "I'd gone there (New York City) with the goal of every young actor: to make my way in the theater. To make my money last, I ate almost nothing: hot water for breakfast, a roll for lunch, rice for dinner. It was hungry work, making the rounds of casting agents, mile after mile on the unyielding sidewalk, and I used to wonder fervently just how God was going to provide manna in this man-made wilderness. At last came the day when I was literally down to my last dime. I stood in front of an automat gazing hungrily at the plates of food behind their little glass doors. The trouble was that one of the agents had given me clear instructions, 'Phone, don't come in,' which meant that five of my 10 cents would have to go into a telephone box instead of opening one of those little doors. With dragging feet I went into the drugstore next door and changed my worldly wealth into two nickels. I shut myself in the phone booth at the rear of the store, inserted one of the precious nickels — and then waited in growing alarm for the operator's voice. Half my fortune was in that phone, and nothing happened — the coin was not even returned to me! I jiggled the hook. I pounded the box, but it held tight to the coin that would have bought me a big white roll — and a pat of butter on the plate beside it. As always when I let myself think about food, a kind of desperation seized me. I thrust two fingers into the coin return, clawing the cold metal sides of the tube. They closed on a piece of paper. Though I didn't know it then, I had stumbled onto a familiar racket of those days. Pay phones were built in such a way that a piece of paper inserted from the bottom would trap the money in the chute. All I knew was that as I drew out the paper, a little river of money streamed into my lap: dimes and quarters as well as nickels. In all when I had finished my incredulous count, I had $4.25 . . . The oatmeal and rice it bought lasted until I got my first part."

She does go on to say that she paid back the telephone company with interest and believed that it was God, himself, who provided this bounty to her. "Does God drop manna through phone boxes? Of course. Anyone who spends much time with the Bible recognizes humor as one of the surest signs of his presence."

Agnes and Jack were married on June 5, 1930 — which also happened to be Jack's 27th birthday (Agnes joked that they chose that day so Jack wouldn't forget their anniversary). They were married at the Little Church Around the Corner on East 29th Street in New York — close to the theatre district. The church, which had been part of the underground railroad in the 19th century, got its reputation for being "the actor's church" when in 1870 a man named Joseph Jefferson sought to make funeral arrangements for a friend of his, an actor, who died. Jefferson was rebuffed by several churches because of the profession his friend was in. Finally he was told, "there is a little church around the corner that does that sort of thing." The story was spread in show business circles and the church attained its reputation as "the actor's church." Agnes would recall that on her wedding day, Jack arrived late to the chapel because he was appearing in a matinee. Mollie and Dr. Moorehead came in from Ohio for the wedding as did Jack's family from California. Because they were both working, they didn't take a honeymoon.

III

Agnes, in the months and years after the AADA, kept busy as a bit player and/or understudy on Broadway. She also began to get some work on radio — landing a contract with NBC where she played small or featured roles in such weekly series as *Sherlock Holmes*, *Bertie Sees the World* and *The Silver Flute*. But the break she was waiting for didn't really come until the summer of 1931. Phillips H. Lords created a weekly half-hour network (NBC) radio show called *Seth Parker*. In his definitive book on old-time radio, John Dunning describes the show as a "weekly hymn-sing." It had a cast of regulars who became like friends to the radio audience; as the *Forum* described it, *Parker* was built around "the pleasant little conceit that they are all gathered every Sunday after supper in the rural New England home of an old gentleman, Seth Parker. These quaint creatures sing old-fashioned hymns with many dear and charming halts and interruptions while they

An early publicity picture, circa 1930.

josh each other in their very nice and restrained manner. They do their best to conjure up days of long ago, when applejack and bundling were in vogue." The show premiered in March 1929 and became an immediate hit, and at its peak the show had more than 300 clubs formed within the United States and Canada. Lords himself played Seth Parker — the kindly old gentleman, but in reality Lords was only in his mid-20's.

To capitalize on the show's enormous popularity a nation-wide tour was arranged in the fall of 1931 for the *Seth Parker* show cast, who would appear on stage in costume (meaning the 20-something Lords would appear in old age makeup wearing white chin whiskers). Lords' wife, Sophia Lords, appeared on the radio show as Lizzie Peters, an old maid who often provided the comedy relief. Sophia Lords decided that she didn't want to participate in the national tour, so her character was recast (for the tour — not the radio show), with Agnes getting this pivotal role.

On August 15, 1931, the NBC semimonthly, *Feature Service*, published this little tidbit: "Agnes Moorehead, NBC dramatic actress, will be a member of the Seth Parker cast to tour the United States in the fall. Miss Moorehead holds a master's degree from the University of Wisconsin, and has had an extended stage and operatic experience. She is the daughter of a Presbyterian minister and her girlhood ambition was to be a missionary." In short, a perfect biography for somebody who was joining the cast of a show which had strong religious overtones.

The tour began in October in the Midwest. According to one review, "Miss Moorehead's make-up as Lizzie Peters is a work of art in this play. Severe and old-maidish and constantly exercising supervision over her slow-witted brother Cefus, Miss Moorehead frequently caused the audience to howl." One of the "pieces of business" which Agnes performed as

Lizzie Peters, with the actor Bennett Kilpack as her brother, Cefus, involves Lizzie forcing Cefus to "recitate a pome" he is learning under the direction of Lizzie. Cefus stumbles through a third of it, with Lizzie transfixing him with a disgusted stare as she tries to prompt him through it. When the tour came to Dayton, Ohio, the *Dayton Journal* would write, "Agnes Moorehead . . . was the real star of the piece, we thought." A week later in Detroit, the *Evening Times* said, "Agnes Moorehead or Lizzy Peters . . . also played a big part in making the comic side of the playlet a success."

One of the highlights of Agnes' performance as Lizzie was her ability to recite the books of the Bible in "a record breaking" 14 seconds. The tour continued with enthusiastic notices and audiences in Cleveland, Milwaukee, Minneapolis, Omaha (where another notice stated that Agnes "all but stole the show"), Denver, Kansas City, and Toronto and all the way to the west coast. From Toronto, Agnes sent a telegram to Jack: "DARLING IMPOSSIBLE TO CALL YOU SHOW WENT BEAUTIFULLY GOOD CROWD AWFULLY LONELY TORONTO IS BEAUTIFUL WISH YOU WERE HERE HOPE YOUR COLOR IS BETTER PLAY HAMILTON TOMORROW NIGHT WILL WIRE FROM THERE ANY DEVELOPMENTS ON PLAY EXPECT LETTERS AT WM PENN ALL MY LOVE."

By the time the tour arrived in New York for a stint at the Cort Theatre, on Forty-Eighth Street in Manhattan, Agnes was exhausted — the two-hour play had toured 16 weeks and traveled 32,000 miles. "It is hard work, but it's lots of fun," Agnes declared. "Mr. Lords is always changing things and something funny is always happening, but, goodness, I wish that we would stop somewhere long enough for me to get my face clean!"

The tour was successful in establishing Agnes with a new persona as a comedic character actress and would lead to her first major break on radio.

IV

In September 1932, Agnes was cast in a new mystery-suspense radio series broadcast over CBS, *Mysteries in Paris* — sponsored by Evening in Paris perfume and other toiletries. The show starred Elsie Hitz as Patricia Barlow, the heroine, described as a "young, beautiful vivacious, orphan American girl without family ties and possessed of considerable fortune . . . came to Paris in search of the excitement her temperament craved." Agnes was cast as Nana, Patricia's "maid, chaperon, guardian and general factotum," who participated in helping Patricia in her mysteries against the "sinister, mysterious, all-powerful criminal of the Paris underworld," known as the

Octopus. Agnes' character is described as "providing much sparkling comedy and human interest" to the stories.

In fact, the character of Nana became so popular on the *Mysteries in Paris* program — the title of the program was changed to *Evening in Paris* within a few weeks — that what was initially a distinctly secondary role was greatly enhanced in the weeks which followed. She also experienced a name change — from Nana to Anna. There was no official explanation but it may have been that the network felt Nana was too exotic a name. In *Radio Fan-Fare* magazine, Agnes explained to writer R.R. Endicott how the character became so popular. "That just shows what can happen to you in this business. A hick character called Nana was written into the first *Mysteries in Paris* shows to give the mysteries comic relief. I got the part and for some strange reason the character became tremendously popular almost immediately. Apparently she reminded listeners of ZaSu Pitts (an early radio/stage/movie comedy character actress who had a tremendous following). At least, hundreds wrote in and said that when they heard Nana they could see ZaSu. Then the whole idea of the program was revised and the name changed to *Evening in Paris*. But the sponsors thought they'd better keep the comic character. They call her Anna now but don't ask me why." Endicott went on to write, "Although Agnes didn't say so, the fact is that Nana, or Anna, stole the show, and instead of having just a few lines as she did at first, the whole dramatic part of the program is now written around her." *Radio Guide* describes the voice she used as Nana/Anna as "simple, unsophisticated, frustrated and quavering with the ZaSu Pitts voice, rustic in her simple nature, but definitely not a hick."

While Agnes was causing a stir as Nana/Anna she was also appearing in a variety of other roles on radio including Peter Rabbit in an adaptation of the A.A. Milne's Winnie the Pooh series, along with her recurring character parts on *Sherlock Holmes* and the *Twenty Thousand Years in Sing Sing* program. She made it clear that she didn't want to become typed as Nana. "I can offer them so many characters just as funny Cockney parts, Scotch, Irish, or what have you." Throughout her career she would fight typecasting, but from the early to the mid-1930's her major roles would be in comedy or "stooge" parts for comedians such as Phil Baker.

Agnes' newfound popularity on radio also seemed to leave Jack behind. By 1933 Jack was still acting, but mainly in stock productions. One newspaper clipping from that year indicates that Jack was working in a candy store which had been held up, so while Agnes was receiving complimentary notices in the press for her acting, the story on Jack described not the actor, but a clerk who coolly cooperated when robbers held up the candy store he was working in. His ego must have been somewhat bruised. A *St. Louis Globe* profile on Agnes ("St. Louis Beauty Makes Good on Big Network Programs," 4/23/33) described Agnes' childhood in St. Louis; her favorite sport as riding; unusual incidents in her life, such as dancing with Henry Ford and being presented to Queen Marie of Rumania; that she lives on Long Island "because it is quiet," and that when she is tired she "stays at home and writes letters." But nowhere in that profile is it mentioned that she is married. Only a few years earlier, Jack was getting a great deal of press in the post-AADA period with the bare knuckles mention of him being "engaged." Now the shoe was on the other foot with Jack receiving no mention at all.

Among the many profiles of Agnes during this time appeared in *Radio Guide* ("Chameleon of the Air") and is instructive: "Agnes likes parties and people, and the only time she goes on a smoking binge of cigarettes is when everybody else is having — er — beer.

Christmas card sent by Jack and Agnes Lee, circa 1935.

You have, she says, to do SOMETHING." In the article she states she is superstitious. "For instance, if she should drop her gloves, she never picks them up. Fortunately, there is usually a young man in the vicinity only too glad of the opportunity to pick them up for her. She always wears an Indian bracelet to broadcasts, and regards a falling picture as an ominous sign." The article states that she suffers from chronic mike fright before, but never during, a radio performance. "Any program is preceded by a wave of nausea, but she believes mike fright scares actors into being constantly on their toes." The article sums her up: "And in a final analysis, Agnes saves money, cooks like an angel, likes to putter around her apartment, reads in bed, never finds money on the street, believes a professional and a domestic life can run along smoothly, prefers dark-eyed men (hmm, again no mention of Jack in this profile — could it have been a publicity angle to present Agnes as an attractive single woman?), doesn't believe in fortune tellers, but thinks they're fascinating and would prefer to live 'out where the West begins.' "

Despite her personal success on *Evening in Paris* the show was not renewed for a second season, but Agnes' career momentum didn't flag. She was now identified as a top character comedian in the industry and soon afterward she joined up with Irvin S. Cobb, a humorist in the Will Rogers tradition, as his "stooge." James Cannon, in the May 2, 1933 *New York World Telegram* ("Cobb Snags Rare Stooge"), describes a stooge as "a guy who is funnier than the comedian he helps." But Agnes was no "wild stooge" (and certainly not a guy), she was "a rare tame stooge. The wild stooge is a stooge because it does not know the ways of civilization and, you might say, never had a chance, but a tame, or blasé, stooge is one who is a stooge and knows better. Cobb's stooge is Agnes Moorehead, a funny lady. Miss Moorehead was an able laugh manufacturer on her own at one time, before she answered the call of the wild and turned stooge." With Cobb, Agnes would appear on radio (often in commercial spots) and personal appearances around the country.

While working with Cobb, Agnes stayed busy elsewhere, and around this time she met a young radio director named Himan Brown, who she would remain friends with for the remainder of her life and work with often. The first time was when Brown was developing a daily comedy series based on the comic strip, *The Gumps.* "I first met Aggie in 1933 when casting *The Gumps,* which was a popular comic strip of that time. I had interviewed two or three other people for the part of Min Gump. When Agnes came in, I interviewed her and hired her on the spot. I didn't give her a script and ask her to read it back to me, I just had a one-on-one talk with her. I was struck by her wonderful voice and her enunciation. I thought she would be perfect as the wife who always has to take charge because her husband (Andy Gump) was a misfit. Aggie knew the comic strip and she knew how to portray Min Gump — knew in her own mind how the character should be played and it was perfection."

Himan Brown became one of the top directors and innovators in radio and had strong convictions on what it takes to be a successful radio actor. "A radio actor has to know how to interpret a script. In radio you have no picture — you only have your voice. You have to listen and create with your imagination. Agnes could do this. She was perfect for that rare quality that radio actors must have — identification. Agnes was a wonderful person who had great taste and knew what to do with words." As Brown got to know Agnes he was captivated by her personality. "Agnes was a rare human being. Considerate, concerned, and she really cared for you. Cared about people. She was a real friend, not some phony — and what a wonderful sense of humor! It was sharp and it was witty and it was unpredictable."

By this time, Brown had been out of college for only a few years and when *The Gumps* was launched, he was still in his 20's. Yet according to one profile, he had already produced seventeen single station or network programs by this time. He had gone to college with the intent of practicing law, but went into radio instead. It was producer-director Brown's intention to make *The Gumps* "a real American family, even though a cartoon one." Interestingly, the writer of *The Gumps* was Irwin Shaw, who later became a best-selling novelist. According to *The Encyclopedia of Old Time Radio*, when Brown hired Shaw to write *The Gumps*, he was working on another radio show based on a comic strip, *Dick Tracy*. Brown would recall Shaw as "sensational."

Cast as Andy Gump, her misfit husband, was Wilmer Walter. Walter was an experienced stage and radio performer who played Andy Gump with all of his "bluff and bluster until Min tells him to keep quiet." Agnes worked with Walter on several programs in subsequent years including *The March of Time* and *The Shadow*. Jackie Kelk was cast as their mischievous son, Chester. For Agnes it was the start of a lifelong friendship with the then-14-year-old Kelk. Brown recalls Kelk as "a young kid actor; he played juvenile roles and he was pretty good, but certainly not in Aggie's league. He never married and he was a dear, dear close friend to Agnes. She would often be gone and Jackie would watch her house in California for her — as a matter of fact he had a small cottage on her property. As I say, they were very good friends from that moment on and she needed someone like him later on when she was alone, for safety sake, and when she was off on the road."

Himan Brown has always maintained that he gave Agnes her first big job in radio, but she had actually achieved that with the role of Nana/Anna in the *Mysteries of Paris* program and was under contract to NBC radio where she appeared on many programs. But certainly the season she spent on *The Gumps* enhanced her career and she benefitted in another way, according to Brown, meeting the man who would be instrumental in furthering her career, Orson Welles. "We did our show around noon," Brown recalled, "it was a 15-minute show, and the show just prior to our's was a poetry reading. A young man who was maybe 17 or 18 years old with a beautiful voice would recite poetry and an organ in the background would play music. The young man with such a beautiful voice was Orson Welles — and we were in the same studio and had about 30 seconds for Orson to vacate the stage and for our actors to come in and begin our program." Occasionally Welles would stay and watch, and unsurprisingly he would be taken by the talented Agnes Moorehead.

Agnes' stint on *The Gumps* lasted for only a season and, as luck would have it, the following season she joined the cast of another radio program and a prestigious one at that — Helen Hayes as *The New Penny*. Lucky, too, since it was her introduction to Miss Hayes, one of the great ladies of Broadway, and another lifelong friendship formed. *The New Penny* was a dramatic series which presented Miss Hayes as "the modern woman" — chic, sophisticated, and not ruled by a man. Agnes was cast as her equally sophisticated adversary. Like *Mysteries of Paris,* this program was scripted by the talented Edith Meiser.

Miss Hayes' son, actor James MacArthur, would recall that Agnes and Hayes were "great friends when circumstances brought them together, but otherwise they might go for long periods of time without having any contact. We lived on the East Coast, Aggie lived in Los Angeles, so get-togethers usually occurred when one or the other was in town or they were attending a common event . . . but while it was mostly a long distance relationship, they were great pals whenever they saw each other, comfortable as though they'd only seen each other the day before."

One of the reasons Helen Hayes got along well with Agnes was her sense of humor. "I remember one story my mother used to love to tell," recalls James MacArthur. "She and Aggie were in Pittsburgh together at some type of lady's luncheon, the DAR or something similar. Before it started, Aggie got up and said, 'Helen, this is what we are going to hear,' and then she proceeded to go through a hilariously funny and outlandish parody of the speech they would hear. And, of course, you know what happened. It was exactly as Aggie had predicted. And they were like churchgoers at a funeral who couldn't laugh. The voice, the gestures, the intonation were all dead-on. Every time my mother would recount this story, she would roar with laughter, tears streaming down her cheeks. My mother thought Agnes had a wickedly wonderful sense of humor."

So fond of Agnes and admiring of her talent was Hayes that around this time she used her clout to arrange a screen test for her, in hopes that Agnes might be launched in a new career in motion pictures. The man who Hayes made the arrangement with was called out of town and, as Agnes would recall, the man who was left in his place "eyed me very critically and the first thing he said was, 'Did you ever have your nose broken?'" After that the man delivered a caustic rundown of Agnes' shortcomings and concluded that a screen test would be a waste of money because she "couldn't possibly make it" in pictures.

Like *Mysteries of Paris* and *The Gumps, The New Penny* lasted only a season, but like these other shows it had enhanced Agnes' career. She often appeared on five or six different radio shows per week in steady demand. She soon became part of an important radio news dramatization program, *The March of Time,* which would reintroduce her to the young man she had met while working on *The Gumps,* Orson Welles, and, with him and an extraordinary group of fellow seasoned radio veterans, would go on to create radio history — with a bit of notoriety in the process.

4

ORSON AND THE MERCURY THEATRE

In the early 1920's an Aunt took Agnes on a trip to New York. They stayed in the old Waldorf-Astoria Hotel. One day Agnes was sitting at a table next to a precocious little boy, probably seven or eight years old, who was chubby and had expressive eyes. The little boy was deep in conversation with, who she thought, was his father and two elderly women. "It was at an afternoon tea," Agnes recalled, "and he was talking learnedly about musical theory." Years later she encountered a young man who reminded her of this young boy but didn't say anything to him because she just didn't think it could be the same person. Some time after that she was reading *Life* magazine, which had an article that greatly interested her; as she turned the pages, she found a picture of the young boy she had encountered those many years earlier at the Waldorf Astoria — she was absolutely convinced it was he. That young boy was the focus of the story she was reading. It was the same young man she found so familiar when she met him years later. Agnes now realized that the precocious young boy was none other than Orson Welles. When Welles was finally told of the incident he began to fondly tell people that he had known Agnes Moorehead "since I was seven years old."

No doubt about it: Orson Welles was a prodigy. He was born George Orson Welles, on May 6, 1915, in Kenosha, Wisconsin. His father, Richard Welles, had been an inventor who had patented headlamps for the first automobiles, and Welles would later say that Booth Tarkington had based the character of Eugene Morgan in his famous novel, *The Magnificent Ambersons,* on his father. Welles' mother, Beatrice, was a musician, who later became one of the first women elected to public office in Wisconsin, when she was elected to the Kenosha School Board. Welles had one brother, who seemingly was not as bright as Orson, and who stuttered; the brother must have experienced a terrible inferiority complex, since the parents lavished praise on Orson, while ignoring him.

Orson's parents divorced when he was six. His father had developed a serious drinking problem and his mother had fallen into an affair with another man — a doctor who had treated Orson's grandmother when she was dying of stomach cancer. When they divorced Orson moved with his mother to Chicago where she helped support them by giving piano lessons while Orson recited Shakespeare. In his spare time young Orson wrote plays, developed an interest in magic tricks and performed in puppet shows. When Orson was nine, his mother died of hepatitis. Orson was devastated and his father was of little help because of his own losing battle with alcoholism. As it turned out, Orson stayed in the care of the doctor his mother had an affair with. They lived for a few years in the Chicago area where Orson was able to enjoy the culture the city had to offer such as attending the theatre or symphonies.

When Orson was 11, he returned to Wisconsin where he attended public schools in Madison living with a friend of the doctor's. Orson had no formal education prior to this, but having been home schooled by tutors he excelled and was advanced from the fourth to the fifth grade. One of his teachers, Dorothy Chapman, later said, "His interests were definitely toward art and dramatics. He disliked arithmetic and found the regular school curriculum much to his disliking. He was permitted to take special art courses, in which he showed marked adeptness." After a year in Madison, Orson was enrolled at the exclusive Todd School in Woodstock, Illinois. At Todd, Orson's creativity flourished and he appeared in numerous plays and shows.

His father died in 1930, alone in a hotel room. During these years Orson did a great deal of traveling — to the Orient, Cuba and Germany. When Orson graduated from high school (at age 16), rather than going to college he went on a sketching tour of Ireland; when his money ran low, he managed to get a job performing at the Gate Theatre in Dublin. He gained much useful experience in Dublin. When he returned to the United States, he joined with Roger Hill, the headmaster of the Todd School, who had been much impressed by Orson's skills as an actor, in forming a touring company and writing a play, *Marching Song*, about the underground railroad.

A break occurred in 1933 when Orson, now 18, ran into the playwright Thorton Wilder, who had recalled Welles from the Dublin Theater. Wilder wrote a letter of introduction for Welles to present to theatrical managers and other influential people in New York. This led to an introduction to the critic Alexander Woollcott who in turn introduced Orson to Katharine Cornell, who cast him as Mercucio in a nationwide tour she and her husband, Garrett McClintock, were undertaking in *Romeo and Juliet.* Jane Wyatt would recall the spectacle of middle-aged Cornell and McClintock playing the teenage lovers and how the theatre came alive when Orson came on stage as Mercucio — "we knew a star was born." In 1934, Orson was introduced to sometime-actor and producer John Houseman, twelve year's Orson's senior, who invited Welles to appear in his play, *Panic.* This led to a partnership between the two which culminated with an all-black version of *Macbeth,* which Houseman produced in cooperation with the WPA's Negro Theatre Project, with Welles directing.

Houseman and Orson continued to work producing plays for the WPA including *Dr. Faustus* and *The Cradle Will Rock.* To supplement his meager income, Orson began to do extensive work on radio His rich, deep voice and perfect enunciation were made for the medium and, like Agnes, Orson had a talent for dialects. He became very much in demand and it was through his work in radio that Agnes got to know Welles, whom she later would remember as "quiet and introverted." "He was always very clean," Agnes would recall, "but with frayed edges on his shirt. He carried a shillelagh and had a marvelous voice and diction. Everyone else was afraid to talk to him, but he fascinated me and we became great friends. One night, he asked me whether I'd join him and Joe Cotten to do the classics on Mutual radio." Houseman and Orson finally left the WPA to form their own repertory company — The Mercury Theatre — and they wanted Agnes on the team.

II

While Orson Welles was finding his way on stage and radio, Agnes was increasingly in demand. She was known by many as a comic "stooge" for Phil Baker, but had shown considerable versatility on radio performing on many dramatic programs as well as comedies. Her versatility helped make her part of the ensemble company of the radio program, *The March of Time.* *The March of Time* dramatized news events using actors to accurately impersonate the newsmakers of the day along with classic radio sound effects to make it seem to the audience that they were actually listening to the real event. Because the show covered all major newsmakers around the world, the best radio voices were needed and wanted to do the show. It was on this and other shows of this period, such as *The Cavalcade of America,* that Agnes got to know and work with some of the other great voices in radio. By the time Agnes joined the *March of Time* cast in 1936, the show had been on for five years. Franklin Roosevelt was president and among those who specialized in impersonating FDR were Bill Johnstone and, nearly twenty years before he sky-rocketed to fame as Ed Norton, Art Carney. Eleanor Roosevelt was one of the first voices Agnes was called upon to do and her interpretation was letter-perfect. She had down Mrs. Roosevelt's high-pitched, often piercing voice — and did so without it falling into parody or, as some people who "did" Mrs.

Agnes as Sarah Heartburn on **The Phil Baker Show, 1936.**

Roosevelt, as a way of ridiculing her. In fact, Agnes would recall that she was performing as Mrs. Roosevelt on a *March of Time* broadcast when she looked into the control room and saw the real Mrs. Roosevelt watching her — intently. Agnes was a bit shaken as she continued her performance and was, afterward, apprehensive of what the First Lady would say to her. She was relieved when Mrs. Roosevelt congratulated her and said that she felt Agnes did the best job of anyone she had ever heard impersonating her. Agnes was always very proud of that accolade from a woman she came to admire very much.

In addition to Mrs. Roosevelt, Agnes also performed over the years in a number of other parts on the show. *Life* magazine ran an advertisement for *The March of Time* which featured Agnes and included pictures of her impersonating, Madame Chiang Kai-Shek, The Dutchess of Windsor, Eleanor Roosevelt, and Yetta Rothberg. The ad is interesting since it illustrates how Agnes (and many of the other actors on the show) prepared for their roles. "The poignant, tragic simplicity of Madame Chiang Kai-Shek, wife of China's dictator, the gay sophistication of "Wally," the Dutchess of Windsor, The ebullient energy of Eleanor Roosevelt, or the pathos of plain Yetta Rothberg of the Bronx — Agnes Moorehead, who plays these and many other part in *The March of Time,* is acknowledged as radio's most sensitive, most versatile, and most authentic artist in re-creating the characters of living women. A familiar sight in the *March of Time* studio is Agnes Moorehead listening in tense concentration to a recording of one of the voices she is to reenact, following it with her own voice, learning inflection and accent, perfecting tone and timbre."

Elliott Reid was barely 16 when he joined the cast of *The March of Time.* He recalls Agnes as a "handsome woman, which was my first impression of her. I was new and not totally at ease." As he got to know her, he came to recognize her as a "brilliant actress. On that program she did a number of impressions of world-famous people. She specialized in Eleanor Roosevelt — very nice and not exaggerated — she did it very accurately. Agnes would get up and do a sketch and rehearse it very shrewdly and perform it tastefully. She was a very tasteful person in everyday life and it spilled over, into her acting." Reid would recall that they didn't have time "to struggle with the method" since they basically had to rehearse a show in an hour. "We couldn't take all day to get an effect, we basically had to get it on the first reading."

Reid would become a lifelong friend to Agnes and besides working with her on *The March of Time,* they also did a short-lived series called *The Mighty Show,* about life in a circus. But most significantly they made many appearances together on another landmark radio show of this time, *The Cavalcade of America.* Reid recalls *Cavalcade* as specializing in "Americana"; they did many shows on historic events and people. Agnes appeared on more than 70 episodes and was considered a member of its ensemble cast from 1939–1940 (she would return for an occasional appearance in later years). Reid was another ensemble player on the show, often doing juvenile roles, and he appeared with Agnes more than 30 times — often performing two or more parts in the same episode! On *Cavalcade* as a part of an ensemble, Agnes would one week be the star of the program (such as "The Story of Nancy Hanks," where she played Abraham Lincoln's mother, the focus of that week's episode) and then play a supporting or bit part the following week.

Reid has fond memories of many of the people he and Agnes worked with on *Cavalcade of America.* John McIntyre was a particular favorite; he became known years later to television audiences as the wagon master on

Wagon Train. "He was one of the great people. Wonderful actor, superb voice — one of the most delightful hosts. He and his wife (the equally talented radio performer Jeanette Nolan) were very warm and expansive. Jeanette was a wonderful cook and she would cook these huge meals. Very loving." He recalls that many radio people, including Agnes and Jack, would often go out to Malibu where the McIntyres' lived for wonderful get-togethers and huge meals.

Reid was close to Agnes and he got to know her husband. "Jack was a very unsuccessful actor, I never knew him to have a job. I never knew him to do a lick of work, not that he didn't want to. A marriage would be in trouble if the wife is doing well and the husband isn't. It led to some serious drinking. He was a handsome man and a perfect escort. Agnes liked that. She loved to sit in the first row, center aisle, of any theatre she came into. She and Jack were always in the same seats. I don't know how she managed it. Agnes was a good friend to people if she was your friend. Jack seemed well-mannered, gracious and charming. The inner truth of that marriage — inbalance — Agnes being so successful and Jack so notably unsuccessful, were the seeds to the trouble."

Reid also recalls that another lifelong friendship Agnes formed was with a fellow juvenile actor, Jackie Kelk, who played her son in *The Gumps* as well as appearing with her on other radio programs. "Jack was very close to Agnes. In later years, Jack lived with Agnes and she even invited me to live with her, something I later regretted not doing. It was always platonic. They were good friends. Agnes liked having people she knew from the old days around her and she was loyal to them. Part of it was loneliness, she was a woman alone, only with these two women servants living with her, and she felt more secure if there was a man around the house." Reid decided not to live with Agnes despite her invitation because he thought that such an arrangement would change the dynamic of their friendship. "Agnes didn't drive and I thought I would become a chauffeur — it would take over my life. I'm not proud of that thought, but I had always been used to having my own apartment; but, in retrospect, I kind of wish I had taken her up on it when I came out here (Hollywood) for short visits to do a film or TV program."

III

The Shadow was one of the most successful radio programs of all-time and one of the most remembered of "old time radio." The series was well known, and still today, by its famous signature phrase: *Who knows . . . what evil . . . lllurks in the hearts of men . . . The Shadow Knows!* The show debuted in 1930 and had gone through several incarnations — originally known as *The Detective Story Hour* with James La Curto and then Frank Readick. In the early years the character of "The Shadow" was only the narrator of the suspense-filled episodes, but by 1937 the Blue Coal Company, which sponsored the series, decided that "The Shadow" should have an identity other than just the shadowy figure who narrated the proceedings. The creator of the series, Walter B. Gibson, had, in a series of pulp novels, given the character a name, Lamont Cranston. He was described as "a man of wealth, a student of science, and a master of other people's minds, devotes his life to righting wrongs, protecting the innocent, and punishing the guilty . . ." One Welles biographer likened Orson's interpretation of Cranston as a Noel Coward character, "a suggestion of silk dressing gown and cigarette holder."

Cranston's superpowers were not as advanced as say, Superman's, but they did come in handy. He had the ability to use hypnosis to "cloud men's minds so that they cannot see him." The new program called for a new voice and according to *The Encyclopedia of Old-Time Radio*, 22-year-old Orson Welles, "a regular toiling in anonymity on *The March of Time*," auditioned and won the role. Orson's contract with Blue Coal "allowed him to go on without as much as a prior peek at his script: thus, as he told film director Peter Bogdanovich, when he was thrown into a snake pit, he didn't know how he'd get out till the show ended." Initially the identity of the new "Shadow" was to be unknown, but, as always with Orson, his ego couldn't permit him to perform such a plum role anonymously — it soon "leaked" out. Without a doubt, *The Shadow* is what firmly established Orson on radio.

To give the show some feminine appeal, another character was created, Lamont Cranston's "friend and companion, the lovely Margot Lane . . . the only person who knows to whom the voice of the invisible Shadow belongs." Margot was no "damsel in distress"-type, but joined Cranston in his many adventures, showing admirable courage and ingenuity along the way. Cranston and Margot weren't a "couple" though some fans wished they were. But in listening to the episodes, it seems to me there was a certain amount of sexual tension below the surface. Agnes was signed for this plum role — one created solely for the radio show, and not included in the novels.

The first episode of the Welles/Moorehead version of *The Shadow* premiered on September 26, 1937 and told the story of how the Shadow uses his mental telepathy to exonerate a man scheduled to be executed. Besides Orson and Agnes the supporting cast included three other actors who would become part of the Mercury Theatre — Ray Collins, Paul Stewart, and Everett Sloane. In addition, future stage and screen director Elia Kazan appeared more than once on *The Shadow,* in the premier episode playing the character of "Lefty Collins." William Johnstone, who would succeed Welles as the Shadow the following season, also appears on this first broadcast.

Perhaps Mutual Radio chose Orson and Agnes because they had just completed a project which had generated great buzz in the industry, a seven-part radio adaptation of Victor Hugo's classic novel, *Les Miserables.* Welles proved himself to be an innovator on this project, per his biographer Simon Callow: "No one in the history of the medium has ever unleashed such tidal waves of adrenalin as Welles. *Les Miserables* is electric from start to finish, his own gruff and very credibly aged Valjean leading the excellent group of actors (Agnes Moorehead, Ray Collins, Martin Gabel, Everett Sloane, Chubby Sherman)." Callow goes on to point out that for the incredible scenes which take place in the sewers, Orson "dragged his crew into the men's room, where Ray Collins and Everett Sloane played their scene over a urinal," to simulate the echoing sound and running water of a sewer. Agnes could have been auditioning for the role of the mother in *Citizen Kane* with her role in *Les Miserables.* She expertly played the shop owner who tries to sell her own daughter to Valjean.

Due to the success and innovation of this show, Mutual approached Welles to write, produce and direct a weekly series of hour-long dramas; the program, initially titled *First Person Singular,* would feature actors who had worked with him in Mercury Theatre stage productions as well as on other radio projects. With his association over the last couple of years with Agnes on *March of Time, The Shadow* and *Les Miserables* and his admiration of her talent, there is no doubt that Orson wanted Agnes to be part of this new and exciting program. Arthur Anderson, who at 14, was cast by Orson in an opera titled *Second Hurricane,* and went on to work in Welles' classic modern dress version of *Julius Ceasar* on Broadway, was the youngest member of the Mercury Theatre. He states that Orson and Agnes got along well because "Orson recognized great talent and great voices. Agnes had both."

The new program would, as the title signified, tell the story in first singular with Welles narrating in the first person. Like the program which had inspired the show, *Les Miserables,* the stories would exclusively be from literary works, many of them favorites of Welles' from his childhood — among them *Dracula* and *Treasure Island.* Orson said the purpose of *First Person Singular* was not to bring the theatre to radio but "our own individual interpretation of radio to the listeners. The idea is only experimental. It may prove a failure but it is only by trying new methods that radio drama will ever achieve any independence and eventually discover a satisfactory art form of its own."

Agnes Moorehead, 1938.

While her career was on the upswing with the Mercury Theatre, Agnes received devastating news in the late spring of 1938. Her beloved father died on Sunday, May 22, while he was presiding over a service at his latest pastorate at the Kohr Memorial Presbyterian Church in Columbus, Ohio. The *Reedsburg, Wisconsin Free Press* (5/27/38) reported that Dr. Moorehead was sitting in his chair near the pulpit, shortly before he was to begin his sermon. The choir was singing "Safe in the Arms of Jesus" when John slumped forward. According to a Columbus paper, Mollie, who was singing in the choir, went over to him and, finding him unconscious, she "begged him to speak." At Mollie's request, the congregation quietly and quickly left the church. A physician who was in the congregation examined him and pronounced him dead of a sudden heart attack. The man Agnes revered more than any other was gone. She was deeply saddened but as always when faced with tragedy or heartache, Agnes threw herself into her work

First Person Singular premiered on July 11, 1938 with a classic theme to complement its choice of material, Tchaikovsky's piano Concerto No. 1 in B-flat minor. The music was conducted by Bernard Herrmann, who would go on to a rich career in Hollywood; in addition to working with Welles on *Citizen Kane*, he also did the music for several Hitchcock films (including *North by Northwest* and *Psycho*). The first presentation was an hour-long version of Bram Stoker's "Dracula." Welles was very proud of this adaptation because of his fidelity to the novel; such as telling the story with three narrators, as the novel does. Orson, naturally, was Dracula (as well as Jonathan Harker), Martin Gabel was cast as Van Helsing, with Agnes given the plum role of Mina. The show won good reviews from *Newsweek*, which called it "adventurous," and the *New York Times,* who described the episode as "realistically broadcast: the characters living electronically."

This adaptation of *Dracula* is astonishing, and in many ways it's more eerie and terrifying than the classic Bela Lugosi film version. Frank Brady, in his biography *Citizen Welles,* writes: "All of the performances were beautifully and realistically underplayed. Each actor added to the visual details of the tombs, produced action on the ship, change the locale to Dr. Seward's living room, shifted to the stark terror of a confrontation with Dracula, all with the salutary exercise and control of his voice." Brady called Welles' performance as Harker "convincing," but his Count Dracula, "masterful." As for Agnes, her Mina is described as "superb," and one scene in particular captures the erotic undertones that *Dracula* always oozed. Orson as the Count is about to give the bite to Mina, turning her into his bride, and whispers seductively to her: "Flesh of my flesh, blood of my blood, blood of my blood." He then bites her and Agnes gives a deep and almost orgasmic sigh. Orson's sign-off on the first broadcast highlighted his genius at showmanship. "Just in case Count Dracula's left you a little apprehensive, one word of comfort: when you go to bed tonight, don't worry. Put out the lights and go to sleep. (*A wolf howl.*) It's all right, you can rest peacefully, and that's just a sound effect. There! Over there, in the shadow, see? It's nothing. Nothing at all. Nothing at all — I think it's nothing. But always remember (*Now as Van Helsing*) Ladies and gentlemen, there are wolves. There are vampires. (*As himself again*) Such things do exist." This was Welles' way of saying "Boo" months before Halloween — but by that Halloween of 1938, he had an even more elaborate prank to pull on the American listening public.

Arthur Anderson made his debut the following week as Young Jimmy Hawkins in "Treasure Island," with Agnes cast as his mother. "She used a very authentic cockney accent, she was wonderful at dialect," he would remember. Anderson recalls the routine of the show as very casual. "We would do a first reading around a table, then we would do a mike check for special effects. A dress rehearsal would then be done with the orchestra led by Bernard Herrmann, who had been rehearsing prior to this. Then Orson always recorded the dress rehearsals on discs and he, John Houseman (the producer), and Paul Stewart would sit around, probably while eating dinner, and argue it out on what to cut or change, then the actors would be brought in again and told what was decided." Anderson would also recall that at this time Orson and Houseman worked efficiently together, but later they went their separate ways and were estranged for the rest of their lives. Anderson remembers being told (he wasn't present) that the Mercury actors were called into a meeting by Orson to set the record straight about which man — he or Houseman — ran the Mercury Theatre. "There is some dissension about who is in charge," Welles was reported to have said. "Well, *I* am the Mercury Theatre."

Elliott Reid, who also worked in several Mercury productions, recalls Houseman as "A portly gentleman (who) spoke beautiful English, having been brought up over there. He was a charming person, highly intelligent; I liked him and admired him. He was producing the business side of Orson Welles — he had a little cubby-hole office — a little hole in the wall."

For all his admiration for Orson, Anderson considers Welles "The supreme egotist; actors who were twice his age could be intimidated by him and he would take them aside and say, 'shame on you,' if they did something wrong. My opinion is that Orson was usually right." Welles is also credited by Anderson as "very clever and creative as a director — he didn't mind doing outrageous things and then changing them if they didn't work out, which any good director would do." As an example of Welles' innovations, Anderson would recall that he was cast as the Ghost of Christmas Past in the Mercury adaptation of "A Christmas Carol." "Here I was only 15 and I'm playing this part, but that was the innovator in Orson."

Elliott Reid also credits Orson as a creative radio director, but adds: "He didn't go in for directorial flourishes. He had people who he knew could do it or he wouldn't cast them in the part, so he trusted them. He did direct the actors at times, but technical things were what he concentrated on. But perusing the inner life of a character or artsy direction — No. I can't recall Orson ever saying, 'Now this guy . . . ,' and telling his background." As a director, Reid recalls that Orson liked to keep things relaxed. "He would come to the table with a good deal of bantering, before the reading of the script, and then we would get to it. I looked forward to being in one of Orson's shows." When directing the Mercury shows, Reid says that Welles "had earphones so he could hear the actors from what it sounded like in the control room. Very rarely did he direct from the control room itself — he liked to be with the actors because he generally was acting as well as directing, and so he stood on a platform and would cue us and so forth."

Reid recalls that Welles had an easy rapport with his Mercury players and seemed especially fond of Agnes. "They had a very warm relationship. Agnes was very gracious and charming and loved to laugh and was a wonderful actress, and Orson liked to laugh and wanted good actors and naturally he wanted Agnes. They knew each other in a different way — he and Agnes had a very warm and relaxed relationship."

Among the other actors, besides Agnes, who were linchpins of the Mercury productions was Welles' good friend Joseph Cotten. "He was a great friend of Orson's," says Reid. "Really, Orson gave him his career or at least got it started. He was a struggling actor in New York when he came to Orson. Very charming, delightful man." Agnes, too, came to know and befriend Cotten and would work with him many times on radio, film and stage in the years to come.

Ray Collins, who was already well into his 50's when he joined the Mercury Theatre, is recalled by Reid as "A delightful man, loved to kid, loved to laugh. Because I was so young, he would tell stories which might get a blush out of me. They didn't really shock me that much. A charming guy, but very right-wing (Reid and most of the Mercury players were well to the left, except for Collins and Agnes), and such a wonderful voice."

Everett Sloane was another mainstay, but is recalled by Reid as having "a dark view of life." Reid emphasizes this was his own limited view of Sloane, but others have also confirmed this, including Agnes. Reid remembers that years after the Mercury experience he and Sloane worked together on an *Alfred Hitchcock Presents,* "and it was nighttime and we had to do a scene on a street at night; not pleasant to do. Everett and I had to make an entrance and we were waiting, and were waiting for an electric light to cue us to go in. So we were standing behind this fake door, outdoors, chilly, and Everett was unhappy over it and says, 'Can you believe we are standing out here at 9:30 at night doing this Goddamn thing?' I said, 'At least we are working.' He seemed to like to complain."

Another semi-regular Mercury player, who worked often with Welles and Agnes, was Karl Swenson. "He got known on Broadway in a show called *New Faces*," Reid says. "Very handsome, Scandinavian blood — very good actor (Agnes and Swenson had done a radio version of *Way Down East* together). He had a severe hearing problem, but he was always able to do his work, to get his cues — but away from work you had to be careful when speaking with him so he could hear you."

Martin Gabel was another friend and Mercury semi-regular who would have a long association with Agnes. He occasionally directed Agnes and Welles in *The Shadow* and also directed Agnes in the 1947 film *The Great Moment,* and tour for several months with her in 1957 in the play, *The Rivalry.* "Marty was very nice to work with," says Reid, "but I think he was diminished somewhat by a tragedy — he was a physical fitness fiend so he had these dumbbells which were small but very heavy. It was spring or summer and he and Arlene (Francis, his wife) lived in a high-rise apartment and the window was open and accidentally one of these dumbbells rolled off the table and out the open window and killed a man."

These were all very talented actors with great voices and they all got along well. Yet in their spare time they did not necessarily socialize. Welles described the Mercury Company as " . . . an Anglo-Saxon type family where the members leave each other pretty much alone. We had our fun together during working hours — and it was fun, you know. The atmosphere was like a sort of house party. To give you an idea, we always kept a good jazz-piano man on the set. Between jobs, though, we tended to go our separate ways."

IV

First Person Singular was a summer series which ran from July 11–September 5. Agnes didn't appear every week. After the first two episodes, "Dracula" and "Treasure Island," she didn't appear again for three weeks until "Abraham Lincoln," where Agnes appeared as Mary Todd to Orson's Abraham. She was then absent for the rest of the season. Part of this was due to Agnes having a very busy radio career beside Mercury. It wasn't that Agnes wasn't wanted on Mercury on a regular basis. The female parts in many of the pieces which were adapted were often scarce, and between Agnes and Arlene Francis they had to fight for the few feminine roles available.

When CBS offered Orson *First Person Singular,* he opted out of continuing on as Lamont Cranston on *The Shadow*. Mutual hired veteran radio actor William Johnstone to replace him, but Agnes continued on as Margot Lane. Johnstone would become a great friend to Agnes, who would also befriend Johnstone's wife, Georgia. Georgia Johnstone would soon become Agnes' secretary and, by the mid-50's, her New York theatrical representative. The change from Welles to Johnstone on *The Shadow* didn't diminish the ratings of the show; in fact, ratings improved and many listeners felt that Johnstone made a more effective Cranston than Orson. Anthony Tolin, *The Shadow* biographer, later wrote that "Johnstone brought a mature sophistication to the role of Cranston and a commanding authority as The Shadow that often eclipsed the performances of his illustrious predecessor." *Radio Daily Magazine,* in November 1938, wrote of the new *Shadow*: "Bill Johnstone . . . does a thoroughly good job, up several notches from last season's interpretation by Orson Welles."

CBS was very pleased with *First Person Singular,* even if the ratings were not overly high — it gave the network a certain amount of prestige to present these weekly plays. After the summer run, the show returned with a name change, *The Mercury Theatre of The Air.* But the formula was the same — literary works adapted for the radio listener. The first few weeks of the show didn't include Agnes at all, and the one show where she did "appear" she didn't have any lines at all, but she was instrumental in providing some of the atmosphere of this

(Courtesy of Wade Ballard)

A lovely Agnes Moorehead in the late '30s.

particular show; she is heard several times screaming. The date was October 30, 1938 and that evening's presentation would make broadcast history and eventually lead to a Hollywood contract for Orson which would benefit nearly everyone involved in the Mercury Theatre — especially Agnes.

The War of the Worlds by HG Wells was about Martians landing in the United States. *Mercury Theatre of the Air* was up against Edgar Bergen and his wooden sidekick, Charlie McCarthy. The Bergen show was a huge rating's success; according to Hooper radio ratings, Bergen got ratings in the mid-30s while *Mercury* was struggling on with a 3.5 rating share. But something very odd happened that evening. *The Mercury Theatre of the Air* began as always that evening with an announcer stating: "The Columbia Broadcasting System and its affiliated stations present Orson Welles and the Mercury Theatre on the Air in 'The War of the Worlds' by H.G. Wells. Ladies and gentlemen: the director of the Mercury Theatre and the star of these broadcasts, Orson Welles." Welles then went on to introduce the set up to the night's broadcast. For those who started with the broadcast from the beginning they understood what they were hearing was, in fact, a play.

After the introduction by Welles the script called for a phony weather bulletin, followed by a minute or so of ballroom music, so that if anybody was casually switching stations they might think that they had come upon a show featuring dance music. If so, they were the ones caught in the trap that Orson had sprung. Suddenly, a newsflash interrupts the music announcing that Professor Pieson (Orson) of the Princeton Observatory had observed an explosion of gas on Mars. After this "newsflash," the music resumed — the music (Ramon Raquello and his orchestra) keeps getting interrupted at regular and longer intervals.

It seems that about halfway through the Bergen show his guest, the popular operatic singer Nelson Eddy, began a song; for some that seemed to be a good time to switch stations. For those who switched to CBS — Hooper later concluded that 12 percent of the Bergen audience, or four million listeners, may have switched to CBS — it was just in time to hear, according to Frank Brady, "amidst crowd noises and police sirens, the concerned and authentic-sounding voice of a 'newscaster,' direct from Wilmuth Farm in Grover Mill, New Jersey, painting a word picture of the strange scene of the projectile half-buried in a huge hole" with creatures emerging from the hole and sending out rays which ignited anything in its path. Suddenly the voice of the newscaster goes silent and the air is filled with static.

Despite an announcement about 40 minutes into the program that the audience was listening to a dramatization, panic soon spread. According to *The Encyclopedia of Orson Welles,* "Priests were called to deliver last rites. Police stations were swamped as well. A half hour into the program, panic had seized thousands of people who were in flight, speeding along highways to try to distance themselves from the Martian menace." At the end of the program, just as police were knocking on the doors to try and bring an end to the program, Orson closed the proceedings: "This is Orson Welles, ladies and gentlemen, out of character to assure you that 'The War of the Worlds' has no further significance than as the holiday offering it was intended to be . . . the Mercury Theatre's own radio version of dressing up in a sheet and saying 'Boo! . . . '" The show, and the panic it caused, brought great publicity, and not all of it good. The FCC banned the use of fictional news bulletins in radio dramas, for instance.

Asked later by Peter Bogdanovich if he had expected that kind of response from the broadcast, Welles stated, "The kind of response, yes — that was merrily anticipated by all of us. The size of it, of course, was flabbergasting. Six minutes after we'd gone on the air, the switchboards in radio stations right across the country were lighting up like Christmas trees . . . ." Welles also acknowledged that the broadcast proved beneficial for him and the program. "Well, it put me in the movies. Was that lucky? I don't know. Anyway, thanks to the Martians, we got us a radio sponsor, and suddenly we were a great big commercial program."

Indeed they did get a sponsor, Campbell Soups. The final Mercury program was broadcast on December 4, 1938 and on December 9, *The Campbell Playhouse,* premiered. According to the authoritative *Encyclopedia of Old Time Radio,* under sponsorship from Campbell soup the show "moved up to first-class status." It certainly did get bigger budgets which afforded it the opportunity to utilize big name guest stars such as Margaret Sullavan, Gertrude Lawrence, Helen Hayes, Paulette Goddard, Charles Laughton and Lucille Ball. The "Mercury players" continued to be utilized: Agnes, Ray Collins, George Coulouris, Paul Stewart, Everett Sloane, Joe Cotten and so on, but they became overshadowed by the big names and budgets. The show lost the intimate feel it had for those glorious months it was known as *The Mercury Theatre of the Air.* Interestingly, once the show became *The Campbell Playhouse,* Agnes began to appear more. It is worth remembering that Agnes had appeared in only a handful of the *First Person Singular/Mercury Theatre of the Air* programs — most effectively and memorably in "Dracula." As for the most famous broadcast, "War of the

Worlds," she had only provided sound effects. This was nothing against Agnes — the Mercury Theatre was, by and large, chauvinistic. Most of the members were men and so the scripts were dominated by them. With a new sponsor having more input, it appears that a greater variety of female roles opened up and Agnes benefited from this. One of the most effective of the *Campbell Playhouse* scripts would be an adaptation of Daphne du Maurier's novel *Rebecca,* which became the first episode of the newly named show.

David O Selznick owned the film rights to the novel, but Orson was able to obtain the radio rights and it is a remarkably faithful adaptation. Orson played Maxim DeWinter, with guest star Margaret Sullavan cast as the heroine with no name (identified as "I" in the novel she narrates). Agnes had the plum role of the evil Mrs. Danvers, who believes no one could ever replace the dead mistress of Manderley (the DeWinter estate), Rebecca. Mrs. Danvers intentions with "I" are to make her feel as inconsequential as possible when compared to Rebecca as the mistress of Manderley, and for the love of Maxim. Agnes' performance is every bit as effective as that of Judith Anderson, who played the part in the 1940 film. Had Agnes been established in Hollywood earlier than she had, it is possible that Selznick would have considered her for the film based on her performance in the radio play, but Anderson, at that point, was a bigger name. The show concluded with Orson and Margaret Sullavan speaking by transatlantic phone with Miss du Maurier, who "enjoyed it enormously." Welles lso introduced a new trademark on this first episode by signing off, "obediently yours."

In all, 61 episodes of *The Campbell Playhouse* would be produced, with Agnes appearing in seventeen. Among the highlights were "Our Town," "The Things We Have" (an original story by Welles about a young immigrant who discovers the uniqueness of America), "Peter Ibbetson," "Ah, Wilderness!," "Lilom" and "Vanity Fair" (both with Helen Hayes). The show finally left the air on March 31, 1940. The final episode was an adaptation of "Jane Eyre" with Vivien Leigh, but without Agnes (who would later appear in the 1944 film with Welles and Joan Fontaine). The reason for Orson leaving the show was due to what he felt was sponsor interference. The sponsor wanted Orson, for instance, to hire actress Irene Dunne to appear on the show, but Orson refused, apparently because of her outspoken Republican politics. He also didn't like the "blue-penciling" of the scripts. "I'm sick of having the heart torn out of a script by radio censorship," he said. But in the end, the reason may be simply that he had other eggs to fry. By this time, due to his increased notoriety, Welles had signed a contract with RKO to act in and direct two motion pictures. He and his "Mercury" companions were going to take Hollywood by storm.

V

RKO Pictures signed Orson Welles to a deal which gave him something few actors or directors had — creative control of his projects without studio interference. "Welles could produce, direct, write and star in his projects or any combination of those roles he chose, and he alone would have virtually complete control of the final film. Welles could shoot what he liked, spend studio money any way he liked (up to $500,000 per picture), and with only minimal input from the studio, make the finished film just as he wanted it." Welles' main booster was RKO studio head, George Schaefer.

That many in the Hollywood community were resentful of this brash 23-year-old upstart coming into *their* town cannot be understated. Many longtime Hollywood observers believed that RKO committed a huge gaffe in signing Welles. "RKO is going to rue its contract. I would be willing to bet something that Welles will not complete a picture," huffed the *Hollywood Spectator*. But RKO was a studio willing to take a chance. It was a major, but not in the same league of MGM, Paramount, Warners or Fox. They had made some impressive films and they were the home studio of the hugely popular Fred Astaire-Ginger Rogers musicals, but overall their output didn't break even — they often ended the year well in the red. So they decided to gamble on someone different, like Welles.

They gave Welles the run of the studio. According to David Thomson, in his book, *Rosebud,* "Mercury had a group of bungalows on the lot in Culver City; Welles had his own steam room, as well as a masseur. He had his private cook, who made lunches for everyone: hamburgers, several inches thick, made from fat-free sirloin, and homemade tapioca pudding. Then he would hold court, sitting at his ease, telling gorgeous stories about himself."

At first it seemed that *The Spectator* and others were right. It was taking forever for Welles to finalize what his initial project would be. Initially, Welles had thought of filming Joseph Conrad's classic novel, *Hearts of Darkness,* but that fell through due to the limits of how much he could spend. Then he wanted to do an original film titled, *The Smiler with a*

Knife. But that fell through because he couldn't get the leading lady he wanted — first Carole Lombard and then Lucille Ball.

The studio was paying salaries for the Mercury members on a weekly basis and had nothing yet to show for it, so by Christmas, 1939, they sent Welles a letter informing him that unless he had something concrete on the table for them by New Year's, they would go off the payroll. A meeting on the situation was held in Chasen's and led to a major fight, but not a total break, between Welles and John Houseman. Welles apparently said he wanted to make sure everybody got paid, even if he had to pay for it out of his own pocket — but because his business managers were robbing him blind, he didn't have the money for payroll. To Houseman, this was the height of hypocrisy. Welles had spent money like there was no tomorrow since he had arrived in Hollywood and now he was blaming others for there not being enough money. He challenged Orson. "What are you going to do?" Welles angrily asked Houseman what *he* was going to do. Houseman told Orson to "tell the truth for once." Orson flew off at Houseman: "I don't lie to actors. I've never lied to an actor in my life! You're the one who lies! That's why they hate you! You're a crook and they know it!"

In the end they had no choice but to try and come up with a project as soon as possible. Enter Herman J. Mankiewicz, who was a screen and radio writer, including for *The Campbell Playhouse*. Houseman later recalled Mankiewicz (or "Mank" as he was commonly called) as a ". . . neurotic drinker and compulsive gambler, he was also one of the most intelligent, informed, witty, humane and charming men I have ever known." Welles employed Mank to help come up with an idea for the new film.

It was while Mankiewicz was recuperating from an automobile accident in February 1940 in Victorville, California that he recalled an idea he wanted to film years before: the story of a man's life recalled in flashbacks by the people who knew him. Welles liked the idea and together he and Mankiewicz began to brainstorm ideas on whose life they could base their script on. " . . . we started searching for the man it was going to be about. Some big American figure, but it couldn't be a politician, because you'd have to pinpoint him. Howard Hughes was the first idea. But we got pretty quickly to the press lords." Initially the project was named by Mankiewicz, *American*.

Eventually a screenplay was fashioned and titled *Citizen Kane*. It is the story of Charles Foster Kane, a publishing tycoon who dies at his extravagant mansion, Xanadu. As he is dying, his last word is "rosebud." A reporter is assigned to find out the meaning of Kane's last word and doggedly interviews several people who knew Kane to find the answer to that puzzle.

That the film was a thinly veiled biography of publishing mogul William Randolph Hearst cannot be disputed. Certainly it includes elements of Hearst's own life. Hearst, like the character Kane, had once been a crusading newspaper publisher who moved steadily to the Right. Hearst, like Kane, had an elaborate home called San Simeon which, like Kane's home, also had a private zoo. Hearst, like Kane, got involved in politics and was defeated. Hearst, like Kane, had a mistress he helped bankroll. But where Susan Alexander was a no-talent opera singer, Marion Davies, Hearst's mistress, was a talented comedy actress, who was well known even before she hooked up with Hearst. Still, many people accused Welles of basing Susan on Davies. Welles later admitted he felt bad about that. Welles himself later told Peter Bogdanovich: "He (Hearst) was right! He was dead right. Why not fight? I expected that. I didn't expect that everyone would run as scared as they did."

(Courtesy of Wade Ballard)

Agnes in her first film, Orson Welles' *Citizen Kane*.

Agnes was cast as Kane's mother. There could be no question of what role Agnes would get. She obviously was an important member of the Mercury team, and would be included. But there were few female roles and the only one which, in Orson's opinion, suited Agnes, was that of the mother. She lacked the youth (Agnes was pushing 40) and physical beauty to play the first Mrs. Kane, Emily. She also was not quite suited for the part of Susan Alexander, Kane's mistress and later his second wife.

Principal photography began on July 30, 1940. Agnes would begin four days of filming for what would be her first motion picture on September 13. The sequence opens with the reporter reading Thatcher's unpublished memoirs — the section on Charles Foster Kane. The scene then dissolves from the pages that the reporter is reading to a snow-capped landscape and happy, playful music as we see a child merrily sledding down a hill. Is this the last happy moments of Charles Foster Kane's childhood? The camera then backs up through the window to where Bernstein the banker is presenting a paper for Mary Kane to sign giving him guardianship of her only son. Her husband is putting up a rather weak fight, but Mrs. Kane is adamant and signs the papers. For those who feel that Agnes' acting is stoic and unsympathetic, they are missing two key points which betray that. There is a moment where Agnes says to her husband, "It's going to be done exactly the way I've told Mr. Thatcher . . . I've got his trunk all packed. I've had it packed for a week now." When she comes to the line, "I've had it packed for a week now," a look of regret and a hint of sadness and agony register in her speech. David Thomson, in his fine biography of Welles, *Rosebud,* writes of this moment in the film: "Moorehead looks like a Madonna, but a cold, imperious, adamantine one — she has the eyes of a saint, yet she could play Miss Murdstone in *David Copperfield* or Mrs. Danvers in *Rebecca."*

The other key moment for Agnes occurs only a moment later when she moves over to the window and watches Charles at play; she suddenly opens the window and, in a look of that is both stoic and agonized, she piercingly calls out his name to summon him, "Charles!" Thomson would later write that Agnes figures in two of the most "indelibly humane" moments in the work of Orson Welles — and this is one of those moments.

The scene concludes outside in the snow with Mrs. Kane introducing her son to his guardian and Thatcher telling Charles about how much fun they will have and all the different places they are going to travel. But Charles wants to know if his mother is going with him. He clings to her. "Why aren't you coming?" he asks. He, nor the audience, get a satisfactory answer. The scene dissolves with Mary Kane holding her bewildered son and attempting to reassure him. "You won't be lonely, Charles."

Frank Brady writes in his superb biography of Orson Welles "Although Agnes Moorehead appeared on the screen for only a few moments in *Citizen Kane* it was obvious that she was born to the medium." She gives a performance so assured that it is hard to believe it is her first film. Her acting in this film secured her future as one of the most important and influential character actresses in Hollywood. With her first two films for Welles it is not surprising that Agnes would go on to have the most enduring career in films of any of the Mercury actors.

When the film was completed, it was hinted that the story was thinly based on Hearst. He wanted confirmation of this and assigned his star Hollywood reporter, Louella Parsons to discover the truth. Louella attended a private screening and before the screening was over, she went to the brass at RKO and told them in effect that they better shelve the film or Hearst would put them out of business. She reported back to Hearst and he put his considerable newspaper chain on notice to ignore the film and if they were to publish anything regarding Welles, it was to be of a negative nature — no more "boy genius" fluff pieces. He also made it clear to RKO that unless they shelved the film he wouldn't publish anything in his papers regarding any future RKO productions. Hearst also arranged for Louis B. Mayer to offer RKO a sum of money to buy the film print and then destroy it. To his credit, RKO studio head Schaefer stood his ground and didn't give in; he released the picture. Thanks to that gutsy move — one of the greatest, and in many critics and movie lover's opinions *the* greatest film of all time, was released. It certainly is the most influential.

Years later, probably in the early 1970's, Agnes was attending a cocktail party at a friend's home. The party host's teenage son and a group of his friends arrived home, not realizing a party was going on. The host introduced the kids to Agnes, and while they were well-mannered, they were not particularly in awe of meeting her. The host thought that they were a bit rude and took them aside to tell them so. One teenager was used to meeting celebrities since his father worked in the industry and told the host he didn't think it was a big deal "to meet Endora" from *Bewitched,* adding, "It's not like she was in *Citizen Kane!*" Suddenly, behind him, he heard "one of the most cutting laughs I've ever heard from a woman's throat." The boy turned to the host and slowly questioned, "She . . . was . . . in . . . *Citizen Kane?*" The host was now laughing and nodding his head "yes." The boy and his friends apologized to Agnes, who graciously told them it was okay, as their "awe" level increased.

5

FANNY

Following *Citizen Kane,* Agnes went back to New York "and did a lot of little things," she would recall, "but nothing spectacular." About a year after completing *Kane* Welles called her back to Hollywood. He had another film role for her and believed that she was the only actress who could do this pivotal role justice.

Orson Welles had presented an adaptation of Booth Tarkington's famous novel, *The Magnificent Ambersons* on his radio show in 1939. He loved Tarkington's work and did radio adaptations of several of his books including *Seventeen, Clarence* and *Alice Adams.* Interestingly, none of Orson's radio adaptations of Tarkington's work featured Agnes. In the radio version, the character of Aunt Fanny, who is so prominently featured in both the novel and the later Welles film, is not utilized at all.

Orson's original contract with RKO called for four pictures; he delivered his first, *Citizen Kane,* which became one of the most celebrated and maligned films of its time. But outside of New York City It didn't deliver in box office potential. The Hearst boycott was effective, but even in large cities like Chicago, Boston and San Francisco, which supposedly had more sophisticated audiences, it didn't match box office expectations. Was it too different for contemporary audiences? In an effort to sell the picture, RKO put the actors in contemporary clothing and filmed a trailer that seemed to be trying to sell the film as a love story. Even Agnes, who plays a withered frontier mother in her five-minute sequence in the film, is shown in the new trailer wearing a sophisticated outfit and glamorous hairdo talking on the phone (to whom?). "Of course I love him, I gave him $60,000,000." It didn't help box office receipts. They would have been wiser to try and cash in on the controversy and sell the film as "The Must See picture that they tried to stop," or more effectively utilize the overwhelmingly favorable critical reaction to the film.

RKO studio head, and Orson's main booster, George Schaefer was under pressure. Some studio executives felt that they should cut their losses and do away with Orson all together. Others felt that for Orson's next picture the studio must have tighter control and the right to a final cut. After months of indecision Orson finally determined that the next two pictures he would make would be *The Magnificent Ambersons* and *Journey Into Fear*. He would direct, but not act in, *Ambersons* and, if he got his way, he would co-write (with Joe Cotten), produce and not direct or act in *Journey*. Orson convinced Schaefer to give a green light to *Ambersons* after he played the studio head a recording of the 1939 *Mercury Theatre of the Air* version.

Orson also allowed himself to sign a new contract dated July 7, 1941, which called for him to make *Ambersons* and *Journey Into Fear,* but with RKO getting script and casting approval. They also insisted that Welles keep within a reasonable budget — $850,000. Also, and most important, RKO would get the *right of final cut* (though the studio would allow a cut of Orson's choosing to be shown at the first preview). Orson wrote most of the script, dictated to a secretary, while on director King Vidor's yacht off of Catalina. Orson's script follows the novel with great fidelity, but he did write an original ending — an ending he felt best wrapped the story up.

The Magnificent Ambersons tells the story of a wealthy and powerful Indiana family which has lived in this Midwestern city (probably Indianapolis) for generations. The patriarch of the family is Major Amberson, who has a lovely daughter, Isabel. Isabel is courted by two suitors, Wilbur Minafer and Eugene Morgan. But Eugene loses Isabel when he shows up on her doorstep to serenade her drunk — embarrassing her. She marries the steady but mundane Wilbur. They all live together in the fabulous Amberson mansion.

Other family members include Isabel's brother, Jack, and Wilbur's unmarried sister, Fanny. Isabel and Wilbur have a son, George, who is doted on by Isabel. Stuck in a loveless marriage, she overindulges "Georgie" and only sees his fine qualities as he grows up to be an arrogant and obnoxious young man. Georgie is sent away to school, but returns after graduation. There is a glittering party in his honor held at the Amberson mansion with everybody who is anybody in town invited. Among those invited are the widowed Eugene Morgan and his pretty young daughter, Lucy. Georgie is taken by Lucy, who, despite Georgie's arrogant manner, is also smitten. At first, Georgie doesn't realize that Lucy is Eugene's daughter, and he deeply resents Eugene's obvious attention to his mother.

Eugene is an inventor and intent on opening a factory to produce automobiles — an idea which Georgie scoffs at. Meanwhile, Aunt Fanny is hoping that Eugene will become reacquainted with her — after all, Isabel is a married woman. Soon afterward, Wilbur dies and it becomes apparent to everyone, including Fanny, that Eugene is interested in Isabel. While Georgie is still interested in Eugene's daughter, he opposes Eugene's courting of his recently widowed mother. Aunt Fanny doesn't help the situation by telling Georgie that "people are talking" about Eugene and Isabel. Georgie tells Eugene to stay away from his mother. Fanny, seeing the damage she has done, tells Georgie that she was a "fool" and that "Eugene never would have looked at me even if he'd never seen Isabel." But Georgie remains opposed to his mother seeing Eugene. Isabel, who worships the ground her son walks on, accepts this. Georgie loses Lucy, and he and Isabel decide to take a long trip abroad. By the time they return Isabel is very ill, and soon dies without seeing Eugene one last time. Because of a bad investment, the Ambersons go broke and lose their home. Fanny and Georgie move into a seedy rooming house, Uncle Jack moves away to find work, Eugene is a wealthy automaker, but Lucy, still in love with Georgie, despite everything, is unmarried. Georgie must find work to support himself and Fanny. In an ironic turn of events Georgie is seriously injured after being struck by an automobile — George Amberson Minafer finally gets what the town has been hoping for since he was a young boy — his comeuppance.

Casting would not be a problem for Welles and RKO. Though the studio probably would have preferred a top name star, they accepted the fact that with the budgetary limits imposed on Orson, that would not be a possibility. They also believed that Orson's Mercury stock players were very fine actors indeed. Some of the Mercury players in the months since the end of *Kane* had moved onto other projects and couldn't appear in *Ambersons*. But returning in the lead role was Joseph Cotten, ideal as Eugene Morgan. Ray Collins is Uncle Jack and Agnes would play Aunt Fanny. Welles toyed with the idea of playing Georgie (as he had in the radio version) but decided that due to his age and girth that another actor should be selected. He chose Tim Holt, who up to this time had mainly appeared in B westerns. It was an inspired choice. For the role of Isabel, he brought out of retirement Dolores Costello, who had appeared in silent films and had the kind of fading beauty essential to the part. As Lucy, 18-year-old

Anne Baxter was selected and her beauty and vivaciousness are huge assets to the film. As Major Amberson, Orson cast 68-year-old Richard Bennett, whose career had hit a patchy stretch and was, by this time, quite ill (he would die soon after completion of the picture).

That Agnes would play Fanny Minafer was never in doubt. Orson wrote the part with her in mind. "There was never any question about it," Welles would recall to Peter Bogdanovich years later. "How could there be? She'd been all those years with us — it was going to be her great part, and indeed it was."

Orson decided that, prior to filming, the cast should get acquainted with the elegant set and the feel of their characters, so they spent several weeks rehearsing and just roaming the massive set of the Minafer mansion, becoming familiar with its rooms. This house is as much a character in this film as any. It is usually seen in dark tones — some have

(Courtesy of Wade Ballard)

Agnes as "Aunt Fanny" in her finest screen performance, in The Magnificent Ambersons (1942).

suggested it has the look of a haunted house. Indeed the house is haunted by its past — a glorious past, but as the money runs out it becomes darker and falls into decay.

Orson decided that as an economy measure the actors would record their lines and, when shooting began, they would simply mouth the words. He felt that by recording the soundtrack in this way it would eliminate the need to stifle the usual studio noise which might cause scenes to be reshot.

In a lecture delivered on December 3, 1945 at the Actors Lab, Agnes spoke about the elaborate rehearsing which preceded filming: ". . . Before we started shooting we studied and read aloud around the table for a month. A lot of the lines that weren't comfortable for the actor were changed — Mr. Welles is always very kind to the actor. We knew the story and the script thoroughly, from beginning to end. Then, we memorized our parts and recorded the scenes, then played them back. This, of course, isn't necessary, but it is a wonderful thing because there is nothing like hearing yourself, although I do think that an actor loses something when he tries to be critical of himself. Then we went on the set and became acquainted with the sets. We went upstairs and downstairs, through all the rooms. When we actually started shooting, it took very little time; during the whole production we only had to stop for fluffing of lines three times; because we knew our parts so well and we only had to stop for technical things."

What Agnes doesn't say in her lecture is that when they got around to using the soundtrack on the first day of shooting (October 28, 1941 — the scene where Georgie tells Eugene that automobiles are a "useless nuisance"), the actors found it very difficult to show expression, timing and characterization with this approach. It was abandoned. The first day's shooting lasted until 7:45 at night. Orson shot one scene with 20 set ups and recorded three minutes and twenty seconds of the script.

The pace over the next several days was slow — which exasperated Welles, who felt that the cameraman, Stanley Cortez, spent too much time lighting the set. He couldn't get his favored cinematographer, Gregg Toland, who had filmed *Kane*. Furthermore Welles felt that Cortez was pretentious; Cortez was an art lover and collector and would make suggestions to Orson for certain scenes by referencing great pieces of art. "Why don't we see if we can produce a Goyan 'black painting' in the scene with Aunt Fanny by the boiler," he would say. But Cortez also knew his stuff and the photography of *Ambersons* is in every way as impressive as *Kane*. While sets were being lit, Orson continued to rehearse his actors.

The cast and crew spent nine days filming inside a rented ice house in Los Angeles. Orson decided to shoot at an authentic ice house because he wanted to see the breath of his actors as if they were really outdoors in midwinter. (The snow scene in *Kane* which featured Agnes bothered Welles because you couldn't see the actors' breath.) The ice house smelled of fish and the actors wore longjohns under their costumes. Welles made sure there was plenty of hot coffee, hot chocolate and soup to warm the actors up between scenes. Joseph Cotten made cocktails for the cast toward the end of the day to warm the actors up. These measures didn't work on everyone — Ray Collins caught pneumonia and was hospitalized, missing several days of work. As for Orson, he gained back a great deal of the weight he had lost for *Kane*. His reason? Nobody would see him on camera.

But the scenes filmed during those nine days are among the lightest in *Ambersons*. Eugene is driving his "horseless carriage" on the snow packed roads with Isabel, Fanny, and Uncle Jack when they are passed by Georgie and Lucy in a sleigh driven by a horse going at a high speed. The sleigh overturns (with Holt and Baxter doing the scene themselves, as Orson didn't believe he could get the kind of shot needed with doubles performing the stunt). The car stops to help them, the young people are fine and join their elders in the drive back to the Amberson mansion. The car needs help getting started and eventually, to get it to move, they have to push it — a task Georgie reluctantly helps with. Eventually the car goes on its own power with the cast happily singing "The Man Who Broke the Bank at Monte Carlo," with Agnes' fine voice heard to particular advantage. The scene has a neat fade-out — a happy, light scene in a film which from this point forward grows increasingly pessimistic and dark.

The famous boiler scene from *The Magnificent Ambersons.*

Agnes has many fine scenes in this film and the most demanding is near the end of the picture when the Amberson fortune is gone. Georgie feels obligated to look out for Fanny, who has spent the day walking all over town looking for clean and affordable lodging for the two. The scene is commonly referred to as "the boiler scene" since it takes place in the kitchen by the boiler of the old Amberson mansion they would soon be vacating. Fanny is sinking down to the floor by the boiler staring up to Georgie — she is emotionally at the end of her rope and as the scene progresses she grows more hysterical:

FANNY:	You want to leave me in the lurch!
GEORGE:	Get up, Aunt Fanny.
FANNY:	I can't. I . . . I'm too weak. You're going to leave me in the lurch!
GEORGE:	Aunt Fanny! I'm only going to make eight dollars a week at the law office. You'd have to be paying more of the expenses than I would.
FANNY:	I'd be paying . . . I'd be paying . . .
GEORGE:	Certainly you would. You'd be using more of your money than mine . . .
FANNY:	(*laughs hysterically*) I have twenty-eight dollars. That's all.
GEORGE:	You mean until the interest is due again.
FANNY::	I mean that's all. I mean that's all there is. There won't be any more interest because there isn't any principal. I know, I told Jack I didn't put everything in the headlight (company), but I did . . . Every cent except my last interest payment and . . . and it's gone.
GEORGE:	Why did you wait until now to tell me?
FANNY:	I couldn't tell till I had to. It wouldn't do any good . . . Nothing does any good, I guess in this old world! I . . . I knew your mother wanted me to watch over you and try to have something like a home for you . . . And I tried. I tried to make things as nice for you as I could . . . I walked my heels down trying to find a place for us to live . . . I walked and walked over this town . . . I didn't ride one block on a street car . . . I wouldn't use five cents no matter how tired I . . . (*laughs wildly-hysterically*) Oh . . . And now . . . You Don't want . . . You Want . . . You want to leave me in the lurch! (*she laughs wildly*)
GEORGE:	(*impatiently*) Aunt Fanny! Aunt Fanny . . . Get up! Don't sit there with your back against the boiler . . . Get up, Aunt Fanny!

FANNY: Oh, it's not hot. It's cold. The plumbers disconnected it. I
           wouldn't mind if it burned . . . I wouldn't mind if it burned
           me George!

In her lecture at the Actors Lab, Agnes spoke of this scene. "Take for
example the scene by the boiler . . . When we did it, it ran from the kitchen
through the door into another room to the hall. I did it twelve times
though there was no fluffing. Sometimes it was because the lights weren't
right or the sound. The first time I did it, he (Orson) said that was all right,
now we'll do it as an insane woman and the next time as a drunk. I saw
what he was driving at. Everything you did and every time you did it, you
used a little more and in the end they all merged . . . At least four times that
we did the scene, he changed the perspective and the final time I did it, I
didn't know what I was doing. That is really wonderful for the actor . . . "

Years later Agnes did another elaboration on this pivotal and much-
remembered scene. "Orson would say during rehearsal, 'Agnes, why don't
you play it as if you were drunk? I'd play it that way. 'Okay,' he'd say, 'now
as if you were numb.' Then like a little girl . . . a meticulous old maid . . .
I didn't know what he was doing. Hours later he said, 'Now, Agnes, go play
it in one take!' I didn't realize until then that what he really wanted was a
little bit of all four. When it was over someone said, 'Agnes, you must be
worn out.' Worn out, ha! I was so excited I couldn't sleep for a week."

Peter Bogdanovich once asked Welles about this scene. "Is it true that
you rehearsed Agnes Moorehead so often in her scene by the boiler that she
really did become hysterical?" Welles replied, "Well, she became more and
more real. I didn't put her into a state of hysterics; I don't work that way
with actors . . . Aggie was just that good. Why she didn't get an Academy
Award for that performance, I'll never know."

Another extraordinary scene which thankfully wasn't cut from the
completed film — though many at RKO wanted it to be — is the one
where Aunt Fanny is feeding strawberry shortcake to Georgie and taking
pride in the fact that he enjoys it so much. Agnes, in her lecture at the
Actors Lab, said this was her favorite scene in the movie. "You probably
noticed that time was taken and there was no pressure, you had time to
think what you were doing and to move when it was exactly the right time.
That scene was ad-libbed and we did it ten times until poor Tim Holt was
green. Orson Welles came to me and said this is good, but it really needs
something else — until finally I got the idea from those little things that

you do when you are sitting at dinner with your family: she had time to watch him even though her main action was to try and find out something. Those things were my own adlibs and Tim said, 'For God's sake, don't forget and let me keep on eating!' We did it for the eleventh time and Orson loved it, but he said, 'let's do it once more.' So we stretched a scene that really took two or three minutes to eight minutes. The twelfth time we did it was a take." This scene is a wonderful character study as it becomes clear to Georgie that Fanny is clearly interested in Eugene Morgan and so, naturally, he has to tease her about her attraction:

GEORGE: I shouldn't be a bit surprised to have him request an interview and declare his intentions are honorable . . . and ask my permission to pay his addresses to you. What had I better tell him? (*Fanny starts sobbing, knowing that Georgie doesn't really mean a word of what he is saying. She rushes from the room, crying.*) It's getting so you can't joke with her about anything anymore . . .

UNCLE JACK: (*gently admonishing him*) . . . I think maybe we've been teasing her about the wrong things. Fanny hasn't got much in her life. You know, Georgie, just being an aunt isn't really the great career it may sometimes seem to be. I really don't know of anything much Fanny has got except her feelings about Eugene.

But according to Orson Welles, the finest piece of acting Agnes did in the film was never seen by audiences except at the initial preview. It was his original ending. Fanny Minafer is residing with a bunch of similarly beaten down women in a rooming house. Georgie has been taken to the hospital after suffering his car accident. Lucy has rushed to him as does Eugene Morgan. Eugene stops by the rooming house to see Fanny, who is in the parlor playing cards with the other women. All her hopes have long evaporated. She has lost all — her money, her family — and is now living with a bunch of other maiden ladies. The man she once hoped would love her comes to call. She takes him into the sitting room. She is stiff and formal. She barely looks at him. Eugene barely notices. Eugene asks her how she is, she murmurs, "Fine . . . fine." Fanny sits down in a rocking chair and as Eugene does most of the talking, she rocks back and forth. Eugene;

never understanding nor realizing that Fanny had at one time cared for him. He tells her of his making up with Georgie at the hospital, and Georgie telling him, "You must have known my mother wanted you to come here today so that I could ask you to forgive me." He tells her that Georgie and Lucy will in all likelihood marry. Eugene is now a wealthy car manufacturer; Georgie and Lucy are back together and will marry, but what of poor Fanny? In the final fade out, as Eugene exits after wishing her a "good night," the mirror reflects Fanny watching him leave as the women at the table in the parlor playing cards watch her. Fanny turns and slowly walks back to them. She will end her days alone and living with women just like her. The narrator (Welles) says, "Ladies and Gentlemen, that's the end of the story."

Orson Welles later said, ". . . If only you'd seen how she wrapped up the whole story at the end . . . Jo Cotten goes to see her after all those years in a cheap boarding house and there's just nothing left between them at all. Everything is over — her feelings and her world and his . . . the end of communication between people, as well as the end of an era . . . Without question it was much the best scene in the picture." But after a disastrous preview, the scene was eliminated because the powers-that-be at RKO felt it was too much of a downer for audiences.

In the midst of filming, but on a day off for the actors, Sunday, December 7, 1941, the Japanese attacked Pearl Harbor. The film wasn't delayed as the United States prepared to enter the Second World War. On December 8, the actors, including Agnes, shot the scene where they tour Eugene's automobile factory — another splendid scene. Eugene's attentions are squarely on Isabel as he escorts Isabel, Fanny, Lucy and Georgie on this tour of his factory. Yet look at Agnes' face at the very edge of the screen, as if all the life is sucked out of her when Eugene tells Isabel he is thinking of taking up writing verse again. "I'm almost thinking I could do it again, to thank you for making a factory visit into such a kind celebration."

Welles and Agnes had a close director/actor relationship. He also did the unexpected with her to get the performance he wanted. One day Welles was directing Agnes in an emotional scene where Fanny gets hysterical and has to cry. "Blow the glycerin into those classic orbs!" yelled Welles. The make-up man blew, and Agnes had giant tears rolling down her face. Orson yelled, "Now Aggie, *Action!,*" and Agnes posed for her close-up — but it didn't meet Orson's satisfaction. He called cut. He walked over to Agnes and said, "Aggie, listen to me." He leaned over her, as if he is whispering into her ear, then he jerked down and bit into her neck! Agnes screamed and Orson bellowed, "Aggie! You adorable irresistible creature — *Cry!*" He walked back behind the camera and called "Action!," but this time she didn't need the glycerin blown in her eyes; the tears were real. On another occasion Orson said to Agnes, "You must have a mustache and more lines on your face. I love women with mustaches!" Welles grabbed a make up pencil himself and began to apply the lines and an almost unnoticeable mustache.

The picture finished principal photography in mid-January. Orson soon left on a State Department project in Central America and he cabled his instructions to editor Robert Wise regarding the cutting of the film. At least initially Welles must have been encouraged by the studio's reaction to the picture. Schaefer enthusiastically cabled Welles about the film, and especially Agnes:

PLEASE FORGIVE ME FOR NOT HAVING WIRED YOU IMMEDIATELY ON MY RETURN FROM THE COAST TO TELL YOU OF MY HAPPINESS AS A RESULT OF WHAT I HAVE SEEN OF YOUR CURRENT PICTURE. EVEN THOUGH I HAVE ONLY SEEN A PART OF IT, THERE IS EVERY INDICATION THAT IT IS CHOCK FULL OF HEARTTHROBS, HEARTACHES AND HUMAN INTEREST. FROM A TECHNICAL STANDPOINT IT IS STARTLING AND I SHOULD NOT FORGET TO MENTION ESPECIALLY THAT AGNES MOOREHEAD DOES SOME OF THE FINEST PIECES OF WORK I HAVE EVER SEEN ON THE SCREEN. ALTHOUGH I SAW ONLY PART OF THE PICTURE HER WORK IN PARTICULAR MADE A TREMENDOUS IMPRESSION ON ME. AGAIN, I AM VERY HAPPY AND PROUD OF OUR ASSOCIATION. CONGRATULATION AND BEST WISHES.
GEORGE J. SCHAEFER

There was a preview of the picture at the Fox Theater in Pomona, California on March 17; the preview was still basically Orson's cut. As always in a preview the audience doesn't know what to expect. Is it a musical? A comedy? Drama? Suspense? What? The preview was held following the showing of *The Fleet's In*, a patriotic musical starring Dorothy Lamour. The result was not good. Of 125 preview cards only 53 rated *The Magnificent Ambersons* positively. Among the comments on the negative side: "We do not need trouble pictures, especially now . . ." "It stinks," and "No, it's as bad if not worse than *Citizen Kane*." But others saw the greatness of the film: "This picture is magnificent. The direction, acting, photography, and special effects are the best cinema has yet offered. It is unfortunate that the

American public, as represented at this theatre, are unable to appreciate fine art." And, "I think it was the best picture I have ever seen." Some people showed their disdain for the movie by walking out. Did showing such a bleak, yet brilliant film, after a patriotic, breezy musical-comedy help seal its fate? Was this the reaction the studio wanted anyway, so that they could cut the film the way they wanted? One wonders.

Needless to say, Schaefer once again contacted Orson, this time by special delivery mail. "Never in all my experience in the industry have I taken so much punishment or suffered as I did at the Pomona preview. In my 28 years in the business, I have never been present in a theater where the audience acted in such a manner . . . It was just like getting one sock in the jaw after another for over two hours."

A second preview, in Pasadena, with a slightly older audience was held shortly after the first. A few minutes had been cut, but the results, while somewhat more positive, were still not what the studio was hoping for. The audience had a hard time following the various relationships in the film. Was Fanny an Amberson or not? Who was Uncle Jack?

But Orson's cruelest jab must have been when he received a heartfelt letter from his best friend, Joe Cotten: ". . . Dramatically, it is like a play full of wonderful, strong second acts all coming down on the same curtain line, all proving the same tragic point. Then suddenly someone appears on the apron and says the play is over without there having been enacted a concluding third act. The emotional impact in the script seems to have lost itself somewhere in the cold visual beauty before us and at the end there is definitely a feeling of dissatisfaction."

Welles, still in South America, cabled revisions to the studio. "I was bargaining. 'I'll give you that if you'll leave me this.'" The studio wanted an upbeat ending. Orson tried to oblige and cabled this idea to RKO on April 2, 1942: "To leave audiences happy . . . remake cast credits as follows and in this order: First oval framed old-fashioned picture very authentic-looking Bennett in Civil War campaign hat. Second, live shot of Ray Collins . . . in elegant white ducks and hair whiter than normal seated on tropical veranda ocean and waving palm tree behind him — Negro servant serving him second long cool drink. Third, Aggie blissfully and busily playing bridge with cronies in boarding house. Fourth, circular locket authentic old-fashioned picture of Costello in ringlets looking very young. Fifth, Jo Cotten at French window closing watch case obviously containing Costello's picture tying in previous shot: sound of car driving away, Jo turns, looks over shoulder and waves. Sixth, Tim Holt and Anne Baxter in open car — Tim shifting gears but looking over shoulder — as he does this, Anne looking same direction and waving, then turn to each other then forward both very happy and gay and attractive for fadeout. Then fade in mike shot for my closing lines as before." It was all in vain.

Anne Baxter, Tim Holt, Agnes, Donald Dilaway in _The Magnificent Ambersons_.

The actors were called back to do retakes to try and make the ending more upbeat, at least in the eyes of the studio. On April 18, 1942, Agnes and Joe Cotten shot a scene in the hallway of the hospital where Georgie had been taken after his accident. In the scene, Aunt Fanny arrives at the hospital just as Eugene Morgan comes out of Georgie's room. Much of the dialogue in this scene is the same as in the original final scene that Orson shot with Eugene telling Fanny that Georgie told him, "you must have known that my mother wanted you to come here today . . . ," and Georgie and Lucy reconciling. The difference is that the dramatic tension and the sense of isolation and bleakness which Fanny had in the scene originally shot by Welles is lost. As directed by Fred Fleck, the dialogue was now mere words with little meaning behind them. Cotten and Moorehead walk down the corridor together with schmaltzy music playing as if they are walking out into the sunset — looking up with serenity written all over their faces.

All in all, the studio cut forty-four essential minutes from *The Magnificent Ambersons*. The film was released, and is still shown today, at eighty-eight minutes long. It is a mangled masterpiece. It still has brilliance especially the first half of the picture, which is spared the most. The second half is disjointed; partly the work of Welles, with brilliant shots interspersed with the work of various others who directed retakes such as editor Robert Wise and assistant director Fred Fleck. Welles, years later, saw *The Magnificent Ambersons* at a theater in Paris and at first thought, "hmm, this isn't that bad." But as the picture proceeded, he said "all hell broke loose." He was talking about his baby.

The amazing thing about the film is that even today in its butchered state it still works, and at times, is even better than *Kane* — especially in terms of performances. Agnes Moorehead's performance survives — it is a performance for the ages. One of the best performances ever recorded up to that time, one that still rings true. Author James Naremore sums up her performance well: "Throughout the film Moorehead conveys Fanny's torment in every bird like gesture of her body, frequently drawing the spectator's eye into little corners of the frame, where she dominates the screen without saying a word. In the brief scene at Morgan's automobile factory, she can be seen bestowing an adoring look on her beloved as he tells Isabel that he feels like writing poetry again; the glance speaks volumes, but is delivered at the very margin of the playing area and is ignored by the other actors." Over the years, other critics have testified to the greatness of this performance. Pauline Kael would later write: "As the nervous, bitter, hysterical old maid aunt, Agnes Moorehead just about belts you out of the theatre." Charles Higham said, "Agnes Moorehead moves deeply inside the frustration and misery of the character, she conveys in high-pitched whines, in querulous outbursts of rage, and in her whole taut, cramped, tightly corseted body and pinched, hawk like face, in every movement of her hands, in every fit of hysteria, a life wretched on the rocks of repression." The British critic Kenneth Tynan, who first saw the film as a sixteen-year-old movie lover and who began a pen pal relationship with Welles, later wrote that Agnes' performance "seemed to me then (and seems to me still) the best performance of its kind in the English-speaking cinema." That Tynan did indeed love the film and Agnes' performance as a teenager is confirmed in a letter he wrote to a friend on 4/11/43: "The acting through-out is exquisite but of course the real star is Agnes Moorehead. That performance is the finest I have ever seen particularly when she sits down and laughs at Tim Holt and the scene where he taunts her for being in love with Cotten and she screams at him from behind her bedroom door — her entire performance was logical hysteria, which is rare — very rare."

The contemporary reviews of the day were mixed on the film, but mostly quite positive regarding Agnes' performance. Upon the films release in July 1942, *Newsweek* wrote that *Ambersons* "falls considerably short of matching . . . *Citizen Kane*," but said the cast was "fine," particularly "Anne Baxter as the attractive Lucy Morgan and Agnes Moorehead as George's hysterical, repressed Aunt Fanny." *Commonweal* said that Agnes gave "a splendid portrayal as the frightened, frustrated Aunt Fanny." The *New York Times* referred to Agnes' performance as "splendid." The *New Yorker* said she was "especially fine as George's Aunt Fanny." The critic for the *Detroit Free Press* wrote: "Miss Moorehead's performance is a gripping and thrilling piece of acting which marks her for stellar honors."

While he was still filming *Ambersons* by day, Welles began to shoot the third Mercury production *Journey into Fear* by night. This film was to be a departure from *Kane* and *Ambersons* in that it was considered to be a purely commercial film. The film was co-written by Cotten and Orson. The story concerns a married couple, played by Joseph Cotten and Ruth Warrick, in Turkey where the Cotten character, Howard Graham, has been working to upgrade Turkish munitions. In a bar for a farewell drink, an assassin (played by Jack Moss) makes an attempt on Graham's life but ends up killing a magician (Hans Conried) instead. The head of the Turkish secret service, Col. Haki (played by Orson), puts the bewildered Graham on a freighter leaving for Batum (his wife stays at a hotel). At this point Graham interacts with the various other passengers on the freighter including Josette (Dolores Del Rio) and Gogo (Jack Durant) who were entertainers in the bar where the attempt on Howard's life had been made. While there is sexual tension between Howard and Josette, Howard is faithful to his wife. Among the other passengers are a German archeologist, a tobacco salesman and Mr. and Mrs. Matthews (played by Agnes and Frank Readick). Mr. Matthews is a socialist while his wife, a French woman, is not — and deplores it when he talks politics. Also on board is the assassin, actually more than one.

Orson produced the film and gave the directing credit to Norman Foster, though many Welles fans believe that the direction has many classic Wellesian touches. But, as Welles himself noted, he was out of the country during much of the filming (his role as Taki is actually quite small). He always gave Foster his due as director, but admits that he "supervised the planning" of many of the shots. Originally, Welles didn't want to act in the film and was hoping to get the veteran character actor Thomas Mitchell to portray the head of the Turkish secret police, but he proved unavailable. The film is tense and well made, playing like a Hitchcock suspense film. One of the best scenes in the picture is when Graham, escorted ashore by the assassins and driven away, uses a penknife to create a commotion by sticking it in the car's horn to create a diversion. Graham grabs the wheel, crashes the car and flees. It is a superbly directed scene. The Hitchcock comparison was made by other critics as well, including *Time:* "Welles shows himself a careful student of Alfred Hitchcock, but he falls far short of the old master. *Journey into Fear* also falls short of the best Orson Welles." The film also has elements of *film noir;* it is dark, cynical, full of characters who seem to have something to hide, and ambiguous heroes. Agnes is fine in her small role and plays it with a realistic accent, but there are no shining scenes like she had in *Kane* and *Ambersons.* The film belongs to Cotten and especially Jack Moss as the silent assassin. Once again, though, this film would be recut by RKO and Welles would later say the film had "lots of brilliant character performances which all got chopped out and thrown out." Welles, himself, thinks he was pretty "awful" in it.

While *The Magnificent Ambersons* didn't do well at the box office (and *Journey into Fear* would be also be a failure — making Orson a three-time loser with RKO, who would soon terminate his contract), the film, and particularly Agnes, received critical plaudits. The *National Board of Review,* on Christmas Eve, 1942, would list Agnes' performance as Aunt Fanny as one of the best of the year. But the high point in critical reaction would be the announcement of the New York Film Critics' choices for Best Picture, Best Actor and Best Actress. The winners were announced on December 26, 1942. A patriotic British war picture, *In Which We Serve,* was named Best Picture. James Cagney was named Best Actor for his energetic performance in *Yankee Doodle Dandy* and, in a stunning upset, Agnes was named Best Actress for *The Magnificent Ambersons.* It was an upset because many fans and critics believed the winner would or should be Greer Garson for *Mrs. Miniver.* The critic for the *New York Herald Tribune* wrote: "I must admit I was a bit startled by the critics' vote. Agnes Moorehead gave a brilliant and thoughtful portrayal . . . but I definitely preferred Greer Garson's modulated performance." Apparently, Garson led on the first ballot with 7 votes, compared to 3 each for Agnes and Katharine Hepburn (for *Woman of the Year*). But it wasn't enough for a victory. On the sixth ballot Agnes prevailed with 11 votes, with 7 for Garson. Louella Parsons, wrote in the *LA Examiner:* "The award given Agnes Moorehead for best performance of the year by New York writers, was received with uplifted brows in Hollywood, to put it mildly. She was eerie and different, but compare her with Greer Garson or Bette Davis or Teresa Wright, and in most people's opinions she wouldn't be in the same class." This was expected since Louella was writing for a Hearst newspaper and Agnes appeared in a Welles picture and was identified mainly at the time as being one of his Mercury players.

Agnes received word of the critics' decision by telegram and attended the awards ceremony held on January 3, 1943, at the Barberry Room of the Berkshire Hotel in New York, and carried live over the NBC radio network. The award was presented by director John Farrow, and she delivered a gracious acceptance speech: "Thank you, Mr. Farrow. It is a great honor for me to be here this afternoon. It would be untrue if I said that I had not hoped that someday, I might win the New York Film Critics Award for a performance. I don't think there is any actress who hasn't dreamed of it. But there is a great difference between keeping an illusion alive, and seeing it become an actuality. I know that all this must be happening to me, because I am on this program, and because on Wednesday morning, I received Mr. McManus' wire informing me how the New York Film Critics had voted. If nothing else, I have the wire for proof. I have read it many, many times and it still says the same thing . . . In accepting this honor in playing Fanny Minifer in *The Magnificent Ambersons,* I cannot accept it for myself alone. A great lady of the theatre once said that a performance depends on three things — an actor, a part, and a director who understands both. In all honesty, I must say that the part I was given to play had a great deal to do with my performance, and even more than the part was the creative understanding of the director of *Magnificent Ambersons,* Orson Welles. I have been fortunate enough to have worked with Mr. Welles for many years, in radio, in the theatre and in motion pictures. I am in motion pictures because of Mr. Welles. It would take a much longer time than I am allowed to tell you how much he has had to do with whatever achievement I have made. I can say it best perhaps, by accepting the New York Film Critics Award for him too. Thank you."

David O. Selznick thought *The Magnificent Ambersons* was a tremendous achievement and was particularly impressed by Agnes, sending her a congratulatory telegram when he heard that she was honored by the New York Critics:

DEAR AGNES PLEASE ACCEPT MY WARMEST CONGRATULATIONS ON THE WELL DESERVED AWARD OF THE NY CRITICS I AM VERY HAPPY FOR YOU. DOS.

It is interesting that the New York Critics made no distinction between best actress and supporting actress. They named Agnes best actress over such worthy competition as Greer Garson, Katharine Hepburn, Bette Davis, Teresa Wright, and Rosalind Russell. The Academy of Motion Pictures Arts and Sciences did make such a distinction. On February 8, 1943, Agnes was nominated for her first Academy Award. It was not in the best actress category, though it can be persuasively argued that Agnes was the lead actress in *The Magnificent Ambersons*. The Academy thought otherwise, nominating her in the Supporting Actress Category, probably because they thought that was where she belonged; not only her part in the picture, but by her looks and status in the industry at that time. Her competition was Teresa Wright for *Mrs. Miniver,* Gladys Cooper for *Now, Voyager,* Susan Peters for *Random Harvest* and Dame May Whitty, also for *Mrs. Miniver.* It would not have been unrealistic to think that because there were two actresses nominated for *Mrs. Miniver* that it might split the *Miniver* vote and allow Agnes to win. In any other year that might have happened. But young Teresa Wright was having a banner year. She had also been nominated for Best Actress for her performance as Mrs. Lou Gerhig in *The Pride of the Yankees*. The Academy was prepared to honor the number one film of the year and the actress they felt gave the year's best performance, Greer Garson as the long-suffering *Mrs. Miniver.* They also felt they should honor Wright in some way for giving two memorable performances in the single year, and she ran away with the supporting award.

In addition to Best Supporting Actress, *The Magnificent Ambersons* was nominated for three other Academy Awards: Best Picture, Cinematography and Interior Decoration, but came up short. Without a doubt *The Magnificent Ambersons* is a personal triumph for Agnes. It capped an incredible year and established her in Hollywood. By the time she was nominated for the Oscar, Agnes had already appeared in four releases over the past two years: *Kane, Ambersons, Journey into Fear,* and *The Big Street* (Agnes' first non-Mercury film, based on a Damon Runyon story, and starring Henry Fonda and Lucille Ball; Agnes' first comedy role in pictures), and while

Agnes in her first screen comedy role, opposite Lucille Ball in *The Big Street* (1942).

Hollywood was suspicious of Welles they would embrace Agnes. Welles would always be an outsider, and indeed would be exiled for over a decade, but Agnes would flourish and grow into one of the most respected and in-demand character actresses in the industry. Former detractors like Hedda Hopper and Louella Parsons would soon come around and embrace her as well, as she emerged from under Orson's enormous shadow and established her own identity.

While she emerged from Orson's shadow, Agnes always remained his biggest booster. "My association with Orson was and is a close association for which I am extremely grateful," she would later write, "because he is a fantastic director — a genius, as far as I'm concerned — and I think I've done my best work for him. He isn't flawless (are any of us?) but his virtues far outweigh his faults. I can only think of what he's accomplished — his great ability, his great imagination. There isn't anything he can't do. A marvelous man. I've worked with many fine directors out here, but the one thing I can say about Orson is that he never does things anyone else would do. He's an original, and I've found, whenever I've put myself in his hands, that I've done far better work than I imagined I could do — work I couldn't conceivably have done by myself. He's been my Svengali." Orson did offer one bit of advice which Agnes said she was unable to take. "He used to say to me 'be a clinging vine, Agnes.' But I never learned how."

6

"THE FIRST LADY OF SUSPENSE"

Up until the time Agnes went to Hollywood in 1940 to shoot *Citizen Kane*, radio had been the mainstay of her career. Now with *Kane, Ambersons* and *Journey into Fear* under her belt she was in high demand by many studios for character parts. Radio would still be a huge part of her career during the 40's but it would have to compete with motion pictures.

She was still closely associated with Orson Welles. Three of her first four films were Mercury productions under Orson's supervision. Furthermore, they still continued to work together on radio. Agnes didn't mind being associated with Welles, a man she would always consider a "genius." She would later say of Welles, "He keeps an actor on edge. He goes beyond the limits of what an actor can do and brings out something extra." She was aware that the press, primarily the Hearst press, went out of its way to describe Welles as an egomaniac and that the studios were beginning to turn on him due to the unprofitability of his first three films. In the press and in private Agnes was always Orson's biggest booster.

She did have one tongue-in-cheek complaint about working with Welles. "I think Orson is determined to make me the ugliest girl in pictures . . . when he asked me if I wanted to come to Hollywood and appear in his pictures, I thought, 'Ah, now I'll get the Hollywood glamour build-up.' But in my first picture, *Citizen Kane*, I wasn't allowed a smitch of make-up and I played the role with gray lips. Then in *Magnificent Ambersons* Orson ordered all the irregularities of my face brought out with certain lighting. And in *Journey into Fear* Orson gives me big hips and puts warts on my face." While Agnes was generally joking, she did like the idea of getting away from "plain-Jane" types of roles and when the occasion came up where she could be glamorous she would jump at it. But, generally, producers did tend to type her as mothers or repressed old maids. Due to her hawk-like face she also would get plenty of opportunities to play "meanies." Agnes was an actress first and wasn't exaggerating when she said, "They could yank my teeth out, if it's for a good part."

Due to the critical acclaim Agnes received from *The Magnificent Ambersons,* she was in high demand by virtually all the motion picture studios in Hollywood. Orson advised Agnes to go back to New York and "wind everything up" and then to come back to Hollywood for a movie career. Agnes followed this advice. One studio which courted Agnes was Twentieth Century-Fox. They offered Agnes a contract which paid $650 a week. Agnes thought the money sounded "fabulous," but before she made her decision she spoke to Orson. "No, you can't take that — I paid you $1200 per week for *The Magnificent Ambersons.* I'm not going to let you settle for half that amount. That would be terrible." Though she thought she was "mad" to do so, she turned Fox down. Two weeks later she signed with MGM and at nearly twice what Fox offered — $1,250 per week.

MGM was considered the biggest and best Hollywood studio; a place where even their B pictures had strong production values and name stars. The first picture they put her in was a B titled *The Youngest Profession.* Agnes played the part of the governess of a movie-starstruck teenager (played by Virginia Weidler). The governess comes to the conclusion that the teenager's father (played by veteran character actor Edward Arnold) is having an affair with his secretary because both the father and secretary have colds! The script isn't much, but it is pleasant, glossy and fun. It also had a gimmick — guest appearances by such big MGM stars as William Powell, Robert Taylor, Lana Turner and, in their first film with Agnes, Greer Garson and Walter Pidgeon. It would also be the first throwaway part of Agnes' career; she would have many in the upcoming years.

Welles had tried to make each of her parts different and character-driven. At MGM, like the other studios, it was a factory, and contract players were commodities. They chose the parts the actors played and if the actor didn't accept the part they could be put on suspension, without pay. Agnes would acquire the reputation of being a team player who didn't make waves and accepted everything the studio offered her. This wouldn't be uncommon, however, because Agnes was a character actress and not a lead. Stars with strong box office appeal like Bette Davis, James Cagney, Olivia de Havilland could (and did) make waves and may even be put on suspension; ultimately they would win more than lose because the studios needed their names to sell their films. Agnes had no such clout.

Agnes with Lionel Barrymore on *The Mayor of the Town*, 1943.

Radio provided Agnes with the star roles that films denied her. In the late summer of 1942 Agnes signed on to co-star with Lionel Barrymore in what became a long-running radio comedy-drama, *Mayor of the Town*. Set in the picturesque Midwestern town of Springdale, Barrymore was cast as the crusty but warmhearted Mayor. Agnes was cast as Marilly, the Mayor's gossipy housekeeper, the comedic foil of the show. Typical shows dealt with everyday themes and extolled patriotism, in a time of war. The first show, telecast on NBC September 6, 1942, dealt with a young man in Springdale who quits law school to join the Navy. Another show dealt with the town tomboy, Amy Lou, who joins nurses overseas and serves in Bataan. But typical domestic comedy themes were developed, such as the Hollywood movie studio which runs a contest that the Mayor wins.

The first episode of *Mayor of the Town* received generally favorable reviews. "The premier airing indicated the script would tilt markedly to the war, that the typical small American community of Springdale gravitates from its mayor and leading personality (Barrymore) and that the appeal is to the whole family," wrote *Radio Digest*. "It is evident from the script and announcements that the program will be varied, and often amusing. If the performances of future programs measure up to the first, folks are going to stay home Wednesday nights during the winter." Agnes' debut as Marilly was less well received. "Agnes Moorehead, the housekeeper, will probably become a source of kitchen humor, though she is a bit weak as constant foil for the lead character."

The first few shows featured extensions of the Mayor's family, such as his granddaughter, but it was thought helpful to bring in a young boy with Barrymore to interact with. They created the character of Roscoe Gardiner, who would be commonly called "Butch" by the Mayor and Marilly. John Dunning in his essential book, *The Encyclopedia of Old Time Radio*, would recall the origins of the "Butch" character and the evolution the show took from that point on. "Butch . . . had come live with the Mayor (after the first season) when his mother died and his dad went to fight with the Seabees. On warm nights he liked to play under street lamps, chasing fireflies with his friends . . . Often the stories were coming-of-age pieces, focusing on the Mayor's special relationship with Butch. They fished together and swam at the hole near Rock Creek. Marilly entered the stories with complaints about the mayor's tardiness or repeating the gossip of her friendly enemy, Abby Peters." While he was "Butch" to everybody when he was behaving, to the Mayor and Marilly, "Butch" was called by his full name when he was misbehaving. Often a scene would begin with the crusty Marilly calling Butch in for lunch:

BUTCH:	Yes'm. (*Door Opens*) Gosh — it's really gettin' hot out. (*Door Slams*)
MARILLY:	ROSCOE GARDINER! IF YOU SLAM THAT SCREEN DOOR ONE MORE TIME . . . !
MAYOR:	Aw, doggone it, Marilly — there's no sense in picking on him all the time.
MARILLY:	If you could see how that bangin' sets off my whole nervous system . . .
MAYOR:	Oh, sure, sure.
MARILLY:	Bang from the top of my head right down to my toes!
MAYOR:	Fine. Why don't you enter your name as Miss Atom Bomb of 1946?
MARILLY:	Oh, you may laugh — you may wax ironical, Mayor — but you won't think it so terrible funny on the day I fly to pieces and they deliver my straitjacket.

For the part of "Butch," the producers selected twelve-year-old Conrad Binyon.

Binyon doesn't remember his first meeting with Agnes, but recalls that when he worked with anybody who was famous in the industry — including Agnes and Barrymore — he would do his best to be "worthy of that opportunity. "(Agnes) was nice to me and I respected our professional association." Binyon has fond memories of both associations, of Barrymore he would recall, "My friendship with Mr. Barrymore stemmed from my great respect for his work, and that I was to be a part of that work in supporting him in his roles when we worked together." He remembers that Barrymore, in private or rehearsals, often used salty language. "His expletives were numerous but not smutty." Binyon recalls Agnes as "quite down to earth. We always sat next to each other on stage in the cast chairs during the times we weren't on mike . . . I did not find her to be a secretive type of person. She'd always give me an answer if I ever questioned her about anything I wanted to know of herself. Of course I didn't go around prying into her private life, for it was none of my business, but she never said that to me."

Interestingly, Binyon says that years later Agnes would reach back and use bits of Marilly in her interpretation of Velma Cruther in the film, *Hush . . . Hush, Sweet Charlotte.* Certainly there were similarities. Marilly, like Velma, didn't take guff from anybody and didn't hesitate to put her employer in his place. Marilly also has a country accent, but not as exaggerated as that of the New Orleans-born Velma.

Barrymore and Moorehead's relationship, Binyon recalls, was "very good . . . I never saw the slightest animosity between them." Agnes would later state, "I can think of no one I would rather be associated with (than Barrymore). He's one of the finest actors and personalities I know. He's a great artist in the theatre and a fine musician (Barrymore composed music). He's generous of spirit and a rare sense of humor."

As for Barrymore, he was as much a curmudgeon as many of the characters he portrayed. *Radio Life* did a profile of him and *Mayor of the Town*: "Arriving early (to a rehearsal) we found 'the mayor' had not yet put in his appearance so (with a sigh of relief over our temporary reprieve), we collapsed meekly in an inconspicuous corner to await his entrance. Conrad Binyon, "Butch" of the show, came in and surprised us by sitting down at the piano and delivering an ear-pleasing rendition of 'Clair de Lune.' Agnes (Marilly) Moorehead entertainingly related tales about her new film assignment . . . Time was passing pleasantly when Mr. Barrymore came on-stage, installed himself in his chair at the microphone and, beneath furrowed brow, spouted a series of profane utterances. This over, the great actor took script in hand, smiled benignly at all assembled and the rehearsal began. For the next hour we watched with unwavering fascination while Barrymore and company performed, once through the script for 'practice,' and then immediately again for the preview audience. It was a tremendous treat. The most skilled of ad-lib actors, Barrymore and Moorehead vied for laughs — he with his 'Mayor's' grumble and she with 'Marilly's' whine. Obviously, both of these experienced performers thoroughly enjoy their weekly ether antics."

Conrad Binyon, Lionel Barrymore and Agnes on *The Mayor of the Town*, circa 1949.

After initially airing on NBC for the first six weeks of its run, *Mayor of the Town* moved to CBS where it aired on Saturday nights. On air night the actors would perform the script twice, which was common practice. The show was broadcast live with a studio audience in Studio C at CBS studios in Hollywood. The actors gathered the Thursday prior to the Saturday show, in the late afternoon, to do a read-through of the script and then another reading at the microphones for timing and sound effect rehearsals. Then a "preview" audience was allowed in and the script was done for them to gauge their reaction, with changes made based on their response. On the actual air date, another audience was brought in for a six o'clock live performance for the east coast (nine o'clock in New York) and then another show was performed at nine o'clock for the west coast. In the two-plus hours between performances, the cast would sometimes leave for home, or socialize at Brittingham's, a restaurant located on the lower floor of Columbus Square — the CBS complex in Hollywood.

The show proved highly successful and ran for seven years. Initially Agnes would be paid $300 per week, and every season it was on the air she received a $100 per week pay raise; by the end of its run in 1949, Agnes was earning $1,000 per week for her work on *Mayor of the Town.*

II

Once she became established on *Mayor of the Town,* every movie contract that Agnes signed had a provision included stating that if she was shooting while *Mayor of the Town* was in production she had to be released on Saturdays by noon. The provision was necessary and used many times in the next seven years due to the fact that Agnes was working constantly in films at this time.

In 1943 in addition to *The Youngest Profession,* she was lent out to Twentieth Century-Fox to shoot *Jane Eyre* for producer William Goetz, who was also the son-in-law of MGM studio head, Louis B. Mayer. This film reunited Agnes with Orson Welles, who was cast as the darkly handsome Edward Rochester. To be believable as the romantic lead in this film, Orson went on a crash diet and steam bath regiment, as well as wearing a corset under his wardrobe. As the adult Jane, Joan Fontaine was cast. Peggy Ann Garner was cast as young Jane and Margaret O' Brien, in her first film with Agnes, played Adele, who the adult Jane eventually becomes

Margaret O'Brien and Edward G. Robinson with Agnes in *Our Vines Have Tender Grapes.*

governess of. Agnes plays Mrs. Reed, the harsh aunt of young Jane, who shows Jane no affection and eventually sends her to the Lowood Institution, where Jane would spend ten years. The script was developed by David O. Selznick, and then sold to Twentieth along with Fontaine (who was under contract to Selznick). It is faithful to the Charlotte Bronte novel. Welles wasn't enthusiastic about doing the film, he was only a "hired gun" actor, but on his radio shows over the years he had performed adaptations of the Bronte novel many times and considered it an "old warhorse" of his. Welles did have one bit of advice for Agnes, though; he suggested that she play Mrs. Reed "along the lines of Aunt Fanny." There is a certain resemblance, but where Fanny was at times a gossip with devastating results, she was generally a good person who longed for love. Mrs. Reed is out-and-out pure evil; Agnes' first truly despicable character on film.

Welles and Fontaine didn't get along during the shooting and this may have influenced Fontaine's attitude toward Agnes, who was still at the time considered a "Welles protégée." Years later, once Agnes had carved out a career independent of Orson's, they did work together again and, while never friends, did become friendly acquaintances.

Jane Eyre would be the fourth and final film that Agnes would make with Orson Welles. It wasn't that Welles and she had a falling out. They would continue to work together for a time on radio, but Orson was falling out of favor in Hollywood, while Agnes' star was rising. There were other opportunities for them to work together. Orson directed the 1946 film, *The Stranger,* where he portrays an ex-Nazi who assumes another identity and settles down in New England. He is dogged by an FBI hunter, played by Edward G. Robinson. However, Welles wanted Agnes to play this part. "I wanted the Robinson civil-servant part to be played by Agnes Moorehead. I thought it would be much more interesting to have a spinster lady on the heels of this Nazi." But the studio balked. Too bad, it would have been a different and challenging role for Agnes and would have permitted Welles and Agnes to share the screen together. In all their film collaborations they had never actually performed a scene together. In later years, Welles would also pursue Agnes for both the stage and screen roles of Lady Macbeth in his production of *Macbeth,* but, due to her busy work schedule, it couldn't be arranged. In the early 60's Orson had been the original choice to direct Dino De Laurentiis' production of *The Bible,* and had approached Agnes to play the part of Sarah, but again it didn't pan out. Up until the deaths of Tim Holt in 1973 and then Agnes in 1974, Welles had toyed with the idea of filming a new ending to *The Magnificent Ambersons* with the still living characters, thirty years later, speaking to the camera about what had happened to them in the intervening years. This, too, like many Welles projects, never materialized.

Following *Jane Eyre,* Agnes went almost immediately into the production of David O. Selznick's massively sentimental film, *Since You Went Away.* Selznick, another son-in-law of Louis B. Mayer's, was a hands-on producer who supervised every element of his pictures, sometimes even writing the screenplays (here under the name Jeffrey Daniel — the combined names of his two sons).

A glamor shot of Agnes for David O. Selznick's *Since You Went Away* (1944).

Selznick hand-selected his cast: Claudette Colbert, Joseph Cotten, Jennifer Jones (whom he would later marry) and Shirley Temple. Jones' then-husband, the troubled but talented actor, Robert Walker, was cast as Jones' love interest. Selznick also personally cast the smaller roles as well. He chose Agnes for the part of Emily Hawkins, a snide and gossipy friend who tells the Colbert character (who has two daughters, played by Jones and Temple) that her 40-year-old husband was "irresponsible" to leave his family behind and enlist into the service. The film, clocking in at nearly three hours, is full of pathos and patriotism, dealing with the homefront and the loves and tribulations of the mother and her two daughters. The mother is tempted by love in the form of Joe Cotten, but remains true to her husband and is gratified at the end when, at Christmas, she receives word that her husband is returning home. With this film it was becoming clear that Agnes was becoming typed in unsympathetic roles: the mother who willingly gives up her child in *Citizen Kane,* the repressed aunt who spreads gossip to her nephew which helps ruin his mother's happiness in *The Magnificent Ambersons,* the evil Mrs. Reed in *Jane Eyre,* and, now, this unsympathetic

Agnes with Greer Garson in *Mrs. Parkington*.

characterization in *Since You Went Away.*

It was with this knowledge that Agnes actively campaigned for and received the role of Aspasia Conti in the film *Mrs. Parkington.* The film tells the story of Suzie Parkington (Greer Garson) who marries a mine owner, Major Agustus Parkington (Walter Pidgeon), and they move to New York from Nevada. Major Parkington believes that Suzie needs tutoring in how to be a "lady" and requests aid in the form of his former mistress, Aspasia (Moorehead). Suzie and Aspasia become lifelong friends. It is a warm, sympathetic performance by Agnes and one she would consider her favorite for years to come. Agnes would later expand on why it was the part she liked best. "I'd love to say that my favorite role was forced on me over my polite protests. But if truth is to struggle to light here, it must be admitted that the part of Aspasia Conti in the picture, *Mrs. Parkington,* came to me only because I put up a fine battle to get it. After playing a series of women who were either strained, neurotic or mousy, I was eager for a good, normal role, and this was it. So I went to producer Leon Gordon and asked for it. 'I don't think Aspasia is an Agnes Moorehead kind of role,' he said, 'But there's a drunken duchess I'd love to have you play.' 'Why not test me for Aspasia?' I said. 'Then, if you don't like the test, I'll play your drunken duchess.' I got the test and then I started scurrying around. I found that Greer Garson was wearing a dark wig, so I got a blonde one. Then I had a sheer nightgown fixed up, as the test was a bedroom scene. Fortunately, my French was fine, and the day after the test Leon told me the part was mine. After all this effort, one might suppose the mere playing of the part would be an anticlimax. But it wasn't. I thoroughly enjoyed being a worldly French baroness who not only was attractive and intelligent but who also had great wisdom and a great heart. I also learned to know Greer Garson and formed a lasting friendship. So, all in all, the role was worth the battle I put up to get it, and I'm

Her favorite role, as Aspasia Conti in *Mrs. Parkington*

quite happy to name it as my favorite." Her French was so good, in fact, that a visitor on the set asked director Tay Garnett, "Where did you get the French dame?"

Upon completion of her part in this film, Leon Gordon, the producer, sent her a note: "Had I realized that you were finishing on Saturday I should most certainly have been on the set to tell you how much we all enjoyed working with you both as an actress and as a person. It is my sincere hope that in the near future I shall have a picture and a part worthy of you." They never worked again, but Agnes did campaign to get another part in a Gordon film, *The Green Years,* as Dean Stockwell's grandmother. Again, Gordon felt she wasn't right for the part, and again Agnes insisted she could play it and arranged a screen test; this time the results didn't work out in Agnes' favor and Gladys Cooper got the part. Gordon broke the news to her in a letter dated July 2, 1945: "If I were not such a terrific fan professionally and personally, this note would be easier to write, but I have looked at the test very carefully and given it a great deal of study and have come to the conclusion, Agnes, that I was wrong in asking you to make it because of the physical aspect. I know you can play anything you can, but it's asking too much for a woman of your age to look convincing as Grandma. In the final analysis it would give you an unreality which would be a handicap both to you and the picture. Please forgive me, but I know you don't mind my being perfectly frank. And I can say to you in all honesty that the fact that you won't be in it is a disappointment to me . . ."

Mrs. Parkington opened in October 1944 and, like the previous teamings of Garson and Pidgeon in *Mrs. Miniver* and *Madame Curie*, was a big hit at the box office. *The New York Sun* called the picture a "good strong drama. It pulls out all the stops. It does not hesitate to call for tears, for laughter, for a sneer or two." *Variety* also lauded the picture and called Agnes' performance "great." It is a very good performance and it is certainly understandable why Agnes was so high on it. She was able to convey sex appeal and sincerity, and was not drab, neurotic or nasty. She was nominated for her second Academy Award nomination. But of all of her Academy nominated performances, it is her weakest. *In Ambersons, Johnny Belinda* and *Hush . . . Hush, Sweet Charlotte*, she has more to do, with more complex characterizations. But in each of them she is drab and unattractive. It is my feeling that she was nominated primarily because she gave a performance which was much different from the usual Agnes Moorehead persona and Hollywood recognized that and decided to reward her for it. Her competition was strong: Jennifer Jones, *Since You Went Away*; Angela Lansbury, *Gaslight*; Aline MacMahon, *Dragon Seed*; Ethel Barrymore for *None But the Lonely Heart*. Barrymore won the statuette (undeservedly over Lansbury). It is interesting to note that two of her fellow nominees were from films which Agnes had also appeared in, *Since You Went Away* and *Dragon Seed*. Might this have affected Agnes' chances? Perhaps, but it also probably affected the chances of Jones and MacMahon as well. Barrymore in all likelihood got her Oscar because of her renown as a stage star who was "slumming it" by appearing on screen. As a consolation prize, Agnes did win the Golden Globe award for her performance as Aspasia.

III

One afternoon, writer Lucille Fletcher needed to get milk for her six-month-old baby. Fletcher made a trip to the local store and made her selection.

She got in a check-out line where behind her an elderly woman began to loudly rant about Fletcher being at the front of the line. The woman demanded to know what made her so important that she was in front of her. When she got home, Fletcher began to think about that angry woman and how she might make an interesting character in a story. She began sketching a character based on that woman, who eventually became Mrs. Elbert Stevenson in a radio script titled, *She Overheard Death Speaking*.

In her long career Agnes made hundreds of radio, film, television and stage appearances. In many of these she was singled out for praise and saluted for all she added to the production. In each medium she left a large legacy which her reputation is most identified with. In film, it is Fanny in *The Magnificent Ambersons;* on stage, Donna Ana in *Don Juan in Hell;* and, on television, she attained lasting immortality as Endora on *Bewitched*. In radio, despite her wonderful work as a member of The Mercury Theatre of the Air, no role would be more associated with Agnes than that of Mrs. Elbert Stevenson in "Sorry, Wrong Number" (what "She Overheard Death Speaking" was retitled just days before it was aired).

If Agnes was a true star of any medium, it was radio. And on radio it was her association with the popular anthology series *Suspense* which truly immortalized her. So associated with this series was Agnes that she became known as "The First Lady of Suspense."

Suspense made its debut on June 17, 1942 on the CBS radio network. The show was tightly constructed, lasting only thirty minutes with usually a commercial by its sponsor about halfway through. Each episode was introduced by the "Man in Black" (veteran radio actor Joseph Kearns) stating, "The CBS radio network brings you tales well calculated to keep you in *(dramatic pause)* Suspense!," followed by its dramatic theme. It was a radio show which name motion picture stars had little apprehension of doing. In fact, many did do the show and loved it. Cary Grant said in 1943, "If I ever do any more radio work, I want to do it on *Suspense,* where I get a good chance to act." Indeed it allowed many stars the opportunity to stretch. Comedians like Jack Benny and Fibber McGee and Molly did dramatic episodes as did singers like Frank Sinatra and dancers like Gene Kelly.

The man who had the most to do with the success of the show was its producer William Spier, who, according to *The Encyclopedia of Old Time Radio*, "personally guided every aspect of the show, molding story, voice, sound effects, and music into audio masterpieces." Another major reason for the success of *Suspense* was its sound effects team headed by Berne

Surrey. Surrey and Spier would go through each script, "as if the two were plotting it themselves." Special effects were important on a medium like radio, where imagination is key. In Martin Grams, Jr.'s book *Suspense: Thirty Years of Chills,* the role Surrey played is well described: "Sound effects artist Berne Surrey had many challenges working on *Suspense.* The difficulty was that over the microphone, many sound effects don't register to the ear like they do in real life. If water dripping from a spout in a sink is required then real water from a real sink wouldn't do. Surrey used balls of wet sand being dropped into a huge metal tub to create the desired effect."

As for Spier, he was the heart and soul of the show. Elliott Reid appeared a number of times on *Suspense* and other shows helmed by Spier and recalls him as "a highly intelligent man with a wonderful sense of humor. He was also an accomplished pianist who could play anything almost at a concert level. He brought this intelligence to his work — he was wonderful." Reid also recalls Spier as a perfectionist who "liked to rewrite, and we would discuss the script and change the script right up to airtime — but he trusted his actors and we trusted him."

Although Agnes became strongly associated with the show she didn't make her debut on it until nearly a year after it premiered. She was cast in the play "The Diary of Sophronia Winters," which aired on April 27, 1943; this, too, was written by Lucille Fletcher. Agnes plays a woman who marries a man she had only met days before on a beach. Her new home is a deserted hotel in the middle of nowhere and her new husband (played by Mercury veteran, Ray Collins) locks all the doors leading to the outside. She discovers she has married a psychopath. There is a good example of using just the right sound effect in this show. At the conclusion, Agnes must kill her new husband by using an ax. Spier and Surrey came up with the idea of using a cabbage as the head and an ice pix as the ax — it made a convincing and chilling sound. But in the process of performing this sound effect, Surrey accidentally stabbed himself in the hand. According to Martin Grams, Jr., Agnes commented after the program that while the special effect was expertly done, "he didn't have to add the real blood."

Fletcher was a regular contributor to the *Suspense* program and indeed wrote many of the best plays presented on the show. The script she based on that demanding old woman told the story of a nervous, high-strung, invalid, Mrs. Elbert Stevenson, no individualized first name is given to her, alone in her apartment one night while her husband is presumably at his office working late. She phones her husband and gets a busy signal on the first two attempts. She finally persuades an operator to dial the number for her a third time, and is astonished to discover that she has cut into a conversation between two men making plans to murder a woman. She is cut off and, appalled, calls the police, who don't believe her story and end up hanging up on her. After a while it becomes clear to her, due to the clues she overhears, that the men are planning to kill her.

She goes through more attempts to reach her husband and the police, but gets nowhere. She becomes demanding with a telephone operator, who responds unsympathetically. She tries to have a nurse come out and stay with her, without success. Her paranoia and nerves rise with each rejection and reach its peak when she hears footsteps coming up the stairs making their way toward her bedroom. She is waiting for the police to call her back as the killer enters her bedroom — she lets out a terrifyingly piercing scream just as a train is going by, which muffles the sound as the killer plunges his knife into her. Then for a moment there is silence, interrupted by the phone ringing. The killer picks up the receiver. A police officer identifies himself. The killer responds by saying, "Police Department? . . . Oh, I'm sorry, you've got the wrong number."

It was a brilliantly executed script with heightened tension exhibited by Mrs. Stevenson as each moment passes. Lucille Fletcher believed that the voice of Mrs. Stevenson was vital. It should be shrill and demanding, yet at the same time make the listener feel the tension and terror that this invalid is experiencing, to make the listener empathize with this unsympathetic woman. Fletcher also believed that the story was an "experiment in sound and not just a murder story with the telephone as the chief protagonist. I wanted to write something that by its very nature should, for maximum effectiveness, be heard rather than seen."

As she was writing the story it became clear to Fletcher that Agnes was the only actress who could do the script justice and capture the essence of its heroine. "In the hands of a fine actress like Agnes Moorehead, the script turned out to be more the character study of a woman than a technical experiment, and the plot itself, with its O. Henry twist at the end, fell into the thrilling category . . . it is as I see it, a simple tale of horror." Fletcher didn't have to do much convincing of Spier to send the script to Agnes.

When Agnes read the script, she realized what a tremendous opportunity it was for an actress. Yet she almost turned it down. She later said, "I couldn't even finish reading it because it made me so nervous. I was afraid it was too morbid and people would turn it off." If it was too morbid and nerve-wracking for her as an actress, how could the listeners be able to sit back and enjoy the program? Only through the intervention of Fletcher did Agnes finally agree to do the part.

On air day, May 25, 1943, Agnes spent up to six hours working with Spier and Surrey to make sure that the timing was in tune with the sound effects. Agnes later spoke on the importance of coordinating her efforts with the sound man. "The sound man is extremely important. A mood can be projected expertly, you know, in the mere dialing of a telephone. Also, the various telephone voices — each must convey just the right tone. For instance, we had trouble once because a girl playing the telephone operator couldn't keep a note of sympathy from her voice while I was pleading with her for help. I always 'tune up' my scream with the sound man's whistle, to be sure we'll hit the same note. I have to get set psychologically each time." (Incidentally, Agnes was considered to have one of the best "screams" in the business. As mentioned, she was used in Welles' "War of the Worlds" broadcast as a "screaming woman," and one week she did an unbilled appearance on *Suspense,* in an episode which starred little Margaret O'Brien, titled "The Screaming Woman" as the title character, though only her scream was heard.)

That night she performed "Sorry, Wrong Number" first for east coast listeners, giving an emotionally draining performance. Everything was going well until the very end, when one of the most famous gaffes in radio history occurred. The actor who played the killer forgot to say his final line, ". . . Sorry. Musta been a wrong number." It confused the listeners who were already on the edge of their seats. It took a lot out of Agnes emotionally to do that performance. "Moorehead played the invalid Mrs. Elbert Stevenson with such terrified realism that she sometimes collapsed across the table at the conclusion," according to radio historian John Dunning. Two hours later the show was repeated again live for the West coast. The West coast audience that night heard the entire show, gaffe-free.

In the days following the broadcast CBS was bombarded with thousands of letters and phone calls from listeners questioning what had become of Mrs. Stevenson! During the following week's broadcast Spier had Joseph Kearns, in his guise as the "Man in Black," address the situation. "The producer of *Suspense* felt it was incumbent to reply herewith to the many inquiries to the solution of last week's story of the woman on the telephone titled, 'Sorry, Wrong Number,'" explained Kearns. "Due to a momentary confusion in the studio, an important line cue was delivered at the wrong time and some of our faithful listeners were uncertain to the outcome of the story. For them, they knew that the woman, so remarkably played by Miss Agnes Moorehead, was murdered by a man whom her husband had hired to do the job. We would also like to announce that, in response to the many hundreds of requests, this *Suspense* play will be repeated within a few weeks." The show was repeated again on August 21, 1943 — only three months after the first airing — an almost unprecedented act in radio at the time.

The many moods of Agnes Moorehead performing *Sorry, Wrong Number*.

"Sorry, Wrong Number" became an instant classic. It also terrified people who listened to the broadcast, not unlike the famous Martian scare that Orson Welles sprung in 1938, but this audience knew they were listening to a dramatic program — yet the realism of Agnes' performance was chilling. Greer Garson and her mother listened to the show one night. They were alone and after the conclusion of the broadcast they spent considerable time going through their home locking windows and doubly bolting doors. Agnes even got a chill herself shortly after performing in "Sorry." One night her husband, Jack Lee, was gone and Agnes was alone when she picked up the phone and got "crossed-wires" and heard two men discussing "the end of the world." Her experience performing the play was still fresh and it terrified her. One funny story which might have had a tragic outcome, but didn't, concerned a man who was driving along Sunset Boulevard in Hollywood listening to "Sorry, Wrong Number" on his car radio. He got so caught up in it that he crashed his car into a telephone pole. Agnes and Spiers heard about this and took up a collection to pay for the $20 in repairs his car required. Perhaps what makes it so terrifying to so many people is that unlike most *Suspense* episodes the killer(s) get away with it. The show ends with the murderers seemingly prevailing.

In the program's first three years, Agnes made nine appearances on *Suspense*. Of those nine appearances, four were performances of "Sorry, Wrong Number." So popular was this play that for the first few years after its initial airing it was presented annually on *Suspense*. But Agnes also performed it on other shows as well, for instance in 1946 she did a condensed version on *Radio Hall of Fame*. Agnes became identified with the role of Mrs. Elbert Stevenson and "Sorry, Wrong Number." In 1952 Agnes released a disc version, which became the third highest selling record that year for Decca records.

Many stories have been told of Agnes' emotionally draining performance in "Sorry, Wrong Number." One such story involves how, when performing, Agnes would get so nervous and emotional that without knowing it she would have her hair pulled down over her eyes, her blouse would be pulled out and she would remove her shoes and jewelry. Conrad Binyon, her *Mayor of the Town* co-star, recalls viewing her through a window during a *Suspense* broadcast, and discounts this particular story. "I never saw Agnes during any performance on radio that she didn't maintain an immaculate decorum."

While she was always in demand to perform "Sorry, Wrong Number" on radio, and hers is considered the definitive performance, she was not considered for the part of Mrs. Stevenson when producer Hal Wallis bought the rights for a motion picture to be produced by Paramount in 1948. Agnes went to Wallis and asked to be considered, but Wallis told her no. He didn't feel Agnes was a big enough name at the box office, but he did offer her a supporting role in the film, which she wisely declined. Barbara Stanwyck got the part and did a good job, but padding out a 24-minute play to an 80-minute motion picture took much of the dramatic tension out of the story. Agnes later said she wasn't "bitter," but "of course, I wanted to play it. I did all I could do to get the part. But they had Barbara Stanwyck and I hear she gives an Academy Award performance. It's a fine part and a fine script. When you add a fine actress like Barbara Stanwyck, it should be a great performance. Well, those things happen and it's useless to grow resentful. I did the broadcast eight times, after all, and the records. Wasn't I foolish not to tie it up then, when it had been written for me?"

Interestingly, in 1949 both Stanwyck and Agnes were nominated for Academy Awards; Barbara, for *Sorry, Wrong Number*, and Agnes, for *Johnny Belinda* — though in different categories. Both lost, but some wags in Hollywood believed that Stanwyck's loss (her fourth and final Oscar nomination without a win) was due to comparisons made between her interpretation of Mrs. Elbert Stevenson (she is given the first name Lenora in the film version) and Agnes' . . . and that Agnes came out on top.

7

HOLLYWOOD'S LEADING CHARACTER ACTRESS

When World War II broke out, the Hollywood community got firmly behind the war effort, and Agnes was no exception. During the war years Agnes participated in war bond rallies and helped promote the Red Cross. She also volunteered at the Hollywood Canteen, a club jointly opened by Bette Davis and John Garfield, where servicemen visiting Hollywood could enjoy being waited on, served, and entertained by celebrities. Agnes waited tables, washed dishes, chatted and danced with servicemen. Bette Davis let Agnes know how much her efforts were appreciated in an October 24, 1944 letter: "We thought you should know how very happy you made the service men, when you visited with them at the Canteen recently. We are doubly indebted to you for the spirit of cooperation you have shown towards this organization."

Agnes also joined with Orson Welles and Joe Cotten in an enterprise to raise money for the USO called *The Mercury Wonder Show*. Welles later described the "Wonder Show" to Peter Bogdanovich. "It was like a circus . . . All the servicemen got in free, and they were 90 percent of the public. We had twenty-five or thirty seats which was called the Sucker Section and cost $30 each; they were for the Hollywood celebrities who wanted to come and see it — this small, highly paying public that got hell from us every night. We broke eggs over their heads and gave them blocks of ice to hold and demeaned and humiliated them in front of the servicemen. There was one seat that cost $70, and that was behind a pole so you couldn't see anything. Everybody'd want to get that good seat, and they always ended up straddling the pole — they had to look around from either side." This "luxury" seat usually went to such powerful Hollywood producers as Louis B. Mayer or Sam Goldwyn, who turned out to be good sports about it.

Welles spent about $40,000 of his own money on *The Mercury Wonder Show*, which. according to Welles biographer Joseph McBride, included "red circus wagons, sawdusted floors, a live lion, tiger, and leopard, a group of barnyard types, and an assortment of clowns, acrobats, and other circus-touched performers." For seventeen weeks, mostly during the period when he and Agnes were working together on *Jane Eyre*, Welles rehearsed "stooges" to make the magic seem effortless. Welles would recall The Mercury Wonder Show as "fun" and proudly say, "It's one of our great works, as any and all who were concerned will say. We're as proud of that as anything we ever did. Ask Aggie Moorehead or Jo Cotten."

The Mercury Wonder Show was held in a tent at 9000 Cahuenga Boulevard in Hollywood. Welles, an amateur magician, called himself "Orson the Great" and did feats of magic with his assistant and soon-to-be wife, Rita Hayworth, until her studio boss, Harry Cohn of Columbia, put a stop to her participation. Then Orson recruited his great friend, Marlene Dietrich to assist him. Cotten also did feats of magic and billed himself as "Jo-Jo the Great," while Agnes was known as "Calliope Aggie" due to her playing the calliope out front to draw customers. The Wonder Show was staged in August of 1943 and ran for over a month with each performance lasting over two hours. The shows were highly successful and usually sold out, with nightly audiences totaling more than 2,000 people. Later, Welles and company would take the Wonder Show around the country in a successful tour of army camps.

Agnes frequently appeared on radio during the war years to raise money for war bonds. For instance, shortly after *The Mercury Wonder Show* closed its tents, she appeared in the guise of Mrs. Dithers, from the *Blondie* radio show, in a *Treasury Star Parade* show which was syndicated across the country. And only six days after D-Day on June 12, 1944, Agnes joined Orson Welles, Walter Huston, Keenan Wynn and President Roosevelt for an hour long War Loan Drive which was written by Welles and presented over the CBS radio network. She was also vocal and highly visible in giving her voice and time toward supporting a state for Israel. For movie houses, she and Margaret O' Brien shot a short film at MGM (five 1/2 minutes long) which was played in theaters around the country, *Victory in Europe*. Agnes plays a woman who learns that her husband has been killed in the war, and Margaret was cast as her young daughter. The intention of the short was to provoke audiences to support war relief charities.

During the Second World War Agnes, like most actors working in Hollywood during this time, made several "patriotic" motion pictures. The studios went out of their way to keep morale up and support our troops as their contribution to the war effort. The first of these films was a frothy comedy, *Government Girl*, which was released in 1943 by RKO and starred Olivia de Havilland and Sonny Tufts. The story concerned an automobile executive who is recruited by the government to oversee airplane bomber production during the war. De Havilland plays a government secretary he ultimately falls in love with. Agnes plays a Washington socialite. The film was not very good, but it kept wartime audiences entertained.

In Oriental makeup for *Dragon Seed*.

On the other end of the spectrum was David O. Selznick's all-star *Since You Went Away*, released in 1944. This film was meant to stir up audiences. Set on the homefront during World War II, it tells the story of a middle-aged mother (Claudette Colbert) whose middle-aged husband decides to enlist into the service, leaving her home to support their two teenage daughters (Jennifer Jones, Shirley Temple). To make ends meet the mother has to take in a border, exasperating her "friend," gossipy Emily Hawkins, glamorously and unsympathetically played by Agnes, who utters, "All these irresponsible 40-year-old fathers dashing off into uniforms." The film also co-stars Agnes' old friend Joseph Cotten, playing a Navy officer who also happens to be an old boyfriend of the Colbert character. There is still sexual tension between the two, but it is never acted upon; Colbert represents the perfect wife and mother during the war years — longing for her husband to return, safe and sound. The film was very successful.

Agnes' next patriotic film featured her for the first and only time with Spencer Tracy. *The Seventh Cross* is the story of seven prisoners of war who escape from a German concentration camp in 1936. The commandant of the camp orders seven crosses constructed so that they will be used to display the bodies of the seven escapees. Agnes has a sympathetic part as a costume shop owner who provides clothing for one of the escapees (Tracy). While she displays a "Heil Hitler" salutation to Tracy as he leaves her shop, he discovers that she put money in the clothes she gave him to help him escape.

Agnes next appeared in a little known film released through United Artists in 1944 called *Tomorrow, the World!*, which was based on a play, adapted by Ring Lardner, Jr. The film tells the story of a 12-year-old war orphan, whose father was put to death in a German concentration camp. The boy is brought to the United States by his uncle (Fredric March), a professor. The boy has been brainwashed by the Nazis and tries to break up the marriage of his uncle to his part-Jewish girlfriend (played by Betty Field). The boy is presented as thoroughly wicked: he lies, causes disturbances in school and even tries to kill a cousin. Agnes plays March's spinster sister who is verbally abused by the boy. Ultimately, the boy is redeemed in a typical Hollywood happy ending. The film did get its share of good reviews. *Newsweek* called it "engrossing." *Time* lauded the actors: "Nearly all the supporting performances, especially those of Fredric March, Betty Field and Agnes Moorehead as a confused spinster, are warm and sympathetic; and young Skippy Homeier captures as remarkably as ever the pathetic, frightening overtones of the poisoned, pernicious little hero he created on the stage."

Her final "war effort" film is another frothy comedy, *Keep Your Powder Dry*, released by MGM in 1945. The film focuses on the efforts of three female enlistees played by Lana Turner, Laraine Day and Susan Peters. They are assigned to Fort Oglethrope where the women make it into Officers Training School. Their commanding officer is played by Agnes. The film is not much more than passing entertainment, but during the filming Agnes became close to young Susan Peters. Peters, shortly after *Keep Your Powder Dry* wrapped, suffered a serious spinal injury in a hunting accident which would ultimately end her career and eventually lead to her untimely death in 1952. When she heard about Peters' accident, Agnes sent flowers and her best wishes, to which Peters responded, "Your flowers were truly beautiful and I enjoyed them more than I can tell you. Knowing that you were thinking of me has added so much to my recovery. Love, Susan." Agnes visited often during this period. This is not an isolated incident either. Joe Cotten would later write that Agnes, in an effort to lift his spirits, was a frequent visitor in the period after his first wife died.

II

Publicity shots of Agnes at home, early 1940s.

Agnes and Jack were now living in a beautiful home in the picturesque Cheviot Hills area of Los Angeles. The house was described in a magazine profile of Agnes: "Room by room, it is one of the most unforgettably lovely homes in California, where beautiful homes grow ticker'n orange trees. What makes the house exceptional is that rather than a mere background, it is an actual part of the woman who did every inch of it. The part you don't see on the screen — the gay, imaginative, rebellious side of the actress best known for her frustrated, bitterly drab females."

In addition to the California home, she and Jack, particularly Jack, spent time on the farm in Ohio. Jack, frustrated at not finding work as an actor and jealous over the attention given to Agnes, oversaw the farm as the couple increasingly spent time apart from one another. The farm was not for show, but was a profit making enterprise since the Lees raised alfalfa, wheat, and soybeans, and they would also journey to Argentina to buy Hereford cattle stock.

Occasionally they would travel. "We wanted very much to see the Grand Canyon,"Jack said. "We planned it for quite a while before we actually got there. After traveling all that distance, Aggie took one quick look into the gorge and turned away. S'help me, she was eavesdropping on some other women who were seeing it for the first time — more interested in watching and listening to their reactions, than in the biggest ditch in the world!"

On another occasion, the Lees were invited to observe military maneuvers off of Santa Barbara. "The sky and the sea were incredibly beautiful," recalled Agnes. "I thought how beautiful they must look to a real landing expedition when many of the boys are taking their last look, and know it. The landing barges were loaded with men, and even though it was just a practice landing, the ships were throwing out a protective barrage that split the air all around us. It was beautiful and exciting."

In a radio interview Agnes spoke of she and Jack wanting to adopt children. ". . . we expect to adopt three children. Two boys and a girl. You see I want a really big family." When she was asked what Jack thought of that idea Agnes replied, "It's as much his idea as mine. He's back in Ohio now, getting our farm in shape, and as soon as everything is ready, we'll see what we can do about a family. We both feel that it wouldn't be fair to one child, to say nothing of three, not to prepare the proper home and background in advance.

We don't expect to do anything elaborate, of course, but we do want to have the farm fixed up comfortably, and make sure that we will be able to give our children a simple and wholesome background." By this time Agnes and Jack were already becoming estranged and indeed had separated a couple of times only to reconcile. Jack was drinking increasingly as his career was being eclipsed by Agnes'. Yet, it appears that he and Agnes were still working at trying to make the marriage work. Certainly with Agnes' religious views she didn't welcome a divorce, so at an age when most parents are seeing their children off to college (both Agnes and Jack were well into their 40's), they were talking of adopting three children.

Conrad Binyon occasionally visited the Cheviot Hills home and got to know Jack. "I always liked Jack due to his and my mutual interest in aviation and flying," recalled Binyon. "He gave me for Christmas a navigational handwork E-6B military computer, and invited me out to their Cheviot Hills home to swim in their pool and have lunch." Binyon says he had no idea that Jack had been or was an actor himself. "Jack never discussed his status as an actor. In fact, I never knew much about it existing at all. I was totally surprised when I saw him in a small role as the Army Captain on the Berlin Express in the movie of the same name." Their mutual interest in aviation bonded Binyon and Jack, but Conrad doesn't believe that Jack himself was a pilot. "I figure he'd have told me if he had been licensed. I'm thinking he perhaps may have taken lessons pursuing a license, because the computer he gave me I could see had been used and perhaps had been his at one time prior to his passing it on to me. Of course, if he had been licensed and owned a plane he'd certainly taken me flying with him, for that's what most pilots love to do . . ."

III

Following the war, and while still under contract (though nonexclusive) with MGM, Agnes signed with Warner Brothers. Her first role was in producer Jerry Wald's *film noir Dark Passage*. The film tells the story of Vincent Parry (played by Humphrey Bogart) who is wrongly convicted of murdering his wife and is sentenced to San Quentin. He escapes and is taken in by a San Francisco artist named Irene Jansen (Lauren Bacall). She had followed his trial and believes in his innocence. By coincidence, Irene and Vincent have a mutual acquaintance, Madge Rapf (Agnes), who had testified against Vincent at his trial. Up to this time, Bogart is heard but not seen since the camera point of view is seen through his eyes, but after getting plastic surgery to change his appearance he emerges as Bogart. Madge becomes hysterical because she believes that Vincent will kill her for testifying against him. With his new face, Parry goes to see Madge, introducing himself as a friend of her boyfriend's. Madge flirts with Parry — not knowing who he really is. But she gradually comes to recognize something about him — "you remind me of someone," she says to him — perhaps his voice. Parry has found out information which links Madge to the murder of his wife and a trumpet-playing friend, who was protecting him, and tries to convince Madge to sign a paper admitting her guilt. She tells Parry, "You won't be able to prove anything because I won't be there." With that she jumps out a window and falls to her death.

Agnes is magnificent. She is rotten to the core, more so than in any of her previous films. She is also beautifully made up and wears fashionable clothes. She is no repressed old maid here, but an experienced woman who has used men all her life. She completely steals the film from the leads, Bogart and Bacall. Her Warners contract paid her $2,500 per week and she certainly earned her paycheck.

Her producer, Jerry Wald, was also impressed and expressed his admiration in a letter on February 5, 1947: "We ran the first rough cut of *Dark Passage* yesterday. These few lines are to implore you to put me at the head of your long line of fans. Despite the fact that you haven't too many sides in the film, the scenes you do have are without doubt the finest job of acting I've seen on the screen or stage in years. You're truly a great artist . . . Why we haven't worked together before is something beyond my powers of comprehension, but in the future this must be changed. Just tell me what parts you'd like to play, and you've got them. If there is any role that you like of any pictures I've got coming up, for goodness sake, just say, "That's for me," and you've got it. If there are some stories that you think would be good screen vehicles for you, please tell me about them. If this note sounds fan-ish . . . it's meant to be . . . " What an incredible letter from one of the leading producers in Hollywood at the time. He was as good as his word. He employed her in three more films, including one which would earn Agnes her third Academy Award nomination.

(Courtesy of Wade Ballard)

While the film did well at the box office, it didn't get critical raves. For instance, the *New Republic* said it was, "so bad that I worry about Humphrey Bogart and Lauren Bacall." But *Time* felt the film had an

A chic and beautiful Agnes.

"unusually good script and direction by Delmer Daves." The review went on to laud Agnes: "Daves knows how to break players effectively out of type (Agnes Moorehead who usually plays embittered spinsters, does handsomely in a sexy role)."

Shortly before filming *Dark Passage* Agnes was again asked to return to Broadway, this time in a revival of Lillian Hellman's classic play, *The Children's Hour.* The producer, Jane Broder, sent an urgent telegram to Agnes with the news that Hellman herself would act as director. Agnes, though flattered, had to turn the play down. "Present commitments make acceptance impossible. If you have good new play for future please contact me."

By this time Agnes was also making amends with Louella Parsons. Louella still worked for the Hearst press, and still took her job of hounding Orson Welles seriously. But as Agnes was establishing her own identity as an actress, separate from Orson Welles' Mercury players, Louella, like Hedda Hopper, would begin to champion her. By November of 1945 Agnes was even attending cocktail parties in Louella's honor.

Orson Welles hand drew this Christmas card for Agnes is his then wife Rita Hayworth and their daughter Rebecca.

Welles was in the east mounting a huge stage production of *Around the World in 80 Days.* On March 22, 1946, Welles wrote to Agnes: "…After the opening of *Around the World* which I think is going to be wonderful, I will be out there for some sort of picture. Nothing is definitely set, but one of the things we are thinking of has a fine part for you. I don't think, however, that you should let it interfere with the scheduling of your year's commitments. I will certainly write again the moment I have anything definite. All my love, always Orson."

She joined Orson on one segment of his *Mercury Summer Theatre* that summer in a half hour (!) version of *King Lear*. It would be their last major radio program together. Agnes' contract with MGM and Warner Brothers as well as her radio work — which was extensive — kept her from accepting Welles' offer of Macbeth (in the pivotal role of Lady Macbeth) which was staged in 1947, for Utah's Centennial Celebration at University Theatre in Salt Lake City. Welles set up this four-day engagement partly as a rehearsal since he had signed with Republic to make a film version shortly thereafter. Had Agnes accepted she would also have done the film, so it was a missed opportunity for Agnes on two counts: one, to work with Welles again in a film he directed *and* as his leading lady, and two, to appear in a Shakespearean classic in one of the great female roles. Jeanette Nolan played the part instead.

But Orson wasn't through trying to tempt her. He sent her a telegram, dated February 3, 1949:

DEAREST AGGIE ARE YOU FREE AN WILLING TO BE THE GREATEST EMILIA IN THE HISTORY OF OTHELLO STOP WE BEING IN PARIS IN ABOUT A MONTH WIRE ME HOTEL LANCASTER ALL MY LOVE ALWAYS ORSON.

Othello is one of Welles' masterpieces, but it was also one of the films he would shoot a few sequences here and there until he ran out of money, then have to work in a film to raise more money and reassemble the cast again to shoot more sequences. The film he invited Agnes to be in starting in March 1949, and wasn't released until 1952. Once again Agnes had to turn Welles down due to other film and radio commitments.

IV

Producer Walter Wanger (*Stagecoach, Foreign Correspondent*) made a deal with Universal to film an adaptation of the 1888 Henry James novel, *The Aspern Papers*. It is the story of an American publisher named Lewis who searches for the love letters of the late Jeffrey Ashton, a poet who disappeared decades earlier. He is told that Ashton's one-time lover, Juliana, now a weathered old woman of 105, is in possession of these letters. Jeffrey assumes the false identity of a young writer from America in need of lodging. He plans to steal the letters. At the house he meets Juliana's niece, Tina (in the original novel it is her sister), who tries to discourage Lewis from staying in the house. The household staff tells Lewis that Tina is evil. Juliana also tells him that she fears that Tina will kill her. Juliana tells Lewis that she doesn't have the love letters. They are in Tina's possession, and that the letters have apparently taken possession of Tina. They are the reason she believes herself to be Juliana. She begs Lewis to get the letters back from Tina. Lewis steals the letters from Tina's room and is about to leave with them himself when he hears an argument between Tina and Juliana. Juliana admits she killed Jeffrey Ashton when he told her he was going to leave her. A fire breaks out, Lewis is able to save Tina, who has fainted, but in the process he drops the love letters and the letters are destroyed in the fire and Juliana, who earlier told Lewis she would never leave the house alive, is killed.

This was an ambitious story to film. For the part of Lewis, Wanger very much wanted Rex Harrison or Charles Boyer, but both proved to be unavailable. Finally, in a bit of offbeat casting, light comic leading man Robert Cummings was signed for $15,000 per week. For Tina, Wanger cast his beautiful and talented contract player, Susan Hayward. For the pivotal role of the 105-year-old Juliana, Judith Anderson, who played the wicked Mrs. Danvers in *Rebecca,* was considered. In the end Agnes was signed at $5,000 per week.

It was a difficult shoot for Agnes, who wore a mask which made her utterly unrecognizable as the 105-year-old Juliana. The procedure she had to endure every day became one of the key selling points of the film and generated a great deal of publicity. *Life* magazine did an article on the five-hour daily procedure she endured: "In preparation for the camera, Miss Moorehead arrives at 5 each morning in her dressing room where Make-up man Buddy Westmore spends five busy hours remodeling her. To begin with, a rubber mask is attached to her face with spirit gum. Then liquid adhesive and urbber grease are spread on, wrinkles are etched in and the whole business is heavily powdered. This operation takes almost three hours. The remaining time is used to prepare the Moorehead hands, with small rolls of cotton as veins. By 10, she is all ready to act and by 3 p.m. she is ready to go mad inside the mask. When it is finally removed at 6, the spirit gum which has been burning her face all day tears out all the downy hairs on her cheeks. This daily ordeal has already taken seven pounds off Miss Moorehead."

The working title of the film was not *The Aspern Papers,* but *Lost Love.* By the time it was released it was retitled, becoming *The Lost Moment.* The

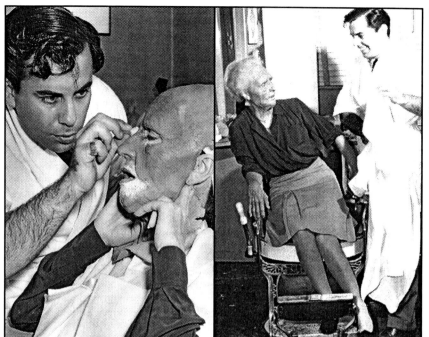

Agnes being made up for *The Lost Moment*, and the end result.

picture was in production from March 10–May 19, 1947. A preview of the picture was held in Studio City on September 9, and the results were pretty good. Of 34 preview cards, 9 rated the film "Excellent"; 11 rated the film "Very Good"; 10 rated it "Good"; 3 rated it "Fair"; only 1 rated the film as "Poor." An analysis of the preview stated, "Enjoyment of preview audience exceeded its anticipation." The words selected by the audience as descriptive of the picture were: "dramatic," "held interest," "well acted," and "emotional." Interestingly, the preview summary pointed out that "Persons under 18 years of age, however, had a higher level of enjoyment than those who were older"; enjoyment was highest among people who were 12 to 30 years of age, and females.

Agnes received quite a few compliments from the preview audience — especially among women. Her name was also a draw. Robert Cummings and Agnes received a greater percentage of mentions from those who "especially wanted" to see the picture than from those who were not particularly interested. Among the comments regarding Agnes on preview cards, a 16-year-old female listed Agnes as the person she most enjoyed in the film. A male, 22, also listed Agnes first as the player he especially enjoyed and wrote, "Any scene with Agnes Moorehead" in the section which asked the audience for their "favorite scene." Another male, age 21, wrote: "The reason I pick Moorehead is because at her age I think she did very well even if it was only acting." A 17-year-old female wrote, "I liked the cast and especially Agnes Moorehead. I think she is a fine actress, and the make up job was excellent."

Wanger could have expected good word-of-mouth to lead to strong box office based on the preview comments, but when the film was released in October 1947, the reviews were, on the whole, quite savage. *Newsweek* wrote, "Frankly, the admirers of Henry James have cause for complaint, and the average moviegoer will probably complain of boredom." *The New Republic* was devastating: "Robert Cummings . . . gives a performance that is probably meant to be sensitive but turns out to be unctuous; Agnes Moorehead . . . is called on to do no more than shiver slightly from time to time." The *New York World Telegram* wrote, "*The Lost Moment* is a ponderous, majestic and thoroughly dull picture." The Box Office slant of the Showmen's trade review wrote, "Extremely off the beaten track, *The Lost Moment* will puzzle the average audience . . . Give an A for effort, anyway, to Wanger for his production." The word of mouth that Wanger thought would be favorable sank his picture, which went on to lose money at the box office.

Agnes was shooting a western in Arizona, *Stations West,* when, on September 17, 1947, she dubbed her final lines for *The Lost Moment* by phone: "I killed him. He was going to leave me so I killed him," and "Father buried him in the garden by the bower." Agnes liked the picture; perhaps for enduring five-plus hours of make up and physical discomfort, she felt she had better like the picture!! The film is not as bad as the contemporary reviewers said, but it is patchy. Robert Cummings is miscast. It is a shame they didn't get Boyer or Harrison for the lead, but both Hayward and Agnes give good performances. Agnes would later say of *The Lost Moment,* " . . . It was . . . a class of movie they don't make anymore, with romance and beauty, culture — wonderful music, piano — and fantasy. What is wrong with fantasy?" Miss Hayward was less enthused with the finished product. "Their name for it should have been *The Lost Moment* but after I saw it I called it 'The Lost Hour and a Half.'"

It was while filming the western, *Stations West,* that Agnes had a rare run-in with a director, Sidney Lansfield. Usually Agnes was considered a director's dream. Always prepared and always cooperative. Lansfield, though, had a reputation for being acerbic and belittling actors — perhaps it was his way of getting a performance out of them? The film starred Dick Powell and Jane Greer; Greer was not his first choice, Marlene Dietrich was, and he never let Greer forget it. Greer endured it, but when Lansfield turned his fire on Agnes, he was up against a more formidable force. Greer would recall that one day, after shooting a scene, Lansfield told Agnes, "Do you ever think before you say a line, hatchet face?" Without responding, Agnes simply walked off the set. She phoned Dore Schary, who was at the time RKO's executive vice president in charge of production, and got another director to supervise her scenes from that point on.

V

Shortly after she had filmed *The Lost Moment,* Agnes was cast in a picture at Warner Brothers, one that became one of her favorite and most popular. *Johnny Belinda* was set on Cape Breton Island in Nova Scotia in the fictional village of Carcadio, a little community on a small bay which depends on income from fish and lobster from the sea for survival. Belinda McDonald is a deaf mute. She is cut off from contact with others except her father, Black, and her stern Aunt Aggie. Into this community moves Dr. Robert Richardson, a man of great intellect, who is devoted to his profession. He meets Belinda, when on a rainy night Aunt Aggie comes to fetch him due to a medical emergency, which turns out to be the birth of a calf. He takes an interest in Belinda and begins to teach her sign language so that she will be able to communicate with the outside world and end her life of isolation. Dr. Richardson goes to Belinda's father and urges him to allow Belinda to be sent away to school, that she is a bright girl. The father explains that he needs Belinda to help tend to the farm, and, besides, everybody including him and Aunt Aggie refer to Belinda as "the dummy." Aggie is called away to tend to her sick sister; when Black takes her to the train, a drunken townsman, Locky, goes to the farm where he viciously rapes Belinda. Dr. Richardson later discovers that she is pregnant. Aunt Aggie returns and the news brings out another side of her personality; she now becomes protective of Belinda. Because of his interest in Belinda, many people come to believe that Dr. Richardson is the father. When the baby is delivered, Belinda names him Johnny. Belinda's father soon discovers that Locky raped his daughter and the two have a fight, which ends with McDonald falling to his death. The town, which has always had a snobbish attitude toward the McDonalds, believes that Belinda is an unfit mother and they want to give the baby to Locky and his new wife, who is Dr. Richardson's assistant. Locky comes and tries to forcefully take the baby from Belinda. Belinda kills Locky and is then arrested and tried for his murder. Locky's wife eventually admits that Locky told her he was the father of the baby. Belinda is acquitted and is granted custody of the baby. Belinda, Dr. Richardson (who discovers he loves Belinda), Aggie and the baby leave the courtroom together at the conclusion.

For the part of Belinda, Warner Brothers cast Jane Wyman, who had since the thirties endured frivolous comedy roles at the studio. Wyman had scored big in the past two years with strong performances in *The Lost Weekend*, for Paramount, and *The Yearling* at MGM. This was to be the first real role of substance that her home studio would give her. For the part of Dr. Richardson, Lew Ayres was cast. Ayres was best known as "Dr. Kildare" in a series of films he did for MGM. He had spent the duration of the war as a contentious objector, which at first seemed to hurt his career. But he turned public opinion around by bravely serving in the ambulance corps. As Black McDonald, the venerable character actor Charles Bickford was cast. True to his word of wanting to work with Agnes again after her stellar performance in *Dark Passage,* producer Jerry Wald cast Agnes as Aunt Aggie. In the script Aunt Aggie is described as a "gruff, austere spinster living with her brother. Bleak as her existence, nevertheless there's a kind streak, a sympathetic heart buried beneath her forbidding exterior." In short, it was perfect for Agnes.

The filming went smoothly under the direction of Jean Negulesco. The actors got along well. Wyman and Agnes formed a strong friendship and admired each other as actresses and individuals. Miss Wyman would recall that Agnes had a "marvelous sense of humor." Wyman also recalled that between scenes, and in the evenings when filming on location in Mendocino, California came to an end, the cast would "get together to joke around — just laugh. It was such a fun set." She also found Agnes to be a "warm individual," yet possessing a "very dramatic" personality. As an actress Wyman believed that Agnes could act "any kind of part." She believed that Agnes had a "very difficult part and studied it hard. Aggie was so versatile — each (part) was different. Each character was different from each other." Agnes also got to know Wyman's then-husband, Ronald Reagan, whom she served with on the Screen Actors Guild — and attended parties at the Reagan's just as they would attend parties at the Lee's. Wyman recalled Agnes as "a wonderful hostess. A party at Aggie's was the event of the season." Wyman had warm words for the others connected with the picture as well, calling Negulesco "an artist" who allowed his actors to work out scenes themselves, giving them leeway. This would be the first of five films that Agnes would work in with Wyman. "I was always happy when Aggie was cast in one of my pictures."

Agnes recalled the experience on *Johnny Belinda* as a happy one as well. "We all had such a wonderful time. Jane Wyman, of course, had the principal part . . . but Lew Ayres, Charles Bickford and I had good parts too. We loved them. We loved the whole picture. And we each honestly admired each of the others as a good actor. We each became so interested in the picture as a whole that we used to discuss it and our work in it all the time. I don't suppose there's ever been another picture where one actor could stop another and say, 'Look, Aggie, don't you think maybe you could make it a little clearer by doing it this way?' or 'Charlie, I don't understand what you mean. How about your saying it like this?' . . . We were always suggesting things to others about their parts. And no one took offense . . . the director, Jean Negulesco, was so delighted he just let us go ahead with the criticisms and suggestions. Now we're all eager, the five of us, to do a second film."

The studio realized they had a marvelous film on their hands but they didn't rush to release it. While the film had completed principal photography by late 1947, the film wouldn't be released until September 1948, By then it was getting considerable hype as one of the biggest films that would be released in 1948.

Agnes had plenty to keep her busy. The New Year began with a major radio performance. Agnes portrayed Regina Gibbens on *The Theatre Guild of the Air* presentation of Lillian Hellman's *The Little Foxes*. Supporting Agnes in this starring performance would be Thomas Mitchell and Zachary Scott. *The Little Foxes* had been immortalized on the stage by Tallulah Bankhead and on film by Bette Davis. It tells the story of a cold-hearted woman who deliberately allows her husband to die of a heart seizure by coldly walking out on him as he begs for his heart medication. The performance aired over ABC on January 4, 1948. The response was excellent. Helen Hayes wrote Agnes on January 19, gushing, "I listened to you on the *Theatre Guild* and was thrilled by your 'Regina,' and then a few nights later a thrilling, pixilated 'Marilly' who has become such a real person in our lives, truly amazes me! Your 'Regina' brought a vivid picture of you, yourself, to my mind, and I won't be happy now until I see you some day play that part." This letter had been typed up to this point, and then Hayes writes in her own hand, "You would look so much better than Tallulah did." Her friend and publicist, Peter Opp, wrote, "You wuz wonderful. I'm working now on a retirement fund for Bankhead and Davis." While she was in New York preparing for *The Little Foxes*, Agnes took time out to attend a Saturday matinee of *A Streetcar Named Desire* at the Ethel Barrymore Theatre on January 3. The show made a star out of a young actor from Nebraska named Marlon Brando.

Agnes received an intriguing offer to replace Judith Anderson on stage in *Medea*, with Hume Cronyn directing. Judith Anderson was renowned for her interpretation and anybody who stepped into the role would have very large shoes to fill. Hume Cronyn, on behalf of the producers', spoke privately of having Agnes replace Anderson in the stage play and Agnes said she would consider it. But in April, the producer Robert Whitehead wrote to Agnes with the news that they decided to close the show at the end of May, "otherwise you would have heard from me before this as I am a great admirer of your work and I do hope I will sometime have the pleasure of being associated with you." It was another lost opportunity to do one of the great parts on the legitimate stage in a lead role.

Agnes did take an active interest in trying to move beyond supporting roles in motion pictures. She did attempt to get the lead in *Sorry, Wrong Number*, when it was being made into a movie, on the basis that the part had been written for her. She also read a novel she felt would be tremendous for her, *Friendly Persuasion*. It is the story of a Quaker family during the Civil War. Agnes wanted to play the part of the mother. She even inquired to the author Jessamyn West about buying the screen rights to the novel. She was disappointed when she was informed by Miss West's publisher that the screen rights had already been sold to Frank Capra for his Liberty Pictures. But Capra, himself, would never film the novel. Instead, he sold it and *Friendly Persuasion* was later filmed in 1956 with Gary Cooper, with Dorothy McGuire in the part Agnes wanted to play.

Hedda Hopper reported in her March 4, 1949 column that "Agnes Moorehead is writing her own experiences as a Wisconsin school teacher into a screenplay titled, *The Golden Land*. It's about an earthy, unusual character Aggie would like to portray on the screen. Warners is interested." Nothing came from this effort.

In the summer of 1948, Agnes and Jack discussed the possibilities of opening a professional school of the dramatic arts along with a first-class summer theatre. They discussed locating it with Monterey Peninsula College in Monterey, California, where the Lees had property and some of Jack's relatives lived. They discussed associating with the college and indicated that some of their friends in Hollywood and New York would help teach and fund such a school. They went as far as to discuss such items as good will with existing theatre groups, possibilities in recording, training for the studios, outlets for frustrated actors, equipment, financing, administration. They had Remsen Bird, a consultant with Monterey Peninsula College,

(From Moorehead papers, copy from Author's collection)

Jack and Agnes invited to a party by their friends Lucy and Desi.

write to a Mr. S.F. Morse to interest him in helping to fund such an endeavor. In a subsequent letter to Agnes, Bird would write that "As you know, Jack certainly does, he (Morse) owns everything in these parts." Apparently Mr. Morse was interested. Bird later wrote to Agnes again (interestingly the letters are all addressed to Agnes and while Jack is mentioned in the letters he isn't part of the salutation), stating, "There is considerable interest in the Monterey Peninsula College in the field of the dramatic arts and it might be that a plan could be worked out that would be suited to what you plan and what they plan. It looks like we would be in Los Angeles sometime in the latter part of this month and if we come down we shall hope to see you and Jack. If what Mr. Morse has written strikes a fire with you perhaps you will come up and we can have a little conference." But apparently plans did fall through. The "Moorehead School" (again one wonders how Jack felt about a school in which he was involved was named after Agnes without any mention of him) never did open. But Agnes never gave up the hope of such an enterprise and would later successfully open her own acting school.

Jack had some unexpectedly good news, which may explain why plans

Summer Holiday (1948).

for the school never did jell. He received a featured part in the touring company of the play *Command Decision*. He was cast as a war correspondent. It was a good part and must have lifted his spirits to some extent. Perhaps because of the good news, the Lees also began to think about adopting a baby again.

Agnes returned to MGM where she was cast as James Stewart's mother in the film *The Stratton Story*. It is the inspiring story of Monty Stratton, who lives with his mother on a cotton farm in Texas. Stratton meets a baseball talent scout (played by Frank Morgan) who eventually takes Monty to California to join the Chicago White Sox training camp. While in California he meets Ethel (June Allyson), who becomes his wife. Monty is signed by the White Sox and becomes an all-star. Then, tragedy strikes and Monty is injured in a hunting accident. Due to the injury his leg is amputated. Monty fights despair and depression and eventually gets fitted with an artificial leg. He battles to come back and ends up pitching in an all-star game which ends with him retiring the opposing side in the final inning, winning the game. The film was well made and enjoyable. The part of Mother Stratton was not demanding but, significantly, Agnes met on the set a man more than twenty years her junior, a handsome young actor named Robert Gist, who has a small part as Larnie. Within a year she and Jack would separate and within two years Gist would be accompanying Agnes on tour with the stage production of *Don Juan in Hell* as stage manager — at Agnes' insistence.

Muskingum College, which only a year earlier had presented Agnes with an Honorary Doctorate of Literature, now wanted her monetary support. Her friend and the president of the college, Robert N. Montgomery, sent her a pointed letter: "Well, I am trying again . . . as you know, I have written you a number of times expressing the hope that you would make a gift to Muskingum. But my letters haven't had what it takes because as yet

I have failed each time. You have already indicated two or three times that you will do something, but evidently the matter has been overlooked. I recall that when I was out in California two years ago you mentioned to me that your income placed you in the top bracket as far as maximum income tax was concerned. Since that is the case, it means that a gift to Muskingum would cost you relatively little because you would have to pay so much of it in income tax anyhow. I do not know, but my guess is that you would be one of three or four of our graduates who are in the top income bracket." That was the hard-sell, now he switched into a soft-sell by mentioning somebody he knew she might respond to — her father. "I wonder if you have ever thought of starting a memorial fund in memory of your father. The Moorehead name has been an honored one in Muskingum history for many years. I would love to see a Moorehead Memorial Library on the campus . . . " Agnes' instructions to her secretary are written on the back of this letter: "ans. Ruth, not this (just skip)" — Ruth was Dr. Montgomery's wife and a dear friend of Agnes' who had recently written a chatty, friendly letter.

VI

Johnny Belinda was released in the early fall of 1948 to enthusiastic reviews. *Variety* called the film, "a compelling, adult drama, told with sensitive taste." Jane Wyman's performance was called "boff" and "compellingly artistic." Lew Ayres was called "of equal worth" and, in their supporting roles, Agnes and Charles Bickford were lauded for their "commanding performances." Most reviews particularly lauded Wyman's brilliant performance as the deaf mute but the entire cast and the film were also handsomely praised. *Time* stated that Bickford and Moorehead did a "solid job." The *St. Louis Globe-Democrat* would write that Lew Ayres, Agnes and Bickford are "equally earnest." The *New York Times* would put the picture at number one on its list of best films of 1948. The film also became one of the top-grossing of the year.

By the time the film premiered, Ronald Reagan and Jane Wyman had separated and were in the process of divorcing. To show his support for his estranged wife Reagan had attended the Hollywood premiere of the film — going stag — and it led to rumors that the couple might reconcile, but it wasn't to be. When *Johnny Belinda* premiered in London in late 1948, Reagan was in England shooting the film *The Hasty Heart*. On Savoy Hotel stationary he hand wrote a letter to Agnes dated January 1, 1949:

Dear Agnes,

Happy New Year and Thanks for your nice letter. We are hard at work on the picture now after a few weeks of taking a bow here and there. I'm trying to keep an open mind but must para-phrase a line or two from *Annie Get Your Gun* and sing, "Anything they can do we can do better."

Enough of that! Must'nt sound like a colonial. Don't know whether you've heard but *Johnny Belinda* is "standing room only" and is being held over. It received great reviews in papers that ordinarily are anti-American in policy.

I guess I'm a country boy at heart but Calif. is going to look awfully good one of these days. Give my best to that guy of yours and save some "sunshine" for me. Best Ronnie

P.S. Some of our "bleeding hearts" on the board (SAG) should try this "life under socialism," they better hurry though because these people don't talk like they are going to try it much longer.

It is clear by this letter that Reagan and Agnes shared an increasingly conservative viewpoint. Obviously Reagan felt a political kinship with Agnes or else he wouldn't have referred to "bleeding hearts" on the Screen Actors Guild in the way he did with her. It is also clear that Reagan, a long time liberal, was already evolving in his political views — contrary to those who have argued that it came about through his courtship with the conservative Nancy Davis, who would be his second wife, but who he hadn't even met as yet. He also doesn't display any bitterness toward Wyman and speaks proudly of how her film is doing.

The Lees were still together. On Agnes' 48th birthday on December 6, Jack, on tour with *Command Decision,* sent a telegram to Agnes: ALL MY LOVE DARLING ON THIS BIRTHDAY AND ALWAYS. JACK.

Agnes flew to Detroit to spend Christmas with Jack, their last together, who was appearing there in *Command Decision.*

Noxema, the chemical company which was sponsoring *Mayor of the Town,* would end its sponsorship of the show when it launched its sixth season. The President of the company, GA Bunting, wrote to Agnes expressing their admiration for her. "Your fan mail is indicative of the great popularity you enjoy among your audiences, but as sponsor . . . I personally want to add this bit to let you know just how much we at Noxema feel you contributed to the program and how you endeared yourself to us all."

It was not surprising when, in February 1949, it was announced that *Johnny Belinda* was nominated for twelve Academy Awards including Best Actress, Actor, Supporting Actor and Agnes as Supporting Actress — her third nomination. Agnes' competition was Barbara Bel Geddes, *I Remember Mama*, Ellen Corby, *I Remember Mama*, Jean Simmons, *Hamlet*, and Claire Trevor, *Key Largo*.

Agnes at the Oscars, 1948.

The Oscar ceremony was held at the Academy Theatre in Hollywood on March 24, 1949, hosted by Robert Montgomery. In the book, *Inside Oscar,* Montgomery is described as acting like "the host of a bachelor party as he drooled over every actress presenter." When he introduced Ava Gardner, he winked, "you must admit that Mother Nature lingered over the job."

Prior to the awards ceremony each nominee got special instructions for the 21st Academy Awards: "As a nominee for an Academy Award you will be seated near one of the two center aisles. If your name is announced as a winner, please rise promptly and approach the stage by the nearest aisle. A spotlight from the balcony will follow you on stage. When receiving your award, please acknowledge the applause first and shake hands with the presenter. Your thanks, to be spoken clearly into the microphone, must not exceed one-half minute of air time. Exit STAGE RIGHT (your own right as you face the audience). You will then be taken to the press photographer's room and to the press room for a brief interview." It was signed William Dozier, General Director, and 21st Awards Program. Dozier would later be the head of Screen Gems at the time Agnes agreed to do the pilot of *Bewitched.*

The day before the awards producer Jerry Wald wired Agnes:

DEAR AGGIE WIN LOSE OR DRAW THURSDAY NIGHT ALL OF US CONNECTED WITH BELINDA HAVE HAD THE SATISFACTION OF KNOWING THAT WE DID A FIRST RATE JOB THAT WAS RECOGNIZED BY THE PUBLIC AND

PRESS. I KNOW WE'LL DO IT AGAIN. WARMEST PERSONAL REGARDS. JERRY WALD.

Edmund Gwenn, who had won an Oscar the previous year for his performance as Kris Kingle in the film *Miracle on 34th Street,* presented the Best Supporting Actress category. He prefaced his announcement of the nominees by stating, "I'm just about able to venture down the street without being mobbed by small children." He read the list of nominees and the winner was — Claire Trevor for *Key Largo.*

Trevor was a popular choice and indeed her performance as the boozy moll in *Key Largo* is a highlight. But it was just one more disappointment for the *Belinda* nominees. Of the 12 nominations, the film would only win one — for lead actress Jane Wyman. Wyman was excited, but she later said when her name was announced, the first thing that came to her mind was, "Did I or didn't I put on my girdle tonight? Then I thought, so what? Let it bounce." Her acceptance speech was short and funny: "I accept this for keeping my mouth shut for once. I think I'll do it again."

Agnes was disappointed, but probably relieved that Barbara Stanwyck, nominated for Best Actress that night for *Sorry, Wrong Number,* had also lost. Had Agnes lost and Stanwyck won for a role which Agnes was so associated with, it might have made a disappointing evening even worse. After the ceremony, Agnes and Jack gamely attended a small dinner dance Warner Brothers' studio head, Jack Warner, was giving at the Mocambo. While she didn't win, she and the other *Belinda* nominees consoled each other that night — and they all were happy for Jane.

8

"THE HIGHLIGHT OF MY CAREER"

Professionally, throughout the 30's and 40's, the bread-and-butter of Agnes' career was her work in radio and films. She would still work in both, as well as television in the 1950's, but the stage now became her favored medium. After Orson Welles, two men would establish themselves as the major influences in her career: the tall and handsome producer Paul Gregory, and the short, fat, but brilliant actor Charles Laughton.

During the 40's, Agnes appeared in such varied and important films as *Citizen Kane, The Magnificent Ambersons, Journey into Fear, Jane Eyre, Dragon Seed, Mrs. Parkington, Our Vines Have Tender Grapes, Dark Passage, The Lost Moment,* and *Johnny Belinda.* She won three Academy Award nominations in the process as well as the New York Film Critics Award and the Golden Globe award of 1944 from the foreign press. During the 50's she would appear in some good films, but really no exceptional ones — for every *Caged* or *Fourteen Hours* she would appear in, she would follow it up with the likes of *The Adventures of Captain Fabian, Captain Blackjack, The Blazing Forest,* and *The Conqueror.* She was still in great demand as a motion picture actress during the 1950's — she released 27 films during this decade — but without a doubt the quality of her films dropped and she would not be nominated for the Academy Award again until 1964. Instead, she would mount a three-year run in one of the most spectacular stage experiences of her time, begin touring with her own one-woman show and do two more stage productions before the decade was out. In her mind, Hollywood was a "place to earn enough money to be able to do the sort of stage acting one wants to do." Personally, the new decade would bring the desolation of her 20-year marriage to Jack Lee, the continuation of her romance and eventual marriage to Robert Gist, and she would take in a foster son.

With Eleanor Parker in *Caged* (1950).

Caged would be Agnes' only film release of 1950. It was an important film — released by Warner Brothers and directed by veteran John Cromwell, who had also helmed *Since You Went Away*. It was a message picture with Agnes cast as a well-meaning progressive warden in a woman's penitentiary who tries to bring reform. Eleanor Parker stars as a young woman who is sent to prison for helping her husband rob a gas station — the husband is killed during the robbery and the widow is also two month's pregnant. Agnes, as Mrs. Benton, assures the young woman, Marie, "I want you to know that we're all here to help you. I want you to believe that I'd like to be your friend." Her baby is delivered prematurely and, because she is in prison and her family won't take care of the baby, it is put up for adoption. During Marie's stay she sees suicide and has to deal with a sadistic matron, Harper, played by Hope Emerson. In this world of brutality Marie finds a bit of hope in the form of a kitten that she keeps and takes care of — but the evil prison matron attempts to take the kitten away from her, the end result being that the kitten is killed. Mrs. Benton has tried to get Harper fired in the past and writes to the commissioner of prisons to recommend her firing again, only to be thwarted by Harper's connections. Harper retaliates against Benton by spreading rumors about her which causes the commissioner to ask for Benton's resignation — which she avoids by telling the commissioner that if she is fired she will take him and the crooked penal system down with her. The evil Harper is eventually killed by another inmate and Marie is released, but, by now, the once innocent Marie is hardened by prison life, and it is clear to Mrs. Benton where she is headed. The final line in the film is Benton telling her secretary to keep Marie's file active. "She'll be back."

Agnes was justly proud of *Caged,* even though it seems a bit dated today. She told author Boze Hadleigh that it was an important film, "because it helped ameliorate conditions throughout the penal system. I was assured." Prior to shooting this picture, Agnes got the Los Angeles County Sheriff's Office to intercede on her behalf so she could do research at the California Institution of Women in Tehachapi. The Sheriff's office wrote, "Miss Moorehead is well and favorably known to this office and any courtesies extended her will be very much appreciated." She visited the institution and conferred with Alma Holzschuh, the Superintendent at Tehachapi, as well as touring the facility and meeting many of the inmates. In her interview with Boze Hadleigh, Hadleigh points out to Agnes that *Caged* is a "lesbian cult classic," and goes on to say, "It was one of the first movies to bring up lesbianism, although in an unsavory context and even though each Sapphic character had to express interest in men." Agnes points out to Hadleigh, "My character was the film's conscience — she had nothing to do with sex, one way or another."

Caged boasts an excellent supporting cast; along with Emerson, there is Ellen Corby (twenty years before she became Grandma Walton), Jan Sterling, Lee Patrick, Jane Darwell, and numerous other lesser known actresses who excel even in the smallest of parts. The film was released in June 1950 and the reviews were quite good. The *New York Herald* called Eleanor Parker's performance as Marie a "tear-jerker." They said that Agnes, "exhibits the best control as a keen, aggressive prison superintendent trying to substitute education for the rubber hose as a corrective measure." The *New York Daily Mirror* pointed out that *Caged,* "explores a woman's prison, as *The Snake Pit* did a mental asylum." *Time* made note of John Cromwell's direction, saying the film "has some unblinkingly realistic moments." The *New York Times'* Bosley Crowther wrote, "John Cromwell manages now and again to bring individual scenes to throbbing life . . . but on the whole *Caged* is a cliché-ridden account." The film went on to do decent, but unexceptional, business at the box office — it was probably too bleak for many moviegoers. The film was nominated for four Academy Awards, although none for Agnes; Eleanor Parker for Best Actress, Hope Emerson for Best Supporting Actress, as well as the screenplay and the story.

Just prior to the film's opening, Hedda Hopper announced in her column that Agnes filed for divorce after 19 years of marriage to Jack.

Hopper reported that if a property settlement could be worked out, Agnes would go to Las Vegas "immediately" to obtain a quick divorce. If it couldn't be worked out then the divorce would proceed in California, which meant it wouldn't be final for a year. The property settlement was not worked out and Agnes did not go to Las Vegas — instead the Lees would spend the last year of their marriage living separately and waiting. Jack, having toured in *Command Decision* during the late 40's, had enjoyed a return of some of his confidence during that time only to see it elapse again once the tour was finished and no further job offers were on the horizon. He again retreated to the bottle. By this time, though, Agnes had had enough and having fallen in love with Robert Gist, she wanted to marry him.

Jack and Agnes had spoken publicly of adopting children. Perhaps because they felt their marriage was teetering, they believed a child could bring them closer together. But they never did adopt. By 1950, they had separated. While Agnes was visiting a children's hospital, she came across twin siblings — a boy and a girl. They were toddlers — a year-and-a-half-old, and from a large family which could no longer afford to care for them. Agnes would recall that they had already been in two or three foster homes. They were both ill, but the boy, Sean, was the sickliest. Debbie Reynolds, who became a close friend in the last twelve years of Agnes' life, later wrote that Sean's "eyes were crossed and he was almost dying of malnutrition." Agnes recalled that the boy suffered from anemia and had a spot on his lung. When Agnes saw the baby, "she couldn't resist the urge to help him," according to Reynolds. She asked if she could take the young boy home with her. "What a poor little thing he was . . . I didn't care what he looked like, if he wasn't perfectly healthy. He was mine."

After some legalities and paperwork were completed, Agnes became the foster mother of young Sean. Many articles claim that Agnes had adopted Sean, but that was not the case. In the early 1950's it was rare for a single woman (with Agnes going through a divorce) to adopt a child. For whatever reason, Agnes took the boy but not the girl, who was later adopted by another prominent Hollywood citizen, according to both Reynolds and Paul Gregory. Agnes later said that the first thing she did when she got legal custody of Sean was to take him to a well-known pediatrician. "Oh my, that doctor's reaction," Agnes recalled. "He examined Sean and said, 'Miss Moorehead, you've taken on an awful big responsibility.' I answered that I didn't care. 'Let's just see what we can do to make him well again, to give him a zest for living.'"

Agnes didn't do much on radio in 1950, but she did appear on *Cavalcade of America* for the last time on March 7 working with Claude Rains in the drama, "Mr. Peale and the Dinosaur." It is the story of the man who started the Museum of Natural History in Philadelphia taking the advice given to him by Benjamin Franklin to heart: "such a museum could help the American people to realize and appreciate the great wonders of the new world." Agnes played his wife, Elizabeth. A month later she made her almost annual appearance on *Suspense,* in a much more interesting role than the one she just did on *Cavalcade.* In the story, "The Chain," Agnes plays a mean spirited woman who sends a chain letter to a woman who dies shortly after receiving it. Her husband leaves her and she is soon alone with the dead woman's husband waiting outside to kill her. William Conrad, who would soon become the voice of Matt Dillon on radio's *Gunsmoke* (and later become best known as *Cannon* on television during the 70's), plays her husband. Agnes would repeat this story on *Suspense* again in 1958 with John McIntire.

Soon after, Agnes filmed a picture for Twentieth Century-Fox, *Fourteen Hours,* for one of her favorite directors, Henry Hathaway, whom she lauded for his solid craftsmanship without pretension; not making himself the star of his films, for Hathaway, the story was the main attraction. The film is the tense story of a young man who climbs out on the 15th floor ledge of a hotel and the attempts of various people, including a police officer (played by Paul Douglas), a former girlfriend (Barbara Bel Geddes), his hysterical mother (Agnes) and the father who abandoned him (Robert Keith), to talk him down. The young man is well-played by Richard Basehart, whom Agnes

(Courtesy of Wade Ballard)

Fourteen Hours (1951).

had corresponded with and encouraged in his career for many years. While this is the main story, a backstory is being told of other people with their dramas occurring at the same time in this hotel. Grace Kelly had her first important film role as a woman who is divorcing her husband only to reconcile with him as the drama above her unfolds; her performance in this film would favorably impress producer Stanley Kramer who would cast her in his next film, *High Noon.* Fox contract players, Debra Paget and Jeffrey Hunter have winning roles as young people who meet and fall in love. The film was based on an actual true story about a man who stayed on a ledge for many hours. But real life didn't have the happy ending that *Fourteen Hours* eventually had — he jumped to his death. Agnes was already in Europe shooting another film when her agent, Felix Ferry, wrote her on 9/15/50: "Henry Hathaway showed the picture, *Fourteen Hours,* last night at a private showing at 20th — I can't tell you how impressed I was . . . I wouldn't be surprised if you got an Academy Award nomination for this. It is really a gem."

The picture that Agnes was shooting in the south of France in the summer of 1950, when her agent wrote to her about *Fourteen Hours,* was *The Adventures of Captain Fabian.* She held the picture in no great esteem but believed it an inexpensive way to visit Europe. The film was co-written and produced by its star, Errol Flynn. Also appearing was another old friend, Vincent Price. Flynn, true to form, was a month late arriving on the set. One reason for this was Warner Brother's belief that Flynn's appearance in this film, produced by Republic, was a breach of his contract. The other reason, according to Vincent Price, was that the notorious rogue Flynn was, "disengaging a princess at that point, and apparently she was hard to break off with."

To keep themselves occupied until Flynn showed up, Agnes, Price and his wife Mary toured Europe, "covering it like three vacuum cleaners." After a few weeks of this, Flynn finally did arrive and the picture began shooting. Flynn was showing the effects of his hard drinking and promiscuous lifestyle. Still Agnes had a soft spot for him. She knew him at Warners and, like many women, found him charming and processing an intellect greater than he was given credit for. Flynn was well read and cultured. For his part, Flynn was flattered that an actress of Agnes' stature would consent to appear in his film.

The shooting was moving along briskly to make up for lost time when one day after a shot had been completed Agnes was handed a cable. It intrigued her since it was from one of her acting idols, Charles Laughton. Charles explained that he, Charles Boyer and Sir Cedric Hardwicke were planning a cross-country tour of George Bernard Shaw's *Don Juan in Hell.* Charles explained that he and producer Paul Gregory wanted Agnes to play Donna Ana, the lone female in the quartette. Without hesitation, Agnes cabled Laughton back with a resounding "YES." Agnes later explained that she "couldn't resist working with these great interpreters" of the theatre. Interestingly, this theatrical offer by Laughton wasn't the only one Agnes received while abroad. She had been offered *Ethan Frome,* probably the part of the wife, which would be opening in New York, per the wire she received, in January or February, 1951. While ordinarily she probably would have been ecstatic about the prospect of *Ethan Frome, Don Juan in Hell,* was different and would represent a departure for her.

At this point it is probably best to back up to a cold, winter night in 1948 when a junior executive with Music Corporation of America (MCA) stopped off at a bar in New York City. It was a Sunday night and the bar was packed with people probably due to the presence of a television set, still a novelty for much of the country. On the television was Ed Sullivan's *The Toast of the Town.* All eyes at the bar, including the junior executive's, were on the set where a portly and unattractive man, yet with undeniable presence and a hypnotic voice, was doing a dramatic reading. The young man soon fell under his spell. The reader was Charles Laughton. He was reading the "fiery furnace" passage from the Book of Daniel. During this reading the young man with MCA noticed that not a single sound was uttered and few people picked up their glasses. The agent was so impressed by what he saw and what he felt that he ran out of the bar, hailed a taxi, and arrived at the theatre just as Laughton emerged from the stage door.

This was Charles Laughton's first encounter with Paul Gregory. It was only by luck that Gregory was able to stop into the bar in the first place. He had been expected to pick up a client, singer/actor Dennis Morgan at the train station, but Morgan's train was delayed by a snow storm in Buffalo. Gregory had time on his hands and, as they say, the rest is history.

Paul Gregory was born James Burton Lenhart in 1921. He was an exceptionally bright child who was skipped ahead in school. At eleven, he earned money as a carrier for the *Des Moines Register and Tribune.* At fourteen, he had a radio show in Des Moines where he read from the classics. At sixteen, he won a national essay contest which awarded him a scholarship to Drake University. (Gregory would later say that he spent only one day at Drake where, he says, on his first day he met a professor who spent more time gazing at his crotch than teaching.) At nineteen, he arrived in Hollywood and began acting, but within a couple of years he realized his true talent was in recognizing talent in others and promoting them. He was twenty-five when he joined MCA and launched tours for Ralph Edwards, Tommy Dorsey and Spike Jones. He was now twenty-seven, and he had a brainstorm.

Charles was blown away by Paul. He was brash and, at 6' 2", 170 pounds with black hair, blue eyes and a dazzling smile, Charles found him irresistible. Charles later told his wife, Elsa Lanchester, "Don't be deceived by Paul's looks. He is over handsome. He is right up in the Gregory Peck school of good looks." Besides his good looks, Charles found Paul persuasive and even brilliant.

Charles Laughton was born in Scarborough, England in 1899. His family owned a hotel and it was expected that Charles would help run it when he came of age. This plan was interrupted by the First World War, in which Charles served with distinction. After the war he returned to Scarborough and began working in the family business. He found it respectable but boring. As an outlet for his creative energies Charles enrolled at the Royal Academy of Dramatic Arts in 1925. Within a year Charles was awarded the Bancroft Gold Medal, the highest award given by the institution, and the offers began pouring in. During the next few years Charles would appear in a wide range of roles on the stage. While appearing in the play, *Mr. Prohacle,* Charles met a vivacious beauty named Elsa Lanchester. Charles was self-conscious of his bulldog face and short, stout body. He was also homosexual. Elsa was a free spirit. She had been a dancer, model (sometimes in the nude), teacher, painter and actress. In Elsa, Charles found someone who was, in the words of his biographer, Simon Cowell, "a friend; a companion; someone to confide in; someone to lavish his attentions on — all complete novelties for him." They formed a strong bond and came to depend on one another, but it is unlikely that it was more than a platonic relationship. They married in 1929. Soon Charles came to New York and appeared on Broadway, and that led to Hollywood where he became one of the leading character leads of the 1930's in such films as *Henry the VIII, Ruggles of Red Gap, Mutiny on the Bounty, Jamaica Inn,* and *The Hunchback of Notre Dame.* Charles continued to work in Hollywood when his native country went to war — a fact not lost on Britain and one which would come back to haunt him at a later date. At the time of his meeting with Paul Gregory, Charles' film career had lost some of its luster. He needed a new challenge and, as Elsa would later state, "Paul Gregory came along just when Charles needed him most."

Paul convinced Charles that his future lay in going around the country doing readings such as he performed on the Sullivan show; readings from Shakespeare, Dickens, Kerovac, Thomas Wolfe, and the Bible. He convinced him of how lucrative a cross-country tour could be. It would be a one-man show, *An Evening with Charles Laughton,* and Paul would book it into college auditoriums or have it sponsored by various civic groups or clubs around the country — many in locales which rarely had a name act visit. The initial tour proved successful beyond even Paul's expectations and subsequent tours also went well. The meeting that cold Sunday night turned into a rendezvous with destiny for both men and eventually for Agnes.

II

Don Juan in Hell is the third act of Shaw's *Man and Superman.* It is a dream sequence that many companies decide to cut because it takes the focus away from the main story. More likely than not it is cut to save time since, in its entirety, *Man and Superman* ran more than five hours. It is difficult to get even the most devout theatergoer to sit for five hours. *Don Juan in Hell* is essentially an argument in which Juan's vision of a higher plane is pitted against Satan's concerns for more immediate pleasures. It is a morality play, a debate on idealism vs. realism. Shaw saw the hero of the piece as Don Juan, who holds forth philosophical discussions that go on for great lengths between Satan (Laughton), The Commander (Hardwicke) and his daughter, Donna Ana (Agnes), whom Juan had an affair with in life. Shaw, himself, summed up the Hell scene. "I have thrust into my perfectly modern three-act play a totally extraneous act in which my hero's ancestor appears and philosophizes at great length with the lady, the statue (the commander), and the devil."

After a couple of years of doing his one-man show Laughton wanted to do something different and suggested the "Hell scene" from *Don Juan in Hell* to Gregory, who also liked the idea. Paul would produce the piece and Charles would direct. The play begins with the recently-deceased Donna Ana finding herself, to her chagrin, in Hell rather than in Heaven. This is jolting to her since she has always believed herself to be a woman of virtue.

She meets up with her former lover, Don Juan, and her father, the Commander (who is only visiting Hell because he finds Heaven a bore), who was killed by Juan when he came to defend his daughter's honor. The Commander, to the astonishment of his daughter, finds Hell an immensely satisfying place to spend eternity and much preferable to Heaven, which he finds stuffy. He also holds no malice against Juan for killing him. Finally the Devil appears and each expresses his view on the nature and purpose of existence. When casting the quartette, Laughton maintained that, "we didn't necessarily need the best actors, but the best voices in America." Certainly he and Paul were successful on all counts.

How did Paul and Charles come to the conclusion that Agnes was the best actress to play the part? Well, she wasn't the first choice. According to Elsa Lanchester the original choice was Madeleine Carroll, the cool blonde heroine of Hitchcock's *The 39 Steps*. Carroll was eliminated, according to Paul, because she didn't process the sense of drama that the character needed. At one point Fredric March and his actress wife, Florence Eldridge, were considered as a package; March as Juan and Eldridge as Donna Ana. But that was eventually discarded. Laughton was also pushing Elsa. "Charles wanted Elsa," recalls Paul Gregory, "but I thought her voice was all wrong and that she possessed no romantic quality." As gently as he could, he persuaded Charles not to cast Elsa. The aged character actress Beulah Bondi was also considered, but ruled out as unacceptable due to her inability to perform as the 27-year-old Donna Ana. Paul Gregory believed Agnes was right for the part because "she was bigger than life and could convey womanhood, rejection and love." Laughton perhaps summed it up best of all. "She is with us because Anna has to change from an old wizened woman of 77 to a young lady of 27. The actress will only have her voice to convince the audience of this transition — Aggie will do it." Hedda Hopper later asked Paul Gregory why he chose Agnes for the part of Donna Ana, and Paul replied, "The answer is simple. First, I consider her one of the very finest actresses in show business. She's extremely cooperative."

The other members cast were also inspirations. There would be no doubt that Laughton would be perfect as the Devil. But some have asked, why Charles Boyer? He was a fine actor, but with a heavy French accent; Don Juan is Spanish. On the other hand, Don Juan is a great lover and Boyer's screen persona was that of the great lover. In reality, Boyer was hardly the caricature of the French lover; he was totally devoted to his wife and when she died in 1978, he quietly put his house in order and committed suicide.

"Boyer is a master of the tirade," recalled Laughton, "and as such is invaluable to our play — not every actor can handle that difficult of dramatic speech." Gregory concurred, "Charles had great facility for the written language." The Commander is often a comic character with certain Col. Blimp-type stereotypes. Sir Cedric Hardwicke, according to Laughton, "could speak an author's lines as if they were fresh from his own brain." Gregory also recalls Hardwicke as a man of great humor and warmth; both traits he felt were called for in this role.

(Author's collection)

Don Juan in Hell cast: Charles Laughton, Charles Boyer, Agnes, Sir Cedric Hardwicke, from 1952.

Agnes' reasons for accepting the part of Donna Ana are clear. First, it was a prestigious production with actors she respected. Second, and perhaps the primary motivator was that it gave her an opportunity to be more glamorous than she was usually allowed to be in films. "I sometimes wonder how they saw me in such a glamorous role for usually I am relegated to those dreary, drab characters that are completely void of charm and beauty, though I must say they are usually the meatiest roles to play. Nevertheless I was complimented to be their choice for Donna Ana — they have my undying gratitude."

It was believed that the public might turn out to see such an impressive cast, but how would they react to such high-minded material? Agnes had the idealized opinion that the theatre had an obligation to be more than a "place of amusement." She felt that audiences would respond to intellectual material which, "widened their sympathies and broadened their intellects and sweetened their hearts." She believed it was a worthwhile experiment.

For Gregory and Laughton, it was important to keep the economics of such a venture as low as possible. No Dali-type recreations of Hell for this show. The set would be simple. Laughton would have the four actors sit on high stools, with reading stands in front of them, and dressed in evening clothes from their own wardrobes. The tour would involve only six people: the four actors, a stage manager, and a crewman. According to Paul Gregory, Agnes "insisted" that Robert Gist be made the stage manager because she wanted to "keep him on a short leash." This was granted and Gist did a credible job. The use of the reading stands with scripts propped on them, with the actors turning the pages, gave the illusion that the actors were reading. This was not the case; in fact, the actors had all memorized their lines prior to rehearsals. The pages were turned to relieve the eyes of the audience, for with so little movement from the actors on the stage it was felt the audience could become tired watching them so intently. Movement of the actors, or rather the lack of it, was important. Charles believed they must not move except for effect.

(Courtesy of Wade Ballard)

Boyer, Laughton, Paul Gregory, Hardwicke, and Agnes during the first run of Don Juan in Hell.

Don Juan in Hell would formally open on February 1, 1951 in Claremont, California, but a "dress rehearsal" was held a few days prior in Hollywood before an invited audience. From November 1950 thru early January 1951, Agnes would play the role of Parthy Hawks in the color MGM remake of *Show Boat*. While shooting the picture by day, she and the rest of the *Don Juan* company would get together to rehearse at night. Rehearsals generally went well and the actors bonded. Agnes called Laughton, "a big bear with a big pink plush heart." But it's not that there weren't any problems. According to Paul Gregory, Charles wasn't sure of Agnes' stage technique so he spent "weeks" working with her. He recalls that Charles strived to make Agnes become "emotionally involved" rather than relying on "phony" tricks such as a British accent she initially affected for her character.

Show Boat was one of MGM's major films of 1951. It was assigned to the studio's most prestigious musical producer, Arthur Freed, and lavishly cast. In the pivotal role of Julie, the studio originally wanted Judy Garland, but by the time the film went into production, Judy had been fired from MGM. The new head of MGM, Dore Schary, wanted Dinah Shore. "He talked to her about doing it and actually promised it to her," Freed would recall, "but she was wrong for the part. I sent for Dinah, 'Dinah,' I said, 'I'd love to do something with you, but you're not a whore, and that's what the part is.'" Ava Gardner eventually landed the role. Joe E. Brown was cast as Cap'n Andy Hawks, Parthy's husband, with Agnes' good friend Kathryn Grayson cast as their daughter, Magnolia, who is wooed by a riverboat gambler, Gaylord Ravenal, played by Howard Keel. The film was expertly directed by George Sidney and included the great score by Jerome Kern and Oscar Hammerstein II, including "Ol' Man River" performed by William Warfield playing Joe. His rendition was marvelous, but didn't overshadow Paul Robeson's in the 1936 film version produced by Universal. All in all, $2.4 million was spent on this film and it shows with carefully constructed sets and lavish costumes. The film would more than make back its cost, grossing well over $8 million and becoming one of the biggest hits of 1951.

Don Juan in Hell had its first tryout in the small California town of Claremont. While there rehearsing, Laughton went into a deep depression exasperated by a terrible case of nerves. He became convinced that the show was going to be a disaster. Over drinks one night he told Gist, "I've destroyed these actors. I've fucked up their careers." He almost broke his health by spending up to twenty-hours per day on the show. Boyer asked him if he ever rested. "Why rest?" replied Laughton. "There's all eternity to rest in." His dedication was total and according to one biographer, "Laughton took pains over every word, every sentence, and every nuance" of the show.

The show opened in Claremont on January 27, 1951. Paul Gregory sent a wire individually to each cast member. To Agnes, he wrote: "I cannot begin to tell you how deeply I cherish all that you have contributed toward this idea which has captured all of us." That evening, Laughton came out

The First Drama Quartette: Charles Boyer, Agnes, Charles Laughton and Sir Cedri Hardwicke.

first to warm up the audience. He explained how Shaw had written the play fifty years before and how it was not usually performed by companies which staged *Man and Superman* — but that it stood alone and could be appreciated as a solo piece. He also went into the Don Juan legend. After this brief introduction he would leave the stage for a moment and then reemerge in the company of the other actors all carrying big green folios which they placed on their music stands. The covers would open and the play would commence. Two hours later the play concluded and the results were electric. The preview audience was small (according to Elsa Lanchester, only forty people attended), but those fortunate few had witnessed great theatre. The reviews confirmed this. *Variety* proclaimed it "one of the most exciting experiences of this and any other season." The First Drama Quartette (as they called themselves, coined by Paul Gregory) was off and running. They would zigzag across the United States and into Canada. They played in small and large cities at universities and colleges and in high school auditoriums and coliseums. The show would become a great success due to the genius of Paul Gregory. As Elsa Lanchester put it, "It was his sheer invention to book tours all over the country and be hailed in every town — and then go into New York." Paul believed this put the New York critics on the spot. If they panned a show, with the rest of the country embracing it, it would expose them to the criticism of being highbrow snobs. But, with *Don Juan*, it really didn't matter. The New York critics would be expected to praise such an intellectual theatre of the mind; the real triumph was that critics and audiences everywhere from Peoria to Shreveport, Salt Lake City to Baltimore, loved the show. The cast traveled by bus, automobile, train and occasionally plane. To say they covered a great deal of mileage is an understatement. Here is their itinerary just for the month of February:

FEB 1:   Stockton, Ca.
             (That Agnes and Gist were a couple by this time, even before the divorce was final with Jack, is evident from some of the letters and telegrams which Aggie received as the tour began, including one from a friend on the night of the Stockton opening: "Dear Agnes just to wish you, Bob and your Star group the greatest success on this tour.")
FEB 2:   Fresno, Ca.
FEB 3:   Sacramento, Ca.
FEB 4:   San Francisco, Ca.
FEB 5:   Oakland, Ca.
FEB 6:   Travel
FEB 7–10:   Salt Lake City, Ut
FEB 11–13:   Travel
FEB 14:   Denton, TX.
FEB 15–16:   Houston, TX.
FEB 17:   Dallas, TX.
FEB. 18:   Shreveport, La.
FEB. 19:   Alexandria, La.
FEB. 20:   Traveling
FEB. 21:   Manhattan, KS.
FEB. 22:   Stillwater, Ok.
FEB. 23:   Fayetteville, Ark.
FEB. 24:   Memphis, Tn.
FEB. 25:   St. Louis, Mo.
FEB. 26:   Columbia, Mo.
FEB. 27:   Bloomington, Ind.
FEB. 28:   Urbana, Il.

They would have two more months of this before they took a break and would resume again with a fall tour.

Agnes and Sir Cedric Harwicke in *Don Juan in Hell*

While it was exhausting for the actors, the Quartette did gain strength from the reception they received. They took part in local activities and suffered through many after-show parties. Hardwicke especially found these parties tedious primarily due to the lack of hard liquor. He began calling the tour, "The Cranberry juice circuit." Yet, for all of his moaning about the cranberry juice, Sir Cedric would remember the camaraderie fondly. "Our discomforts are forgotten in the fun of rushing to catch a train or returning to our hotel, scraping together what supper we can find in a small town at that hour, packing and unpacking and particularly solving the problem of laundry. Boyer and I have a contest to see how long we can make our dress shirts last between laundries. Miss Moorehead, being the only woman naturally has a rough time of it, but she more than holds her own. I don't have to tell you that one woman is vastly more clever than three men."

The travel from city to city was chaotic. Gregory called it "a nightmare"; some wanted to fly, others wanted to take a train, and some wanted to take the bus. A bus was actually the most practical solution and most used when they traveled short distances. In his book, *Charles Laughton: An Intimate Biography,* Charles Higham recounts Boyer's nervousness when traveling: "Gregory reserved a bus, which normally traveled 80 people, for himself, the four actors, two staff members . . . Boyer was extremely nervous, sitting just behind the driver, jumping up and complaining loudly everytime the bus traveled at more than 40 mph. Laughton and Agnes Moorehead used to sit on either side of the aisle and exchange wisecracks about Boyer's terror of speed. Finally Charles (Laughton) told the driver, 'discount the speedometer.' He did. Whenever Boyer asked what exact speed the bus was traveling at, the driver would say, 'forty' or 'thirty-five.' Boyer settled back, feeling perfectly comfortable, even though the bus was rushing along at 60 mph."

For his part, Laughton would often appear before civic groups giving talks or reciting the Gettysburg Address. He was invited to judge a beauty contest and was startled when Agnes, as a gag, appeared as one of the contestants. He promptly declared her the winner. When the Quartette made a stop in Moorhead, Minnesota, Agnes was presented with a bouquet of flowers from the Chamber of Commerce of her namesake city. While Agnes was in Oklahoma with the Quartette her friend Greer

(Courtesy of Wade Ballard)

As Donna Ana in *Don Juan in Hell* (1951).

Garson wrote: "Was thrilled to hear about the wild success you are having with DON JUAN IN HELL. It must be a really exciting experience and I am awfully glad that you are doing it; you four must be a terrific team and I hope you will repeat the program locally when you come back to the coast."

For Agnes, one of the most gratifying moments of the tour occurred in Sacramento. Two farmers came backstage after the show asking where they could get copies of the play. She asked one of the farmers if he had enjoyed the program. His reply would stick with her for the rest of her life: "I was just struck by it. Sometimes it was a little quick. That's why I want to get the play so I can memorize parts of it." Another remembrance she often quoted for comic effect occurred in Kansas City where all the actors (while on stage) became covered by streams of ants coming down from the rigging. "Try to perform while these creatures were in your hair, down inside your costumes, just everywhere, it was unnerving. The graceful gesture becomes a little forced." For audiences who recognized Agnes primarily due to her film work, seeing her in person dressed in an elegant lilac evening gown with a small golden crown atop her red head was a revelation. One critic described her as an "elegant lily." Paul Gregory recalled hearing people at intermission say, "Isn't that Agnes Moorehead gorgeous?"

Agnes, Jane Wyman and director Curt Bernhardt on the set of *The Blue Veil* (1951).

While the tour was underway, *Fourteen Hours,* which Agnes had filmed the previous summer, was released in March to good reviews and solid box office. *Newsweek* called it "easily one of the outstanding film achievements of the current season." *Time* called it "tense" and the script, "ingenious." The *New York Times* raved and, in fact, Bosley Crowther put the film on his ten best list for 1951. It must have been sweet for Agnes to simultaneously be receiving widespread praise and audience approval for *Don Juan* while at the same time appearing in a critically applauded and well-received film.

When the initial domestic tour of *Don Juan in Hell* came to a close at the end of April, Agnes made her way back to Hollywood where she began work on the RKO film *The Blue Veil,* which starred Jane Wyman. It was a woman's picture, written by Agnes' old friend from radio, Norman Corwin. Charles Laughton also appears in the film, but he and Agnes do not share any scenes. Wyman plays a pregnant woman who becomes widowed during the First World War and, compounding her tragedy, her baby dies soon after birth. She becomes a governess so she can be around children. The film is episodic, telling her story over the course of forty years. Agnes plays one of the women who puts Wyman's character in her employ. During the course of the film, Wyman turns down two marriage proposals so she can devote her life to being a governess. The film's conclusion is a tearjerker. Wyman is old, penniless and alone. One of her former charges finds her and a party is held in her honor, attended by many of her former charges; she will never be alone again. After Agnes completed her part in the film in early June, the film's producers Jerry Wald and Norman Krasna sent her a letter of appreciation: "Thank you for the superb job you did for us . . . While it was a short job, it was an impressive one."

While shooting *The Blue Veil,* Agnes went to court to win her release, after more than twenty years, from her marriage to Jack Lee. The publicity for both was ugly. According to Jack, after Agnes had won her first Academy Award nomination in 1943, she "went Hollywood," giving the maid orders to answer the telephone by saying, "This is Miss Moorehead's residence." He also said Agnes began to criticize the way he talked, dressed and ate. Jack also alleged that Agnes began talking in a "corny" manner around the house, "displaying her thespian talents and emotions." He said that Aggie made him sleep in another room rather than sharing the master bedroom. Jack said the "last straw" occurred on June 15, 1949 when he came home one night to find a "strange man" (Gist?) sitting at his usual spot at the dinner table. Agnes' response was to tell him they were "just rehearsing a play" and to pack his bags and get out. Jack asked the court for all the community property, which he estimated to be valued at $200,000.

For her part, Agnes charged Jack with "mental cruelty." But the cruelty in question occurred in 1945, causing Superior Court Judge Frederick F Houser to rule that since Agnes had lived four years under Lee's roof, "a reconciliation was evident." However, the next day, Agnes' attorney brought into the courtroom the houseman, Marion McGuire, who testified about some of the cruelties which had occurred since 1945:

- Lee had called Agnes dirty names.
- Lee played the radio loudly and slammed doors when Agnes was trying to study her scripts.
- Lee forced Agnes to sleep in his room despite her fear.
- Lee fired pistols from his firearms collection.
- McGuire testified that Jack was "drunk practically all the time" and heard him "browbeating" Agnes.
- Jack's drinking "got so bad he hid his bottles in bushes and a grandfather's clock."

Agnes also testified that on the following occasions Lee struck or threatened to strike her:

- APRIL 3, 1949   Struck her at their Monte Mar Terrance home.
- APRIL 27, 1949   Threatened her with bodily injury.
- MAY 5, 1949   Lee threw a table at her.
- MAY 17, 1949   He told her he no longer loved her and threatened to get a divorce.
- JUNE 14, 1949   He again struck her.

Agnes also testified that Jack struck her at "other times."

This second day of testimony was enough and Judge Houser granted the divorce. The property settlement also was in Agnes' favor. She retained $100,000 in property, plus a Cadillac, while Jack got $5,000 cash, a $40,000 apartment house and $11,000 in insurance, as well as a Ford.

Most people who know Agnes say that Jack was an abusive alcoholic who used Agnes as a "meal ticket" since his career was clearly not going anywhere. Over the years it appears that Jack, once a rising young star in the AADA and on the stage, saw his career decline and Agnes' eclipsed his. This caused resentment on Jack's part and his self-esteem dwindled. He increasingly turned to the bottle. But Paul Gregory has a slightly more sympathetic view of Lee. "He was a nice man, but she was a meat grinder. He didn't have a chance with Agnes. She was a tough, tough, tough woman. She was driven like no one I ever knew. Her little husband never had a chance. The more successful she became, the deeper the wedge between them. She was on her way up and he was on his way down."

Agnes with her second husband, Robert Gist, circa 1953.

Agnes' good friend, Jack Kelk, sent her a telegram of congratulations upon the news: "Congratulations and best wishes for health, happiness and newborn freedom." The initial tour of *Don Juan* completed, a new film completed, and a divorce granted, Agnes was off to England traveling with Robert Gist aboard the *Queen Mary* to begin a tour of *Don Juan* in Britain. One blurb in the press would say of Agnes and Gist, "Those who have seen them around London say he's the Don Juan of Aggie's personal life."

<h1 style="text-align:center">III</h1>

There was a distinct possibility that one member of the Quartette would not make it to England. Sir Cedric was having tax problems and the IRS barred him from leaving the United States. In fact, Boris Karloff was announced to be his replacement for the tour of Britain. Just as quickly, though, Hardwicke was back in. He explained, "What proved to be a complete misunderstanding with the tax collector has been cleared up — even more promptly than I had hoped." How it was cleared up, in actuality, was through the intervention of Paul Gregory. Gregory advanced him the money in an effort to keep his original Quartette in tact. Paul certainly had a great deal invested with his stars. He took the further guarantee of taking out an insurance policy on each of his four players. If any of them died in the next year, he would collect $213,000.

The tour of England would have to be made, to the chagrin of all, without any appearances in London. The Festival of London was presenting John Clement's production of *Man and Superman,* and Laurence Olivier, the executive officer of the theatrical arm of the festival, supported Clement's belief that the rival show would adversely affect ticket sales for the Festival's presentation. Clement had also waited more than two years to present his production and wasn't about to let Laughton steal his thunder. Laughton would never forget this and held Olivier in contempt for the rest of his life. Agnes weighed in, "I can't think why John Clements should be perturbed, on Broadway no one would be worried at three Hamlets playing at once!"

While London was out, the show was hardly consigned to the sticks. The Quartette would appear for a week each in the provincial cities of Manchester, Birmingham, Edinburgh, and Liverpool. Boyer let it be known that he was, "quite happy to play the provinces." Still, not to appear with the show in London's West End was like being booked into Albany instead of New York City. It hurt.

For Laughton, the British tour was bittersweet. He was home for the first time since 1939. His return brought enormous press — much of it positive — and brought out his own sly sense of humor: "There for the grace of

THE FIRST DRAMA QUARTETTE

Starring

CHARLES BOYER
CEDRIC HARDWICKE

CHARLES LAUGHTON
AGNES MOOREHEAD

Opening June 18 at

The Festival of Britain

"One of the most fascinating and provocative theatrical demonstrations of this or any other season . . . each of the four readers walked off the barren stage covered with individual glory." —VARIETY

"The occasion is one for rejoicing . . . the brilliant artistry of the players provokes the onlooker to applaud again and again. Their elocutionary artistry is a display of its own." —HOLLYWOOD REPORTER

FALL TOUR COMMENCES SEPTEMBER 23
OPENING NEW YORK NOVEMBER 28

1951

Directed by
Charles Laughton

Produced by
Paul Gregory

God goes a hotel keeper." Yet Charles was also haunted by his belief, with justification, that the British public had not totally forgiven him or Elsa for sitting out the war in the United States, despite helping to raise enormous sums of money for the British war effort. Compounding the feeling of desertion was the fact that he and Elsa had received American citizenship in April 1950. Laughton's biographer, Simon Cowell, best summed up Charles' feelings: "It saddened and enraged Charles to feel he was regarded as a foreigner; his espousal of American citizenship had been an act of love for that country, not a renunciation of England." In many ways Charles believed the London snub was pointed at him.

Prior to the provincial tour, beginning on June 18, Agnes had several days to relax and see the sights with Gist. It was their first time together outside the United States, but not her first visit to England. Together they toured London, spending a good deal of time at museums or shopping for antiques. The other part of the time was spent granting interviews with the other members of the Quartette to help publicize the tour. She was asked in one interview with the *Manchester Evening Chronicle* who she thought was the most beautiful woman. Agnes chose one of her acting idols, Dame Edith Evans. "I see her and I know there is a woman who thinks beauty, and because of that it belongs to her." She was asked her thoughts on Englishwomen: "Well, I have many English woman friends, and I find them so comfortable, less demonstrative and a little more conservative — but very good friends." She spoke about her high regard for her colleagues. Of Boyer, she said: "He has a tireless capacity for work, after all, for DON JUAN he overcame the difficulties of a foreign language, and mastered a part longer than HAMLET." As usual, most of her praise went to Laughton. "He knows at once what mood you are in, and he plays on the moods of the audience like a master on a violin." Of herself, she said, "I'm a blotter — I absorb impressions and atmosphere. For instance, five months — five years from now, I could remember your face and the clothes you are wearing — I've trained myself to do it. People are the raw material of my work."

The first performance was in Manchester. The theatre held 2,200 seats, and the show was not sold out. Britain was still recovering from the War, and inflation was quite high. There were shortages on food, and wages and prices were still being regulated. Ticket prices for the show were blamed for the lack of a sellout. Still, nearly 2,000 people attended and saw Agnes appear in a shocking pink gown with a tiara on her red head. The next day the *Manchester Daily Dispatch* called the performance a "triumph" and singled out Agnes: "Agnes Moorehead, like her three companions, achieved success with a minimum of gesture. Here outraged Donna Ana . . . was perhaps the most inspired portrayal." As good as this review is, it takes a back seat to the notice she received a week later when the show performed in Birmingham. "Her Donna Ana is a radiant, terrifying example of what we poor men are up against. She is magnificence itself." Agnes couldn't have put it better had she wrote it herself.

But the icing on the cake was a handwritten note she received from one of her favorite actresses, Vivien Leigh. Leigh apologized for not being able to come backstage to express her "admiration" in person, but wanted to let Agnes know that "it was really a wonderful experience in the theatre." The tour continued playing to solid, if unspectacular, box office and strong reviews. What pleased Agnes most was to be part of a touring company of international actors — two born in England and one from France, with Agnes being the only American, and to be so warmly accepted by the British public. She hated leaving, but was hopeful that in 1952 the Quartette would return to play an engagement in London, a desire which would go unfulfilled. As she and Gist sailed back to the United States after the conclusion of the tour in mid-July, she would have a break from the almost nonstop work of the past year. But in the fall the *Don Juan* troupe would hit the road again, culminating in playing the creme de la creme — Carnegie Hall.

When the papers announced the Carnegie Hall engagement, all 2,800 seats sold out within eight hours. The Quartette would perform only one show at Carnegie Hall and then take a month off and reopen on Broadway at the Century Theatre on November 29. It would be the first production of *Don Juan in Hell* to reach Broadway.

The fall tour of the Quartette was launched on September 23 in Amarillo, Texas, and would go west to Denver then east to Nebraska and north to Minnesota. In mid-October, just before the Carnegie Hall appearance, the troupe made its way into Wisconsin where, on October 18 playing at the Memorial Union on the University of Wisconsin campus, Mollie finally got to see her daughter in all of her glory as Donna Ana.

The show played at Carnegie Hall on October 22. Prior to the performance Agnes received many telegrams, but two probably meant the most to her. One was from Robert Gist, by now her fiancé: "This is the big one. My thoughts are of you. Good Luck. Love Robert." The other was from Charles Jehlinger, still running the AADA after more than fifty years: "Welcome

Home — all our best wishes tonight." As expected, Carnegie Hall was a smash. The Quartette had no less than five curtain calls. It would seem like one curtain call for each of them individually and one for them as a quartette. The audience refused to let them leave. *Time* magazine's critic first paid tribute to the usually omitted Hell scene, ". . . It is not only the finest thing in *Man and Superman,* but the most brilliant talkfest, the most glittering dialectical floor show of modern times . . . The characters score their points like polished duelists, flash their rhetoric like master showmen, make ideas hiss and coil and spring like creatures of melodrama . . . Charles Laughton, Charles Boyer, Cedric Hardwicke, and Agnes Moorehead standing in evening clothes in front of the mikes, they merely read the scene with an apparent absence of acting that conceals a great fund of it."

Over the next two years there would be more tours of *Don Juan in Hell* to the delight of many more audiences, but, compared to this first tour, the others would pale in comparison. These four actors — and Paul Gregory — were the big winners, but another winner was the Hell scene from *Man and Superman.* The Hell scene would no longer be treated as an unwanted stepchild. It would be staged with more regularity, and usually as conceived by Laughton and Gregory. This was their unique contribution to the modern theatre and more shows would be produced which depended on the written word and little else such as *John Brown's Body* and *The World of Carl Sandburg.* That they, and others, were successful is a lasting contribution of the First Drama Quartette. Agnes would sum up her feelings years later. "I must have given over three hundred performances in plays and films but I really consider the role of Donna Ana in *Don Juan in Hell* as the highlight of my career." She never failed to thank her lucky stars for this part or expressing her gratitude to Laughton and Gregory for selecting her to play it. Laughton later paid tribute to "his Donna Ana." "Agnes Moorehead is great because, without being a dazzling beauty actually, she is able to create the illusion of queenliness, regal bearing, and sex appeal in its loftier connotation of magnetic femininity. Besides which she is a great talent whose ability is matched by a real, not assumed, modesty, what I think may justly be defined as the humility of genius."

9

"THE FABULOUS REDHEAD"
(1952–1956)

Professionally, 1951 was the highlight of Agnes' career. The recognition she received as part of the First Drama Quartette in *Don Juan in Hell* was beyond anything she had experienced during her career up to that point — including *Sorry, Wrong Number*. The large audiences in the United States, Canada and Britain, and the stellar reviews, generated endless publicity. It also wetted her appetite for more. As early as the initial *Don Juan* tour, both Charles Laughton and Paul Gregory had urged her to create her own one-woman show.

The Quartette would reopen in *Don Juan* in April, appearing through the spring at the Plymouth Theater on Broadway. Prior to the opening Agnes reported to MGM to shoot the anthology film, *The Story of Three Loves*. The film comprises three parts, set on an oceanliner, and Agnes appears in the first story, "The Jealous Lover." The segment stars James Mason and Moira Shearer, about a young ballerina who dies of a heart condition. Agnes plays Shearer's aunt, and her small part was completed in a matter of days.

Agnes was increasingly doing quick movie jobs for big paychecks due to her new love — the theatre. Her status in the industry over the years had grown to such a level that Agnes Moorehead had become a draw herself especially among women moviegoers. She wouldn't have films built around her, but like Thelma Ritter and Charles Bickford she was not a character actress who faded in the background; audiences knew her face and name and the studios recognized this. She continued to do her usual professional job in a wide variety of roles, adding quality and name value to any film. But many of the films were not on the same level as the ones she did during the 40's. There are many explanations for this. Hollywood was making a transition, moving from the studio system which kept their actors constantly at work in one picture after another to the era of the independent producer and freelance actor. There was more competition for parts in post-studio system Hollywood and often actors — especially actors of a certain age — had to accept what they could just to keep working. Agnes freelanced at all the major, and some of the minor, studios during the 1950's. Author James Robert Parish summed up this phase of Agnes' career well: "No longer was she the striving actress seeking to reach a higher plateau. She had risen as far as it was possible for a character star. Now she could offer her name and appearance to grace a film, television show, or stage presentation as a celebrity of the first rank."

On April 6, 1952 Agnes, Laughton, Boyer, and Hardwicke reopened in *Don Juan in Hell* in New York City. While it didn't have quite the excitement of the initial New York engagement at Carnegie Hall, the show was still consistently sold out. Agnes was invited to a number of social events that spring, including the annual April in Paris ball. Her invitation called this "the great French party of the year." While proposing not to impose on her, they did: "We do not want to impose upon you by asking if you would appear in the Francois I or the Louis XIV Tableaux, but if you could possibly do so, we will have a superb costume waiting for you when you arrive at the Hotel, and you can either ride a horse or lead one by the reins." Agnes had to decline the invitation as her work in *Don Juan* would conflict. But she did make a champagne supper party for Ethel Merman held at the Pen and Pencil on April 26. That April, she also received word that the Motion Picture Exhibitor's had given her the Laurel Award for her "sparkling performance in *Show Boat.*" She was awarded for giving the top performance by an actress in a character role. The film itself also was selected as Best Musical of 1951.

Meanwhile, Hume Cronyn was wooing Agnes to appear in the play, *Jezebel's Husband.* On May 7, he invited her to meet the author, "if you're at all interested in the play." Her interest was peaked and the wooing continued. On May 24, Cronyn wrote her that he found a director named Sherman Marks and that he and the writer were on Cape Cod discussing script changes: "if you're still interested, I should like you to meet him when he returns to town next week. I do hope you can be persuaded to do the play." About a week later, Cronyn was writing again, this time apologizing about an item which had appeared in the *New York Times* on May 29 which stated, "Agnes Moorehead will play Jezebel," when apparently no contracts had been signed. Cronyn explained in his letter, "I don't believe in this kind of publicity although I doubt that it does any positive harm — unless, of course, it embarrasses you. However, I did not authorize the release and I know that you were not consulted. Consequently, I made a fuss about it . . . I can only pray that it will turn out to be justified . . ." Cronyn's prayer would go unanswered.

Agnes always maintained that actors should not get mixed up in politics. She rarely took a public stand on an issue or endorsed a candidate. She just didn't think that it was an actor's place to do so, once saying it was like "mixing water with oil." One area where she was active, and had been since the earliest days of her career, was in speaking out in support of Israel. She did so again at a New York rally on May 22, 1952.

She had also seen many actors she had known and worked with — especially in radio — fall victim to the Blacklist for real or imagined communist or left wing sympathies. It was the era of McCarthyism, a dark age in Hollywood history. Agnes really had nothing to fear. Politically, she was to the right, but she often voted for the man over the party and had friends in each party. (Adlai Stevenson and Robert Taft, for example, could be introduced as her friends.) Orson Welles, an outspoken liberal, was investigated and, while not found to be a communist, he certainly was not considered a friend of the witch hunters. He was eventually gray-listed and spent a decade exiled from Hollywood working in Europe.

Sylvia Richards was a radio writer and a contract employee for Walter Wanger who had written screenplays for such films as *Rancho Notorious* and *Ruby Gentry*. According to author Victor Navasky (*Naming Names,* 1980), she appeared before the House Committee on Un-American Activities in 1953 as a friendly witness. She admitted to being a Communist, "because I was young and irresponsible and I didn't want to think for myself." She was separated from her husband, also a fellow writer, Robert Richards, whose best-known film was *Winchester '73* and who, ironically, wrote a film called *Johnny Stool Pigeon.* While she did admit to being a communist to the committee she later told Navasky that she did it primarily because she was afraid of going to jail; she had two children and, "my ex-husband was not helping to support the kids." Her estranged husband was also called before the committee and he took the Fifth — refusing to answer any questions. Both of them knew Agnes, but it was Robert who wrote her a startling letter, one which must have been painful for Agnes to read. It was not an unusual letter, and the circumstances that Robert Richards speaks of were common of many people who were accused of being communists, and it deserves to be recounted in depth:

Dear Aggie,

As you may know, I was called, and have appeared, as a witness before the House Un-American Activities Committee. I was not a "cooperative" witness.

I think the main arguments for taking this stand are pretty well understood by most people, whether or not they agree with them.

But as I attended the hearings, waiting to be called, and as I was myself examined on the witness stand, I began to see other reasons which I had perhaps not previously considered as carefully as I might. It seemed to me no longer simply a matter of refusing to aid in the sacrifice of careers — careers of people whom I had known only as fine and decent and loyal Americans — in order to save my own.

The blacklist, it occurred to me, is only a means of creating fear. Fear is only a means of stifling opinion. And I could not escape the terrible conclusion that in attempting to stifle opinion, this committee was actively and knowingly serving those elements in this country who want to force us into war — *aggressive* war.

There were repeated questions on Korea, the implication being all too obvious that any disagreement on this tragic affair or with present foreign policy in general, constituted treason to one's country.

In my own case, for example, the assertion in as positive a manner as I was able to make it that I would defend my country against attack from any source whatsoever, including the Soviet Union, was not considered sufficient by the committee. I was probed further. The phrase 'preventive war' was not mentioned, for obvious reasons, but again the implication was unmistakable that anyone who could not be wholeheartedly behind such a mad (in my opinion) and unthinkable crime was also a traitor to his country.

I cannot help sincerely believing, therefore, that the persons who refused their cooperation to this committee, rather than being in any sense "disloyal," have in their small way rendered a distinct service to their country, and perhaps to the world. For it seems to me that the fear, the attempt to intimidate, must be resisted somewhere, by someone. The Atom Bomb will make small distinction between nationalities or political affiliations.

I am sure you know that many of the persons who took this stand at these last hearings literally do not know how they are going to pay the rent next month. Legal expenses have been necessarily heavy. There have been other expenses — transcripts of the hearing record for purposes of preparation, etc.

I am trying to raise money to defray some of these expenses. And I feel, considering all the circumstances, that I have a right to ask you for a substantial contribution to such an end.

I hasten to add that if, on any grounds, you should "decline," I think you know me well enough to realize that such a declination could never in any way alter my feelings of respect and affection for you personally. I know you would not want to decline.

It is perhaps indicative of the work of this Un-American Activities Committee that many people may justifiably wish to make such contributions anonymously. I leave the methods of such anonymity to you.

I realize this sounds like a very stiff and formal letter. I am sorry. Perhaps it is because these seem like very stiff and formal times. In any event, along with the formality (and the dun) I send you my very best wishes and my love.

Sincerely,

Bob Richards

On this letter is written, "Did not answer." Whether she did help Richards or some of her other friends who may have fallen pray to McCarthyism, anonymously, is not known. What is known is that Agnes never did speak out against it nor did she endorse it. Her friend, writer Norman Corwin, who did speak out publically against the Blacklist, doesn't blame Agnes. "No, she was the most apolitical person I ever knew. Not a political bone in her body. So she never spoke out against the Blacklist, but on the other hand she never joined the blacklisters like some others ended up doing."

II

With her marriage to Jack over and done with, Agnes and Robert Gist were married in Yuma, Arizona on Valentine's Day, February 14, 1953; Agnes was 52 and her new husband, 28. Unlike Jack, Gist was his own man and didn't, according to Paul Gregory, "allow Agnes to run him." To a point, it seems. When Gist accompanied Agnes in her one-woman show in 1954, "so she could keep him on a short leash," according to Gregory, she insisted that Gist dye his hair red so they would have the same hair coloring. He did. It also seems that some of her friends were surprised about the marriage or even who Gist was. Helen Hayes didn't acknowledge Agnes' marriage for more than six months after it occurred. "Shame on me for not writing as soon as I got the happy news of your marriage. Is the groom that attractive man you brought to my dressing room at the Morasco?" That same year Agnes bought, for a bargain price, "the old Sigmund Romberg" mansion on Roxbury Drive in Beverly Hills. It was reported that Agnes was "doing it over room by room." The mansion had high ceilings and a patio "very much like some of our French courter homes" and Agnes was furnishing the home with antiques she had collected over the years. Her neighbors included her good friend Lucille Ball, Jack Benny and The Jimmy Stewarts. She would live in this home for the rest of her life.

In May, Agnes' agent wrote her about dining with Jean Negulesco, the director of *Johnny Belinda,* about using her in his new film, tentatively titled, *My Mother and Mr. McChesney:* "He was very much impressed with this script, thought it was excellent . . . when I told him about your playing the part of the nun, he thought it would be just wonderful as he has always been crazy about you . . ." That summer, following the ending of the *Don Juan in Hell* engagement in New York, she returned to Hollywood to shoot the picture, now retitled *Scandal at Scourie,* at MGM. Norman Corwin was one of the film's three screenwriters. The film reunited her with her good friend Greer Garson and Garson's longtime leading man, Walter Pidgeon, in what would be their last film together. Agnes plays Sister Josephine, who runs a Catholic orphanage near Quebec. A fire burns the orphanage down but one orphan is missing, a little girl. The little girl is found by Sister Josephine and admits to her that she started the fire unintentionally. Sister Josephine tries to find a family to adopt the little girl. Enter Mr. and Mrs. McChesney (Garson and Pidgeon). The husband, however, doesn't want to adopt the child due to her being Catholic; Mrs. McChesney adopts her anyhow. The little girl has a hard time in the Protestant community she now lives in due to religious bigotry and when another fire occurs and appears to be caused by arson, she is accused of it.

By this time, the Garson-Pidgeon teamings were running out of gas at the box office. Agnes and Garson got on very well, but there may have been a bit of professional rivalry on Agnes' part, according to Paul Gregory.

Paul recalls that Agnes would tell him, "I'm as big a star as Greer Garson" to which he would reply, "Agnes, go to the bathroom and get it over with."

"Are you saying I'm full of shit?"

"You bet."

Paul says that Agnes would take this from him because they knew each other for so long and she had a genuine respect for him, but she wouldn't have taken it from others, "especially those she didn't respect — she would have cussed them off."

That fall *Don Juan in Hell* played two weeks in Los Angeles before beginning a two-month cross-country tour with Vincent Price replacing Laughton as the Devil. According to Price, it was Agnes who suggested him to Charles for the part. Laughton had to leave the show due to a film commitment, and rehearsed Price in San Francisco where Vincent was appearing in the play *The Lady's Not for Burning*. According to Price, Laughton had made a pact with the original cast members stating that they would all stick together and, "for some obtuse reason, decided to do it in an underhand way by rehearsing me in it without telling anyone else — except Agnes. She was the confidante of Laughton and the producer, and I was the ignorant, stupidly innocent party. I knew nothing of the original agreement, nothing of Laughton's film — he told me he was ill; I only knew it was a great part and that to work with Hardwicke and especially with Boyer was a dream come true. And Laughton's personal direction night after night during the San Francisco run was one of my greatest theatrical excitements. He was a superb, if eccentric, man and actor, but an enlightenment as a director." There can be no doubt that the change from Laughton to Price was not widely known since most of the theaters on this tour had publicity material and brochures already printed stating that Laughton was appearing as the Devil.

Price maintains that Laughton's deceitful way of rehearsing another actor for the part of the Devil without telling Boyer and Hardwicke "destroyed their respect and friendship" for Charles. Price also later wrote, in his unpublished memoirs, that "I am afraid Agnes's part in the whole affair . . . did nothing for her relationship with any of us." He says that he came to the conclusion that Agnes resented the good notices he received. "Our long friendship chilled to the bone and it was a bone which never entirely buried. I should have been grateful to her for suggesting me for a great experience. Instead, I sympathized with the other's feelings of betrayal."

Still, Price loved the show and working with Boyer and Hardwicke. He would recall that all of them, including Agnes, enjoyed reading murder mysteries. "We had a tacit understanding that if the girl wasn't seduced by page fifteen or if there hadn't been a murder by page ten, the book was thrown out the window." This latest tour took the Quartette to the Midwest: Iowa, Chicago, Detroit, Washington, D.C., Baltimore, Philadelphia and then into New England for stops in Connecticut and then a week in Boston before heading west again with stops in Pittsburgh and several cities in Ohio before ending with another two days in Chicago a week before Christmas.

Agnes spent a good deal of her spare time while traveling with *Don Juan in Hell* toward developing her own one-woman show. She found the idea hugely appealing. Laughton had proved that such an undertaking could be lucrative and Agnes had legions of fans who knew her work from films, radio and the stage willing to spend a few dollars to see such a distinguished actress in person. Paul Gregory, who would produce Agnes' one-woman show, says the origins of the show were pure and simple economics. "Actors go through dry spells in Hollywood. So I said to Aggie let's do a one-woman show which we would present in New York and if it turns out very well we decided it would be a good idea to do a tour titled, *An Evening with Agnes Moorehead.*"

It appears that as early as 1949 Agnes had been toying with the idea of doing a one-woman show at Charles Laughton's urging. Laughton wrote Agnes on 6/5/49, telling her: "I am almighty serious about this reading thing . . . it would be nice to meet and talk about it again some time." He added, "I do love you every time I see you. The moist look in the eye isn't phony." The following month he wrote her again, "I hope to goodness you persist with the reading thing. I am so terrified. It gets into the wrong hands. People like Ray Massey and Basil Rathbone could kill the whole bloody racket. I have no doubt you know some females who could do the same thing for you."

She spent a great deal of time trying to select material for the new show. It was a cinch to include an excerpt from the program which most people still identified with her — Mrs. Ebert Stevenson in *Sorry, Wrong Number.* In fact, that would be the dramatic climax of the show. Agnes loved the color lavender, so one of her choices was a reading of James Thurber's "Lavendar with a Difference." Now, the piece really has nothing to do with the color; it was Thurber's reminiscence of his mother, still her identity with the color must be one reason she decided to include it. This piece would remain steadfast in her one-woman shows to the very end. She had a great love for Thurber and collected many of his books in her personal library. She once asked Thurber for permission to use his material in her shows and his reply gratified her: "You and Lionel Barrymore gave me so much pleasure that you can use anything of mine. Free." He later thanked Agnes for helping him sell many more books through "your popular readings."

Another of the highlights was the reading of the letter from Queen Elizabeth to the Bishop, Dr. Richard Cox, done with power and flourish, that caught the attention of a critic: "She read Queen Elizabeth's imperious letter to the Bishop of Pike in 1573, sounded like the rolling of drums in her opening phrase, 'Prrroud Prrrrelate . . .' when she finished the brief role, the actress said, 'Elizabeth!' and grinned at the audience — and the audience couldn't help grinning back."

Other selections included Marcel Proust's "Remembrance of Things Past" and the story of "Moses and the Bullrushes" as told by a Negro maid, with an exaggerated stereotypical dialect. (Later in the 60's Agnes would continue to include this piece, but changed the dialect to that of a heavy southern dialect; she would introduce it by saying it was her cousin Daphne from Louisiana). Usually after this piece she would do a dramatic reading of the story of the flood from the Bible. She also delivered Ring Lardner's "Some Like 'em Cold."

One of the comic highlights of her show was "Household Hints Down Through the Centuries." These included a 14th-century recipe for a dish called Cocyatrice, a 16th-century cure for bruised withers and, from the 17th century, "How to cure canaries of asthma." Many of these would continue to be staples of her one-woman show for the next twenty years, but she occasionally varied things. By the late 50's, "Sorry, Wrong Number" was out; it was just too elaborate to stage every night, not to mention what it took out of Agnes physically to execute it every performance. Replacing it would be a speech she always admired, one delivered by Laughton in *Don Juan in Hell*, "The Devil's Speech on Destruction." Her recitation never ceased to induce a thunderous standing ovation. When her mood dictated, she would also recite Robert Frost, Rupert Brooks ("These I Have Loved") and on one occasion, according to Warren Sherk in his book on Agnes, even the phone book.

The show opened in Salt Lake City on January 30. The reviews were good. In Salt Lake City the *Tribune* critic wrote: "It was an evening of smiles, chuckles and laughs, of serious attention and meditation and some dreaming. Miss Moorehead made it a completely artistic evening." In Oklahoma City, over 2,000 people attended the concert and the reviews acclaimed Agnes as a "great artist," presenting a program which "ranged from the hilarious to the lofty, and her performance evoked tears one moment and laughter the next." By the time the tour reached Ottumwa, Iowa it had a new name, coined by Paul Gregory, "The Fabulous Redhead."

Gregory said he overheard a member of the audience refer to Agnes in this way and that he thought it would make a good name for her show.

Prior to the Salt Lake opening, Charles Laughton, her director, wrote her a letter of directorial advice:

Agnes Dear,

I will not come to Salt Lake. I am not feeling well and will spend two days in bed and fly to Minneapolis. It is probably just as well as Paul and you might fuss about me a bit when there should be no concern in Salt Lake but you. You are splendid and thrilling and beautiful and it is all much better than ever . . . but of course I can't resist a last poke or two. Brooke and Proust and Shaw are poetry and the inspiration of the poet should flow through you unsimplified by your mind or any performance of thinking . . . *Keep your chin down* . . . In *Sorry, Wrong Number* don't get hysterical too soon — it makes it hard for you at the end. *Mind your projection when you're on the bench* . . . The only script doubt I have is that maybe the entrance to Thurber is milder than you would have done it naturally — alter it if you want. Keep your chin down. What a lucky audience its going to be . . . *Mind your projection when you're on the bench.*

Charles xxxxxx

Paul Gregory says that despite Laughton's written advice, Charles didn't really do much directing. "All Agnes wanted him to do was view the show and say, 'you were wonderful, darling,'" Gregory maintains, "She didn't take direction, she would speak too quickly and editorialize between pieces — charmingly so, but it prolonged the evening. It could have been a stimulating night of theater in a third less time. Charles warned her of this, but she did it her own way. But it did turn out to be very profitable."

The New York opening at the Academy of Music on March 13 was a huge success and the reviews were gratifying: "Displaying an assured, attractive personality and a sense of humor which you could never guess from her many neurotic roles in films, as well as a distinguished titian-haired beauty . . . she doesn't actually read her program, for she has almost all of it committed to heart, glancing only occasionally at her book." (*Brooklyn Daily Eagle,* 3/14/54).

The Fabulous Redhead, or simply "the one woman show," became an endeavor she would enjoy more than any other and which, over the next decade, would be a major source of revenue and bring her closer to many new fans. In her personal library at home, inside the book *The Thurber Album,* which includes "Lavender with a Difference," she made notes for speed and emphasis. She also wrote: "Learning now to do a thing is the doing of it, and as my father used to say, 'I am buying some sandpaper to sandpaper my soul,' for the tour that is looming ahead (Fabulous Redhead) hoping that I can in some way follow in Charles' (Laughton) wake trying to reach man's heart." The overwhelming verdict, based on the record of reviews, profitability and the thousands of fan letters she received over the years, was that she more than succeeded.

Gist had begun touring with Agnes for the first few weeks, primarily participating in the *Sorry, Wrong Number* selection but also handling some of the tour manager's duties. When Paul offered him a part in the play *The Caine Mutiny Court-Martial,* he jumped at it. He wanted to be more than Mr. Agnes Moorehead. Paul maintains that Agnes "threw a fit" when he offered Gist the part. She may have been insecure at what temptations a man more than twenty years her junior could find when hundreds of miles away from his wife. In July Gist informed Agnes that he was leaving her and he was "interested in another woman," and urged her to get "a 24-hour divorce." The news devastated Agnes, who later said she had to withdraw from a film due to the emotional wallop she had received. For whatever the reasons, Agnes didn't follow through on a divorce for another four years. In that time, they were separated and living apart but still legally married. Larry Russell, who lived as a child with his grandmother near Agnes in Beverly Hills and befriended Agnes, would recall that he felt that Gist "felt like a guest in that house," and that young Sean "was like a little lord at times; so Gist felt left out." Others have maintained, and Agnes herself would later state, that they felt that Gist had used Agnes to get ahead in his own career and once he secured a foothold he dumped her.

To occupy her time after the separation she pushed herself into more work. She appeared in six major films between 1953 and 1955: *Scandal at Scourie, Those Redheads from Seattle, Main Street to Broadway, Magnificent Obsession, Untamed,* and *The Left Hand of God.* Of these films, it would be *Magnificent Obsession* which would be far and away the most popular. This was a remake of an equally popular 1935 film which starred Irene Dunne and Robert Taylor. The story was based on a novel by Lloyd C. Douglas, of a devil-may-care playboy, Bob Merrick (Rock Hudson), who, while recklessly driving his speedboat, has an accident. The town apparently has only one resuscitator, and the good Dr. Phillips, who has helped countless

Agnes with Those Redheads from Seattle (1953).

Torn between Tyrone Power and Susan Hayward in *Untamed* (1955).

people in the community, suffers a heart attack and dies while Merrick is being saved. This causes resentment, particularly from the wife of the doctor, played by Jane Wyman. When Merrick finds out what happened, he thinks that writing a check for $25,000 to Mrs. Phillips will square things, but he offends the doctor's widow. Otto Kruger has a supporting role as a friend of Dr. Phillips' who introduces Merrick to the doctor's philosophy of life — that he should do good deeds for people anonymously without seeking reward or recognition. Merrick decides to take up this philosophy, but still thinks that it is only by giving money away that one finds true happiness. He tries to make up with Mrs. Phillips, but offends her again when she feels that he has vulgarized her late husband's philosophy. She tries to escape from him by jumping into a cab, only to have Merrick

Adjusting her lip liner between takes on _The Left Hand of God_ (1955).

follow her; as she tries to get away from him, after exiting the cab, she gets struck by a car and is blinded. Guilt-ridden, Merrick tries to make it up by secretly depositing money into Mrs. Phillips' bank account so she can maintain a life of comfort. He also goes to medical school and ultimately he performs the surgery which restores Mrs. Phillips' eyesight.

Agnes plays Dr. Phillips' level-headed nurse and family friend, Nancy, and has little of substance to do in the film except be sympathetic to the Wyman character. The film was directed by Douglas Sirk and produced at Universal by Ross Hunter, whose films of this period included such "women's pictures" as _One Desire, Imitation of Life,_ and _All That Heaven Allows,_ which would reunite the team of Wyman, Hudson, and Moorehead. Wyman would recall Sirk as "a wonderful director who was open to anything — any suggestion." She also enjoyed working with the more inexperienced Hudson, whose first major dramatic film this would be. "He was a very warm individual," Wyman would say of her co-star. As for Agnes, Wyman was "always hugely pleased when I found out that Aggie would be in one of my pictures. She was simply one of the best." Hudson would recall for the rest of his career the kindness showed by Wyman to a new actor by being patient and encouraging to him. For her part, Agnes also worked with the young Hudson going over lines with him and offering the inexperienced actor tips on how he should play scenes.

While quite popular in its day, _Magnificent Obsession_ does seem a bit over the top in story and production when viewed today. The character played by Otto Kruger seems almost "Christ-like," seemingly with a glow over his head when he speaks, not to mention the "gooey music." Kruger would later tell author Lawrence Quirk that he felt "ill at ease" with his mystical role, feeling that the way actor Ralph Morgan had played the same part in the 1935 version was the better approach. Kruger felt that some of the lines didn't hit the mark. "I recall that naming Jesus Christ as having died on the cross for secret do-gooding was wrong, as Christ made no secret of any of his good works or miracles during his three-year ministry. I felt this was just one of the examples of bad research on this film."

(Courtesy of Wade Ballard)

With her friend and frequent co-star Jane Wyman in the 1954 film *Magnificent Obsession*, one of Agnes' biggest hits.

Agnes felt that "there was something starry-eyed, something out of balance, about *Magnificent Obsession,* and I don't think Sirk really believed in it while he was doing it. The coincidences were stretched, the situations unbelievable, and I for one, felt it was very hard to play. I didn't feel I was at my best in it." The reviews seemed to pick up on this. *Newsweek* would write, "it is reverence before an altar of schmaltz," but *Time* would say, "the new picture easily rates four handkerchiefs." Female moviegoers ate it up in droves.

In late 1954 Agnes undertook something she had not done before professionally — directing. She directed a new tour of *Don Juan in Hell,* one not connected with Paul Gregory. Cast as the Devil was Kurt Kasznar (originally Edward Arnold was cast, but had to withdraw due to poor health), Ricardo Montalban as Don Juan, Reginald Denny as the Commander and Mary Astor as Donna Anna.

Apparently, Agnes did this behind Paul Gregory's back and he later called her "a shit" for doing it. He had produced by this time several successful tours with his own stable of actors doing this show and was appalled that Agnes would agree without consulting him to direct a version independent of him, yet using the same ingredients that the Gregory-Laughton production had: sparse sets, actors seemingly reading from scripts on music stands while seated on stools wearing evening clothes. Mary Astor, in her autobiography, recalls Agnes as "a fine director and was most generous with her own experience in the show." She also said Agnes gave "her lots of little goodies," so it wasn't the case of one actress following "the personal success by another actress." They rehearsed for several weeks at a small playhouse above Santa Monica Boulevard. They opened for three weeks in San Francisco and then played twenty-eight one night stands in a row, in the Northwest and Canada.

While Astor lauded Agnes as a director, she didn't care for the lack of comfort on the road. "Playing every night and hopping by some intercity, single-engine carrier in all kinds of weather, waiting around chilly airports where even a coffee shop hasn't opened as yet, not eating properly — it all took its toll on our small company. I have toured in station wagons and buses and played one-night stands with a Pullman car waiting on a side track with at least food and a decent berth. But never anything like this."

Apparently the toll got to be too much for Astor, as well as what she considered Montalban's overacting and overbearing nature, and she gave her notice. In Minneapolis on Leamington hotel stationary she wrote despondently to Agnes:

Dear Aggie,
You probably have heard that I have given my notice. To avoid discussion of something (the producer) couldn't comprehend I told him that I had an offer that I could not reasonably refuse.

I see no reason to explain to anyone but you; because of the time and effort you put into this production and because of the fact that when it left your hands it was something very fine.

The truth is that I am depressed and sick at heart of what has happened to Ricardo's performance. Whether it is ignorance, bullheadedness or star-itis or all three — I cannot know . . . The tour itself is a bit more fatiguing than normal. My own personal complaints such as dreadful lighting — stuffing my gown into a cardboard packing case with tuxedos and shoes, etc. could be rectified by doing a little screaming. Or born cheerfully because of the thrilling privilege of playing in a great show.

Everyone has done his bit in trying to get through to Ricky (Montalban). Kurt has the most influence, and occasionally, part of his performance is back in line. But the next night it is all forgotten. I gave up trying after asking him if he could — please — during my 'compact pantomine' not make any gestures, and give me approximately the same tempo. It was ignored. I have to start later in the speech or add more details or do it in slow motion . . . I did stop him from pointing at me with his thumb. However, the overall picture is much more serious . . . Juan is now a lightweight; nasty, argumentative, obviously loathing everyone including the audience — spitting anger at the Devil . . . Technically there is none of the carefully constructed form you so painstakingly gave him. He hits the highs of the great speech many times before it. Sometimes it gets applause — after a bad moment!

Now that he is completely sure of himself, he underscores and italicizes every phrase and draws pictures not only of 'houses' but of the surrounding country-side! I can try to find reasons but it doesn't solve anything. I believe that Kurt's skill, bewildered him — and his reviews added fuel — he is trying to keep his 'superiority' by fighting back with quantity: more voice, more emphasis, more movement and more gesture — which is futility of course.

The three of us are well 'jelled' although Kurt is forced to some dog fighting. But we sit, miserably on our stools, just waiting for it to end. I waited to decide what to do till I was well rested in the two day stopover in Appleton. I thought perhaps a session of rehearsals with you might save it — but I am convinced it would not — it would be all right as long as you were around but I know he would get unglued after one good notice — Carnegie Hall?!!

I am sorry that I can't stick it out. I believe I am doing the right thing by leaving, and am not condoning bad theatre. The financial side is as bad for me as the others. I know that for practical reasons one has to put up with the mediocre but I have been in this business too long to know the amateur . . .

Love,
Mary

Agnes, however, stuck by Montalban. In the 70's when she toured with another production of *Don Juan in Hell* it was with Montalban again cast as Don Juan. She later called Astor "illiterate" regarding literature.

III

By the mid-1950's radio drama programs were fading. The competition was television. Some programs, such as *The Jack Benny Program* and *Gunsmoke,* were broadcast both on radio and television at the same time. Eventually both, and others like it, went exclusively to television — following the consumers and the sponsors. Agnes, one of the great radio actresses of all-time, and an authentic star of that medium, followed suit. During the 50's Agnes, who at one time was appearing on six radio shows daily and a regular on three weekly shows, was down to making one or two appearances on the radio show which still considered her their "first lady," *Suspense.* During the 1950's Agnes would make 18 appearances on *Suspense.* On two of those occasions, in 1952 and 1957, she would repeat "Sorry, Wrong Number." These 18 appearances on *Suspense* would represent the bulk of her radio work during this decade — and would come to a virtual stop in the early 1960's.

But *Suspense* allowed her starring roles in showy parts that motion pictures and television weren't giving her. Here is a rundown of the parts afforded Agnes on *Suspense* during the 50's:

4/27/50: "The Chain Letter." Agnes plays a woman who sends a chain letter to somebody who dies shortly after receiving it. Her husband leaves her and she finds herself alone with the husband of the woman who had died — who is waiting to kill her.

2/15/51: "The Death Parade." Agnes as a woman who finds a letter addressed to a Miss Sheela Manix. The letter warns of a murder which will take place soon and names a time and place. She spends the day trying to locate this woman.

9/10/51: "The Evil of Adelaide Winters." Agnes as a medium who uses fake séances to profit through the pain of others until she gets her comeuppance.

1/14/52: "The Fall River Tragedy." Agnes plays Lizzie Borden in a play which tries to determine if the children's rhyme ("Lizzie Borden took an ax gave her mother 40 whacks and when she saw what she had done gave her father 41") is true.

9/15/52: "Sorry, Wrong Number." Agnes plays Mrs. Ebert Stevenson for the seventh time on Suspense.

11/17/52: "Death and Miss Turner." Agnes as a woman who suffers a memory loss and can't remember her name or the reason why she lost it.

3/23/53: "The Signalman." Agnes as a newspaper writer who returns to her hometown and visits the old train station she used to play in and meets with a signalman who tells her of the ghost trains which haunt the station.

9/21/53: "The Empty Chair." Agnes plays a teacher who becomes concerned about a student's safety when driving.

11/30/53: "The Wreck of the Maid of Athens." A ship catches fire and sinks, leaving passengers and crew shipwrecked on a deserted island. They come to believe that the captain's wife (played by Agnes) is a bad omen and decide to kill her to eliminate the bad omen.

5/19/57: "Death and Miss Turner." Repeat of the show which Agnes did on 11/17/52.

6/30/57: "The Yellow Wallpaper." Another repeat of a performance Agnes did on Suspense in the 40's, about a couple who move into a house where the wife claims the yellow wallpaper upstairs has patterns which are coming off the wall and coming toward her — driving her mad.

10/20/57: "Sorry, Wrong Number." It seems every so many years she would have to repeat this stellar performance.

3/9/58: "The Chain." Agnes gives yet another repeat performance of an earlier script done in 1950.

8/31/58: "The Whole Town's Sleeping." Written by Ray Bradbury, this is the first original script Agnes did for *Suspense* in five years that wasn't a repeat of an earlier performance. A strangler is on the loose and Lavinia Nebbs (Agnes) insists she's not afraid and to prove it she walks home alone after dark.

1/4/59:   "Don't Call Me Mother." Agnes plays a possessive mother who kills her son's fiancée and tries to make it look like an accident.

Television was taking over. At first Agnes was cautious, making her debut on an anthology series called *Revlon Mirror Theater* on October 3, 1953. She did nothing more in the medium for another two years until she appeared on *The Colgate Comedy Hour* in an hour-long special of the musical-comedy *Roberta* on April 10, 1955. Part of the reason for her caution was, like many film actors in those early days of television and (even today), she felt that by appearing in a medium where people could see you for free would diminish her bankability and allure in motion pictures. Another reason is that many studios didn't want their actors appearing on television since it was in direct competition with motion pictures and had caused box office totals to plummet from a high that had been achieved just after the War. But by 1956, and for the rest of her career, Agnes would appear with increasing frequency on television as the studio system was dying or long dead and actors of a certain age found more regular work in television than they did in motion pictures. In Agnes' case, though, that is not necessarily the case, as a strong character actress she was still in demand and, in fact, would appear regularly throughout the late 50's and into the early 60's in several films. But television, like radio, did allow her the opportunity to do more challenging roles, often in lead parts that eluded her in films.

One part on television, like the film version, which Agnes didn't get, was *Sorry, Wrong Number.* For an actress acclaimed for this role, it was her lot that there would be no visual recording of her anguished performance. John Houseman, in the early 50's, had been given "carte-blanche" to do a half-hour television drama and he selected "Sorry, Wrong Number." In his book, *Front and Center,* Houseman would recall, "The doomed solitary heroine had been played on radio by Agnes Moorehead; she was back in California and we couldn't afford to bring her back (to New York)" Mildred Natwick got the part.

In 1956, Agnes had appeared in no fewer than six major studio films: *All that Heaven Allows, Meet me in Las Vegas, The Conqueror, The Revolt of Mamie Stover, The Swan, Pardners* and *The Opposite Sex.* None of these

Trying to protect Wyman's reputation in *All That Heaven Allows* (1956).

films can be considered masterpieces or even very good, but most of them did well with audiences — the exceptions being *The Conqueror* and *The Revolt of Mamie Stover.*

All that Heaven Allows reunited Agnes with Jane Wyman and Rock Hudson, along with producer Ross Hunter and director Douglas Sirk, in a followup on the big box office hit *Magnificent Obsession.* Agnes felt that this second film was much more intelligent, and gave the actors more to chew on than the first. Wyman plays a middle-aged widow who falls in love with her younger gardener, Hudson. The film takes place in New England and the color photography is truly magnificent. Hudson plays a character with a bit of the spirit of Emerson in him, not caring much for material items, while Wyman's friends are the country club set, who behind her back disparage her affair. Agnes plays her friend who walks the thin line between being supportive and being somewhat aghast herself about the May–September romance. Overall it is a sympathetic performance delivered by Agnes. The film also includes a delicious knock on television. At Christmas, the Wyman character's children present her with a television set so she would have something to occupy her time during the long, lonely nights. Fortunately, for middle-aged women everywhere, Wyman has no intention of whiling away her hours in front of the set when the handsome Hudson is pining for her. The resulting film was as much of a gold mine for Universal as the original, and Hudson, now a much more experienced actor, gives a more assured performance than he did in *Magnificent Obsession.*

Meet Me in Las Vegas allowed Agnes to play Dan Dailey's mother — a strong-willed woman named Miss Hattie. It is a musical about a Nevada rancher (Dailey) who falls in love with a ballerina (Cyd Charisse). Miss Hattie at first disapproves of Charisse, but is ultimately won over by her. As a musical, it would never rival *Singin' in the Rain,* but it is a pleasant piece of fluff to occupy a couple of hours. The Las Vegas setting allowed for cameos by such Vegas performers as Frank Sinatra, Eddie Fisher, Debbie Reynolds, Sammy Davis, Jr, and Lena Horne.

The Revolt of Mamie Stover, shot at Fox, was based on the true story of a prostitute who builds a large following among servicemen in Hawaii during the Second World War. Of course, Hollywood couldn't allow her to be identified as a prostitute, so Jane Russell plays Mamie Stover as a dance hall hostess, the same way that Donna Reed was sanitized in *From Here to Eternity.* Agnes plays the proprietor of a dance hall named Bertha — wearing a garish blonde wig. Richard Egan co-stars as a writer who disapproves of, but falls in love with Mamie. Shooting this film was quite pleasant for Agnes, who truly appreciated the workman-like talents of veteran director Raoul Walsh, and she found Egan an interesting and attractive man. She and Egan spent time between scenes discussing religious theologies; Egan was a devout Catholic, and Agnes always appreciated someone who was a true believer regardless of their faith.

The Swan, shot at MGM, is best remembered (if at all), as the last film of Grace Kelly, who, ironically, plays a princess whose mother wants her to pursue a Prince, colorfully played by Alec Guiness. However, Kelly finds more in common and a great deal more attraction for her tutor, Louis Jourdan. Agnes has a small but sparkling part of Guiness' autocratic mother, Queen Maria Dominika. The production is lush and was personally produced by studio head Dore Schary and directed by veteran Charles Vidor. The performances were good, particularly Guiness', who provides much of the humor. But overall the film is a bore, a very pretty, competently played two-hour bore.

Pardners was the next to last film to feature Dean Martin and Jerry Lewis together as a team. Agnes plays Lewis' wife Matilda in the opening scene of the picture where both Martin and Lewis play the fathers of the characters they would portray in the remainder of the picture. After this scene, Agnes is the Lewis character's mother. Lewis played his typical dweeb who decides to become independent of his domineering mother, who is trying to arrange a marriage for him, by going west and proving he is as much a real cowboy as his father and his friend Slim (Martin). After the first few minutes of this picture, Aggie is not seen again. The film itself is actually pretty good for its type and, like all the Martin and Lewis films up to this time, it was a huge box office hit.

The Opposite Sex was shot at MGM and is a remake of the classic 1939 film, *The Women*. The leading roles in this remake went to June Allyson (in the role originally played by Norma Shearer) as the good wife, with Joan Collins (in the part played originally by Joan Crawford) as the bitchy other woman. Also in the stellar cast is Ann Sheridan, Ann Miller, Leslie Nielsen (in a change from the earlier film, men do appear in this film), Charlotte Greenwood, Alice Pearce (in a terrific bit as Olga, the Russian hair dresser), Carolyn Jones, Jim Backus, and Dick Shawn. Agnes plays a colorful Countess whom the Allyson character meets on a train heading to Reno full of other women intent on divorcing their husbands. She has some good lines especially when offering Allyson some champagne and advice: ". . . Oh, don't take it so hard, Cherie. Wait til you've had four like me. Husbands, I mean, not champagne."

The Conqueror may be the worst film Aggie ever appeared in and she is in good company. In the leads are John Wayne and Susan Hayward and it is hardly their most auspicious moment in motion pictures as well. Produced by RKO, when Howard Hughes was still in charge and systematically ruining this once great studio, the film cast Wayne as a 12th-century Mongol warlord. *Time* summed up his performance: "He portrays a great conqueror as a sort of cross between a square shootin' sheriff and a Mongolian idiot." As for Agnes, author Lynn Kear (*Agnes Moorehead: A Bio-Bibliography*, 1992) sums up her performance

(Courtesy of Wade Ballard)

As John Wayne's mother in *The Conqueror* (1956).

thusly: "Agnes Moorehead, as Genghis Khans's mother plays her role as though she is in a Shakespearean tragedy." This film is so bad it has acquired a camp following due to its laughable dialogue: "I feel this tartar woman is for me. My blood says take her," says Wayne of Hayward. With this cast, which also includes Pedro Armendariz, William Conrad, Lee Van Cleef, and Dick Powell directing, not to mention a $6 million budget, it is a shame that they couldn't have found a script better suited to all the talents involved.

This film also has a terrible legend surrounding it. Many of the people in the company later developed and died of cancer. Most prominently are Wayne, Hayward, Moorehead, Powell, and Armendariz (who killed himself before allowing the cancer to consume him). A big portion of this picture was shot on location in Utah near an atomic test site and the soil was full of radioactivity. When the company moved back to Hollywood, tons of this soil was shipped back with them so that it would match the sand used on location. Mollie Moorehead would later say that it was working on this film which led to Agnes' death. When Debbie Reynolds was asked if she believed in the connection between the high death rate of actors working in this film and the location where the picture had been shot, she replied, "Wouldn't you?"

Agnes was so busy traveling to movie locations or performing her one-woman show that some of the letters that her young foster son, Sean, sent to her during this time sound like a cry for attention: "Dear Mother. I miss you. I love you. I will give you some of my toys. Come home. I am a good boy and I have my lesson every day. I want to send you a kiss." Then another begins, "Dear Mother, I miss you very much. I love you and want you to come home." She missed one birthday, but remembered him with several gifts. "Dear Mother, I am very happy about all the gifts that you gave me. Thank you very much. I am sure I will have a lot of fun with my bicycle. I like my gun and punching bag and all the presents you gave me. I love you very much. Your son Sean." Sean spent summers on the farm. "Dear Mother. I am having a nice time. I hope you are feeling well, we have a new calf. Say hello to Freddie and Polly (Agnes' maids) and Uncle Jack (Kelk)" But Sean's situation was not much different from that of most other children of celebrities. One or both parents were off working or traveling and the children were in the care of others. In Agnes' case she was Sean's sole support and to maintain a home and give Sean the things she felt necessary she needed to work. She needed to work not only for Sean's sake but her own — it was her life.

10

(Courtesy of Wade Ballard)

With Jeff Chandler in *Jeanne Eagels* (1957).

Having appeared in seven films in 1956, Agnes would do three more in 1957 — *The True Story of Jesse James, Jeanne Eagels* and *Raintree County.* Of these three, the most interesting was *The True Story of Jesse James,* which was released in February. The film was produced by Twentieth Century-Fox and was yet another telling of the Jesse and Frank James saga. But in the hands of a revisionist director like Nicholas Ray, fresh off the success of *Rebel Without a Cause,* the film attempted to be a sympathetic view of the James' and why they turned to a life of crime. In short, it seems the Yankees drove them to it. Agnes is cast as his elderly mother who tells the story in flashback. John Kreidl, in his book *Nicholas Ray,* writes: "While not exactly an avant-garde western, *Jesse James* does call for a revolution of the James brothers and specifically examines the violence inside them. To some extent they are portrayed as rebels without causes, their violence and their good reasons to be violent are posed against each other in a tense way."

According to writer Gavin Lambert, who befriended Agnes while on this film, Ray initially was very enthusiastic, but about half way through he "lost interest and was drinking heavily." Bernard Eisenschitz, in his book *Nicholas Ray: An American Journey,* writes that first Ray wanted Elvis Presley, then a newcomer to the screen, to play Jesse. According to Lambert, "(Ray) was interested mainly because he was to have Elvis Presley play Jesse James. He saw Presley as another kind of James Dean . . . probably Fox tricked him and pretended to be interested in Presley, but always wanted to use their contract players Robert Wagner and Jeffrey Hunter." Lambert adds that eventually Ray was "very happy" having Wagner cast as Jesse.

(Courtesy of Wade Ballard)

Agnes and Hope Lange in *The True Story of Jesse James.*

One of the most dramatic scenes in the film is when Jesse is whipped in front of his mother and his neighbors, and expelled from Missouri by union soldiers. The scene had to be rewritten and reshot, according to Eisenschitz, in part because Ray "felt Agnes Moorehead was excessively hysterical as the mother."

After appearing in ten films in little less than two years, Agnes was more than delighted to entertain an offer in January 1957 from Paul Gregory to appear in a new play he was producing, written and directed by her old friend Norman Corwin, *The Rivalry.*

The Rivalry dealt with the famous 1858 Illinois Senate race between Stephen A. Douglas and his opponent Abraham Lincoln, told from the point of view of Douglas' wife, Adele. Initially, Brian Donlevy was cast as Douglas but he couldn't memorize his part. With the play opening in just a matter of a week or so, an urgent SOS went out to Martin Gabel, who replaced Donlevy. For the part of Abraham Lincoln Gregory and Corwin had to look no further than 6' 4" Raymond Massey, who had played Lincoln numerous times on stage, films (*Abe Lincoln in Illinois*) and television. Agnes was cast in the smaller but pivotal part of Adele Douglas.

Even though Agnes was busy working in one picture after another she still had an actor's fear of where her next job would come from. She had enormous debts which worried her; the farm in Ohio and maintaining the Beverly Hills mansion and the opulent lifestyle of a Hollywood celebrity were important to her. The divorce from Gist was also financially draining; Agnes ended up selling some stock she owned as part of a settlement with him. Gregory helped by offering Agnes a weekly salary of $2,750 for a show which was scheduled to tour 16 weeks. In addition he would furnish Agnes with a maid or secretary of her choice (her longtime stand-in and secretary Kathy Ellis), who would receive a salary of $100 per week, plus $50 weekly for living expenses and transportation. She would also be second billed:

RAYMOND MASSEY · AGNES MOOREHEAD · MARTIN GABEL
IN
THE RIVALRY

The star billing, above the title, greatly appealed to Agnes.

Agnes found that she could usually count on Paul Gregory to come through for her. She needed a loan to meet some of the expenses of her various households and Paul proposed to her accountant, Harold Williams, "you and I had better get together and work out the details on the loan to Agnes if it is to be worked  out at all. Or, should you like, I can pay her in this year $1,750 per week and hold $1,000.00 per week of her salary until after the next of the year, then pay her that money so that she gets it next year."

Paul also wrote a character reference on Agnes' behalf to St. John's Military Academy in Los Angeles, where Agnes was applying for admission for Sean. "It is my understanding that application has been made for the Fall term enrollment at your Academy of Sean Moorehead, seven-year-old son of Agnes Moorehead," he wrote. "Please know that I have been associated, both professionally and socially, with Agnes Moorehead for most of her son's life and as a result feel fully qualified to recommend your approval of Sean's application. I firmly believe that you will find the young man a worthy addition to your roster and Agnes Moorehead a most cooperative and understanding parent." Sean was admitted.

Despite his praise for Agnes in this letter, Paul Gregory didn't consider her a model parent by any means. He thought Sean a "very dear and very sweet natured boy," and that Agnes "wanted him to be Little Lord Fauntleroy, sometimes dressing him in short pants and sending him to boarding schools, getting him well educated and speaking several languages — good things, but what he really wanted and needed was a loving mother and I think Agnes failed him on that count — not that she didn't love him in her own way, but she didn't demonstrate it — Poor Sean — she acted like she was a general in the army and he was some little grunt." Yet despite criticisms of Agnes' parental skills, and other shortcomings, Gregory still maintains a spot in his heart for her. "She was a unique person and she was an enormous part of my life. I loved her and I still miss her — she could be grand fun."

Rehearsals for *The Rivalry* began on Monday, August 26, 1957, at the Rainbow Studios in Hollywood. When compared to the parts of Massey and Gabel, Agnes didn't have nearly as many lines and often was simply seen sitting quietly on stage as an onlooker at the Great Debate between Lincoln and Douglas. But, according to Norman Corwin, as Mrs. Douglas Agnes, "opened the play — provided commentary midway and closed it — she cemented the piece." He maintains that despite her comparatively small part she never complained — "she just wasn't that way."

As with *Don Juan in Hell*, the sets were not lavish; just a few chairs, two tables, and the three actors. But the material, as expected with a Norman Corwin play, was topical. The issues the play confronted were blazingly alive in 1957 — civil liberties and segregation. In fact only a week prior to its opening Paul Gregory sent each of his stars a letter which reflected on the controversial nature of the play: "As you know, *The Rivalry*, is based upon a very controversial subject and the headlines today and every day are carrying constant accounts of the tragedy of this subject matter as it applies to modern day living. There are many passionate views stated in *The Rivalry* by Mr. Lincoln and Mr. Douglas, and I am sure each one of you have your own personal views. It is in this respect that I feel it is extremely important that you guard very carefully what is said by any of you outside the theatre pertaining to these issues. Perfectly well meant remarks could be misconstrued, and at all costs we want to avoid the actors, as individuals, becoming embroiled in any kind of misunderstanding which would make for newspaper copy . . . All of our passions pro and con for the subject should be spent in the performances." While Agnes had always been a very fairminded person who disapproved of segregation she didn't believe actors should speak out publicly on political matters. This letter was most likely meant for the more liberal and outspoken Massey and Gabel.

The rehearsals went well and the play held its world premiere at the Georgia Theatre in Vancouver, B.C. Prior to the show, Martin Gabel's wife, well-known television personality Arlene Francis, wired Agnes: HAVE A GLORIOUS SUCCESS DARLING MRS DOUGLAS AND BE GOOD TO YOUR HUSBAND UNTIL HE COMES BACK TO HIS WIFE MRS GABEL. Paul Gregory also wired his sentiments to Agnes prior to the opening: AGNES DEAR AGNES IT WOULD BE IMPOSSIBLE TO PUT INTO WORDS THE GRATITUDE THAT I FEEL TOWARDS YOU AND EVERYONE IS RAVING HOW MAGNIFICENT YOU ARE AS ADELE I PRAY THIS EXPERIENCE SHALL MEAN AS MUCH TO YOU AS IT DOES TO ME REGRET I AM NOT THERE TONIGHT I WILL BE IN JUST A FEW DAYS MUCH LOVE = PAUL.

The show was sold out before an audience of 2,200 and the reviews glowed. "There was a great deal to listen to in *The Rivalry*. Not all of it was important. Most of it was pertinent, either in forwarding the issue or in establishing the character and personalities of the Democrat Douglas and Republican Lincoln," wrote Les Wedman in the *Province*. "Playwright Corwin, writing in spurts of inspiration, moved his play gracefully from poetic vein to straightforward, powerful prose . . . *The Rivalry* just as decidedly is a giant step of progress in modern theatre."

The *Vancouver Sun* praised each actor, particularly Agnes. "Of the three-some, Agnes Moorehead, one of the last of the great ladies of the American theatre, won honors for acting hands down. So great was Miss Moorehead's vitality it was impossible to ignore her even when she sat silent for minutes at a time."

After Vancouver, *The Rivalry* continued to play to packed houses in the lower 48 states and the reviews were still quite good, especially for Agnes. The *Seattle Times,* on September 25, 1957, proclaimed, "Agnes Moorehead fairly steals the show with a thoroughly charming, irresistible performance as Mrs. Stephen Douglas." In Portland more than 3,000 people "thrilled to one of the most timely dramas the theatre has offered in recent years," according to the critic of the *Oregon Journal*. In that hotbed of liberalism, Berkley, California, Agnes was called, "beautiful and accomplished" by the *Berkley Daily Gazette*, which summed up its review by saying, "You wonder what would happen if it were presented at Central High School in Little Rock" — a reference to the recent events when President Eisenhower called in troops to enforce integration at the Arkansas high school. But not all the reviewers were captivated; in late October the troupe made its way to Iowa and received one of its harshest reviews for a performance in Waverly: "Drama came to the Artist Series stage, and after last Sunday's performance it may never return." Agnes was accused of trying to upstage Raymond Massey. "Miss Moorehead, who held the spotlight only about a fourth of the time, tried to counteract the situation by constant attempts at scene-stealing. Straightening her wig and waving her fan, Miss Moorehead distracted the audience while Lincoln was delivering his speeches." On the whole, however, *The Rivalry* and Agnes were a huge success.

The stars got along well enough. Agnes had known and liked Gabel for years and performed with him on radio many times. She was less taken by Massey, though she recognized he made a perfect Lincoln. The actors often traveled by car and Agnes once told her *Mayor of the Town* co-star Conrad Binyon that in the close quarters she occasionally found Massey's body odor offensive. More galling to her was when she read in a New York newspaper that Massey had referred to *The Rivalry* as his and Gabel's show. She immediately wrote Paul Gregory: "Mr. Massey must be alerted that there are 3 stars and not one or two! Working with an Italian company is about as bad as working with Raymond." (She was shooting the film *The Tempest* in Rome when she got wind of Massey's comments.) Gregory contends that Agnes needed to keep up with Massey publicity-wise. "If Ray Massey had an interview; she had to have one too."

By Christmas the cross-country tour had concluded. As it turned out, it ended both Massey and Agnes' association with the show when both decided not to go with the show to Broadway; each had other projects they wanted to pursue. Richard Boone and Nancy Kelly replaced them. It turned out to be a smart move because *The Rivalry* died a quick death in New York, closing after only eight performances. Paul believed that while the show did well on the road, a historical drama was not the type of show that New York audiences were looking forward to seeing.

In December 1957 Paul Gregory gave Agnes news which he says gave her "an absolute fit": he cast her soon to be ex-husband Robert Gist in his film, *The Naked and the Dead.* To appease her he wrote a letter in which he insisted that Gist was cast "completely against my wishes," and that he couldn't control director Raoul Walsh, who insisted on screen testing Gist. Paul told her that he was the only one of five officials who saw Gist's screen test "who did not want him," but that his test was "colossal" because, "being the bastard he is," Gist was perfect for the part of the "heel." But Paul assured Agnes that when Gist returned from the location filming in the Panama jungle, "he will have a bite or two on his rosy you-know-what if I have to plant the bugs in his Pancho." In reply, Agnes joked about the casting of Gist: "He's the malaria kid in every sense of the word — which part is he playing 'The Naked' or 'The Dead'? May I say he's dead-naked!" Then she added, "Doesn't Robert have money enough now to buy my stock back that he says he sold?"

In January 1958 Agnes received an offer from Producer Dino De Laurentiis to appear in *The Tempest,* based on two novels written by Alexander Pushkin, to begin filming in April in Yugoslavia and then Italy. Set in 1770's Russia during the rein of Catherine the Great, Agnes would play the pipe smoking wife of a captain who commands a fort in the middle of nowhere, which a group of travelers stumble upon during a fierce storm. The money was good and Agnes, as always, enjoyed traveling and happily accepted De Laurentiis's offer.

To occupy her time before leaving for Europe Agnes appeared on two live 90-minute TV dramas. The first was an ambitious adaptation of "A Tale of Two Cities" on the *Dupont Show of the Month,* with Agnes cast as Madame DeFarge. Agnes picked up on Madam DeFarge's habit of knitting shrouds for her victims and in true "method" acting style began knitting herself. "I haven't stopped knitting since I picked up the script four weeks ago, and I'm getting paid for it," she told columnist Kay Gardella. Agnes was intent to play Madam DeFarge as "a villainess . . . the meanest of my career, and I've played some real meanies." She was surrounded by a first-rate cast — Gracie Fields, Denholm Elliott, Fritz Weaver, Rosemary Harris and George C. Scott. Directing the program was a veteran of live television who would later make a name in motion pictures — Robert Mulligan, who was only five years away from directing the screen version of *To Kill a Mockingbird.*

The rehearsals were long, exhausting and physically demanding; Agnes sprained her ankle while rehearsing a scene, but, ever the trouper, she went on in intense pain, but seeing her doctor daily. Most taxing to all was the constant script changes and the learning new lines; "hours and hours of confusion," she called it. She was glad when the program was broadcast and over with, calling the experience "bedlam" and that "live TV can go — but far, far away." Paul Gregory sent his congratulations. "You were magnificent — my God, how could you sustain that character for ninety minutes?" He added something he knew she would appreciate: "The next time I use you, however, I want you to be beautiful again. I hate them always making you look like an old hag . . . for some reason they always want to do this to my lovely Aggie." *New York World Telegram* television critic, Harriet Van Horne, didn't think that Agnes' Mme. DeFarge was up to par. "I have always regarded Miss Moorehead as a fine, sensitive actress. But her Mme. DeFarge lacked the vengeful quality — the touch of Lady Macbeth — that Dickens gave her. Her great denunciation scene seemed merely shrill and spiteful . . ."

Prior to leaving for Rome she taped two more television appearances which would be broadcast during the spring of 1958 — a *Playhouse 90* with Paul Douglas and Patty McCormick, "The Dungeon," and on *Suspicion* with William Shatner and Jack Klugman, an episode titled "Protegee," which had elements of *All About Eve* due to its theme of an older actress being upstaged by her much younger protégée.

Just prior to leaving for Rome she received a tantalizing offer — to play Ben-Hur's mother in the MGM film *Ben-Hur* which would also be filming in Italy shortly after Agnes finished with *The Tempest.* The opportunity to be cast in one of the biggest films ever produced certainly appealed to her, but not really the part itself. "The part of the mother in *Ben-Hur* isn't so great — it's only long," she wrote to Paul Gregory, and told him that if anything else came along which was "bigger and better," to keep her apprised, as she would prefer something with more substance as compared to doing yet another mother role. "I must know what you are going for, as you know, I'd rather be home and work for you than run around after chariots and Charlton Heston!"

Indeed, Paul did have other plans on the fire; one of the most intriguing was a new play, *The Scourge of the Sun,* by playwright Leslie Stevens, a rewrite of *Marlowe.* Paul told Agnes that the part of Queen Elizabeth "is just made for you" and believed that Cedric Hardwicke would play the "older man" with Richard Burton as Marlowe. Paul informed Agnes that if all of these ingredients, including Joseph Anthony as director, fell into place the show would begin touring, but "not quite in the strenuous pattern as the last one" and promised longer rest periods. He anticipated a successful road tour which would culminate in taking the play to New York for a limited Broadway engagement. Agnes, from Rome, was excited, immediately writing Paul, "If you are in New York I hope John (Paul's secretary) will either forward this letter or read it to you via phone. Your letter was exciting . . . I must read the play immediately."

Filming *The Tempest* was moving along well, despite some communication problems. In Yugoslavia, for instance, the crew was made up of Russian and Yugoslavians who spoke no English. Agnes also noticed that on the set the Yugoslavian actors and crew members were "guarded by police from their own country! It's amazing — there is a soldier on the set continually — poor souls." With few exceptions, most of the actors and crew members involved didn't speak English which made it difficult for Agnes and the other American actors to understand what they were saying. "I have no idea what they are saying but instinctively I go on." But she saw the humor in the situation: "I can out-shout the Russians and out-gesture the Italians — so they look at me in complete wonderment and let me alone."

Happily for Agnes much of the filming and dubbing took place in Rome. Accompanying Agnes was her secretary and stand-in Kathy Ellis. In their spare time Agnes and Kathy took on the role of tourists and visited museums and sampled the fine cuisine. Agnes reported that "Kath" is "on cloud nine." When they first arrived in Rome, the film company put them up in a

(Courtesy of Wade Ballard)

With Orson Welles on the set of *Compulsion* (1958).

hotel until an apartment was secured. The hotel was not to Agnes' liking, describing it as dreary, ugly and uncomfortable. But the apartment found for them was another matter; it was "small but charming" with an Italian maid thrown in who couldn't speak English. "It keeps me studying nightly to make my wants known; however, we get along very well. She is exceedingly well trained and cooks dreamily." Also welcome were the visits paid by American friends who also found themselves in Rome, such as fashion designer Don Loper and columnist Hedda Hopper.

Perhaps due to Gregory's optimistic letter regarding the possibility of staging *The Scourge of the Sun,* Agnes declined the offer to play Ben-Hur's mother. But, as it turned out, *Scourge* also fell by the wayside and the team of producer Paul Gregory, director Joseph Anthony and writer Leslie Stevens began work on another production which would ultimately unite all of them in a play featuring Agnes, *The Pink Jungle.* As work on *The Tempest* was coming to a conclusion in the summer of 1958, Agnes was on the lookout for another project. While still in Rome, she received an offer to work in a picture with the Italian actress Anna Magnani, the best actress winner for *The Rose Tattoo,* but this too fell by the wayside as Agnes reported to Paul Gregory: "She has absorbed any scene that is of any consequence and if that is the case it would be foolish for me to stay here to do it."

By early July Agnes was done with the picture and on her way home — via Cairo, Nice, and London. This would be her first visit to Cairo, but not her last; in 1961 she would present her one-woman show there. After a layover with her friend Derek Prouce in London she would go on to New York City and then head home to LA, with a brief stop to see Sean who was spending the summer at the Kitchen Middens farm in New Concord, Ohio. She gave this itinerary to Paul Gregory along with her insecure feelings about her career. Yes, she had just completed *The Tempest* but other things such as *Ben-Hur,* the Marlowe play, and the Magnani picture had not panned out, and as an actress in her upper 50's she was worried about her next job. Paul attempted to reassure her: "Darling, don't worry about making a living — just tell me I have your time to fill and I will see to it that the money rolls in." He then appealed to her vanity by mentioning the visit to Cairo. "If Nasser sees you in Cairo there will be a revolution, for they haven't had such a gorgeous bombshell since poor little Israel tried to seize the Suez."

When Agnes arrived in New York, she found that the religious album she had recorded prior to leaving for Rome, *Psalms of David,* with violinist Ralph Hollander, had been released and was selling well. The *New York Times* review was favorable: "an interesting and honest attempt to heighten the prose of several of the psalms of David . . . aside from the artistic worth of the recording, it would be well for all speech students to listen to Miss Moorehead's enunciation of English, with special ear to her pronunciation of 'hosts'." This review must have cheered former speech teacher Agnes, who did take pride in her enunciation of the English language.

In California, Agnes finally proceeded to legally end her five-year marriage to Gist. Separated since 1954, Aggie testified in Santa Monica Superior Court that Gist told her in 1954 that he was interested in another woman. "He was cold and distant and urged me to get a 24-hour divorce in Mexico. He told me to go home, that he had no further interest in me." Kathy corroborated her testimony. Under terms of the property settlement Agnes did retain the title to the Roxbury Drive home in Beverly Hills, the thing which meant the most to her, and she was ordered to pay a token $1 per month alimony. She wrote out a $120 check for Gist so she "wouldn't have to deal with him for at least another ten years."

II

While Paul was preparing *The Pink Jungle* through the remainder of 1958, Agnes accepted a part in the low-budget feature, *Night of the Quarter Moon,* once again cast as a mother, this time of John Drew Barrymore. It is actually quite an interesting little film, directed by cult favorite Hugo Haas, that had a social theme for its time. Through a series of misunderstandings the wife of the Barrymore character (Julie London) is revealed to be part black. Agnes' character is a closet bigot; at first she warmly welcomes London into her family, but once it becomes known that her daughter-in-law is part black, she viciously turns on her and turns her husband against her as well. All this so she can protect what is really important to her, her social status in the closed-minded community she lives in. At one point the Moorehead character explains, "I always thought we should have equality for all people in the world. Until it happened to me." Boosting the film, more so than the somewhat hackneyed script, is a good cast: Nat King Cole, Dean Jones, Edward Andrews, Charles Chaplin, Jr. and Cathy Crosby. However, it certainly was a product of its time and, as author Lynn Kear states, it can seem "hilariously dated" for today. Overall, the reviews for the film upon release were disappointing, though *Variety* threw Agnes a bouquet: "Agnes Moorehead as the mother who highhandedly brings annulment proceedings despite her son's opposition delivers her usual competent performance." The film went nowhere at the box office.

Agnes made the first of three appearances on *The Shirley Temple Playhouse* in the fall of 1958, as a witch in an hour-long adaptation of *Rapunzel.* Miss Temple didn't appear in the play itself and the leading role of Rapunzel went to a young newcomer, Carol Lynley. Miss Lynley had happy recollections of her time working with Agnes. She recalled Agnes as

Relaxing in the late 1950s.

"great company always — funny, feisty, witty, direct and very professional; just a fabulous lady." But she never really got to know her, despite working with her again the next year in a *General Electric Theater* presentation with Ronald Reagan, and future meetings at social events. "We never socialized on a personal level. There was a big difference in our ages. I think the only person she ever really socialized with who was much younger than she was Debbie (Reynolds)." While they certainly did get along, "She was a private person, she never volunteered information regarding her private life and she never invaded your privacy." Miss Lynley never even knew that Agnes had a son. Still, she cherishes the memory of their professional collaborations. "I think she was one of the all-time great Grande Dames of Hollywood."

Rapunzel did well in the ratings and won favorable reviews. "In view of the approach of Halloween, *Rapunzel* was an appropriate choice for the TV screen. There probably was no new moral lesson in this fairy tale. But if there happens to be a rampion garden in the neighborhood, it probably won't be invaded for a long time by young adventurers. Miss Moorehead might just happened to be hiding there." Carol Lynley was applauded as "lovely and sympathetic." Agnes was not Endora in *Rapunzel,* but a more evil cousin. Some of the dramatic gestures that she uses in *Rapunzel* may remind one of the witch she would immortalize within a decade, but this witch was ugly where Endora was glamorous, evil where Endora was mischievous. By this time Agnes was getting greatly excited about *The Pink Jungle,* and her part in the show.

The Pink Jungle was a musical-comedy about the world of Madison Avenue, and specifically the cosmetic industry. The head of a cosmetic firm, Eleanor West, dies and her son inherits the company. A battle for the succession to the presidency begins, with the main focus being between two vice presidents, Tess Jackson and Chris Taylor, who both also happen to be in love with the son. Agnes was cast as Eleanor West, or rather her ghost, because we never see her as a living being, but rather a specter who returns to watch over the son, the company, and other members of her family. For the part of Tess Jackson, Paul Gregory wanted an actress who not only could handle comedy and the musical numbers but someone whose name would mean box office. He approached Ginger Rogers with an offer of $5,000 per week plus a percentage of the box office. It was too good to turn down and she didn't. The other ingredients were strong with a supporting cast led by Leif Erickson as the "good" son (Gig Young had declined the role), Maggie Hayes as Ginger Rogers' main competitor for the presidency of the firm and the attentions of Erickson, Gavin Gordon as Erickson's father (described as a "nincompoop" in the script), Ray Hamilton as the brother of the Erickson character — a ner'do well, and Louis Nye as a psychiatrist. Joseph Anthony directed, with book by Leslie Stevens, music and lyrics by Vernon Duke and costumes by Jean Louis (including a $32,000 chinchilla trench coat and $8,000 beaded gown worn by Ginger Rogers). With these elements the show seemed to be a good bet for a long run on Broadway.

Rehearsals for *The Pink Jungle* wouldn't begin until the late summer and in the meanwhile Agnes received an offer to appear at the 1959 Vancouver International Festival in the play *Mary Stuart* in the role of Queen Elizabeth. Swedish actress Viveca Lindfors was cast in the title role. The money was good; for two weeks of rehearsals and then two weeks of performances at the festival, Aggie would receive a lump sum of $8,000. There seemed to be a tacit agreement that everything was in place and the Festival artistic and managing director, Nicholas Goldschmidt, made an announcement of Agnes' participation before any contracts were signed. It turned out to be premature when Agnes specified (through Paul Gregory) that she expected the Festival to provide her with an apartment and a maid, at their expense. Goldschmidt said it was their understanding that they were to *find* Agnes an apartment and maid but not pay for them, because it just wasn't in their budget. Despite a prestigious play, above-the-title-billing, and the large fee, Aggie decided not to participate since the Festival was unwilling to accept her other demands.

In April Agnes accepted one of her rare leads in a motion picture, a 12-day-shoot on a low-budget horror film for Allied Artists of Mary Robert Rinehart's *The Bat*. In it she plays mystery writer Cornelia Van Gorder who comes to stay at a mansion in the country called the Oaks to write her latest whodunit. Vincent Price kills the owner of the Oaks while they are on a camping trip after the owner, in confidence, tells Price that he embezzled $31 million from the bank he is president of. Price is convinced that the money is hidden somewhere at the Oaks. Meanwhile, a murderer by the name of The Bat is on the loose, terrifying local women. The film had plenty of atmosphere and the usual murder mystery ingredients including dark passages, hidden rooms, and thunderstorms on dark nights. Agnes is also carefully lit and looks good in this film. In one scene she even wears a low-cut nightgown. This little thriller more than made a profit at the box office when released.

III

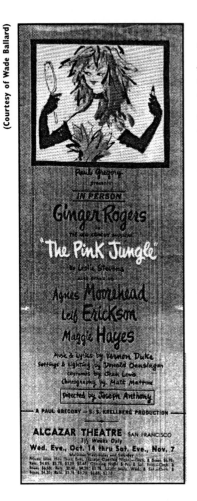

Initially, Paul Gregory was quite high on having Ginger Rogers in *The Pink Jungle.* He based it on her past history as a star of several musical-comedy films, so he was surprised when he got feedback from director Joe Anthony that Rogers just wasn't making the cut during rehearsals. He was told that she rarely arrived on time for rehearsals, often being a half-hour, hour, or even hour and a half late which left the other cast members fuming. Most surprising of all was that Ginger just couldn't master the songs which Vernon Duke had composed. Certainly, she had sung well enough in many of her films, so why was she having such problems now? Then there were the dance numbers, which she also couldn't memorize; one such routine had to be simplified for her and she still was having problems with it. One half of the greatest dance team in motion picture history having trouble with a relatively simple dance routine? Perhaps Paul should have had a forewarning when, shortly after he had signed Ginger, he ran into Fred Astaire. Astaire mentioned that he had read that "Gin" had been signed and asked if she had asked for a dance-in yet, and Gregory, puzzled, said, "No." "She will," claimed Astaire.

Astaire was correct and Ginger did ask for a dance-in. Ginger would observe her dance-in doing the number and then try to copy her, but it was clear that by taking this approach that Ginger was not mastering the routine. She also wasn't memorizing her lines and would often need to be cued. As usual, Agnes was the complete professional and not only knew her lines but just about everybody else's as well. As the ghost of Eleanor West, to gain admission to heaven, she has to perform one good deed. In her efforts to accomplish this appears in several guises including an Irish New York policewoman, a secretary and a telephone operator.

Given the shaky performance of lead Rogers, Paul Gregory was understandably apprehensive when the show made its debut on October 15 at the Alcazar Theatre in San Francisco. But he had seen a star before, weak in rehearsals, turn it around when the curtain went up, delivering a smashing performance — and was hoping this would be the case with Ginger. Unfortunately, it was not. Ginger's name helped at the box office, though it still wasn't a complete sellout, but the reviews were not good — except for Agnes.

Variety pinpointed one of the major faults: a book that was too long (each of the two acts ran 90 minutes), a confusing plot, and the music and lyrics suffered because "none of the leading players can sing." On the plus side, according to *Variety,* was "a marvelously funny performance by Agnes Moorehead who walked off with individual honors." Also on the plus side were the costumes and "elaborate staging." Ginger got kudos for her still "amazing youth and luscious figure." But overall, "Miss Rogers fumbled considerable dialog, probably as the result of too little rehearsal."

While Ginger was a major source of the problems, due to her lack of preparation, the other problem was the length of the show. A three-hour light comedy was at least an hour too long. It was clear that the show would need retooling. Adding to Paul's problem was that Ginger's mother Lela, still the ultimate stage mother for her nearly fifty-year-old daughter, was making demands on Ginger's behalf and also making it well known in public that she and Ginger were unhappy with the show. After the San Francisco premiere, Lela took Paul aside, telling him, "this was not the play we (her and Ginger) bought." Furthermore, she told him that the "one way to strengthen Ginger's part" was to practically cut Agnes out of the play. Paul asked Lela if the Agnes Moorehead part should be eliminated all together, to which Lela replied, "No, but that Agnes was overpowering

Ginger and she (Ginger) couldn't match it." So, if Agnes would just tone down her performance Ginger would, somehow, miraculously improve. In no uncertain terms Paul set the record straight with Lela and through her, Ginger, when he told her, "Agnes was the one keeping the show afloat." He would not tell Agnes to tone down her performance or make any unnecessary cuts just to please Ginger. From then on Paul would keep Lela monitored because he could hear her "denounce what the management was doing to her little girl" to anybody within listening distance. It was a bad situation which didn't get any better; at the end of the San Francisco run, director Joe Anthony quit primarily due to being unable to "evaluate clearly" because he was unable to get a quality performance out of Ginger.

Things didn't improve when the show moved on to the new Fisher Theatre in Detroit. By this time Leslie Stevens had taken on the directing chores as well as doing rewrites which the cast was supposed to learn by day while still delivering the old dialogue at the evening performances. Attendance continued to be good, not great, and the reviews continued to be mediocre at best.

Things came to a climax when *The Pink Jungle* came to Boston and Ginger went public with her disdain for the show, telling the *New York Post* that *The Pink Jungle*, "needs more than a face-lift. They better bury it." Leslie Stevens sent Paul a telegram on 11/5/59 from Boston which starkly presented the problems: "Not one good review during the entire run . . . The more improvements we give Ginger the more visible her acting, comedy and singing shortcomings become." He, too, submitted his resignation and wished Paul luck in finding a director who could work under these circumstances.

This was the last straw. Paul decided to close the show to "retool," but the expenses already

(Courtesy of Wade Ballard)

Backstage at The Pink Jungle (1959).

incurred and the difficulty at this late stage to recast Ginger's part would be too much. *The Pink Jungle* never did reopen. But Paul decided to set the record straight with Ginger. In a "private and confidential" three-page letter dated January 19, 1960, Paul told Ginger he felt she was "laboring under a delusion" as to why the show closed. "The unfortunate fact of the matter is you did not deliver the standards we expected." He went out of his way to stand up for Agnes: ". . . if you were to play Agnes's part and Agnes was to play your part the situation would be just reversed. Instead of Lela crying and complaining about the part of Tess Jackson she would be complaining about the part of Eleanor West. For the fact of the matter is, Ginger, the load in THE PINK JUNGLE was just too much for you . . . if your performance had been sufficiently up to standard I believe you would have gotten far better reviews, comparable to those of Agnes . . ."

After more than 30 years in the business, that must have been a blistering letter for a star of Ginger's magnitude to receive. In her autobiography Ginger has little to say about *The Pink Jungle* except that the playwright, Leslie Stevens, was not as "responsive" as he might have been due to the illness of his wife. She also alleges that she was not being paid in the timely fashion her contract specified and that Paul was not as hands-on as he should have been because he was producing a film in Hollywood: "How could a producer desert his own show at this early stage?" This was enough to cause her to give her notice. "The writer wasn't writing, the producer wasn't producing and the show was standing still." But no mention of her own lack of preparation or generally poor reviews, and certainly nothing about feeling upstaged by Agnes Moorehead. Yet the records of correspondence from those in the show from Paul Gregory to Leslie Stevens to composer Vernon Duke (Duke wrote to Agnes saying that Paul intended to reopen the show, minus Ginger), and the reviews of the time certainly point to one major culprit — and that was Ginger. The question is why was she so unprofessional and unpolished as a comedian and singer/dancer in this show when she had proved to be so talented in other shows, before and after, including stints in *Hello, Dolly!* and *Mame*? Could it have been as Paul Gregory suggested that, "Ginger was very jealous of Agnes — no doubt Agnes stole the show, so Ginger acted very childish and refused to rehearse or dance"? It is clear that in the story of *The Pink Jungle* there was only one winner — Agnes, who won the reviews and the respect of her co-workers and producer. The losers were Paul, who lost a fortune, and, at least temporarily, Ginger Rogers.

11

DEBBIE, COLUMBO & PENGO (1960–1962)

As the old decade turned into the new Agnes was putting herself back on the market. She had fully expected that she would be spending most of 1960 in New York working in *The Pink Jungle* on Broadway. But with the show closing in Boston and not likely to open again she needed to take what she could to garner the income she needed. In 1960 alone, she would appear in nine television dramas or series. One which she enjoyed was an appearance on the anthology series, *Ford Startime* in a piece titled "Closed Set"; the writer was Gavin Lambert, who had worked with Agnes on the film *The True Story of Jesse James,* and they had formed a friendship. Also cast was Joan Fontaine, who Agnes had not worked with since the chilly atmosphere of *Jane Eyre* nearly twenty years earlier. But they had seen each other over the years at various social and entertainment events and had gotten closer — not really friends, but friendly acquaintances.

In February, Agnes would appear on her final episode on *Suspense,* a series she had made well over thirty appearances on, doing yet another adaptation of "Sorry, Wrong Number." She was still referred to as "The First Lady of Suspense." It seemed fitting that as radio drama was coming to an end that Agnes would make one final appearance on this show, one of the last survivors of Radio's classic era, in a part which meant so much not only to the show but to Agnes. With the possible exception of doing a small portion of it in her one-woman show, this would be Agnes' final, full-length, fully realized performance as Mrs. Elbert Stevenson.

Taking a break from the routine of television guest appearances and her one-woman shows, Agnes was offered a part in the new Walt Disney film, *Pollyanna.* Agnes eagerly accepted the supporting part of crotchety Mrs. Snow, a hypochondriac, who it seems can't get along with anyone — until she meets the ever-cheerful and optimistic eleven-year-old, Pollyanna. The cast was made up of veterans: Karl Malden, Richard Egan, Nancy Olson, Adolphe Menjou, Donald Crisp, and Reta Shaw. The role of Pollyanna's stern Aunt Polly would be played by Agnes' old friend, Jane Wyman, in their fifth and final film together. In the pivotal role of Pollyanna, Disney cast Hayley Mills, the daughter of John Mills. This film, and her followup for Disney, *The Parent Trap,* would make Hayley Mills the most popular child star since Shirley Temple.

While Walt Disney had a reputation for not paying his actors top dollar, his films were well made by expert craftsmen, and always had a built-in audience which guaranteed big box office. Karl Malden had fond memories of the film and Disney. "The Disney studios were one of the best studios to work at. It was like a college campus. Between shots people would play volleyball, shoot baskets. It was a relaxed atmosphere. Disney didn't ask for much. He trusted filmmakers and the actors. He tried to get the best and, when he did, he let them do their work without much interference. I did one six-minute speech in one take (where his character, Rev. Ford is delivering a fire and brimstone sermon) and the next day, after he had seen the rushes, Disney came out to me and asked if I wanted a 16mm print of the film because of what I had done! Of course I did and he delivered."

The picture was partially shot on location in the Napa Valley of California and Malden recalls that the actors, himself, Agnes, Wyman, Egan, among others, would all go to dinner together and then while away the night by playing card games or charades. "We all were like a family — full of love like a family." Malden got to know Agnes on this picture, but would spend more time with her later on the long location shoot of *How the West Was Won* and at Screen Actor Guild meetings. "Aggie was a strong, solid person with a strong character. She was a quiet person and quiet people don't get noticed much. Her whole thing was up there, on the screen, and when she wasn't acting she was as normal and quiet and nice and sweet as anyone I knew. It was a pleasure knowing her. I know if she hadn't died we would still be friends today." For her part, Aggie always considered Malden "one of the most talented and considerate actors I've ever worked with."

Wyman also enjoyed this film and her favorite scene in the entire picture is where Agnes, playing the hypochondriac, who always thinks she has one foot in the grave, chooses her own casket. "I just love that scene — only Aggie could make it as believable as it turned out."

While the film certainly did well, grossing about $3.5 million, it was far below Disney's expectations of between 7 and 8 million. Disney historian

Leonard Maltin, in his book *The Disney Films,* says Disney was convinced that the title, *Pollyanna,* was a barrier; females were drawn to it, but men and young boys might have thought it was a "sissy" type film.

For Agnes, *Pollyanna* turned out to be a happy highpoint of an otherwise lackluster year. Her final television appearance for 1960 was on *The Rifleman,* playing "Miss Bertie" a woman who keeps a scrapbook on outlaws. Richard Anderson also guest-starred as an outlaw she tries to apprehend for the bounty so she can retire to a rest home for older women. Anderson recalls Agnes as "very direct and certainly polite. I sensed that she was a private person and I respected it. She would often complete a scene and go to her trailer. Nobody resented it because when she was on the set she was a complete pro and very gracious to everyone."

Anderson had a healthy regard for Agnes' screen presence. "She brought it up — the magic or whatever the magic is that the camera captures — and she could make a poor actor look good. She could take over a scene if she needed to and dominate it so that no one was paying attention to the struggling actor. I thought she was technically as good as they come; the only one who comes close to her in my opinion is Bill Holden." High praise indeed, since Anderson considers William Holden to be the best screen actor he worked with or knew. "I mean, she knew how an actor should translate a script to the audience. She was like Stanwyck, who I worked with often, in that she was always prepared. She didn't make a fuss. Moorehead had it all down — she knew what she was going to do and had it thought out in advance. Her acting was below the radar, which is the highest kind of compliment you can get in this business." Anderson believes that Agnes had a "respect for the people that she worked for which some actors I've known didn't have." Because of her preparation, "the producers and directors knew if you got Moorehead you didn't have to worry about her — she would be one less actor they would have to worry about." This is why, along with her "obvious talent," she was always employed.

During the fall of 1960 Agnes received a script which greatly interested her. It was an episode of the science fiction anthology series, *The Twilight Zone* written by Richard Matheson titled, "The Invaders." The script contained no dialogue until the end, but was full of action and dramatic tension. Her character is described in the script as having "been alone for many years; a strong, simple person whose existence is primitive and whose only problem is acquiring enough food to eat."

The story dealt with a woman who lives alone out in the middle of nowhere in an old farmhouse. While preparing her evening meal, she hears a strident noise and then a crash, which sounds like it came within her home. She climbs up to the attic to investigate and is startled by what appears to be a small flashing flying saucer. As she approaches the saucer-shaped object, a door opens and out comes a small creature, and then another, which she does battle with. The ending is a classic; after she kills one of the creatures (wrapping it up in a blanket and beating it to death — then throwing it in the fire), the other creature

(Courtesy of Julia Devlin)

Agnes on *The Twilight Zone* in her tour de force performance in "The Invaders" (1961).

moves back to the spaceship, and she begins to hack away at the spaceship with an axe. A voice in the ship is heard to say, "Central Control. Come in, Central Control. Do you read me? Gresham is dead. Repeat. Gresham is dead. The ship destroyed. Incredible race of giants here. Race of giants. No Central Control. No counterattack. Repeat. No counterattack. Too much for us. Too powerful. Stay away. We're dying. We're finished. Finished. Stay away. Stay away. Uhhh . . ." The camera then focuses in on the writing on the ship — *U.S. Air Force Space Probe No. 1.*

The episode was directed by Douglas Heyes, who recommended Agnes Moorehead for the lead upon receiving the assignment to direct. "The reason I suggested her was that she had done a radio show called 'Sorry, Wrong Number,' which was a half-hour *tour de force* where she used nothing *but* her voice, and I said, 'Here's a half-hour *tour de force* where the woman doesn't use her voice at all!'" At first, when Agnes met with Heyes about the part, she questioned him about her lines. "She looked at me very curiously when she came in," recalled Heyes. "I said, 'What is it?' She said, 'Well, I've been reading the script and I've been trying to find my part!' Assured that her part was to be done completely without dialogue must have surprised Agnes, but when Heyes explained why he chose her for this part she must have felt both honored and up to the challenge.

The show would become one of the most famous of her career. With the exception of Endora, the woman in "The Invaders" is probably her most recognizable because it is still in syndication and audiences to this day can still view it. *The Twilight Zone* often has marathons of favorite episodes shown, and "The Invaders" is always included. She would always consider this show to be a highlight of her television career.

The income that Agnes earned by performing on television was contributing a bigger percentage than ever toward maintaining the lifestyle which she had become accustomed to. Furthermore television was allowing her to make new fans among people who really didn't know her from the movies, especially among children. She was also impressed by the immediate reaction she received. While she recognized these benefits from working in television, and didn't deem the medium to be below her status like some actors of her era did, she was never completely taken by it either. She found the pace of television exhausting and felt it offered actors little in the way of creative stimulation. "I wouldn't say it is a lark . . . I do think it's very hard work and that you have to be very careful with your creative sense. It is the only sacred thing an actor has and it must be protected and nurtured a great deal. There is very little time to nurture it (on television)." But Agnes, always perceptive, understood the nature of the industry. Actresses of a certain age tend to get offered fewer roles, and television opened up another avenue for her which she both embraced and disdained.

By the early sixties Agnes was looking for a series. She was most excited about doing an anthology which would allow her to introduce every episode and perform in a certain number of them without being obligated to appear in each story. Furthermore it would allow her to showcase all of her talents — heavy drama, light comedy, and even an occasional musical. To sell this idea to the networks Aggie formed a company called Roxbury Productions, Inc. along with her friends, writer Robert J. Shaw and Jack Kelk. Shaw would be the principal writer of the new series and Kelk would act as producer. The program they would attempt to sell was simply, *Agnes Moorehead Presents.*

To sell this project, Shaw, a distinguished radio and television writer in his own right, submitted a simple, yet detailed, proposal in which it was asserted that most pilot proposals were, "ponderous, pompous, promising, and not much more." He promised that the proposal for the pilot of *Agnes Moorehead Presents* would not be and, to a remarkable degree, he succeeded. The proposal presented by Shaw is only thirteen pages long and included five pages of a typical Moorehead introduction of the evening's play along with a conclusion where she would chat with the guest star or introduce a scene to the following week's play.

The proposal suggests that Agnes' main duties beyond lending her name and reputation to the series would be as a tutor and talent scout: ". . . since her reputation speaks for itself, it is pertinent here to mention only that some may not know of her constant and active participation in teaching her craft. There are many thousands in her profession who know her not only as an actress of infinite talent, but also a dedicated teacher. They more than anyone will realize that she is by no means lending only her name or her acting abilities to this enterprise. Selecting and guiding the talent she will present in the series will be, in fact, her personal and primary concern." To accomplish this, Agnes would work with people she knew, including Joseph Cotten, Ray Anthony, Everett Sloane, Jean-Paul Belmondo and Edd (Kookie) Byrnes. She would also utilize students in her acting classes for small or even featured parts depending on their development. It was an idea which thrilled Agnes.

Unfortunately, there were no takers. Anthology series were numerous at this time. During the 1961–62 season, when Agnes' show would presumably have debuted, Barbara Stanwyck would launch her own anthology series. Additionally, there were many already on the air such as *The Twilight Zone* and *General Electric Theater,* and the vogue for such series was coming to an end. While the networks were willing to give a green light to the Stanwyck series, they were hesitant to do so for Agnes. Despite her great reputation as an actress, she wasn't considered a big enough name to headline her own show. It was like *Sorry Wrong Number* all over again with Stanwyck in and Agnes out. But she wouldn't give up hope that one day she would find a series for herself.

Intriguingly, she did audition for a part in a series which would be launched in the fall of 1961 and would enjoy a five-year run. The show was *Hazel,* based on the popular *Saturday Evening Post* comic strip character of the maid who runs the Baxter family in more ways than one. Agnes, along with Betty Field and Shirley Booth, auditioned for the part. According to *Hazel* creator Ted Key the executives in charge of casting were divided over who should be cast, but that he favored Shirley Booth, who had once wanted to play the character in a stage play. Booth, a well-respected stage actress and winner of the Academy Award for *Come Back, Little Sheba* ultimately won the part and legions of new fans. It is hard today to imagine any other actress as Hazel, just as it is hard to imagine anyone other than Agnes as Endora.

II

(Courtesy of Wade Ballard)

How the West Was Won (1961).

During the summer of 1961, Agnes accepted a part in a mammoth motion picture, *How the West Was Won,* which would utilize three directors including George Marshall and John Ford. Agnes' section of the picture would be directed by her old friend Henry Hathaway. The film would feature an all-star cast: James Stewart, Carroll Baker, Debbie Reynolds, George Peppard, Henry Fonda, Gregory Peck, Richard Widmark and John Wayne. The nearly three-hour epic would tell the story of the expansion of the American West through the eyes of the Prescott Family on their move west. Agnes was cast as the mother of Baker and Reynolds, with Karl Malden cast as the father. The family travels both by wagon train and then by raft, and meets up with a mountain man (Stewart), whom one of the daughters, Baker, falls in love with. Along the way the family also tangles with river pirates and gets caught up in deadly rapids. It was not to be an easy shoot.

Location shooting would take place about two hours outside of Paducah, Kentucky. That meant that every morning the cast had to rise at five a.m. to get made up and make the long car ride to the location, then finish up by five thirty or six at night and another long drive back to the hotel that the cast and crew were staying at in Paducah. As usual, when working under such conditions, the cast and crew bonded. The long rides to and from location allowed Agnes to reacquaint herself with Karl Malden and director Hathaway. Hathaway was called "Screaming Henry" by Malden because of his reputation for yelling at actors. "He was a good director, a wonderful director from the old school. He knew how to put a film out and didn't use a bunch of tricks like Hitchcock did, but he screamed at everybody — it was his way to heighten dramatic tension — but I loved him." So did Agnes, who would always regard Hathaway as one of her favorite directors.

Jimmy Stewart also added to the camaraderie on the set. "Jim was a professional," recalled Malden. "Nothing highfalutin' about him — he ate a sandwich with the rest of the cast and crew. There was no temper with Jim. I remember one day on the picture. I was five years younger than he was, yet I was playing this old man, the father of one of the girls he was romancing. I said to him, 'How is it that you are five years older than me and like me you wear a hair piece and yet you still play romantic leads?' He told me he would gladly switch with me if he could have my teeth!"

(Courtesy of Wade Ballard)

Carroll Baker, Agnes and Debbie Reynolds on the Paducah, Kentucky location of *How the West Was Won* (1961).

Carroll Baker would recall one dangerous day when a controlled fire on location went out of control. "In one scene in our movie the family was required to witness a trading post burn to the ground. Karl and Agnes were in the background, Debbie and I were in the foreground nearest the fire, and in between were our two brothers, one of whom was stretched out on the ground with his leg in a splint in order to match an earlier sequence. A *Life* magazine photographer was up a tree ready to capture the action in stills. Henry found the first four attempted fires both unspectacular and unsatisfactory. He lost his temper and began to heckle the special effects men into giving him a fire worthy of Cinerama. Too much oil was used on the fifth take. The fire instantly became a roaring blaze which swept rapidly over the rest of the set and all nearby trees. Debbie and I instinctively grabbed hands, turned and jumped straight into the river. Then Karl and Agnes and the one brother followed suit. The other boy couldn't move because of the splint, and was screaming to be rescued. The *Life* photographer was yelling 'help!,' as he was caught in the middle branches of a tree, which was rapidly burning toward him from the top and the bottom. But Henry was yelling, 'Save the camera! Save the camera!' All eventually were saved, but needless to say the camera was the first out."

But the long location shoot also brought together Agnes and Debbie. They had known each other at MGM and met at parties throughout the years but their friendship really formed on *How the West Was Won*. One of Debbie's first impressions is that Agnes was a serious person, ". . . but I also discovered that she had a very dry 'inside' type of humor and she loved to laugh. At first she could frighten anyone off but after she got to know you, the gate came down." Agnes later said, "You know, it's rare to form a lasting friendship from making a picture together. But Debbie and I have formed a friendship that has lasted." One day, during the long location shoot, Debbie approached Aggie and said, "I admire you so much and I want to be your friend." Agnes, somewhat dramatically, replied, "Then you shall be." One of the things that brought the two together was a similar sense of humor. "Debbie has an incredible sense of humor," said Agnes. "Both Debbie and I manage to see the funny side of things . . . we both have this zany sense of humor. That may surprise a lot of people, I'm sure because I always seem to appear so austere and seem to play those types of roles mostly. We both, Debbie and I have a deep faith in God, too." The relationship blossomed as Agnes and Debbie made the long back and forth car ride to the location set together and often sat together gabbing between scenes and set-ups on the set.

As Debbie got to know Agnes, her admiration grew. "I thought she was quite brilliant. She carried herself with great poise and dignity." Occasionally Debbie, like many actors, would go to Agnes for acting advice. She never came away disappointed, often more hopeful with a better understanding of what the part or scene in question was calling for. Their bond was close and in the eyes of both Debbie and Agnes it was akin to a mother and daughter relationship, especially since Debbie was more than thirty years younger than Agnes. Debbie's then-husband, Harry Karl, also became close to Agnes and, according to Debbie, Harry on more than one occasion tried to play matchmaker and fix Agnes up with one of his friends or acquaintances. "Harry was always trying to find a man who would protect her and love her," according to Debbie. He never succeeded. Nor did Debbie, who, on occasion, would be on the lookout for a possible romantic interest for Agnes. "I tried setting her up a few times, but it always turned out to be quite ordinary men — Agnes needed someone unique. Perhaps someone from a University setting who had intelligence and taste, someone who could stimulate her intellectually. She never found that man. She would tell me, 'you know, Debbie, the way it is going, it is going to be you and I to the end.'" The Karls and Agnes lived a block-and-a-half away from one another in Beverly Hills and, after the picture wrapped, the friendship continued with Agnes often invited to the Karls' for dinner, "sometimes two or three times per week." It was a friendship which would mean more to Agnes than any other in the last decade of her life, as Debbie became one of the few people she would be comfortable in confiding in about her personal life and about her increasingly difficult time with her son, Sean, when the boy hit his teenage years.

After about a month of location work interrupted by storms, illnesses (both Malden and Baker came down with serious illnesses during the filming) and fire, the company moved back to MGM in Culver City to complete shooting. If they thought that things would be easier at the studio they were in for a rude awakening. According to Carroll Baker, the studio utilized a large tank with back projection from the Kentucky location, with "high powered" fans to whip up wind, and wave machines to simulate the currents. They put herself, Debbie, Agnes and Karl on a raft going down a river with technicians rocking it back and forth. "The logs of the raft were slippery," recalls Baker. "There was nothing to brace your feet against, and very little to hang on to for support. Physically, it was hardest for Karl who had not fully recovered from his operation . . . Debbie, Agnes and I were most frightened of being dragged under and getting our long skirts caught up in the mechanism, where we might have been trapped and possibly drowned before we could have been released. Once the camera rolled, they began making the raft leap, blasting us with forty-mph winds and hitting

As the frontier mother in *How the West Was Won* (1961).

As the Judge in *Bachelor in Paradise* (1961).

As she appears in *Jessica* (1962).

us with walls of freezing cold water. No acting was necessary. They simply filmed what our real struggles and our expressions of genuine terror."

The picture soon wrapped and while the shoot was uncomfortable and full of bugs (literally) and dangerous situations on location and off, Agnes came back with a new friend and an excitement for the picture. She anticipated it would be a huge box office hit and would give her film career a needed boost.

In the fall of 1961 Agnes delivered a lecture in Dayton, Ohio that delved into something she normally didn't — politics and current events. "Theater is the best ambassador of peace I know of — but we don't use it," Agnes asserted. Agnes argued for a representative theater, one which the government, thru tax payers, would "subsidize," but "people are repulsed by that word. We subsidize libraries, roads and everything else, if the spirit of mankind is moved to something worthwhile that will make a difference." Agnes emphasized the need to "love mankind, rather than killing mankind . . . people say why fight city hall? Join it. I won't do it, but I'm in the minority. I would try to benefit the heart of mankind. Mankind wants to be needed and loved. What does mankind have without love?"

To finish out the year Agnes made a quick cameo as a judge in the Bob

Hope sex comedy, *Bachelor in Paradise,* and went to Italy at the invitation of her old friend director Jean Negulesco to appear in the comedy *Jessica,* based on a novel *The Midwife of Pont Clery,* starring Angie Dickinson. The scenery was nice and the money good — $4,000 per week for a six-week shoot, but the film did nothing to enhance anyone's film career.

Director and playwright James Clavell wrote to Agnes in February 1962, offering her a part in his film *The Sweet – The Bitter.* "There's a part that I wanted to offer you. You're just about the only person who could do it — and why not, as I wrote it for you in mind? In fact, come what may if you're available, I have to find a carrot to tempt you with . . . as far as I'm concerned you'd bring the role what I need; in fact — quite openly — I've GOT TO HAVE YOU."

The same month theatrical producer Anthony Lyons wrote to Agnes offering her the role of Mary Chestnut in a one-woman show based on Mrs. Chestnut's published journals she kept during the Civil War. These journals were later quoted from extensively in Ken Burns' massive documentary on the Civil War which aired on PBS in 1990.

Unfortunately for Clavell and Lyons, Paul Gregory was waiting in the wings with a pair of stage shows which would occupy her time in 1962.

III

Prescription Murder was the story of Dr. Roy Fleming who murders his wife, Claire, so that he can eventually marry his mistress, Susan Hudson. It is the story of an almost perfect murder especially since the detective assigned to the case, Lt. Columbo, seems incompetent. Agnes was cast as the wife with her old friend Joseph Cotten cast as the murderous doctor and his real-life wife, Patricia Medina cast as the mistress. As Lt. Columbo, Gregory cast the veteran character actor, Thomas Mitchell. Paul's intentions with this play were to make money, pure and simple, and he felt that a suspense-mystery with an all-star cast would be profitable. Historically this play is important since it was the first time the character of Lt. Columbo was introduced to audiences — six years before Peter Falk would immortalize the role on television. Agnes thus had the distinction of playing the first victim of murder investigated by Columbo.

The cast would be well paid for their talents. Cotten, the leading man, received $4,000 per week and 10% of the gross. He would be billed first. Thomas Mitchell would receive $2,000 per week and receive 7.5% of the gross and be billed second above the title. Agnes, who appears in only the first act of the play, would receive $1,750 per week with no percentage but billed in the same type as Cotten in third position above the title. Medina would receive $1,000 per week and be fourth-billed. Rehearsals began just after Christmas, 1961, with the show opening on January 15 at the Curran Theater in San Francisco, where Paul Gregory traditionally opened all of his shows. If Agnes was upset over the relatively small role she had in *Prescription Murder,* she didn't let on. "It never bothered Aggie that she was only in the first act because she completely dominated that act," says Gregory, "and the audience always expected she would return which, of course, she never does, but it added to the mystery and the suspense."

The play opened to strong box office, but poor reviews in San Francisco. Joseph Cotten would recall that the opening night audience "made us feel welcome to the Golden Gate," but that the critical reception the next day "made us feel like hurling ourselves off it (The Golden Gate Bridge)." So outraged by the critical reception was Gregory that he vowed that he would break tradition and never open another of his shows in San Francisco — a vow he would keep. Still, the good box office reception more than made up for the slings and arrows of the critics and the actors enjoyed working together. Agnes particularly liked the Cottens. Joe Cotten would note that Agnes' love of touring "justifiably earned her the title of Queen of the Road," and that "she had truly become everyone's idol, from Eau Claire to Pensacola, from Raleigh to Scottsdale." Agnes felt no competition with Pat Medina and, in fact, Medina would refer to Agnes as "Sis." Still, according to Paul Gregory, it was during the tour of *Prescription Murder* that Agnes exhibited a troubling side of her personality, one he had seen all too often. It was after a performance, which Paul had flown in for, and he, Cotten, Medina and Agnes were bantering in a dressing room. Paul and Cotten were deep in a discussion, as were Agnes and Medina. Suddenly both Paul and Cotten interrupted their discussion and turned their attention toward the ladies as Agnes was describing for Pat Medina the pains of labor she had experienced when she delivered Sean — as if Medina had no idea that Sean was not Agnes' biological child. It was a stunning performance and shortly after it Agnes excused herself from the room and Paul and the Cottens shook their heads and laughed, "Poor, Aggie." Gregory came to feel that Agnes felt a need to attract attention to herself at times even if it meant she had to invent a story to hide behind; she had trouble just being herself.

Despite the good box office Medina would describe the production as "jinxed." Gregory had used a revolving stage which allowed the actors to go from scene to scene without having to close the curtains. During dress rehearsals, just prior to opening in San Francisco, Medina, who was unfamiliar with revolving stages, caught her left leg in the doors as it went around and had to be rushed to the hospital to treat the gash. It was painful, but she was determined not to limp. "I was playing Jo's mistress and Agnes Moorehead was his wife. Between us, we had decided that Jo would choke her to death and run away with me. Therefore, no limping mistress seemed very helpful in planning a murder." Medina would also recall a comical situation on opening night: "Jo murdered Aggie just before my entrance and he pulled her behind the sofa where she lay dead. Enter 'the mistress.' I look behind the sofa and sway in horror (quite easy for me with my gimpy leg). Rushing to Jo, my lover, to hide my face, from behind the sofa came the loudest sneeze I've ever heard (the carpet was new and Aggie was allergic to it)." The perils of live theater.

Following the San Francisco run the cast and crew took a train to their next engagement in Denver, Colorado and happened to be appearing on stage while at a neighboring stage under the same roof the classical pianist Van Cliburn was presenting a concert. Joseph Cotten would recall: "I was slowly pulling on my gloves, about to choke my wife. She was standing, face to the window, back to the audience. The end of Tchaikovsky's third movement was approaching. The crescendo was not only building in volume, it was creeping across the

(Courtesy of Wade Ballard)

hall that separated the two auditoriums and becoming a distinct and clearly audible accompaniment to the action on our stage. I hurried with the gloves, but before my hands could reach Aggie's throat, Van Cliburn ended the concerto with nothing less than an atomic eruption. This was followed immediately by thunderous applause, not only from his audience, but also from ours. Aggie, whose throat was yet untouched, immediately and correctly dropped dead." She figured how she could top Van Cliburn. The dramatic flourish was there and Agnes took advantage of it.

While in Denver, Agnes attended an after-show party and was able to renew her friendship with the author, William Barrett, who had written the bestseller *The Left Hand of God,* which was made into a 1955 film which Agnes appeared in. Barrett decided to offer Agnes a critique of the show which he wrote up in a letter and sent to Agnes: "There is no hatred in it, and the drama of murder, even when coldly planned, is suspended upon hatred. Joseph Cotten, excellent actor that he is, seemed uncomfortable in the role at times." As for Agnes, "Everyone deplored the fact that an actress of your stature should be killed in the first act . . . you are far too likeable and attractive as the wife. You can be attractive but not likeable. The murder of such a woman as you portray is a cold thing and we do not feel emotions that we should feel." His wasn't the only review which commented that Agnes was being under utilized in such a minor role. When the tour came to Toronto, the critic of the *Toronto Globe* stated, "It is a pity that Agnes Moorehead was killed at the end of the first act of PRESCRIPTION MURDER . . . The play, which was creaking even with her magnetic presence, expired with her."

When the tour reached Miami, Agnes created a minor storm when she declared in an interview with the *Miami Herald* that the U.S. didn't have the same level of culture and regard for the theatre as Europe did; adding salt to the wound she mentioned that Sean was attending school in Switzerland so that he could get a better education than was offered in the U.S. She received many outraged letters, one of which was especially scathing: "I have news for you. Your dear little boy in Switzerland may turn out to be a real failure and a snob. There is more art, music and I refer to symphonies in every town and village in America than any place in the cockeyed world . . . You don't know what you are talking about and that goes for a lot of your type who shoot off the hip at these crummy interviews . . . Bring your boy back. He is liable to end up with a pack of deviates in Europe."

The jinx, which Patricia Medina believed the show had, came to a climax in Philadelphia when Thomas Mitchell became seriously ill and had to leave the show. His understudy, Howard Wierum, who had been playing a small part in the play, took over. But, according to Cotten, Wierum was "able and professional, but the play seemed to lose its spine without Tommy, and we abandoned all plans to take it into New York." Which, in Agnes' case, was just as well, since according to her contract she was obligated to leave *Prescription Murder* if *Lord Pengo*, a co-starring vehicle with Charles Boyer, opened that fall on Broadway as seemed increasingly likely.

Agnes' friend Gavin Lambert wrote her in July while she was on the road with *Prescription Murder,* keeping her up to date on the Hollywood scene. "There's not much going on here, that's for sure. The whole atmosphere is a little spooky, with all those huge stages at the huge studios idle, just a few people furtively doing a little TV on what remains of the back lot." The motion picture industry was in a doldrums at this time, particularly Twentieth Century-Fox, which was hit by a double whammy — Elizabeth Taylor, in the very costly

(Courtesy of Wade Ballard)

At home in 1963.

and way-behind-schedule shoot of *Cleopatra* in Rome, and Marilyn Monroe's problems on the set of what was to be her last (uncompleted film), *Something's Got to Give.* "No doubt you heard of poor Jerry Wald's sudden death," Lambert continued. "When you think of all the dodos doddering on, it seems a waste that one of the few people actually doing things should have to go. I'm in the middle of a script for him and have no idea whether Fox (what's left of it) will take over all of his projects or not . . . Otherwise I finished my new novel, which I think is good, and will be out around the end of the year. It's called *Inside Daisy Clover.*" This novel would indeed be a big success and also be made into a motion picture starring Natalie Wood and Robert Redford in 1966. "In the meanwhile, there's a depressing lack of anything going on here, even scandal. And I miss you. Much love, Gavin." Such a letter must have made Agnes happy. She was steadily employed for the next several months — on the stage.

Agnes and her frequent stage co-star, Charles Boyer.

Lord Pengo was based on the true story of art dealer Sir Joseph Duveen and his attempts to establish a national gallery of art, as well as his rocky relationship with his son, who Pengo wishes to follow in his footsteps. The young man has a mind of his own, however, and wants to be an abstract painter rather than an art dealer. Paul Gregory hired the noted playwright S.N. Behrman to write the script and veteran Vincent Donehue to direct. For the pivotal role of Lord Pengo, Paul had only one actor in mind all along and that was Charles Boyer. As Pengo's son, Derek, Gregory cast Brian Bedford. Agnes was cast as Pengo's loyal secretary who never deserts him and may have been secretly in love with him. The cast also included Henry Daniell, and, fresh off *Camelot,* actor Laurie Main.

To this day Gregory considers *Pengo* "a very satisfying show." Even though Behrman was getting on in years and "didn't want to do a lot of rewrites," and Boyer "didn't want to learn any new lines," Gregory loved working with them, calling Boyer "a wonderful man and a marvelous actor — one of the best" and that Behrman "enriched my life." As for Agnes, Paul contends that she was "very excited about the show," but insisted on having billing equal with Boyer's — above the title. Boyer was fond of Agnes, but when Paul went to Charles about Agnes' demand, the Frenchman put his foot down. "Boyer wouldn't let her," Paul recalls. "Really, her part as the loyal secretary didn't call for it either. Charles said, 'Give her as big of billing as she would like UNDER the title.'" Paul contends that Aggie occasionally "seemed to care more about her billing than the part," and, as late as 1973, when she did *Gigi* on Broadway, Paul maintains that "she would bitch to me about not being billed above the title. Sometimes she never let her talent take the front seat — too often her ego did." Paul may have suffered a memory lapse regarding *Gigi* since Agnes is billed above the title and is, in fact, second only to Alfred Drake. Still, one can't blame Agnes for trying. Why is it that Agnes is faulted for caring more about billing than the part when Boyer, himself, insisted on solo billing above the title? Nevertheless, Boyer did keep his solo billing.

A glamor shot of Agnes, 1962.

The part of Miss Swanson, to be honest, was not a stellar one. The character could be considered "long suffering" and cosmetic with no real depth of her own and used mainly as a sounding board for Pengo. Paul and Agnes realized this and Paul, in a letter sent along with the script in July 1962, acknowledges its shortcomings and promised to beef it up: "By no means is it all I hoped for from the standpoint of Miss Swanson; however, I think you will be able to do marvelous things with it. And further, before we even get into rehearsal I feel there will be additions which will strengthen considerably your part as well as the whole play . . . In the meantime, keep the pot boiling. You know I love you, dear Aggie, and please know the only real pleasure I get in all of this hectic carry-on is greatly related to the fact that I know of your devotion, which helps more than I can say." The script was indeed punched up, but not by the degree which would enhance Agnes' part substantially.

During rehearsals for *Lord Pengo*, Aggie befriended the likable British actor Laurie Main, who was cast as Boyer's valet. Main had just come off a successful run in *Camelot* and found that Agnes had seen him in that play and was highly complimentary of his performance. "During the *Pengo* rehearsals we gravitated toward one another." They would often go out to dinner together and found that they shared an interest in books. In fact,

Agnes, at one point in their friendship, promised that Main would inherit her books if she died before him. Main was impressed by the way Agnes came to rehearsals knowing her lines and being prepared, "which is rare for an actor." He explained that many actors find their way during rehearsals but that Agnes seemed to already have her interpretation of Miss Swanson already figured out. He also found her "helpful to other actors," but "she didn't push herself on you. You had to gravitate toward her and ask — but if you did she was more than willing to offer advice."

Main has happy memories of *Lord Pengo* with the exception of the director, Vincent Donehue. He contends that Donehue had no sense of humor and kept trying to make a light comedy-drama something darker. Still, the actors were a "joy to work with" and Boyer and Agnes had a "marvelous relationship — one of mutual admiration." He also enjoyed working with Henry Daniell, even though he was "fast approaching his dotage." He recalls that he and Agnes were in the wings awaiting their entrance for a scene when Daniell suddenly, not realizing that the play had begun, walked out on stage while Boyer was performing a scene. Daniell just stopped, stunned to see the curtain up and a scene underway, and turned around and came off stage muttering, "my mistake," but otherwise unphased.

(Courtesy of Wade Ballard)

Candid shot, 1962.

Paul Gregory kept his promise not to open his new play in San Francisco, where *Prescription Murder* had been butchered by local critics. Instead the show opened on September 25 in Detroit. If Paul thought the change of venue would mean better reviews, he was mistaken. "This is a wordy play which would not be the least bit harmed if about a half-hour were cut from it. Boyer, for example, has been given much too much to say," per the critic of the *Daily Collegian*. But Agnes was singled out with a bouquet: "Agnes Moorehead plays Pengo's secretary with all the artistry one has come to expect of this excellent actress." While in Detroit, Agnes conducted a freewheeling interview with the *Detroit Free Press*, vigorously defending *Lord Pengo.* "I must disagree with some of the critics remarks . . . It is a comedy-drama which develops its characters well, and that takes words and time . . . This is a charming, tender, sensitive and funny play. When the curtain goes down no one goes away feeling depressed." Still, Paul realized that the show needed some retooling and during the Detroit engagement an entirely new first act was introduced "replacing an act which had been found talky and static when the play opened here." The *Detroit News* found the new act an improvement: "the new Act one served as a clarification and enlightenment for the entire play." The reviews remained mediocre when the show moved to Philadelphia but *The Inquirer* gave the play

(Courtesy of Wade Ballard)

Lord Pengo, 1962.

a rave calling it, "highly polished theatre shining with wit and nimble in its plot manipulation." Meanwhile, critic Ernest Schier sniffed, "Agnes Moorehead breaks down and cries near the end because, she says, the Great Pengo is not long for this world. She may be right, at that."

Lord Pengo opened at the Royale Theater in New York City on November 19. Aggie was deluged by telegrams from friends as she made her first Broadway appearance in a play since *Don Juan in Hell* — more than a decade earlier:

Ann Sothern	DARLING GOOD LUCK AND LOVE TONIGHT.
Rita Hayworth	THE BEST OF LUCK. SEE YOU NEXT WEEK.
Baron Polan	AGNES DARLING I KNOW THAT LORD PENGO WILL ONLY PRESAGE THE GLORY THAT IS TO BE. YOU HAVE MY LOVE AND GOOD WISHES.
Joan Fontaine	KNOCK 'EM DEAD, LUV.
Rosalind Russell	DEAR AGGIE. LOVED SEEING YOU LAST NIGHT. YOU WERE A DEAR TO COME. CHEERS, GREAT LUCK AND FONDEST LOVE.

The New York critics were mixed. The *New York Times*, the most critical: ". . . It lacks the indispensable ingredients needed in the theater — the development of character and a story with dramatic tension . . . he (Pengo) is dying and he knows it. He says goodbye to his blunt, loyal assistant, Miss Swanson, in a scene meant to be touching. Agnes Moorehead plays with gruff integrity and Mr. Boyer covers his emotions with a debonair manner. But it is too late. One no longer cares."

But John McClain, of the *New York Journal-American*, countered, "It has been a long time since such skill and charm have been displayed in a role so ingeniously conceived (regarding Boyer) . . . Agnes Moorehead provides magnificent support . . . *Lord Pengo* is stylish and sophisticated."

Basil Rathbone offered Aggie an accurate assessment when he wrote her on 11/25: "What an excellent cast — maybe you all made the play look better than it really is . . . I do think the author has been a little lavish with Lord Pengo and a little sketchy with the rest of his characters."

While the reviews were not what was hoped for, the box office was strong and one night brought to the Royale Theatre one of the most beautiful and fashionable women in the world — the First Lady, Mrs. John F. Kennedy. At the invitation of playwright S.N. Behrman, Mrs. Kennedy accompanied him to see *Lord Pengo* along with Mr. and Mrs. Vincent Price. Mrs. Kennedy was clad in a two-piece gold and white brocade suit trimmed in black and red. Her appearance at the theater generated huge excitement not only from the audience but from the cast. It seemed fitting that this First Lady who emphasized style and elegance as well as an appreciation of art should attend *Lord Pengo.* Yet according to Laurie Main, when the First Lady was presented to the cast the only secure place deemed by the Secret Service was the ladies' room backstage; one by one the cast and crew would make its way into that ladies' room to meet Mrs. Kennedy. Later, Agnes would write Vincent Price, "Not that I want to crowd J. Edgar Hoover out of a job, but didn't I hear your hearty laughter in the audience Tuesday night? If I'm right, you selected a most exciting performance with Jackie Kennedy in the audience. I was told Marlene Dietrich was there too but no one was aware of it until too late. When she can be overlooked, I guess our First Lady is *glamorous.* Were you sitting anywhere near her?"

Lord Pengo was running on Broadway when Agnes celebrated her 62nd birthday on December 6; of course, unofficially, it was her 56th birthday. Paul sent her a telegram: "Dear Aggie, you are so clever. I know you are not as old as you say you are, but it does help in getting character parts. Love you with all of my heart. Happy Birthday and many more. Paul." The cast and crew presented her with a huge birthday cake that night after the performance as the audience serenaded her to "Happy Birthday."

On December 15, Agnes received the sad news that Charles Laughton had died after a battle with cancer. Their mutual friend, Remsen Dubois Bird, later wrote Agnes, ". . . it is good to know he has been freed. So many persons in Charles and we knew the best one."

Despite this, Agnes would end 1962 in high spirits, having participated in two well-received, if not well-reviewed, shows. She was on Broadway, and in movie houses: *How the West Was Won* was opening to strong box office. She felt more confident than she had in some time regarding her career as the New Year approached. The year 1963 would be a key year in Agnes' career, though she really didn't realize it, because of her decision to participate in a pilot for a television series, one that would win her more fame and popularity than she ever dreamed.

12

The Witch of Endor (1963–1964)

As 1963 began Agnes was enjoying her run on Broadway in *Lord Pengo,* but after an initial burst of box office success, attendance began to dwindle and expenses began to mount. The show closed on April 20, 1963 after 225 performances, including the six-week road tour prior to the New York opening. It was an exhausting, yet rewarding experience, but after six months of doing the same play night after night, especially in a part which was less than stellar, Agnes was ready to move on.

Who's Minding the Store?, (1963).

Her first opportunity came when Jerry Lewis offered her a part in his new comedy, *Who's Minding the Store?* This would be Agnes' second film with Lewis, the last time appearing as Lewis' wife *and* mother in the Martin and Lewis film *Pardners,* seven years earlier. She would play yet another mother role in this one too — this time the wealthy owner of a department store whose daughter, played by Jill St. John, falls in love with the misfit typically played by Lewis. The film began shooting shortly before *Lord Pengo* closed and Agnes almost immediately flew on to California to begin filming her scenes. On her first day on the set, Lewis sent her a dozen roses along with a note: "I consider it a privilege to work with such a fine actress, and I hope you enjoy working in 'films for fun'." It was a quick shoot, in a painless role which Agnes could have done in her sleep. The film was, as usual for a Lewis picture from this period, a huge box office success and even got some decent notices, such as this review from *Commonweal:* "With its zany humor and extravagant slapstick, this comedy is sometimes reminiscent of that 'Mad, Mad World' affair. 'Store,' however has the advantage of being much shorter . . ." For some reason, for the three weeks that Agnes shot *Who's Minding the Store?* she stayed at Debbie Reynolds' house. Agnes also reported to her secretary, Georgia Johnstone, "The picture is just getting along beautifully — they couldn't treat me any better if I was Garbo. Evidentially the rushes are good."

For much of 1963 Agnes toured in her one-woman show, which was given the new title of *Come Closer, I'll Give You an Earful.* It was her first performance of the one-woman show in almost two years and Agnes was apprehensive. " . . . it was quite a pressure! But I managed to get through it without mishap and thankful that my feet are on the ground." Typically, for one performance, Agnes was paid between $1,000 and $1,500 per date plus first-class accommodations and transportation. Which means, if she played 75 individual dates she earned well over $80,000, cushioned by an occasional television job and her work in the Lewis film as well as the final months with *Lord Pengo.* All this brought her income for 1963 to about $125,000, not bad in 1963 dollars. But the money seemed to go as quickly as it came in, what with her home in Beverly Hills, farm in Ohio and the staff who worked for her. Financial forms from the office of her accountant, Harold R. Williams, indicate that Agnes still had unpaid advances made from 1953–1957 and interest of over $18,000. She had unpaid advances to the Kitchen Middens Farms made in 1958 and 1959 with interest of more than $11,000, unpaid business management fees of $7,800, and real estate taxes unpaid for the years 1958–1960 of nearly $5,000. But she also needed to keep up appearances — she lived in Beverly Hills and, along with monthly utility bills, she paid $114 per month for a pool service company, $325 per month to fashion designer Don Loper, $122 per month to a florist, and she subscribed to *Variety, Film Daily, Box Office Digest* and *The Hollywood Reporter.*

There was also the more than $500 per month that she was paying to educate Sean, now attending a private school in Wales. But, as she explained to a reporter, she believed that education was "the most important item for one's children's growth . . . a basic, thorough education, a good moral atmosphere and a training in how to stand on one's own two feet." And Agnes felt that Sean would get the best education abroad as well as a better understanding of the world by not attending either public or private school in the United States. She also stressed discipline in raising a child. "Most teenagers (Sean was now 14) are alike, one of their main problems is brought about by adults who either do not, or will not give them attention, approval and discipline which they need and expect."

During the summer of 1963 Agnes went to Israel to present her one-woman show at the Tel-Aviv Israel Festival. Sean took a portion of his summer vacation and traveled with her and in between appearances they enjoyed sightseeing. While in Israel Paul Gregory wrote Agnes with the news that he was preparing a new show for 1964 for her, *One of My Lovers is Missing*. He also was promising other work — if things worked out — such as a picture that he and producer Sol Siegel were planning, "with a wonderful part for you. This would go some time after the first of the year. Too, there is a good possibility of a spectacular on the life of Eugene O'Neill and I would see to it that you are prominently involved in this." None of these projects came to being.

While she was in Israel, Agnes' mother, now nearly 80 years old, was hospitalized at the Mayo Clinic in Rochester, Minnesota, and underwent surgery apparently for intestinal problems. Agnes wrote to Georgia Johnstone that "2 large stones were found and removed from Mother's gastro-intestinal tract, and that she has a new opening in her intestine." The operation was a success but at Mollie's age the recovery phase was prolonged and she was hospitalized for several weeks. Agnes had also told Johnstone that "I only hope and pray that she will have some good normal years ahead of her." Agnes would have no way of knowing that the unsinkable Mollie would live another 28 years and outlive her famous daughter. Agnes was so pleased by the treatment that her mother received that she offered to perform a concert for the staff of the Mayo Clinic. She was taken up on this offer by the head of Surgery at the Clinic, Dr. David Carr, who pointed out that during 1964 the Mayo Clinic would celebrate its 100th birthday, and the Mayo Foundation its 50th anniversary, and one of the events planned related to a special recognition day sponsored by the Rochester Chamber of Commerce. "This is an attempt by the community to pay tribute to the contributions of the clinic and foundation to the city of Rochester." He said a special script was being prepared by "professional script writers and it has been suggested that you might play the leading role in that production." While she didn't do this show, she did eventually present to them a portion of her one-woman show and, of more importance, she constantly gave Mayo good publicity and began to go there for her own checkups.

Also during that busy summer of 1963 Agnes made a guest appearance on the Canadian Broadcasting Corporation's popular talk program, *Flashbacks,* appearing along with Basil Rathbone. She was outspoken about her regard for the modern theatre and her appearance caused a sensation. She asserted that she believed that many present-day playwrights are "pretty sick" and heading her list was Edward Albee, the author of *Who's Afraid of Virginia Woolf?,* which had just won the New York Drama Critics' Circle Award as the best play of the year. According to Agnes, Albee was, "very intelligent, psychologically perceptive but full of hate and revenge." She also felt that *Virginia Woolf* was "not realistic by any means." Adding more salt to the wound, she asserted that, "If Albee's theatre was the only kind then I would get out. He has great talent but he can only wallow in the gutter." Then she went back to the theme of her 1961 lecture about using the theatre as a positive force for peace in the world. "I think that the theatre can instruct, that it can make the human being better, more compassionate, and more understanding." Both Agnes and Rathbone agreed that the present types of "realistic" plays being presented were not enhancing people. She got a lot of feedback, most of it positive. "Thank God for actresses like you," wrote one Ruth Patterson of London, Ontario. A Mrs. Coughlin wrote, "You are the best guest they have had on that program in our opinion," and a Mrs. Harmon Johnson wrote, ". . . She so intelligently, courageously, passionately and positively, expressed her views about the present decadent trend in our dramatic productions."

In the fall of 1963, as Agnes began yet another tour of her one-woman show, she received an offer to play the part of Nora Nash in the musical *A Little Night Music.* Around the same time, she was sent the script of a pilot of a half-hour comedy series where she would once again play a mother, but with a twist — this mother was a witch.

II

In 1963 Screen Gems, the television arm of Columbia Pictures, was developing a series about the whirlwind romance between a beautiful young witch and a mortal that leads to marriage. The studio had a huge success in 1958 with the film, *Bell, Book and Candle,* with James Stewart and Kim Novak, which explored this theme. Veteran producer Harry Ackerman (*The Donna Reed Show, Father Knows Best, Dennis the Menace*) was approached by his superior at Screen Gems, Bill Dozier, about developing a series based on that film. Ackerman liked the idea and set out developing the show. To flesh out this idea, he chose a contract writer named Sol Saks to write the pilot. Saks was a veteran wrier who got his start in radio, most prominently on the successful *Duffy's Tavern.* Ackerman and Saks came up with a character named Cassandra (or Cass for short), a young witch, who meets a young mortal, an advertising executive named Darrin, and falls in love and marries him. All this to the chagrin of her mother who believes her daughter is giving up her way of life — a much preferable one to her mind — to be the wife of a mere mortal. This scenario was titled *The Witch of Westport.*

The Witch of Westport was initially offered to actress Tammy Grimes. Grimes, however, decided that an offer from Noel Coward to appear in his Broadway production of *High Spirits,* a musical based on his play *Blithe Spirit* — another supernatural comedy — was more enticing at this stage in her career. She turned Ackerman down. (Apparently, at the time, the idea was to team Grimes with a young actor named Dick Sargent in the husband role, but as it turned out Sargent was also tied up with another project.) The search was on for a new lead actress.

Around this time the beautiful young actress Elizabeth Montgomery, the daughter of screen and television star Robert Montgomery, and her husband, director William Asher, were shopping around a television series that would allow them to work together. Asher, a veteran director, who helmed episodes of *I Love Lucy, The Shirley Temple Show* and *The Danny Thomas Show,* among others, had developed an idea for a series titled *The Fun Couple,* about a wealthy debutante who marries a mechanic. He brought this idea to Bill Dozier at Screen Gems, who immediately told Asher about *The Witch of Westport,* which had a similar theme as the show Asher was pitching — about a seemingly mismatched couple who fall in love and marry. Montgomery and Asher embraced the new series. The witch now had a new face — that of 31-year-old Elizabeth Montgomery.

If television had a Grace Kelly, it would be Elizabeth Montgomery, for she was certainly Hollywood royalty, growing up in a rich and glamorous lifestyle. She had a regal beauty and a cool exterior much like the blonde Princess of Monaco. She also possessed a sharp sense of humor which drew people toward her. Agnes' friend Laurie Main, who would make guest appearances on three episodes of *Bewitched,* would recall Montgomery as "a lot of fun, and her sense of humor was delicious, which made coming to the set a real pleasure." Elizabeth, known to her co-workers and friends as Liz or Lizzie, was also a very fine actress who had demonstrated her worth in many television productions since she had made her debut some twelve years earlier on her father's popular series *Robert Montgomery Presents.*

With Elizabeth Mongomery in a publicity still from the pilot of *Bewitched* (1963).

Robert Montgomery was a creative force in the early days of television. He was one of the first major film stars to make the leap to television in an age when film stars just didn't appear in the medium. But Montgomery was an innovator who recognized that his days as a romantic leading man were over and understood that television could eventually reach and touch many more millions who would never see him in a motion picture. He was also a tough taskmaster. Young Elizabeth would not have been cast on his show if she wasn't talented enough to perform the part. Montgomery didn't believe in nepotism. In fact, Elizabeth would become kind of a stock player in his company of actors on his show, but if she had not succeeded in that first program she would not have been asked to return. The work she did on her father's series led to other appearances on such "Golden Age of Television" series as *Studio One, The Twilight Zone, General Electric Theatre* and *Alfred*

Hitchcock Presents. She would be nominated for an Emmy for a guest appearance opposite Robert Stack in an episode of *The Untouchables,* the first of nine times with no wins! In the years leading up to *Bewitched* she would mix episodic TV work with occasional roles in motion pictures such as *The Court-Martial of Billy Mitchell* (with Gary Cooper), *Who's Been Sleeping in My Bed?* (with Dean Martin) and as a gangster's moll in the cult film *Johnny Cool,* which was directed by the man who eventually became her third husband, William Asher.

Equally important would be the role of the harassed yet loving mortal husband. The part called for an actor who could hold his own within the framework of the supernatural tomfoolery. He also had to have the right chemistry with Elizabeth Montgomery. The show was balanced as one-third situation comedy, one-third supernatural comedy and one-third romantic comedy. Indeed, the early episodes, which established the characters, would emphasize the romantic nature of the relationship between witch and mortal and would be critical in defining the series. The actors had to make the love story believable for it to work. Enter 34-year-old actor Dick York.

York came to Hollywood from a humble background. Growing up in near poverty in Chicago, he sought work in radio as a teenager to help support his family. It didn't take long before he began getting steady work in Chicago as a radio juvenile, his big break being *Jack Armstrong – The All American Boy.* It was while working in radio as a teenager that he met the young woman who would later become his wife, Joan Alt; he was 15 and she was 12, "an infant," recalled York. Three years later they met again and this time it was love at first sight — "you would be very surprised at what strides a girl can make between 12 and 15."

Dick and Joan (known as Joey) later married and moved to New York City where Dick found work on radio and in the theatre appearing in such shows as *Tea and Sympathy,* directed by Elia Kazan. Kazan's good friend, Karl Malden, who helped Kazan cast this show, later recalled of York, "He was from Chicago and was in New York maybe a year or two and he read for me. I put him down as a definite possibility. It finally came down between him and another actor. He got the part. He was a wonderful actor and a very nice man." Another Broadway show he would appear in was *Bus Stop,* opposite stage legend Kim Stanley. Hollywood soon summoned York and he appeared in a series of films between 1955 and 1960 which demonstrated his versatility, including the musical-comedy *My Sister Eileen,* the slapstick antics of *Operation Mad Ball,* and the western *Cowboy* — all three with another young actor by the name of Jack Lemmon. The high-point of York's film career was in the well-regarded courtroom drama, *Inherit the Wind,* where York was fourth-billed after screen titans Spencer Tracy, Fredric March and Gene Kelly.

But one film would have far-reaching consequences for York, professionally and personally. In 1959, he went to Mexico to film the action-adventure, *They Came to Cordura,* starring Gary Cooper. While he and several other actors were performing a scene in the picture, using a railroad handcar, an accident occurred, causing York to tear the muscles along the right side of his back, resulting in intense pain that would increase with frequency as the years went by. The pain would come and go early on, go for a stretch without any problems, and then suddenly be taken down by a fierce flair-up. It could be excruciating, but he had to work through it because he had a family (which would eventually grow to five children) to support. During the early 60's York continued to work constantly on television in such series as *Alfred Hitchcock Presents, The Twilight Zone* and *Rawhide.* During the 1962–63 season, York was cast opposite Gene Kelly in the TV series, *Going My Way* (based on the 1944 Bing Crosby film). The series lasted only one season but it was a happy one for Dick according to Joan York. He and Kelly had an easy rapport. One day Joan York arrived on the set and Kelly, with that Irish twinkle in his eye, said, "Dick, she isn't as ugly as you said she was." To which the quick-witted Mrs. York replied, "Well, thank you,

With Dick York in a publicity shot for *Bewitched* (1964).

Mr. Astaire." Sadly, the series wasn't renewed for a second year and so Dick was out looking for his next job when his agent, luckily, got wind of the pilot of *Bewitched,* as *The Witch of Westport* was retitled.

York recalls that he came to read for the part of Darrin Stephens before both Harry Ackerman and Bill Asher. As he was waiting to be seen, he caught sight of a beautiful and leggy Elizabeth Montgomery who was going to read with him (she had the part, of course, which apparently Dick didn't know at the time). The reading went well and Asher was immediately impressed by the gangly and expressive York. "He was just too perfect for the part. Once that reading was done we knew we had found Darrin." Impulsively, after the reading, Dick jumped into Montgomery's lap telling all those observing that they looked "cute together." Dick later explained that it was the way he got all of his acting jobs — taking chances.

Elizabeth Montgomery and Dick York were now in place, but there was one other part which needed to be filled, and it was pivotal that they find an actress of authority — the role of Samantha's (as Cassandra was eventually renamed) mother, who strongly opposes her daughter marrying a mortal.

<h2 style="text-align:center">III</h2>

How did Agnes Moorehead get the part which would transform her from respected character actress to cultural icon? Bill Asher says it was fate. He and Elizabeth were shopping in Bloomingdales one day when Elizabeth went off to another department. She caught sight of Agnes and approached her. They exchanged pleasantries. Agnes certainly knew who Elizabeth was and had met her before through Robert Montgomery. Elizabeth suddenly thought of the part of "Mother" and impulsively asked Agnes, "Have you ever thought of doing a television series?," to which Agnes coyly replied, "Maybe, maybe not" (of course she had many times). Elizabeth explained the *Bewitched* premise and arranged to have the script sent to Agnes. Elizabeth then, excitedly, located Asher and told him, "I found 'Mother'!!" This is the story as Bill Asher explained to this author and largely as it appears in Herbie J Pilato's essential biography, *Bewitched Forever.*

Agnes' friend and theatrical producer Paul Gregory, has a somewhat different spin on it. He says that he was the one "instrumental" in getting *Bewitched* for Agnes. According to Paul, he talked Asher into using Agnes on the show, but that the producers were skeptical because Agnes would be more expensive than they had originally budgeted for the part, not expecting

"Endora," 1964.

that the part would be filled by an actress of Agnes' renown. They finally saw the advantage of having Agnes in the part, along with the ratings value of an actress of Agnes' caliber appearing in the pilot.

This is an interesting theory and I have no doubt that Paul did speak with Asher about Agnes, but it is highly doubtful that Asher would need much persuading since he was well aware of her work and had worked with her several years earlier in the episode of *The Shirley Temple Playhouse* where Agnes had played a witch. But Paul does make a good point that Agnes would be more expensive than another less illustrious actress in the same part. In the end, the network, sponsors and the Ashers made the correct decision in casting Agnes.

Bill Dozier sent the pilot script to Agnes and in a letter, dated October 24, 1963, to Georgia Johnstone, Agnes reveals a certain fear about accepting the part. "The script sent to me from Dozier was titled, *Bewitched* and they want me to play a witch in a series! You know this is murder for then all my work and what little talent I have would only be used by others around Halloween. They have so little minds out here, and I would only be thought of as a witch from now on! So I told them I would only guest star and on a certain number. They seem amenable to it — but we shall see." But Agnes couldn't afford to balk too much. The offer was good; if the show became a series she would be paid an estimated $3,000 per episode and even if she appeared in a limited number, like 26 out of 39 episodes, that would accumulate to some very serious money. But in the end she agreed to do the pilot for another reason — she really didn't believe it would sell. "I thought people would rather watch an operation or something." (Medical shows such as *Dr. Kildare* and *Ben Casey* were the rage at the time.)

Agnes insisted that the witch she would play not be considered wicked. She imagined "Mother" (still no name chosen for the character, though Matilda was toyed around with, but it wasn't to Agnes' liking) as only wanting what was best for her daughter. "I'm not at all wicked. I'm quite a sophisticated gal . . . the humans in the script do plenty of things and she loves to show up their foolishness." William Asher said he wanted the character to be "the ultimate Mother-in-law," and that she would be the show's "conflict," to which Agnes was in perfect agreement. "Every time she shows up you know something will happen."

Agnes had some concerns regarding her character which Bill Dozier tried to dispel in a 11/7/63 letter: "Please don't worry about preliminary indications of wild ghost outfits. I assure you we are not going to go in for anything freakish." In fact, Agnes had her own ideas of what "Mother" should wear and what colors they should be, which, as expected, were shades of green and lavender on chiffon for her "flying suit." She also designed her own make-up which she considered "impish" rather than "devilish." Agnes' other concern was regarding the name of her character. She didn't want to be referred to only as "Mother." It was fine for her daughter, but she wanted a name to go with the character. Dozier tried to reassure her on this point as well. "Also, we shall see that this character has a proper identification other than 'Mother.'"

The first cast reading of the script was scheduled for Friday, November 22, 1963 — but without Agnes, who had a long scheduled commitment set for Thursday night in Toronto, Canada, performing her one-woman show. She couldn't make it back in time for this first reading and was excused. Of course on this date, the unspeakable happened, President Kennedy was shot and murdered in Dallas, Texas. It was two hours earlier in California when Bill and Elizabeth, still at home, received word of the tragedy. ". . . The whole thing was very strange," remembered Elizabeth years later to author Herbie J Pilato, "but to keep on working did seem to be the right thing to do. We went ahead and had the first reading of the script. It was very interesting. There wasn't one person who didn't show up. There weren't any phone calls made. It was like everyone on the set just needed to talk with each other." Agnes was shocked and deeply saddened by JFK's assassination. Politically, she was to the right of the young president, but she admired the First Couple's style and charm, two traits she appreciated in people. It was an unforgettable and tragic way to begin what would become an eight-year journey.

The cast reconvened the day after the President's funeral for an additional reading, wardrobe and make up tests and rehearsals. The pilot was shot the first week in December. Screen Gems was thrilled about the results and went off to find a sponsor and a network. Over the Christmas holidays Sean was returning from Wales, but Agnes couldn't get away from California to meet him upon his arrival in New York. She asked Georgia Johnstone to meet his plane and asked if he could spend a couple of days with she and Bill and also arrange for the boy to see a dentist while he was in New York. As it turned out, Agnes did arrange for Sean to fly directly to Los Angeles where she made arrangements for him to see an eye doctor, pediatrician and the dentist, who needed to rewire his braces. Agnes later reported to Georgia that "Sean had a wonderful Christmas . . . I have high hopes for him."

With the pilot completed and *Who's Minding the Store?* hitting movie houses that Christmas, Agnes was offered, in early 1964, a part in a film with more of an acting challenge than the Lewis romp had required, *Whatever Happened to Cousin Charlotte?* But first she had a series of appearances that late winter with her one-woman show to complete. She was mid-tour when she received news from Harry Ackerman that *Bewitched* had sold and the show was scheduled to be on ABC's 64–65 fall lineup. In fact, the network was very high on the series and was planning a huge promotional campaign to sell it.

Agnes' reaction upon hearing the news that the pilot had been picked up was not one of joy. She said many times that she felt "trapped" since she had agreed to appear in the show (at least verbally), should it be picked up. She reported to Georgia Johnstone on 2/20/64, "I found my series was sold. The script is a bore and you know how I hate to be tied down — but one can't look a gift horse in the mouth these days. Shooting begins in August — Elizabeth Montgomery is pregnant! The baby appears in July — so — that is that." She would honor her obligation but still couldn't quite believe that it sold. "How could witchcraft appeal to the general public?" she asked in a *TV Guide* interview. And it does appear she was willing to at least entertain other offers, such as one to appear in the hit comedy play, *Barefoot in the Park*. "Barefoot was offered to me — a year's contract — very little money tho' — I had better stick to the series." Compounding her troubles that spring was when she attempted to lift a heavy suitcase en route to a concert appearance and twisted her lower vertebra causing an intense backache from the sciatic nerve. In April, she was offered the choice part of playing the nurse in Peter Wyngarde's production of *Romeo and Juliet*, which would open in Chicago that fall and then New York in December. Already cast were Alan Bates, Rosemary Harris and Susan Oliver. Again, Agnes turned down the part preferring the money and security the series had to offer.

In the meanwhile, she did come up with an idea for the name of the character she would play in *Bewitched*. Her inspiration came from the Bible — 1 Samuel: 28, to be exact. It tells the story of Saul who consults a medium to summon up the spirit of Samuel. The medium's name is the witch of Endor. She suggested "Endora," which seemed to fit the idea of the worldly character she envisioned her witch as being. Her other issue, which she had made clear at the time she filmed the pilot, was being tied down to appear in every episode. It would mean too much time away from her one-woman shows, her true passion. She also felt too much "Endora" would be harmful to her career as an actress. "I don't want too much exposure. Our audiences are capricious, full of whims. No matter what the talent pretty soon somebody says, 'oh yes, I've seen all of that.'" An agreement was reached where Agnes would appear in no more than 8 out of every 13 episodes. She also insisted that she receive special billing in the opening credits each week, regardless whether or not she appeared in that episode. So, for the first five seasons, her special billing would be "AND AGNES MOOREHEAD AS ENDORA." With the exception of series leads Montgomery and York, she would be the only *Bewitched* actor accorded billing in the opening credits until David White (who would appear in more episodes of *Bewitched* than anyone except Montgomery) got this reward in season six.

IV

As mentioned, in early 1964 Agnes received an invitation from Robert Aldrich to join Bette Davis and Joan Crawford in a film to be titled, *Whatever Happened to Cousin Charlotte?*, based on a story by Henry Farrell, who had also written the novel, *Whatever Happened to Baby Jane?* which

Bette and Joan had starred in two years earlier. While this story would not be a sequel to the very profitable *Baby Jane,* it did contain many of the same ingredients; chief among them, director Aldrich and lead actresses, Davis and Crawford. It was surprising that after all the acrimony in making *Baby Jane* that the two actresses would consider working together again. But they were astute enough to know that a re-teaming would generate big box office receipts and each of them would have a percentage of the picture's gross.

The story takes place on a decaying Louisiana plantation which has been earmarked by the Highway Authority for demolition. Charlotte Hollis (Davis) has lived there all of her life and over time has gradually begun to lose her mind. The old house was once the site of an infamous murder involving a married lover of Charlotte's (Bruce Dern). Charlotte is convinced that her much-loved late father (Victor Buono, another *Baby Jane* alumni) murdered her lover and she believes that if she lets the house go to the developers they will find evidence which will implicate him in the crime. Crawford was cast as her cousin, Miriam Deering, who arrives from Paris on the assumption, by Charlotte, that she will help her keep the house.

Agnes was offered the plum supporting role of Velma Cruther, Charlotte's poor, slovenly but loyal housekeeper. Agnes read the screenplay, retitled *Hush . . . Hush, Sweet Charlotte* (Davis insisted on the title change because she didn't want this new film so closely identified with *Baby Jane*),

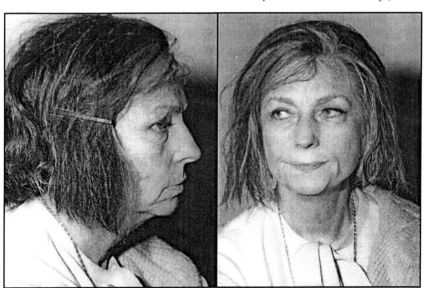

Hair test shots for *Hush . . . Hush, Sweet Charlotte* (1964).

and realized that she had the best part in the film and eagerly accepted. The filming wouldn't begin until May and, with Elizabeth Montgomery's pregnancy, *Bewitched* wasn't scheduled to go into production until August — more than enough time, Agnes believed, for her to complete the picture. Agnes was further excited when her old friends, Joseph Cotten and Mary Astor, were cast in other key supporting parts.

After all her years in Hollywood this would be Agnes' first film with either Davis or Crawford. She had known Davis socially for many years dating back to the early 30's in New York when Agnes and Jack Lee would occasionally go out on the town with Davis and her then-husband, bandleader Ham Nelson. (Nelson, like Jack, grew jealous of a wife whose success eclipsed his own.) Over the years Agnes and Bette would run into each other in Hollywood at social gatherings and exchange letters and Christmas cards. When Agnes came to Warner Brothers in the 40's, Bette was the acknowledged Queen of the Lot — but they never were cast in a vehicle together. Both admired the other as an actress. Agnes believed that Davis was one of the most talented people to appear in motion pictures and yet kept true to her Yankee upbringing and didn't "go Hollywood." Davis felt that Agnes was one of the best character actresses in the business. Coming from Davis, this was high praise indeed since she believed that she, herself, was a character actress first and a star second. Yet, for all of this, they certainly were not close friends who confided in each other. Unlike the cooperative Agnes, Davis had a reputation for being a terror on the set by bullying her directors and belittling her fellow actors. There is truth in that, but mainly with directors who didn't take a firm hand with her or actors she felt were unprofessional. Karl Malden would remember Davis as "very easy to work with and such a professional. A true perfectionist who knew what she wanted. I never had any trouble with her."

Agnes also got to know Crawford at Warners where Joan went after many years as one of MGM's great leading ladies. Crawford was well known for keeping up a staggering amount of correspondence with friends and fans alike. She felt she owed her fans a personal response if they wrote to her because they were the ones who put her where she was — the top. She would occasionally send Agnes little notes on her trademarked light-blue paper, complimenting her on a performance or inviting her to a party. Agnes would respond in kind. Unlike Davis, Crawford epitomized the glamour that was Hollywood in those days: her hair always done up, always wearing the latest in designer clothing and radiating supreme confidence;

Joan was every inch a star. In this regard Agnes was closer to Crawford than to Davis. Joan was also a very capable actress in roles tailored to her persona, but certainly no Bette Davis — or Agnes Moorehead — in range.

After beginning the picture with some location shooting in Baton Rogue, the *Hush . . . Hush* cast and crew returned to Twentieth Century-Fox studios in late May to film interiors. Confronting Davis again made Crawford nervous. To steady herself, Joan always had a bottle of Pepsi laced with vodka stowed away in a flask in her purse. Still, this added stimulant was not enough to calm her for the first scene she shot with Bette. Joan muffed several takes, exasperating Bette who suggested to Joan that she "withdraw and compose" herself. Robert Aldrich began to call himself an "embattled warrior" having to deal with the egos of his lead actresses. After a few days of filming, Crawford began to believe that everyone on the set was against her; she was also exhibiting symptoms of an upper respiratory illness. Crawford entered Cedars of Lebanon Hospital. During her absence the cast would shoot scenes unconnected with her character or around her in other ways. While Joan was hospitalized, Agnes thoughtfully sent an arrangement of garnet roses. Joan, truly touched, and a stickler for good manners, immediately wrote a thank you note which concluded, "Bless you (her trademark phrase) my dear friend. I do hope I shake this pneumonia bug this time, and will be back on the set very soon. Love, Joan."

After a couple of weeks off the picture, Crawford returned to the set with a limited work schedule which required her to work only half days until her doctors felt she was well enough to handle a full day workload. The first day back went fine since it was Bette's day off and Joan was shooting an important scene with Agnes. The scene shot required Miriam telling Velma that her services were no longer required at Hollis House. Velma hisses, "You trying to hand me my walking papers? . . . You can't fool me." To which the perfectly poised Miriam replies, "My dear, with

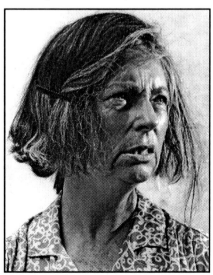

(Courtesy of Wade Ballard)

As Velma Cruthers in *Hush . . . Hush, Sweet Charlotte* (1964).

your keen naive intelligence I wouldn't dream of trying. But the point is, you're fired — you can go." The scene was shot in one take and afterward Joan effused about Agnes to a visiting reporter, "One of the greatest professional thrills I've had is working with Agnes Moorehead." While she was effusive in the press about Agnes, according to author Christopher Nickens, she may have felt that Agnes and Bette Davis were both in cahoots to get her off the film. The assumption is that since they were both character actresses at heart and old confidants that their friendship may have intimidated Joan. Yet in a letter to Georgia Johnstone, Agnes says that while there was conflict on the set of this film, she didn't want to get mixed up in it.

Joan's elation proved short-lived when the next day Bette was back on the set and as unrepentant as ever regarding Crawford, who almost immediately suffered a relapse. Joan entered Cedars again and this time caused the picture to close down production as most scenes left required Crawford's presence. The shut down would cost the studio an estimated $50,000 per day — some would be covered by insurance, but certainly not all. Around this time, Georgia Johnstone sent on to Agnes an offer from the Studio Theatre in Buffalo, NY of $2,000 per week to stage any play of her liking from September through October. Agnes replied, "I will be in the middle of this series — We have only the pilot to go on and we will be shooting back to back for quite a while — especially through September

Confronting Olivia de Havilland in *Hush . . . Hush, Sweet Charlotte* (1964).

and October . . . right now I can't see my way clear to do anything! In fact I haven't finished *Hush! Hush!* as yet. Joan C. is in the hospital again, and Bette D is livid."

A decision had to be made whether to replace Joan. Predictably, Bette was all for it and had a candidate to suggest — her good friend Olivia de Havilland, who had a reputation for playing good-hearted women (such as her Melanie in *Gone with the Wind*), but not murderous bitches. The studio was not totally sold on de Havilland and reportedly Fox approached Katharine Hepburn, who gave a terse "no," and Vivien Leigh who famously replied, "I could almost look at Joan Crawford's face at six a.m. on a southern plantation, but Bette Davis — Never!" The studio finally accepted de Havilland, who flew in from Paris. Agnes did feel certain sympathy for Joan and on this second hospitalization again remembered her with roses — the only prominent member of the *Hush . . . Hush* company to remember Joan in this way. As a matter of fact, no one at the studio even told Joan she had been replaced — she found out only through newspaper accounts. While it is clear this is what Joan wanted, she was still a star and expected to be told by the studio as a courtesy. Upon finding out de Havilland had indeed replaced her, Joan told the press that she was "pleased for Olivia because she needed the part." Joan was grateful to Agnes for the concern she had shown toward her and shortly after being replaced she sent flowers and a note to

(Courtesy of Wade Ballard)

Agnes. "Thank you so much for being so nice to me. I enjoyed working with you more than I can possibly say. It was such a joy to do even the few scenes we had together. I do hope we will be able to work together again sometime very soon. Bless you, and I wish you the great success you so richly deserve in your television series."

Olivia, professional that she was, immediately arrived on the set and the film resumed production. It was essential that steady progress be made since Fox wanted to release the film in Los Angeles by Christmas to qualify for the Academy Awards. Bette, essentially getting her way, proved no problem as filming resumed. For Agnes, the hold up on production was causing some difficulties since it was fast approaching the deadline to begin filming *Bewitched*. Aggie's big scene in the picture had yet to be filmed, Velma's death at the hands of Miriam. It begins with Velma returning to Hollis House to try and rescue Charlotte. She hears Miriam returning and hides in a closet where she witnesses Miriam drugging Charlotte. Miriam leaves, and Velma again attempts to get Charlotte to safety, but is discovered by Miriam. After a confrontation at the stairwell, where Velma tells Miriam she is going to the authorities, Miriam violently knocks Velma down the stairs and kills her.

Meanwhile, also on the Fox lot, Debbie Reynolds was filming *Goodbye Charlie* on a nearby soundstage. In her autobiography, Debbie would recall a difficult scene which involved props. The scene was set in the kitchen where Debbie's character was making breakfast for Tony Curtis. "When it came to the actual shoot, I was already working with so many props, my hands full of coffee and orange juice and eggs, that I didn't know what to do with the toast. Agnes Moorehead, meanwhile, was on another set . . . so I called her. Agnes came down in a house dress, with a turban around her head, a little handkerchief and stage blood on her . . . watch this rehearsal, I said. She watched me go through the whole business, still not knowing what to do with the toast. After the scene, I walked over to Agnes and she said, 'put it in your mouth.'" Debbie would remember how obvious the suggestion was and how quickly Agnes was able to appraise the situation and make her verdict. She did the scene delivering her dialogue with the toast in her mouth, and it worked.

Agnes was pleased to have Debbie around for another reason — had she not, she may well have starved. Agnes described her look in *Hush . . . Hush* as, "a slob, a blob of sagging flesh in a shapeless house dress that had seen better days . . . I looked so awful that I refused to eat in the studio commissary, and I suppose I'd have starved if not for Debbie Reynolds . . . (who) invited me to join her for lunch each day in the privacy of her dressing room." Meanwhile, Agnes glamoured herself up to attend the world premiere of Debbie's latest film from MGM, *The Unsinkable Molly Brown,* on June 25 at the Egyptian Theater in Hollywood, as a special guest of Debbie's. On July 9, Agnes also took time to appear at the Hollywood Bowl doing at a concert of "music inspired by Shakespeare." Agnes would preface various musical compositions with readings from the bard.

With frequent co-star Joseph Cotten in *Hush . . . Hush, Sweet Charlotte* (1964).

By August, Agnes was working double duty going back and forth between filming episodes of *Bewitched* as the glamorous Endora and rushing back to Fox to do retakes and dubbing on *Hush . . . Hush* as the hag Velma. By the time *Hush . . . Hush* finally wrapped in mid-October, it was more than two months behind schedule and had forced Agnes to back out of a role she had eagerly wanted to play in, the satire, *The Loved One.* She was replaced in this film by Margaret Leighton. It was a missed opportunity not to work in that film with her friend Jonathan Winters, but she would later appear in two television specials with him.

V

Back on *Bewitched* in early August, Agnes was working around the clock and as she told Georgia Johnstone, "I am in a literal merry-go-round. They are bickering now about my returning to *Hush! Hush!* — now that I'm deep in a series! These series are for the birds — what a treadmill — the only thing one can be thankful for is the check! And that I am — but one is so tired that one can barely read the figures." Even though Agnes signed on to do only a certain number of episodes per season she does appear in several of the early episodes which helped define the series. In addition to Agnes, Elizabeth Montgomery and Dick York, *Bewitched* had many other veteran actors who would appear off and on over the next eight years to help carry the load — David White, Maurice Evans, Marion Lorne, Alice Pearce, George Tobias, Kasey Rogers (who would join the series after leaving the much steamier *Peyton Place*), and Mabel Albertson, as Darrin's mother, who always ended up with a "sick headache" whenever she visited her son and daughter-in-law. Later, Bernard Fox as the wacky or quacky Dr. Bombay, Paul Lynde as the practical joking Uncle Arthur and Alice Ghostley as the shy and accident-prone Esmerelda joined the cast. Few television shows then or now can boast such a stellar cast or such original characterizations. It is — along with its fine writing — the reason why the show would last as long as it did and continued to do well long afterward in syndication.

(Courtesy of Wade Ballard)

Agnes cleaning up as Endora on *Bewitched*.

In retrospect it worked to the show's advantage that Agnes didn't want to appear on a weekly basis. This gave the writers the opportunity to develop other characters which kept the show fresh. If Endora was the conflict each week the show would begin repeating itself and lose its originality. Instead, these other characters — mainly relatives of Samantha's — could also test the strength of the Stephens' bond. Among the most memorable recurring role would be that of Aunt Clara, played with dithering brilliance by Marion Lorne. Aunt Clara would become one of the most beloved characters on the show and the one relative of Samantha's who accepted the union between witch and mortal. So believable was Lorne's portrayal that some people actually believed that Lorne's halting delivery was intentional to cover up for not memorizing her lines. According to Kasey Rogers, who would play Louise Tate, Lorne was a "very sophisticated and well-informed person." She also knew of the rumors that she didn't know her lines and told her, "Dear, you have to know the dialogue to play it that way."

British stage actor Maurice Evans played Samantha's father, Maurice, with suave haminess. But Evans was not the first choice to play "Daddy" — Montgomery very much wanted her own father, Robert, for the part, but for reasons which are not really clear, Robert Montgomery turned this down as well as an offer to narrate the first few episodes. Still, Evans, with all of his theatricality, was the better choice. What was the status of the Endora and Maurice marriage? Obviously very open.

In addition to the witches and warlocks in recurring roles was the part of Darrin's boss at the advertising firm of McMann and Tate, Larry Tate, played with gusto by David White. White's Tate is shallow, two-faced and only out for one thing — landing the million dollar accounts. Yet he knew he had gold with Darrin — despite firing him countless times over the next eight years. Tate always ended up begging Darrin to return. White's characterization is one of the best supporting jobs by an actor on television during the 60's, and yet he was never nominated for an Emmy — a huge oversight.

In addition to Tate, the other mortal recurring roles include that of the Stephens' neighbors from across the street, Abner and Gladys Kravitz. Abner was recently retired and spent his days lying on a couch reading or listening to a ball game. Gladys was a world-class snoop. But, as played by film and stage comedienne Alice Pearce, Gladys was a snoop you sympathized with. She saw all of these incredible things occurring across the street and could never convince Abner — or even herself — of what she saw. Abner invariably ended up giving her a swig of medicine to steady her shaken nerves. As Abner, movie character veteran George Tobias was a fine counterbalance for the hysterical and hilarious Pearce.

With casting complete and the show in production, the ABC and Screen Gems publicity machine was at its full powers in the weeks before the show's premiere. Countless newspaper and magazine articles were written and Agnes was a good sport, conducting endless interviews and press junkets. When she committed to something, she felt it was an actor's responsibility to try and sell it. The show debuted on September 17, 1964 —

and was the highest-rated new program for the week. For the entire 64–65 season *Bewitched* would rank as the second most watched program, being bested only by perennial favorite *Bonanza*. Ed Scherick of ABC sent Agnes a telegram the evening the show premiered: TONIGHT SHOULD ONLY PROVE WHAT WE HAVE FELT FROM THE START. SOLID SUCCESS. AN IMPORTANT PART OF THAT SUCCESS IS DUE TO THE FINE AND UNIQUE TALENT YOU HAVE BROUGHT TO BEWITCHED. MY BEST TO YOU ON THIS GALA NIGHT.

The reviews were, on the whole, everything a new program would want. Harriet Van Horne, critic of the *New York Telegram,* wrote, "The chief charms of *Bewitched* are Elizabeth Montgomery, an authentic beauty with a cool comic style, and Dick York, who plays with a boyish zest that could slide into cuteness but doesn't . . . In the comparatively small role of Samantha's mother, Agnes Moorehead managed to look regal, sinister, and utterly glamorous." Of Agnes, Kay Gardella of the *New York Daily News* wrote, "playing her mischief brewing mother who has no time for her daughter's journey into marriage is Agnes Moorehead — a case for sure of perfect casting." *TV Guide's* Cleveland Amory wrote, "Between you and me and Halloween, we are Bewitched by *Bewitched.*"

Bewitched was a ratings and critical success and in December 1964 *Hush . . . Hush, Sweet Charlotte* opened to strong box office for its limited run in Los Angeles to qualify for the 1964 Academy Awards. Agnes was with a winner on both television and in films, and finally something which always eluded her had actually happened — she was no longer merely a respected character actress. At age 64, Agnes Moorehead was a star.

13

A Star Is Born (1965–1967)

Bewitched became a ratings phenomenon in its first season. The show captured the imagination of audiences and they loved the weekly romantic chemistry between Liz Montgomery and Dick York. The actors were swamped by fan mail, including one which was passed on to Agnes, Liz and Dick by the sponsor as representative of the type of mail they were receiving: "I have just finished watching the TV show you sponsor, *Bewitched*, and it is so enjoyable that it prompted me to write my first fan letter. Elizabeth Montgomery . . . always appears as a warm, charming, level-headed girl who gave up all the magic in the world just to be with the man she loved. I guess I like her because I'm a happy wife and mother and no enchantments of any kind could entice me away from my husband . . . I like Dick York, too, because he is so adept at comedy he can make this difficult role seem real. It would be so easy to make this part deteriorate into a bumbling boob routine . . . And Endora is superbly done by Agnes Moorehead. She was the perfect choice for what's-his-names's mother-in-law. I like her touch of cynicism that lets the air out of a lot of our inflated ideas about ourselves . . ." But not all of Agnes' mail was as supportive. One Canadian acquaintance wrote, "Oh yes I have been watching *Bewitched* faithfully each Monday evening, but to be quite honest, the series is proving to be very tiresome now, having not improved at all since the initial episode. The fault obviously lies with the writers . . . Elizabeth Montgomery is most appealing, Dick York is quite suitable, and you are quite the most exciting scene-stealer . . . and yet the show is most certainly dull!! . . . you simply must do something other than Endora!" But this opinion was the exception rather than the rule.

Agnes was putting in long hours at the studio which exhausted and exasperated her. She also felt that she wasn't getting enough credit for what she,

With Henry Gibson in *Bewitched*.

as a well-known actress in her own right, was contributing to the high ratings the show had attained. A letter to Georgia Johnstone on October 19, 1964 summed up her exhaustion and bruised ego. "I am so tired, I can't tell you — they can take these series and go some place far away. I know it's remunerative and I thank God for that — *but* the hours and the strain and pressure is unbelievable. Up every morning at 4:45!! And into make up chair at 6am — then we work until almost 8pm — it's a battle every day and Elizabeth married to the director gives me no free agent to appeal to . . . They can't understand why the viewing audience is so big! Some goon comes up to me the other day and said — 'Isn't this wonderful for you — taking you out of the character class and making you a *star*.' I said, 'I've starred since I was 15 years old — my co-stars in *Don Juan* were certainly a different caliber than this show and what's more, I would never do a part without characterization!' I get tired of battling them — but when I come home at night, I fall into a stupor and barely lift my hand to eat, let alone write . . . Have my fans and their friends write in — I don't believe they think I have viewers at all — they think Elizabeth and Dick bring the ratings up so high . . ."

York later told Herbie J Pilato that Agnes' "big debate on the set" was "when do we get to act? She was trained in the theater, so the fast pace of television acting would get to her at times." Said director R. Robert Rosenbaum, "She took direction better than anyone. She took two to three hours in makeup every morning, and was never, never late. She was always ready on the set, and she always knew her lines. She was very prepared and did not respect someone else who didn't come as well prepared as she. The show survived due to her talents, and due to the chemistry between her and Elizabeth."

While the hours working in television certainly were long, the show did establish a routine which tried to be accommodating to the actors' desire for enough time away from the set. Kasey Rogers, who joined the cast in the third season, called *Bewitched* a "luxury shoot," with the cast assembling each Monday around a conference table to read the script, time it, and then do some wardrobe tests. On Tuesdays through Thursdays they would shoot — this is what Rogers meant by "luxury," having three days to shoot a half-hour sitcom "was almost unheard of." If they didn't finish, they would work Fridays — otherwise they were off Friday to Sunday, but the cast was given the next script to begin memorizing.

The show worked on several levels. It most certainly worked as a love story. Elizabeth Montgomery and Dick York made the Samantha/Darrin relationship very passionate. It is hard to imagine another show from that era in which the lead characters — even the married ones — were as romantic and tender together. You got the feeling that they not only loved each other passionately but liked one another as individuals. Dick York said that Elizabeth reminded him of his wife, Joey, which made it very easy for him to both like and love Samantha. Kasey Rogers sums up the chemistry between the leads well when she says that Elizabeth was "every man's idea of the ideal wife. The ideal mother. The ideal friend. She was beautiful, perky, cute . . . Her personality and talent fit the part." York, Rogers maintains, "was a hell of a comedian and his rubber face and reactions were off the wall and very funny."

The show also worked as a standard situation comedy. Bill Asher, the principal director, had enormous experience working with Lucille Ball and Danny Thomas, among others, on their sitcoms and often *Bewitched* devised standard situation comedy plots with the twist of adding magic. For instance, Samantha wants to please Darrin by acting as a "normal mortal housewife," and many of the early shows dealt with her trying to clean the house, cook dinner and attempt to bake Darrin's favorite cake — with less than stellar results. Another perennial situation comedy device is the less than approving mother-in-law, as epitomized by Endora. She scoffs at her daughter's attempts to clean, cook, or even fix a drink "the mortal way" and holds Darrin responsible for the domesticization of her formerly worldly

(Courtesy of Wade Ballard)

A scene from *Bewitched*.

child. She usually gets even with "what's his name" (an early and lasting script device is that Endora acts as if she cannot remember her son-in-law's name, usually referring to him as Darwin, Dagwood, Dennis or something other than his given name) by attempting to expose Samantha to what she perceives as the contradictory nature of mortals — exposing their weaknesses such as vanity, greed, stinginess, egomania, etc. — usually at Darrin's expense. The Endora/Darrin relationship is perhaps summed up in the fourth episode, where Endora and Darrin meet for the first time (Endora uncharacteristically arriving by ringing the doorbell rather than simply "popping" in), when Endora pointedly asks her son-in-law, "Why are you trying to make my daughter something she is not?" In other words, "why can't you accept Samantha the way she is?"

Lastly, *Bewitched* works because it is a supernatural comedy. Usually Samantha has to use the powers which Darrin has forbidden that she use (even sometimes at his prodding) to save the day. Bill Asher explains that the use of her powers is a device which would be used usually at critical moments. "The audience is waiting for that twitch (Samantha's nose and upper lip would twitch when she executed her magic), but we never throw it in merely because it looks cute. We save it until Samantha is so sorely tempted to use her witchery that she can't resist — and that's the point where the audience is usually saying, 'Do Something!'"

The cast got along. Agnes liked Elizabeth, but sometimes her comments could be a tad tart when she referred to the young star of the show. For instance, in a 1965 *TV Guide* cover story Agnes seems slightly dismissive of Elizabeth. "She has quality, charm, warmth, intelligence. Of course, you know she plays herself. When I was an ingénue, we were always characterizing." Quint Benedetti, who worked as the road manager for Agnes' one-woman shows, maintains that Agnes told him that "she liked Elizabeth but wasn't enthralled by her talent. She often mentioned that it might take Elizabeth up to 6 or 7 takes to get a scene right — where Agnes was prepared and ready on take one — it exasperated her." But *Bewitched* historian Herbie J Pilato believes there was "mutual respect between two highly respected actresses." Pilato interviewed Elizabeth for his book *Bewitched Forever* and Montgomery recalled to him, with pleasure, a time when Agnes called her over after she had completed a scene to tell her how proud she was of her. But Pilato does concede that there may have been "a slight professional competition between the two," such as when Agnes was nominated, along with Elizabeth, for an Emmy in the Best Actress in a Comedy Series category. According to Pilato, Agnes "was never crazy about Serena (the brunette cousin of Samantha that Montgomery also played) in the series, because her character was so similar to Endora — especially earlier on when Elizabeth played Serena with a deeper, more arrogant persona as opposed to the kookier, hippy-type that Serena evolved into, later in the series."

Montgomery, for her part, went out of her way to make Agnes feel at home on the *Bewitched* set. She would often send her sweet notes and flowers at the beginning of each season. She would send gag items from newspapers such as a cartoon of an older witch flying on a broom wearing a bikini over

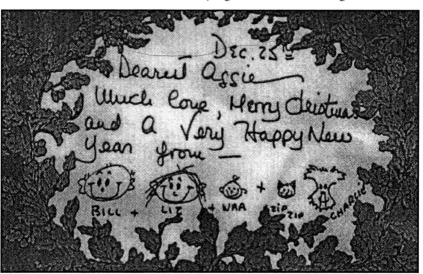

A homemade Christmas card from Elizabeth Montgomery (1965).

(From Moorehead papers, copy from Author's collection)

Miami Beach and write, "Mom over Miami." She always remembered her birthday and sent her cards every Christmas; one of the best and creative was a Montgomery Christmas card which she drew herself, from 1964, showing a caricature of herself and husband Bill Asher (with only a few strands of hair on his head) and their new baby Billy (with even less hair) and their cat and dog. It was an enchanting card. The Ashers also became perennial guests at Agnes' well-attended birthday/Christmas parties during the run of the show.

Both Elizabeth and Agnes won awards from *TV-Radio Mirror Magazine,* and Agnes flew to New York City to accept on behalf of both of them on February 19, 1965. Elizabeth sent Agnes a gracious and funny telegram: "Please tell the *TV-Radio Mirror* editors and all concerned how sorry I am that the *Bewitched* production schedule prevented my being there on this proud occasion. Many thanks to you for your willingness to accept this award for me. Bill and I want to congratulate you on your award. Fly home as soon as you can but do take an airplane this time. Much love, Liz."

Yet, to many, Agnes seemed more in tune with her other co-star, Dick York. Perhaps it was because they both shared a strong spirituality, not that the two were fellow fundamentalist Christians. York was more of a philosopher who was open to many kinds of religions — Christian, Jewish, Hindu, etc. "I believe in God. I'm looking, and I'm open to any and all ideas," York told *TV Guide,* "and thoughts that can come close to pinpointing why all of us are here." Agnes told *TV Guide* about York, "I probably understand him better than the others. He's rather profound, you know. He has a spiritual quality. I am a religious girl. I have great faith. This creates a rapport between us. Actors who have this spiritual quality often understand each other without much communication." She also lashed out at critics who underestimated what York brought to *Bewitched.* ". . . Dick plays a very important part. Nobody can hold up a series by himself or herself . . . Ignoring Dick isn't constructive criticism, it's absurd." For his part, "Dick York absolutely loved Agnes," according to Herbie J Pilato. "Quite simply the relationship between Dick York and Agnes Moorehead was the exact opposite of the relationship between Darrin and Endora." York's widow, Joey, would recall that "Dick admired and enjoyed working with Aggie — they had a similar work ethic." Screen Gems publicist Robert Palmer recalled that Agnes once told him that York was "the one who really held the show together. And that he was the least appreciated, because the hardest job in the world is to react to crazy situations in a believable way."

As always, when she committed to a project, Agnes burst with creative ideas regarding her character and the show; some were adopted (in an early episode, "Paris, Witches Style," it was her idea to do a parody of the American Airlines Commercials of the time with Endora sitting on the wing of a plane with a drink in hand and say, "It's the only way to fly!"), some which were not (Agnes would later suggest that Endora create a playhouse for the Stephens' daughter, Tabitha, that looks quite ordinary on the outside but when you enter, it suddenly becomes a palace with every luxury possible). She also had her ideas of where witches come from — they are created, not born. "Who has ever heard of a witch being born? We won't have any of that. Witches are made out of things like mushrooms and twigs. Everybody knows that." Of course Tabitha was born to Samantha, but that was due to the mixture of mortal and witch. She also had a spin on the Endora/Maurice "marriage": "I have a husband in the series, a warlock who pops in now and then, but there is no great love between us. We can't be bothered with that passion." She also maintained that she never wanted to see Endora flying around on a broom. "No self-respecting witch would use one!" In one interview Agnes said she wanted Endora to have a pet owl, which she wanted to name Jonathan, after her friend Jonathan Winters — "I also want to do the owl's voice." Agnes also maintained that Endora didn't really dislike her son-in-law, "she just brews up trouble to force her daughter into using witchcraft occasionally, lest she become a mortal too."

Agnes would also stress that she didn't see Endora as "hateful." She saw the character as mischievous. "She tells her daughter . . . how frail mortality is. She points out the selfishness and false pride of mankind, and the foibles and failures of the mortal world. She can also bring order out of chaos and we would all like to be able to do that!"

II

In December 1964 *Hush . . . Hush, Sweet Charlotte* had premiered in Los Angeles to qualify for the Academy Awards. Just before its brief LA run, Robert Aldrich sent Agnes a note which deeply touched her: "I don't know if you really understand how completely we all feel about your contribution to the picture. Without your brilliant characterization the picture wouldn't be what it is . . . whatever it is."

The buzz was that while the picture was no *Whatever Happened to Baby Jane?*, it would perform solidly at the box office — as the limited run in Los

Angeles indicated. But much to Bette Davis' chagrin, the performance receiving the most Oscar-buzz was not her own — but Agnes'. Confirmation of this was when the Golden Globes were announced on January 15, 1965. Neither Bette nor the picture itself was nominated, but Agnes was for Best Supporting Actress in a dramatic performance. Her competition was Elizabeth Ashley for *The Carpetbaggers*, Grayson Hall, *The Night of the Iguana*, Lila Kedrova, *Zorba the Greek*, and Ann Sothern, *The Best Man*. The awards were handed out on the evening of February 8 at the Cocoanut Grove in the Ambassador Hotel in Los Angeles during a live telecast of *The Andy Williams Show*. Agnes grew very excited as the date approached as she had been told by nearly everyone that she was a shoo-in not only for the Golden Globe but for a Best Supporting Actress Oscar nomination. Her columnist friends, Hedda Hopper, Louella Parsons and Dorothy Manners, were all talking her up in their columns. The picture and Agnes were receiving tremendous amounts of publicity even though the film had yet to be released nationally. When the big night arrived, Agnes was escorted to the Grove by her friend and frequent escort, Cesar Romero. After Edmond O'Brien picked up his award for Best Supporting Actor for *Seven Days in May*, the Supporting Actress category came up. Agnes sat up in her seat. The nominees were announced by the previous year's winner, Margaret Rutherford. Then, as always happens during such drama, a hush came over the room. Miss Rutherford tore open the envelope. "The Winner is . . . Agnes Moorehead for Hush . . . *Hush, Sweet Charlotte*." Agnes took to the stage and in her brief remarks thanked Robert Aldrich, Bette Davis and Olivia de Havilland. After the ceremony and into the next day her friends and fans alike sent telegrams of congratulations including Debbie Reynolds (also making the rounds of award shows due to her spunky performance as *The Unsinkable Molly Brown*), who wrote, "Dear Agnes — How thrilled I am for you. You are the dearest and deserve only the top honors. Love, Debbie."

Two weeks later, as the sun was rising on the morning of February 23, 1965, the Academy of Motion Pictures Arts and Sciences announced their nominations. The big nominated picture that year was *My Fair Lady* with ten nominations. *Hush . . . Hush, Sweet Charlotte*, surprisingly, was not far behind with seven nominations, but the only acting nomination was accorded to Agnes in the Supporting Actress category. Agnes was enjoying a day off from *Bewitched* and was sleeping in when the nominations were announced. Soon, the ringing phone startled her awake with the news that made her so happy, she later reported she had nearly "fallen out of my bed." She was almost as pleased when she heard that her friend Debbie Reynolds had received her very first Oscar nomination for *The Unsinkable Molly Brown*. She wired Debbie, who was appearing at the Riviera Hotel in Las Vegas: "Dearest Debbie, As far as I am concerned you're remarkable, beautiful, talented and absolutely unsinkable. My love and best luck. Devotedly, Agnes."

Agnes couldn't be faulted if she felt that it was a sign of good luck that she and Debbie had both been nominated in the same year. It would be both of their years. The next few weeks leading up to the Oscar ceremonies would be some of the most exciting weeks of Agnes' career. She received gobs of newspaper print. Twentieth Century-Fox began a campaign on her behalf to help her secure the Oscar; she conducted scores of newspaper and television interviews. Right in the middle of it all, the film she was already Oscar-nominated for was going to have its national release. Agnes truly was the toast of the town.

Hush . . . Hush, Sweet Charlotte opened nationally on March 12, 1965 and, as expected, the box office revenues were good. The reviews, however, were mixed. One of the most enthusiastic came from Judith Crist, the much-respected critic of the *New York Herald Tribune,* who praised the picture but conceded that there were spots of slowness, ". . . but Mr. Aldrich builds his atmosphere so painstakingly and exploits it so beautifully that this devotee, for one, will not complain." She had praise for the entire cast, but particularly lauded Agnes: "Agnes Moorehead — well, Miss Moorehead, just almost walks off with the show as the whining 'po' white trash." On the other side of the ledger, the "Dean" of the New York critics, Bosley Crowther, of the *New York Times,* came down hard on both the picture and its director. "Mr. Aldrich is being touted as a brilliant director in Hollywood. His achievements to date, as I see them, are a couple of second rate freaks." Agnes was not spared. "Agnes Moorehead as (the) weird and crone-like servant is allowed to get away with some of the broadest mugging and snarling ever done by a respectable actress on screen. If she gets the Academy Award for this performance . . . the academy should close up shop!"

The Chicago Tribune, after slamming the picture as "half-baked Hitchcock," singled Agnes out for praise: "best of all is Agnes Moorehead as Charlotte's housekeeper. She's slovenly, nosey, grumpy, and disrespectful and brings it off splendidly." *The Denver Post* opined, "Agnes Moorehead, in one of her strongest portrayals, is the maid and it is no surprise that this performance earned her an Academy Award nomination." However, *Time,* in its review, backed up Crowther, "Oscar nominee Agnes Moorehead, as Charlotte's loyal drudge, is a snarling, scratching sound and sight gag who seems determined to out-overact the best of them." Certainly Velma is an overblown characterization which lacks the subtleness of an Aunt Fanny, but there is no doubt that from her first entrance, to her grizzly exit, you can't keep your eyes off of Agnes even in scenes with Davis and de Havilland. The casting of de Havilland also helps the picture. When Miriam is first introduced, we are to believe she is sympathetic toward Charlotte and only gradually do we discover the truth. De Havilland, more so than Crawford, is able to pull that off.

Agnes believed in signs. In her heart she must have thought that after nearly a quarter of a century as one of the leading character actresses, with three previous nominations under her belt, this would be her year. Everybody told her so. Louella Parsons wrote, "Aggie should be odds-on for Oscar for this." Her friends told her she had their vote and should expect Oscar on her mantle. Finally, she was the only American name on the list of 1964's nominated supporting actresses. She felt that American pride in one of their own would also aid her. In fact, much of the press leading up to the 1964 Academy Awards had to do with the number of foreign nominees for major acting honors. Of the twenty major acting nominations in all categories, only six were American-born; three of the Best Picture nominees took place in England — *My Fair Lady, Becket, Mary Poppins,* and one in Greece, *Zorba the Greek.*

Oscar night, April 5, arrived and the show began its 7pm telecast worldwide over the ABC television network (another good sign for Agnes?), and was held at the Santa Monica Civic Auditorium. Perennial host Bob Hope delivered one of his patented corny jokes regarding all the publicity about the quantity of foreign-born nominees. "Tonight, Hollywood is handing out the foreign aid. Before you can pick up your Oscar, you have to show your passport." The night went predictably, with *My Fair Lady* scoring in almost every category in which it competed. But there were cracks in the armor. Stanley Holloway, up for Best Supporting Actor for *My Fair Lady,* lost out to Peter Ustinov for *Topkapi.* This gave Agnes some hope since she thought that if she were denied the Oscar it would be because of a *Fair Lady* sweep of major acting awards (the only exception being Best Actress where Audrey Hepburn had famously been denied a nomination). During the course of the show, Best Actress-nominee Debbie Reynolds came out on stage to present the Best Score award and did some banter with Hope. She joked that she was "barefooted" under her full-length gown, a subtle joke at the expense of her shoe tycoon husband, Harry Karl. In fact, the show was full of people close to Agnes — Reynolds, her Academy of Dramatic Arts buddy Rosalind Russell, who presented a special award; Greer Garson, presenting the Costume Design Award, and, in an especially good omen, her friend Karl Malden was going to present Agnes' category.

Malden was introduced and, not wanting to keep the nominees in suspense with a lot of needless bantering, he got straight to the point. "I know how your hearts are fluttering so I'll get on with it . . . The nominees for Best Supporting Actress are:

GLADYS COOPER, *My Fair Lady*
DAME EDITH EVANS, *The Chalk Garden*
GRAYSON HALL, *The Night of the Iguana*
LILA KEDROVA, *Zorba the Greek*
AGNES MOOREHEAD, *Hush . . . Hush, Sweet Charlotte.*"

Agnes felt a chill as the envelope was opened.

". . . And the winner is . . . LILA KEDROVA, for *Zorba the Greek.*"

Agnes' heart sank but she put up the usual brave front of applauding for the winner who didn't really believe it had happened. "Has it really happened?" Kedrova asked her co-star, Anthony Quinn, and, assured it really had, she made her way to the stage to pick up her trophy. The rest of the night was also a letdown when Sidney Poitier announced that the Best Actress Oscar went to Julie Andrews for *Mary Poppins* and not to Debbie.

The postmortems began the next morning with Hedda Hopper taking aim at the high number of foreign nominees. "No American actor won. Either the rules will have to be changed or our actors will have to try harder." Robert Aldrich wired Agnes, "To allay any doubts you should know there is no difference in our regards, respect and affection between yesterday and today." Agnes' New York theatre producer and friend, Barron Polan, wrote, "About the Academy I always thought it was a fraud, and now I know it!

I'm about mad enough to chew them out, and I resent that Greek girl something terrible." An old friend, Peter Opp, Jr., now with Disney, wrote, ". . . the entire Oscar presentations now seems to be reduced to a farcical level. I leave you with a salute that you don't need an Oscar to prove your worth as an actress to many of us in the industry." He also left her with a tip that Disney was going to be producing the film *The Happiest Millionaire* in the near future and that there were two plum roles in it, either of which would be perfect for Agnes. As for Agnes, her reaction may have summed it up best of all: "I guess I'll remain a bridesmaid for the rest of my life."

III

Usually by late April or early May when doing a television series, you have completed filming the episodes for the season and are allowed a three-month or so hiatus. This was not the case with *Bewitched* in the spring of 1965 because Elizabeth Montgomery was pregnant again. It was decided after a short break in April to return in late May to film three episodes for the upcoming second season, introducing the audience to the fact that Samantha Stephens (like Montgomery) is pregnant. On the Sunday after filming an episode titled "A Very Special Delivery," where Endora puts a spell on Darrin so that he experiences the same morning sickness that Samantha does, Agnes flew off to Dallas where she was going to spend the next three weeks rehearsing and appearing in the Noel Coward musical-comedy *High Spirits* as part of the 24th Dallas Summer Musicals season.

High Spirits had played 657 performances in New York after opening on Broadway in April 1964. It told the story of Charles Condomine; his deceased first wife, Elvira; his current second wife, Ruth; and the zany medium, Mdm. Arcati, who conjures up the spirit of the first wife who has been dead for seven years. Agnes was cast as Mdm. Arcati, with Michael Evans and Adrienne Angel as Charles and Ruth. The beautiful Iva Withers, who understudied Tammy Grimes in the Broadway production, would play the ghostly Elvira. Given her new popularity on television, along with her recent Academy Award nomination, Agnes was given solo billing above the title as well as a $4,000 per week salary.

Agnes was met at the airport by the director of *High Spirits,* Tom Hughes, who presented her with a bouquet composed of Anthericum and black orchids and covered with artificial spiders — in reference to both the supernatural nature of the play and Agnes' witchy persona on *Bewitched.*

Agnes wasn't pleased as she waved it away exclaiming, "Frightening! Horrible!" She refused to touch them until a photographer insisted.

High Spirits would have many special effects elements, such as Iva Withers flying through the air suspended by wires, tables and chairs seemingly moving by themselves, windows opening and closing on cue, and books flying off the bookcase. Agnes would make her first entrance as Mdm. Arcati on a bicycle connected to a track that would allow her to sing and gesture while riding. Agnes also designed the eccentric costumes she wore in the show, a fact mentioned in an ad for a local clothing store which showed a picture of "the bewitching" Agnes Moorehead, dressed in a checkered hat and jacket she uses when riding her bicycle on stage, with the caption: "Miss Moorehead has always been known for her exotic fashion designs . . . her originally designed costumes steal the show . . . Jas K. Wilson's Ladies departments do not stock Madame Arcadi's wardrobe, but like Miss Moorehead, our ladies fashions are always outstanding."

On opening night Agnes sent a wire to the *High Spirits* company, "May this be the beginning of a wonderful season — Relax and a GoGo." During the opening performance Agnes got a good audience reaction when she ad-libbed a plug for *Bewitched*. It occurred during a scene when Mdm. Arcati is in a trance during hypnotism and absentmindedly whistles the theme to *Bewitched*. This got a good round of applause and Agnes included it in all subsequent performances. Barron Polan sent a cable to Agnes on opening night addressing her as "Aggie Semple MacPherson," and writing, "I wish I could see you on your bicycle! Know you will be great particularly with the Ojai board. Don't summon any of my late friends! Love Baron." The girls' singing chorus of *High Spirits* also sent Agnes a wire, "Our spirits are high tonight because of you. Know you will enchant the audience as you have enchanted us." The audience opening night, according to the *Dallas Morning News,* was "a shade under par," but still a healthy 2,000 in attendance. In its review, the *Morning News* said, "This audience found much to applaud if not shout about, and more to laugh about than to understand. HIGH SPIRITS is a must item from recent repertoires and just now we don't know another summer theater that could convey it as smoothly or professionally." Of Agnes, they wrote, "Miss Moorehead can be hilarious when given scope, as in her boudoir scene while talking to her Ouija board, when going crazily balletic in Margot Fonteyn imitations, in effective delivery of patter songs which intensify the plot, such as 'Something is Coming to Tea' . . . Miss Moorehead . . . can do something all others have missed in words and song. She can play somebody else amusingly besides herself, Noel Coward's Madam Arcati, for instance."

The two weeks of performances flew by and Agnes ingratiated herself with the company. She was there for others and offered kind words and support to her fellow actors in the company. On the day she left Dallas, the chorus from *High Spirits* wrote an "Ode to Agnes": "Bewitching, beguiling — these words are all used to describe our favorite seer. Oh Madame Arcati, we give you this broom in remembrance of your three weeks here. Although you leave us to fly far away, we really want you to see that in witching, conjuring or winning our hearts you'll always be loved in Big D."

The hairstylist for the show, Jimi White, enthused of Agnes, "She is very warm, quick-witted. She is typical of the ones on top, sure of herself, easy to get along with and ready to make everything work out right, with everybody happy." It was a happy experience for Agnes, but would be her final play in theatre for nearly seven years, with the exception of her one-woman shows. Agnes would now take a couple of weeks off to rest before returning to the *Bewitched* set to film several episodes back-to-back throughout July until the second week in September when production would close down for approximately two months while Montgomery was on maternity leave.

Shortly after returning to Hollywood from Dallas, Agnes went to the set of the film *The Chase* to visit her friend, E.G. Marshall, and got to observe the star of the film, Marlon Brando. She wasn't impressed. "A wild set — with the gr-r-reat Marlon Brando," she related to Georgia Johnstone. "You couldn't hear him speak. How do they get on? One take a day practically and he gets $1,000,000 a picture!!! It's beyond me." She was not a fan of what she called "the mumbling school" of acting. "The method school thinks the emotion is the art. It isn't. All emotion isn't sublime. The theater isn't reality. If you want reality, go to the morgue. The theater is human behavior that is effective and interesting."

Again she complained about the "breakneck speed" of shooting *Bewitched* to accommodate Montgomery's maternity schedule. "And this series is getting me down . . . trying to get as many shows in the can before the baby comes. The whole thing is mad and I don't particularly care about arriving on the set *any* morning." Further depressing her was the death of her Mercury Theatre friend and fellow actor, Everett Sloane. She related to Johnstone how she was "depressed" for three days, and then went on to describe Sloane as "strange — turning down work thinking he had every disease in the book." She also called the Watts riots, which were occurring that summer of '65, "shocking, unbelievable actions — I don't know what the world is coming to."

When *Bewitched* went into hiatus again during Montgomery's maternity leave, Agnes accepted the role of Sister Cluny at the invitation of her friend Debbie Reynolds in the film *The Singing Nun* which went before the cameras at MGM in October 1965. It is the story of Sister Sourire who becomes a recording star while belonging to a Belgium convent. Greer Garson would play the Reverend Mother and Ricardo Montalban was

Agnes and Debbie in *The Singing Nun* (1965).

cast as the Father. Agnes wasn't enthusiastic about the script, telling Johnstone, "The script is fair — the best part of it is very dull. They have been after Debbie like mad, and giving her a leading man (Chad Everett) with no name — she is on a rampage . . . It just fit in with *Bewitched* for any minute now Elizabeth will have her baby. She says she will be here Oct. 1, but believe me, she could drop in any minute — she is so huge." For Agnes, the role of Sister Cluny was nothing more than looking disapprovingly at the guitar-playing Sister played by Reynolds. But she was happy to be on the set working with two of her closest buddies, Reynolds and Garson.

Agnes loved the star treatment she received at MGM during the shooting of *The Singing Nun.* "It was a windfall for me," she told Georgia Johnstone, "and I couldn't be happier — my dressing room was all done in lilacs!" While Garson was one of her best female friends, Agnes couldn't help but gloat to Georgia about being billed above Greer in the film. "What a joy it is to work on a picture again . . . and not running a race for time." When

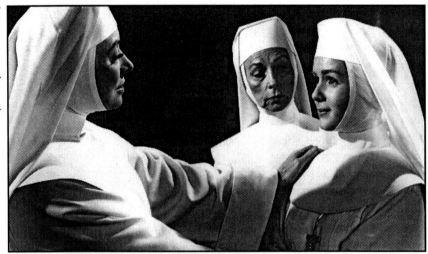

Greer Garson, Agnes and Debbie Reynolds in *The Singing Nun* (1965).

released, *The Singing Nun* did good business at the box office despite weak reviews. Pauline Kael would sum up this film in her book, *Kiss Kiss Bang Bang*: "Ricardo Montalban is a simpering simple priest; and though Agnes Moorehead plays a nun like a witch, she is more than balanced by Greer Garson as the Mother Prioress . . . Debbie Reynolds is less than perfection."

Around this time, Paul Gregory had the idea of casting his wife, former screen actress Janet Gaynor, Tallulah Bankhead and Agnes in a horror film together. Bankhead, with whom Agnes worked with in the film *Main Street to Broadway,* vetoed the idea because she had just completed a horror film and was not eager to rush into another one. But Bankhead would have welcomed working with Agnes again. According to one of Tallulah's biographers, Bankhead called Agnes to propose that they work together on a Broadway show about suffragettes. Apparently Agnes was agreeable, but the project didn't get off the ground.

On October 7, Agnes heard from Shirley Temple Black regarding coming to San Francisco as a guest star at the opening of the ninth annual San Francisco Film Festival. As an honored guest, she would attend a black tie dinner and be introduced onstage at the opening night of the Festival, and then attend a post-opening supper dance at the Fairmont Hotel. The Festival would also fly Agnes and a companion to San Francisco and put her up at the Fairmont Hotel. In a postscript, in a handwritten note to Agnes, Shirley writes, "Please, please come! Last time you were here I tried to

Greer Garson, Ricardo Montalban, Ed Sullivan, Agnes and Debbie in *The Singing Nun* (1965).

contact you, but you were probably too involved. This time, I'll have many interesting people to introduce you to. Fondly, Shirley." Agnes did attend and, while she had a good time, she would later say she was "embarrassed" by all the attention.

Around this time Sean was becoming a bit of a problem. While attending high school at Llandovery College in Wales, he suddenly just up and ran away, which set off a search by police and his fellow students. Agnes was concerned, but didn't fly to Wales herself due to her filming schedule; she did keep in touch with authorities. After four days on the run, Sean walked into the police station at Swansea and identified himself. He was quoted as saying, "I don't know why I ran away, but I didn't walk all the way to Swansea. I had a couple of lifts and one night I slept in the park." Before all of this occurred Agnes had told an interviewer, "Being educated in Europe has made him an adult all the faster. Why he even tells me what to do." She added wearily, "I can remember when I used to tell him." This was basically the crux of the problems which would develop between mother and son in the years ahead — Agnes, firm in her own beliefs, and Sean, having lived so long independently of her, equally strong in his and not wanting to be treated as a child.

In December Agnes held her annual Christmas party which launched the holiday season in grand fashion. Her guest list was always distinguished, but this year it was even more so — perhaps due to her increased profile in Hollywood due to the success of *Bewitched* and the recognition she got from the Golden Globes and the Academy for *Hush . . . Hush, Sweet Charlotte.* Her guest list was glittering, and included such old friends as Henry Hathaway, Betty White and Allen Ludden, The Jimmy Stewarts, The Bob Hopes, Lucille Ball and her husband Gary Morton, Kathryn Grayson, Debbie Reynolds and Harry Karl, and Liz Montgomery and Bill Asher. Yet, according to Cesar Romero, the guest list wasn't only limited to the high and the mighty in the industry. "The annual party was not just for entertainment people . . . she always invited politicians, artists, industrialists, writers, producers, directors, business tycoons and very often, just plain folks." Her servants were always invited. She hired help to come in so that her longtime employees could enjoy the festivities. Prior to the party Agnes would be driven to a location on Alameda Street in Los Angeles, where she would select several newly-cut Christmas trees. "She delighted in choosing and picking several trees for her annual Christmas bash. Nothing but the best for her guests. She was like a child decorating the trees, too," recalled her maid, Freddie Jones.

Elizabeth Montgomery thanks Agnes for an invitation to Agnes' annual Christmas party (1966).

As was her custom, Agnes positioned herself at the front door where she would remain for the entire evening — warmly welcoming her guests upon their arrival and then wishing them a Happy Holiday as they left. The festivities would usually begin around 4 in the afternoon and lasted until about 9 in the evening. According to Quint Benedetti, who met Agnes as a student in her acting class and later became her road manager for the one-woman shows, she would prepare for the party weeks in advance and have professional set decorators come to Villa Agnese and decorate the house, making it look like "a fairyland." Kasey Rogers, who would later attend these parties after inheriting the role of Louise Tate on *Bewitched*, recalls that a sit-down dinner would be served "on her large back patio at tables which seated six or eight. Wine was served in colored glasses, each shaped like a cluster of grapes." At around 8pm, members of the Beverly Hills High School Choir would come in to cap the evening by singing Christmas carols. Laurie Main was another perennial guest at the Christmas parties, recalling them as "grand fun — everyone who was anyone in Hollywood was there." Main remembers one Christmas party in particular and the joke which Agnes had at his expense.

"One year I wasn't feeling well," recalls Main, "so I said, 'I think I'll just stand by the fireplace.'

"Agnes wryly replied, 'Oh, that is brave of you.'

"'Really — why?' I asked.

"'You'll see,' smiled Agnes.'

"When I stood by the fireplace, hardly anyone came near me. Oh, they might have stopped for a moment to say, 'hello' and then they just moved on. I went and told Agnes this and she said, "Well, what did you expect? They thought you were ostracized so they didn't want to be seen with you!.' and then she let out one of her trademarked huge laughs."

Her efforts every year were noted by the Hollywood press — one article called Agnes, "one of Hollywood's most superb hostesses . . . part of Hollywood tradition, in the grand and gala manor of filmdom's golden era."

The year was capped by twin honors accorded to Agnes; the first, by the Academy of Motion Picture Arts and Sciences, which invited her to be a member of the nominating committee to select the Best Foreign Film nominees for 1965. It was somewhat ironic that in a year when Agnes was herself denied an Academy Award in part due to the exceptional performances and films featuring foreign-born actors that she would be selected to be on the nominating committee to select the nominees for best foreign film, but she was honored to be asked and eagerly accepted. The second was her election to the Board of Directors of the Screen Actors Guild, which carried a three-year term with meetings every other Monday night at 8:30 p.m. Often she attended these board meetings in the company of her friend, Karl Malden, who recalled, "Her television series, *Bewitched*, was sponsored by Chevrolet. Every year they gave her a new car. Now Aggie hated to drive. She used that car maybe once a week and had some neighbor kid take her to a store or something. Around that time she became an active member of the Screen Actors Guild and she would call me and ask if I wouldn't mind driving her to the SAG meetings. Of course I didn't mind. So this went on for several weeks. One day as we were driving, she asked me if I wanted a new car. I was surprised and asked her what she was talking about. She explained that Chevrolet gives her a car every year which she never really uses. I told her I would buy it from her as a new car since it only had about 3,000 miles on it. She insisted that she sell it to me as a used car. So we decided to use a dealer. The dealer said he couldn't sell it as used unless it had at least 8,000 miles on it. So she had this neighbor kid using it all the time until the odometer got up to 8,000 miles and at that point I bought it from her as a used car. I used it for many years."

IV

1966 would be a fairly quiet year professionally for Agnes. With the exception of working on *Bewitched* and a few television guest appearances, in addition to a few dates with her one-woman show, she appeared in no major motion pictures (though *The Singing Nun*, shot in the fall of 1965, was released) or stage plays. She did have plenty of time for social functions including a testimonial dinner for Dean Martin in January and a luncheon in honor of Prince Philip held at Twentieth Century-Fox studios in March. Part of this inactivity may have been twofold. First, because she had brought Sean home from Wales. His disappearance from school and reports of other infractions made Agnes feel that it might be best for him to live at home so that she could better monitor his activities and make sure that he was getting the kind of religious instruction that she believed would turn him around. To that end, she enrolled him into Sunday school at Beverly Hills Community Presbyterian Church, where, according to a letter she received from Pastor Samuel Allison, Sean was to be in Sunday school "promptly at 9:30am each Sunday and dismissal at 10:40 a.m." Sean also received "beautifully illustrated books," which the pastor instructed Agnes were to be "read at home with your help and encouragement." She also enrolled him into a private school in Beverly Hills, where she later told the press, "Sean is taking special courses in Algebra, Geometry and Physics. All the teachers are French and he has to learn in that language."

The second and perhaps most understandable reason for her relative inactivity in 1966 may have been because of her health. Toward the end of filming *Bewitched's* second season in April 1966, Agnes was not feeling up to par, her usual energy depleted. She checked herself into the Mayo Clinic in Rochester for a check-up and ended up staying there for several weeks. Correspondence she received at this time indicates that she "went under the knife," but there are no specifics as to what type of illness she had or the reason for the operation. On May 7, 1966, she received a letter from an old friend from New Concord, Ohio who wrote, "thankful that there were no complications," and that she was happy that the care she had at the Mayo Clinic "had won me over . . . so wonderful that you found not only good medical practice but also kindness and understanding." Following her hospitalization, Agnes went on to the Reedsburg, Wisconsin home of her mother for several more weeks of recuperation. There may be a clue, though, about the nature of Agnes' own extended 1966 hospitalization and lengthy recuperation in a letter to Agnes from her friend Barron Polan: ". . . Now, I am only relieved to have had a call from Georgia the Johnstone, telling me that you've already had the knife and are fine! Congratulations . . . But it is important to guard that greatest of possessions, your health. I guess poor Alice Pearce must be a lesson to all of us, for I was told that she was warned, but did not take the time out to see." The original Gladys Kravitz on *Bewitched,* Alice Pearce, had died the previous March after a long battle with cancer. She had heroically worked on the series until nearly the end — the last few episodes she appeared in, especially "Baby's First Paragraph," are somewhat painful to watch. It is clear by her gauntness and the wig she wore that the disease was taking its toll, but her performance never suffered; although her role would later be recast with the talented Sandra Gould, the Gladys character just wasn't the same without Pearce. On Mother's Day, 1966, while in Reedsburg, Debbie Reynolds wrote Agnes:

Dear Agatha,

Was so thrilled to hear from my "lumpy" buddy, and that she seems to be on the upward road. I am so happy for you and your mother to be able to have this precious time together. Betcha there's a lot of bullin going on between the two gals. I tried calling your home today, to wish Sean a Happy Mother's Day and to get your phone number, so I will call again tomorrow. I wanted to wish you a Happy Mother's Day wish on Mother's Day but I guess a sincere wish on paper will do, sweet, dear friend! All is well here and

I know all is well with Agatha too. Please take good care, Much Love to you and your mother.

Mary Frances A.K.A. Debala.

While she was recuperating from her surgery in Reedsburg with her mother, the Emmy Awards were presented in Hollywood. Agnes was nominated along with Alice Pearce for Outstanding Performance by an Actress in a Supporting Role in a Comedy for *Bewitched*. This was to be Agnes' first Emmy nomination, and while she was saddened that she couldn't attend the ceremony in person she was thrilled to be nominated. Also nominated was Rose Marie for her wisecracking and man-hungry Sally Rogers in *The Dick Van Dyke Show*. Rose Marie was a professional acquaintance of Agnes' and they had acted together on the TV series *My Sister Eileen* in 1961. She recalls Agnes as "a wonderful lady and a tremendous actress." Rose Marie considers herself a fan of Agnes'. "You have to understand that stars are fans too, just like regular people, and Agnes Moorehead was one of my favorites; I especially loved her work in radio with *Sorry, Wrong Number*. Agnes was a gracious lady, very professional, never rude and had a great sense of humor, but we never got to know one another outside of work and when we did it was usually a hug and kiss and 'how are you?'" Nevertheless, Rose Marie was thrilled to be nominated in the company of Agnes, as well as Alice Pearce. When the envelope was opened that night neither Agnes nor Rose Marie went home the victor — the Academy bestowed on the recently-deceased Alice Pearce the Emmy for her performance as Gladys Kravitz on *Bewitched*. While Agnes was disappointed, she understood that she would have other opportunities and the industry wanted to recognize Alice. Still, she heard from friends and colleagues who wired their regrets, including Debbie Reynolds: "Sweet Agnes — I know you were pleased for Alice but everyone knew you deserved it. We miss you and love you. Debbie and Harry."

For years Agnes had tutored actors for roles. Debbie Reynolds has told of her taking time out to coach her. Zsa Zsa Gabor was given voice lessons by Agnes. Agnes was dialogue coach to Jeffrey Hunter in the film *King of Kings*. The list can go on. She also felt she was giving something back to the industry by operating an acting school, which for many years she conducted out of her home. Many of the students were the children of well-known performers, but many others were not. Not all were children; many adults were part of her acting school. It was around 1966 that a nearly 40-year-old regional publicist for RCA Victor, who had worked with Eartha Kitt and Perry Como, among others, saw Agnes on a television talk show speaking about her acting school. Intrigued, Quint Benedetti enrolled, and over the next seven years would become an important part of Moorehead's life and career.

Benedetti knew enough about Agnes to realize that she liked "squeakey clean — goody two-shoes types," so he made sure when he auditioned that his hair was cut and combed, and he dressed conservatively. Like all potential students, Benedetti auditioned first for Kathy Ellis, who helped run the school while still serving as Agnes' stand-in and assistant. Benedetti did well enough in his audition for Kathy to warrant an audition in front of Agnes. She approved of the handsome Benedetti and, for $200 per month (a pretty high fee for those days), he became part of Agnes Moorehead's acting school. At the time Benedetti first became a student, the acting school would meet on Wednesday nights and Saturdays. The Wednesday night classes were called, "Musical night" and the students, approximately 10-12 in number, sometimes more, would learn coordination by fencing and doing ballet. Agnes hired a professional fencer and ballet instructor.

Agnes didn't usually attend these sessions but showed up more regularly on Saturdays. The Saturday classes alternated between sessions of 8am to 12pm one week and longer sessions of 8am to 3pm the next week. The curriculum was based on the one that Agnes had learned at the American Academy of Dramatic Arts. It included Technique, Shakespeare, doing scenes, speech, and more dancing, fencing and singing. Benedetti would recall that Agnes often had other teachers assisting her, such as her friends Karl Malden and Laurie Main. He also maintains that she was often promising high-profile guest speakers such as mime Marcel Marceau, "who never showed up." Furthermore, Benedetti says that Agnes would spend less time speaking about the techniques of acting, then she would giving a running commentary of her own career. "Some of the kids made fun of her because they thought she was corny, behind her back — but in front of her they were suck ups." When she wasn't speaking about her own career, she was often quite "outspoken" regarding morals "in and out of the theatre." Every year, according to Benedetti, Agnes would show the students the *Twilight Zone* episode she had starred in, "The Invaders," which she was "very proud of" and considered her best work on television, as well as an effective tool in teaching her students pantomime. In terms of grooming, Agnes expected her students to be "ladies and gentlemen, no slacks for the girls, and good grooming, which excluded long hair on the boys."

Benedetti also maintains that she showed favoritism toward the students who came from wealthy families — "those who were able to pay in full the tuition rather than those who made weekly installments." It is this allegation of playing favorites which prompted one student to write to Agnes after walking out of class one Saturday. In this letter she speaks of "clicks" who won't work with some students (herself among them): "The click although smaller in number still exists and the click is still too good to work with your students — your opinion of the students is meaningless — the only thing that counts is that the click is running things." She also pointedly told Agnes, "I do not have $25.00 a week to pay the rent while your private students control the school." This student suggests that she had "begged" Agnes for three years to talk to her and to get private tutoring to "build confidence. You will not give it to me so I must go elsewhere."

Bernard Fox, who played Dr. Bombay on *Bewitched*, was also enlisted as an instructor at Agnes' acting school, and recalls it as an "excellent drama school," but acknowledges that Agnes' "contribution as far as I could tell was allowing the students to gather around whilst she regaled them with stories of her days with the Mercury Playhouse." He also maintains that "the quality of the scenes her students were presenting was very poor." Fox had charge of her senior students and since he found the quality of the scenes poor, he set about trying to improve it and "to my mind, and the students, I did." But he recalls that one Saturday Agnes dropped in to check the progress and "announced she had seen all of this, evidently not noticing the tightening and the polishing that had been achieved. Anyway, next semester I taught fencing." Fox also says that the students were promised film footage of their scenes and apparently the film instructor was not available so Agnes called upon Fox to take twelve students to USC, "where Agnes said arrangements were made to do the filming. Followed by my twelve goslings, I traipsed around half a dozen classrooms, phoned various departments, nobody knew about any filming — and, anyway, who was going to pay for the footage?" Eventually, Agnes hired a still photographer, who took the students out into the country and took pictures of them in various poses; they were presented with these stills upon graduation, to which Fox recalls remarking to a couple of the students, "perhaps Agnes thought they could stand in front of various casting directors and riffle through them simulating motion!" Fox does say that if a student could not afford to pay it didn't automatically disqualify them because Agnes would provide a scholarship which may have been funded by her "wealthy friends in the industry."

Laurie Main was also called upon by Agnes as an instructor of comedy plays for the school. He has a somewhat different view of the school and Agnes' contribution than Benedetti and Fox. It was Main's observation that the students "doted" on Agnes. He says that Agnes taught the fundamentals of acting rather than directing scenes. He recalls that usually the school ran from the fall until the summer when it would close down for three months or so, but one summer he told the students, "let's keep rehearsing and surprise Agnes in the fall." So they did and in the fall when the school reopened the students were able to present a very "polished" production and Agnes, "was so pleased by what they accomplished." Main says that Agnes, "believed in young people and she began her school because she wanted to give something back to the Hollywood community." While she believed in young people, it didn't stop her from "rebuking someone who she felt was under-dressed or over-dressed — manners were very important to Agnes."

For Benedetti, the turning point in his relationship with Agnes came when she faced a crisis. She had moved her school out of her home and was at a facility on Wilshire Boulevard when she got notice that she would have to vacate that location. She didn't know where she was going to move the school, which had outgrown her home. Up to this point Benedetti had been a shrinking violet in classes, "she never gave me the time of day for acting at all." He pretty much just watched the action and didn't say anything. But when Agnes shared with the class her concern about where the school would relocate, Benedetti thought of the Santa Monica Playhouse where he had appeared in a play the previous year. He boldly told her he would check it out and attempt to work out a deal. Agnes replied, "Well, better men than you have tried, but if you want to try, okay."

Benedetti went out to the Santa Monica Playhouse and, when informed that the space would be for Agnes Moorehead, he was able to make a deal. He called Agnes and told her to come out and see her "new home." She countered — telling Benedetti to come to her home and pick her up and drive her to see the new space, adding, "I don't do freeways." Benedetti picked Agnes up and they drove from Beverly Hills to Santa Monica avoiding the freeways by taking back roads and surface streets the entire way. It was during this extended drive that Benedetti says Agnes "mellowed" toward him and they had their first extended talk — getting to know her not as a grande dame, but as a person. Once they arrived at the Santa Monica Playhouse Agnes quickly negotiated the deal for use of the space and she had a new appreciation for Quint Benedetti. Trusting his business sense, she invited him to be, first, her correspondence secretary, and later work on publicity and bookings for her one-woman shows. In Benedetti's eyes, "the ugly duckling" had made good.

V

Helen Hayes and Agnes had stayed in touch throughout the years. They were friends, but not intimate; they remained in contact mainly through correspondence and would occasionally see each other. "Their friendship was the kind where they were great friends when circumstances brought them together," according to Hayes' son, actor James MacArthur, "but otherwise they might go for long periods of time without having any contact. We lived on the east coast and Aggie lived in Los Angeles, so get-togethers usually occurred when one or the other was in town or they were attending a common event or something like that."

In September 1966 Hayes felt the need to write to Agnes regarding Paul Gregory resurrecting the idea of *Marlowe* as a play. According to Hayes, Gregory had spoken to her son about playing the title role and "Jim has got himself all worked up. I think the lad has got very uneasy sitting around the house waiting for a picture to materialize — so he has latched onto this play." It seems Hayes had some misgivings about her son playing the part. "Don't you think Jim is too American for Marlowe? I think it would be great for him to act this role — but again, I'm loathe to say anything — I'm too close up to see the situation clearly." As if it might lessen her anxiety she inquired as to whether Agnes would be interested in playing the Queen to her son's Christopher Marlowe. Unfortunately, it would be impossible, with Agnes' television schedule, for her to undertake a play.

Years later, James MacArthur acknowledged that Paul had indeed offered him Marlowe. "I was rather taken aback by his offer since I felt it was a very strong part and something a little daunting for someone with my background and skill at that point. I wasn't unwilling to do it, but I was fearful that I wouldn't be able to do it justice." However, Gregory never did mount this production and MacArthur never acted the play, which he describes as "very dark and brooding," adding, "And that's how I remember Paul Gregory as well."

It was during these years of working on *Bewitched* that Agnes spent more time at home. "People don't believe it, but I'm really a homebody" she once said. Prior to *Bewitched*, she toured extensively in her one-woman show or some Paul Gregory play or did one film after another — often on location. Now, with a more or less fixed schedule for much of the year (though she would still hop off in a dreaded airplane for a one-woman show some weekends), she took pleasure in the house she had lived in for nearly twenty years. On Saturdays, when she wasn't spending the day with her acting students, she liked to just "putter" around the house. She would paint, sculpt, play the piano, catch up on reading or even rake leaves — activities which relaxed her and renewed her spirit as well as energy. "She even used to climb a very high ladder to wash windows . . . she must have inherited the trait of cleanliness, because although she had lots of clutter it was clean clutter," recalled her maid, Freddie Jones. She liked to go to the Farmer's Market in Hollywood, near the CBS Studios, to pick out fruits and vegetables. She was a collector too. Everywhere she went, when traveling overseas or to different cities within the United States, she would seek out antique shops. "I prefer Venetian pieces — I select them carefully so they will be appropriate to my Mediterranean styled home." Sundays, true to her religious principles, was a day of rest and renewal. According to Bernard Fox, Agnes would assemble her household staff each Sunday at the stairwell of her home where she would recite passages from the Bible.

In terms of exercise, Agnes enjoyed walking. Occasionally when she was driven to a social gathering at the Beverly Hills Hotel, she would tell the driver, "I think I'll walk back. It'll be easier for everyone and the weather is so nice." For recreation, she was a huge movie fan and saw many of the current releases and, as her scrapbooks indicate, she was invited to the premiers of many films. She also enjoyed attending plays and concerts. For pure relaxation and getting away from it all, she enjoyed nothing more than taking a cruise. She loved the sea air and could have all the privacy she wanted to catch up on sleep or reading in her cabin. She also enjoyed going to parties, and attended many, cocktail or dinner. One party invitation around this time was sent by Aggie's old friend Rock Hudson in honor of Lauren Bacall, who was returning to Hollywood after a stint in New York in the play *Cactus Flower.* "That Broadway Cactus Flower, Lauren Bacall, is coming to town, so I hope that you can join me in welcoming her back Friday night, October twenty-first, at Eight P.M.. Slacks, lounging pajamas are in order. No Ties. Come early and stay late, music and dancing at Ninety Four Zero Two Beverly Crest Drive."

```
WESTERN UNION
TELEGRAM
W. P. MARSHALL,                              R. W. McFALL
Chairman of The Board                        President

CLASS OF SERVICE
This is a fast message
unless its deferred char-
acter is indicated by the
proper symbol.

The filing time shown in the date line on domestic telegrams is LOCAL TIME at point of origin. Time of receipt is LOCAL TIME at point of destination

348A PDT OCT 14 66 LA134
SSK092 L BHA698 BHZ3  BHZ3 NL PD BEVERLY HILLS CALIF 13
 MISS AGNES MOOREHEAD
   1023 NORTH ROXBURY DR BEVERLY HILLS CALIF
  THAT BROADWAY CACTUS FLOWER, LAUREN BACALL, IS COMING TO TOWN,
 SO I HOPE THAT YOU CAN JOIN ME IN WELCOMING HER BACK FRIDAY
 NIGHT, OCTOBER TWENTY-FIRST, AT EIGHT P.M. SLACKS, LOUNGING
 PAJAMAS ARE IN ORDER. NO TIES. COME EARLY AND STAY LATE, MUSIC
 AND DANCING AT NINETY FOUR ZERO TWO BEVERLY CREST DRIVE. PARKIN
 BOYS WILL TAKE YOUR CAR AT LINDA CREST (EAST OFF COLDWATER)
 AND BEVERLY CREST. RSVP BRADSHAW TWO FIVE SEVEN ONE ONE
  ROCK HUDSON.
```

Telegram inviting Agnes to a party honoring Lauren Bacall at Rock Hudson's house.

Lucille Ball, who had first met Agnes in the early 40's on the film *The Big Street*, was a neighbor and friend. She delighted in playing games with her; Lucy loved Scrabble, as did Agnes. "Lucy and I play Scrabble once in a while," Aggie dryly told one interviewer. "I suppose if I needed to borrow a cup of sugar, she'd lend it to me." In one funny postcard sent by Lucy to Agnes from Hawaii she addressed Agnes as "Scrabblehead," and said she was heading home. "Will beat card home even though I'm giving it a head start." In the book, *Lucy in the Afternoon*, Lucy tells author Jim Brochu a funny anecdote regarding Agnes. "I loved Aggie. When *How the West Was Won* came out, I ran to see it, and God was it great. Unbelievable. I called all my friends and told them to rush to see it. I went over to Aggie's house and asked her if she had seen the film, and she said no. I went on and on about it and told her that she had to drop whatever she was doing and see the best movie of all time. Well, about two weeks later, I saw Aggie and said, 'Have you seen *How the West Was Won*? I've seen it twice now.' Aggie shook her head and said, 'No, I haven't seen it yet.' I got so frustrated with her, I shouted, 'Why? I told you to go see it. I begged you to go see it. Don't you believe me when I tell you it's good? Now why haven't you seen it?' Aggie looked at me like I was a first-class dope and said, 'Because I'm in it!' Aggie had played Debbie Reynolds' mother, and she was so goddamned brilliant that I never recognized her."

Agnes had two live-in housekeepers, Freddie Jones and Polly Garland. Freddie, who was with "Miss M" the longest — over twenty years — was the upstairs person, responsible for dressing, clothes, and upstairs house-keeping. Polly tended to the downstairs and did the cooking. According to author Warren Sherk, though, as the years went by and they got to know each well, they would share duties and cover for each other, if need be, at times of illness or vacation. Agnes trusted and respected both these women completely, and they were devoted to her. Despite two maids who did much of the cooking, Agnes also enjoyed dabbling in the kitchen from time to time. Agnes would later say she didn't bother with "mundane cooking," but liked to experiment with gourmet dishes like lobster bisque and minted grapes. "I love to cook . . . not meat and potatoes and fried eggs and that sort of cooking, but creative cooking with herbs and wines." Freddie Jones says that "on rare occasions that she fixed a meal, her favorite was trout, which she prepared with a conglomeration of grapes, almonds, and herbs."

Agnes tried to stay out of partisan politics as much as possible — "I don't mix in politics, I don't believe one should mix oil with water." Over time she had contributed to both parties and was a fervent admirer of Eleanor Roosevelt, but she rarely publicly endorsed or campaigned for a candidate. By upbringing and belief she was a conservative Republican who believed in less government and tax cuts. She would get angered by the fact that the more money she made the more money the government took away from her through taxes.

In 1966, her old friend Ronald Reagan ran for Governor on the Republican ticket and for the first time Agnes publicly endorsed a candidate as well as contributed to his campaign. Agnes told Georgia Johnstone, "I don't think it a good idea to get mixed up in politics — do you? I could be non-partisan about it I suppose. I know Ronald to be an honest, sincere man — and I like him personally. He has the courage of his convictions — well, who knows?" "Agnes Moorehead absolutely loved Ronald Reagan," according to Quint Benedetti. "It was Ronald Reagan this and Ronald Reagan that." Despite Agnes' support for Reagan, it didn't stop leading Hollywood liberals Burt Lancaster and Kirk Douglas from soliciting Agnes to support Tom Braden (the newspaper man who was the inspiration for the television series *Eight is Enough*) in the primary for Lt. Governor. Agnes was very pleased by Reagan's overwhelming mandate that November. Reagan sent a letter of appreciation to Agnes following the election: "There are no words to tell you how grateful I am. Even harder would be to express

Robert Coote, Nanette Fabray, Agnes and Ricardo Montalban in the 1966 NBC TV special, *Alice Through the Looking Glass*.

how proud you've made me. It is sweet to be approved by your fellow man, but when that approval comes from those you hold in affection and esteem, and when that approval is evidenced so unselfishly it makes for a heart-warming and lasting memory. Nancy joins me in a thank you too big for words, but from our hearts. Sincerely, Ron."

In the fall of 1966, Agnes was back on television not only on *Bewitched* but in an NBC 90-minute special broadcast on November 6 of *Alice Through the Looking Glass*. Agnes played the Red Queen, but came into the show at the last minute after the original choice for the part, Bette Davis, withdrew from the production officially due to illness. However, according to Nanette Fabray, who portrayed the White Queen, Davis "chickened out. She thought the idea of singing and dancing was wonderful, then she got a case of the nerves close to the taping — we were all stunned, but she was famous for that kind of thing."

In addition to Agnes and Fabray, the supporting cast was strong: Jimmy Durante as Humpty Dumpty, Ricardo Montalban as the White King, Jack Palance as the Jabberwock, and Tom and Dick Smothers as Tweedledum and Tweedledee. Fabray recalls being "grossly disappointed" about how the special turned out. "I thought it was badly photographed. They put a camera on the floor and had us walk in front of it — they used no imagination at all." While Fabray recalls that there was "no opportunity to mix and mingle" due to the production schedule, she does recall that "Agnes was very authorative in the part and did a fine job, (but) not inspired because the show itself was not inspired." She also believed that Agnes was "a very dynamic woman and her face alone would be worth lots of close-ups." The show was taped, but performed as if it was a live production. The taping itself was very uncomfortable due to the heavy costumes, along with the strong lighting they used in those early days of color television. Despite the air conditioning in the studio, it was uncomfortably hot. Fabray sums up the special, which drew high ratings, as "pedestrian, where it should have been magical."

That same month, Agnes guest-starred on the ABC variety series, *The Hollywood Palace,* which was hosted by Debbie Reynolds' ex-husband Eddie Fisher. On it she participated in a parody of the series, *Batman,* with Agnes playing the Riddler, reciting the dialogue at a lectern bearing a huge script. Here is a sampling of the dialogue:

AGNES: What do we get from a pig? Ham. What goes with ham?
            Eggs . . . I cut your bat-ray with my egg-ray.
BATMAN: Very clever of you, you friend.
AGNES: That's FIEND!
BATMAN: You Fiend.

Not surprisingly, Agnes wrote on the top of this script "Terrible!," but she did it anyway.

In December, Agnes accepted a guest shot on the popular CBS series, *The Wild, Wild West* in the episode, "The Night of the Vicious Valentine." Agnes was cast as Emma Valentine, a matchmaker with a nefarious plan. She matches up women to prominent men and then has the men killed so that women will gain more influence and eventually control of banks, commerce, and the government. Emma explains to James West (Robert Conrad) that she is trying to save women "from domination of the spirit. Economic exploitation. Annihilation of the mind. In brief, all the injustices wrought by men." Since she controls the widows of the men that she matches up, she plans to temporarily reign as Queen of a monarchy; presumably, she has plans to do away with the president as well: "then after time, I shall release this country into a democracy. And allow a grateful nation to elect me president."

The script is witty and full of good dialogue, including this exchange between Emma Valentine and James West: "What do you demand in a woman, intelligence or beauty?" asks Emma. "Beauty, if they are intelligent and intelligence if they are beautiful," responds West.

As Emma Valentine in *The Wild, Wild West* (1966).

West and his colleague, Artemus Gordon, manage to stop Emma Valentine from fulfilling her plan, but they don't capture her and she leaves behind a note. "Roses are red, violets are blue, crime does pay, and I'll show you." While the epilog makes it clear that Emma Valentine is eventually captured by the authorities, it is a shame that she wasn't allowed to get away because she would have been a wonderful recurring villainess for West and Gordon to confront every season or so.

Capping 1966 was an award which left Agnes truly honored — receiving the Human Relations Award from B'nai B'rith for her "personal and dedicated commitment to enhancing individual dignity and respect and promoting better intergroup understanding."

For years Agnes had been wanting to work again with the man she considered the most brilliant and unappreciated director in the industry — Orson Welles. Time and again in interviews Agnes, throughout her career, would make her views about Orson known in the media — and perhaps through them to Orson himself. "I feel it is a disgrace, the way Hollywood and the press let him down, even turned against him. He's an authentic genius — and there are only one or two of those born in each era. He has many quirks, I admit it, but that is what makes him the talent he is. Those quirks give him fantastic imagination. When you take that away from an actor, you've taken the thing that really makes him go . . . makes him different."

But Welles did most of his films in Europe and lived in Spain — making it difficult for the two to see each other. When he did come to Hollywood, it was to make some quick cash to finance his own projects by appearing as an actor in increasingly inferior films for other directors or guest shots on variety shows; Orson appeared two or three times per year on *The Dean Martin Show* and was a regular guest on the talk show circuit. The work was very quick and Orson was often in and out of town — with little socializing. Agnes would occasionally show up in the audience of a show that he was appearing on just to get a glimpse of her old friend. According to Quint Benedetti, Welles seemed to be avoiding Agnes. Benedetti states that on several occasions when Agnes would read in the paper that Orson was in town, she would have Quint call him to invite him over for lunch or dinner, but that Welles "kept making excuses" to avoid seeing her. He speculates that perhaps Welles felt that over the years Agnes had allowed herself to "go commercial" by doing things like *Bewitched*, instead of more artistic work that he knew she was so capable of doing. After all, this was the same actress he considered the best in the world. But, somehow, if that is the case, it doesn't explain why Welles would fail Agnes for increasingly turning to more commercial projects when he, himself, had done the same — unless in Orson's case he felt that he *had* to do it to finance his own more ambitious artistic projects while Agnes had no excuses. Furthermore, it's not like Welles would not ever want to work with Agnes again. In the early 60's, Orson was announced by producer Dino De Laurentiis as the director of his ambitious film *The Bible* and Welles had approached Agnes about playing Sarah, but somehow Orson and De Laurentiis had a falling out and he never directed the film. (John Huston later did, but without Agnes.) Among Orson's never realized film projects was to update *The Magnificent Ambersons* thirty years later with the original cast, Tim Holt, Joseph Cotten, Anne Baxter and Agnes, reprising their original roles; once Tim Holt died in 1973, and then Agnes, the following year, this idea was naturally abandoned. It's a pity it was never done.

But there was one member of the Welles family who surely didn't want to distance herself from Agnes — Orson's 12-year-old daughter, Beatrice, who wrote to Agnes on April 25, 1967:

Dear Mrs. Moorehead,

I am Beatrice, Orson Welles's daughter and I have seen you in *Bewitched* and I thought you were wonderful. I see it every Sunday night, and I just read the letter you sent to Daddy, you say in the letter that you are going to London and then probably to Spain, I do wish you would come to Spain so I could meet you — all my friends have seen you in television and they like you very much (just you wait and see, when I will tell them that you may come to Spain they will go hysterical). Daddy at the moment is in Paris working very very hard and he comes and goes so he really doesn't see me a lot neither Mummy. I am at home alone because Mummy went to take some driving lessons and I could not go because I am going to study at six thirty, I am sorry now it is six twenty so I have to say goodbye.

Kind regards,
Beatrice Welles

Agnes was honored by her peers in the industry in 1967 with two Emmy nominations. She was nominated for Best Actress in a single dramatic performance for her role as Emma Valentine on *The Wild, Wild West* and, most interestingly, for Outstanding Continued Performance by an actress in a leading role in a comedy series for *Bewitched*. This was most interesting because this put Agnes in direct competition with Elizabeth Montgomery in the same category. The previous year Agnes had been nominated for *Bewitched* in the supporting category — but for some reason for the 66–67 season the Academy decided to put her in the best actress category. In the years to come, Agnes would be Emmy nominated four more times for *Bewitched*, but always in the supporting category. Nominated along with Agnes and Elizabeth were Lucille Ball for *The Lucy Show* and Marlo Thomas for *That Girl*. It is really no surprise though that neither Agnes nor Elizabeth emerged victorious (Lucy won) because they no doubt cancelled each other out. Elizabeth, in fact, would be nominated five times for an Emmy for *Bewitched* and lost each time. Sometimes the choices made by the television academy were maddening. In both 1969 and 1970 Elizabeth lost to Hope Lange for the much inferior *The Ghost and Mrs. Muir*. Agnes was equally unlucky with *Bewitched*. The years she probably had her best shot of winning the Emmy for playing Endora were 1966, when she lost to the recently-deceased Alice Pearce, and 1968, when she lost to fellow *Bewitched* actress Marion Lorne who also had recently passed away. There can be no doubt that in a sentimental town like Hollywood the fact that both actresses had recently died influenced the voting — despite the consistently wonderful performances by both Pearce and Lorne. According to Quint Benedetti, never winning the Emmy for *Bewitched* did disappoint Agnes, but it was nothing she would openly admit.

So she was not victorious for *Bewitched*, but she had an ace up her sleeve with the *Wild, Wild West* nomination. Ironically, it was Elizabeth

Robert Culp, Agnes and Elizabeth Mongomery, who presented Agnes with her only Emmy Award, 1967.

Montgomery, along with Robert Culp, who announced the category of Best Supporting Actress in a Drama series. Agnes' competition was Ruth Warwick for *Peyton Place* and Lucille Benson for *Cavalcade*. The award went to Agnes — her first and only Emmy. "She was very proud of that — she loved playing that character — Mrs. Valentine," said Quint Benedetti. She made a short speech of acceptance and thanks, as well as "surprise," before the beaming Montgomery. Telegrams and letters of congratulations came in by the dozens including one from Joan Crawford:

Agnes dear,

Congratulations on winning the Emmy for *Night of the Vicious Valentine*. I'm so happy for you. You were so beautiful on the Emmy awards show and your acceptance speech was so gracious. You added such elegance to the whole evening. Bless you, and my love to you.

Joan

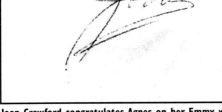

JOAN CRAWFORD

June 16, 1967

Agnes dear,

Congratulations on winning the Emmy for "Night of the Vicious Valentine". I'm so happy for you. You were so beautiful on the Emmy Awards Show and your acceptance speech was so gracious. You added such elegance to the whole evening.

Bless you, and my love to you.

Joan Crawford congratulates Agnes on her Emmy win.

She also heard from her old *Mayor of the Town* co-star Conrad Binyon — serving in the United States Air Force — writing to tell her, "it was simply a beautiful experience for me to see you awarded your Emmy. I just loved it when you said, "I don't believe it!" Well, I believed it and so did all the others who were pulling for 'The Fabulous Redhead.'"

Winning the Emmy was one of the highlights of Agnes' career and certainly the highlight of 1967. Overall, it was a relatively easy year. Her major work was on *Bewitched* and an occasional performance of her one-woman show. In between she was enjoying her home and the newfound wealth and popularity she had gained through *Bewitched* — especially among children who recognized her as Endora. On one occasion while visiting her mother in Reedsburg, Wisconsin, she and Mollie went to the Presbyterian Church that her father had once preached in for a Sunday service. In the pew ahead of her was a family consisting of a mother, father and a very restless little boy. As many children do when in church the little boy began to look around and finally he turned and came face to face with Aggie seated directly behind him. The boy's eyes opened wide and he tugged on his mother's sleeve, "Mommy, Mommy — it's that witch!"

In her spare time she was also taking lessons in sign language from a private instructor. Her eventual goal was to incorporate it into her one-woman shows and present special programs to schools for the deaf and mute. "I'm learning sign language when I can . . . I think it is marvelous what the people can do. I've seen them (deaf people) put on plays . . . it would be really exciting to be a part of this." But, perfectionist that she was, she knew that sign language had to be "expertly done" and she wouldn't do it unless she was proficient at it — unfortunately she never did utilize this into her one-woman shows.

All in all, the last few years had been quite satisfactory especially on a career level. The next few years would be more challenging on both the home and career fronts. As the 60's were coming to a close it seemed that children and their parents were often clashing on morals, beliefs and styles — and Agnes wasn't immune. Career-wise, she would continue to be part of a popular show but one which would soon be shaken when its leading man would suddenly depart mid-season. The times were a-changing, but Agnes wasn't, and she would, often quite outspokenly in the years ahead, lash out loudly against what she saw as declining morals and attitudes and a lack of faith which was tearing the country apart. As she was reaching her own late 60's, this lioness would have plenty to roar about.

14

THE LIONESS IN WINTER (1968–1971)

Paul Gregory believed that Agnes was ill-equipped at being a mother. Her career came first and everything else, including Sean, was secondary. Quint Benedetti says that Agnes could be "over indulgent" with Sean maternally, but strict in other areas — such as what clothing he should wear, the length of his hair and who his friends should be. Benedetti and Debbie Reynolds both agree that Agnes didn't allow Sean to "be himself" and, as a consequence, the boy became very "strong-willed" as he and Agnes were often on a collision course. But she could be very protective of the boy, even when tough love may have been the best course. Benedetti recalls that when they were on the road with the one-woman show that Agnes received a call from her maid, Freddie. Freddie told Agnes that her safety-deposit box, stored in her safe at her home in Beverly Hills, had been broken into. Freddie wondered if she should call the police. "No," Agnes responded. "It was Sean who did it." Benedetti believes that Agnes had a hard time demonstrating her affection not only toward Sean, but toward people in general. "I wouldn't say she was hard, but she was always very much in control of herself."

But, while Sean may have lacked the maternal love he needed, he, nevertheless, did live the privileged life of a celebrity's child. Larry Russell knew Sean off and on over the years when he and his brother came to live with their very wealthy grandmother in Beverly Hills. His brother became especially close to Sean — who liked to call himself Eric. "He told my brother once that he called himself Eric because he didn't want to be Sean." Occasionally, Agnes would also call him "Eric" to humor him but, "it was usually in her *Agnes Moorehead voice.*" Russell recalls that he and his brother were always welcome at Agnes' home. "She never talked down to me. She wasn't too fond of my grandmother, though, as she thought that gran was a 'libertine.' And if I was in Chez Agnese, I'd say that I was visiting because with all those houses (his grandmother owned several homes), my grandmother was cleaning. But she (Agnes) would laugh and say, 'She's never cleaned anything in her life, dearie, not even her own jewelry!' and then she'd give me an 'Endora' look and we'd both laugh." He says that Agnes taught him how to pour and serve tea and that they both used to joke that they were so good at it they could serve Queen Mary. "That harridan bitch on the screen bears no resemblance to the real person," Russell says of Agnes.

Russell speculates that Sean was possessive, that he wanted Agnes to belong only to him. He also believes that, like many adopted children or foster children, Sean grappled with abandonment issues. Agnes was often away from him, either on the road or when he was away at school, and that may have made him feel more abandoned and insecure. He says that when Agnes was gone, Sean could be very "bossy" and possessive of toys or even food when other children were over. Russell recalls that he occasionally helped Agnes in her garden, but when he came over once and Agnes wasn't there, Sean became very "snitty" with him, "but I just ignored him." Agnes once asked Russell if he liked Sean. "No," Russell honestly admitted, to which Agnes sighed, "Neither does anyone else."

Debbie Reynolds recalls Agnes as a "strict disciplinarian. She expected that from everyone around her — including her little boy." When Sean came home from Europe, where he was attending school, to live with Agnes in Beverly Hills in 1963, Reynolds recalled that like other teenagers of that era he wanted to grow his hair long but Agnes forbid it saying, "As long as you're in my home you'll behave as I say." She says that eventually Sean ran away for about three weeks (it has been speculated that he went to San Francisco) and that when he came back, his hair was long and Agnes told him, "I'll take you back as long as you cut your hair — but otherwise, no." He cut his hair but wasn't happy about it and, according to Debbie, an "ongoing duel of wills" erupted between the two and he wasn't about to bend and neither was she. Occasionally Reynolds did attempt to speak with Agnes regarding her inflexibility. "I told her that she didn't allow him any breathing space and if you really loved him to let him be a young person and she would say, 'No, my way is the right way.' I would agree with her but added, 'He has to learn and accept that on his own.'"

It was Debbie who Agnes called upon when Sean, at age 17, wanted to quit school and enlist in the military and go to Vietnam. Agnes was dead-set against it, wanting Sean to finish school. Debbie took Sean to a Veterans Hospital, where many Vietnam War vets were being treated so that he could both talk to the men and get a first-hand understanding of the realities of war. It seemed to work and Sean abandoned his efforts to enlist. Debbie felt she was able to accomplish more as a friend "talking straight" to Sean than Agnes often could as a demanding mother. Debbie felt sympathetic toward Sean. "I didn't find Sean to be unusual. Some people really think he was difficult. I found him to be well-spoken and nice with me and my kids and very sweet. He went to the best of schools. He learned to play piano and spoke French beautifully, but, when he rebelled, Agnes wouldn't allow it. She was inflexible."

Agnes blamed "outside influences" mainly from the type of people Sean wanted to associate with for causing a breech between them. Agnes would try to steer him away from them but the more she did this the more he would rebel and run away from home. He was influenced by the culture of the times. Young men wore long hair and wild clothes and Agnes forbade both. She didn't approve of the type of music which he wanted to listen to. "He wanted to be on his own, with his own friends," Agnes would recall. "We drifted apart." He wanted to experiment with alcohol and drugs, obviously something Agnes wouldn't condone, so like many teenagers he began to sneak it in. Debbie Reynolds wrote of Agnes finding empty beer cans in his room. When he graduated from high school in 1966, Agnes expected that he would go to college, but Sean didn't want to. He wanted to experience life a bit. Agnes tried to dissuade him. "He wouldn't listen . . . It was a shame, too. Because he is so bright so very bright."

After graduation, Sean left home. "Sean is nowhere to be found," Agnes wrote to Georgia Johnstone. "The police have a warrant out for his arrest as he evidently was cited for a traffic violation and didn't show up. As far as I know, he hadn't a license to drive. It's quite a heartbreak — he is absolutely out of his mind — but I've done all I can. I'm only grateful I didn't adopt him. My lawyers say I am not liable for anything he might do. It's tragic — life deals some difficult blows. It's depressing, Georgia." Johnstone sympathetically responded, "Barron (Polon, AM's New York theatrical agent) called me when he returned from L.A. and told me about the latest difficulty with Sean. It is so hard for me to believe this young man could turn out this way after having had so many wonderful opportunities. He has had the best; you've given him everything money could buy. What in the world is the matter with him? Perhaps he was given too much Agnes.

This so often causes a person to make no effort of their own." Johnstone goes on to add that Agnes must be "depressed" with this "disappointment" and summed it up, "You have done your best. If Sean is so stupid as to throw away all the advantages he's been given one can only hope that one day, when this reliably old world has given him the knocks you and I know he will get, he'll look back and realize what a wonderful life he had with you." This letter was sent to Agnes in September; a month later, Agnes was still worried about Sean and Johnstone wrote back, "Please try not to worry about Sean. I hope and pray everything will turn out well. You never can tell about children. Sometimes they suddenly become responsible people."

According to Debbie Reynolds the break finally came when Agnes found a dismantled gun in Sean's room. "She knew he was very angry at her, and finding a gun made her afraid of something drastic. She confronted him about it and he denied it." She took Sean up to his room and opened the drawer where she had found it, and "with that, she told him to leave." Asked what she thought happened to Sean, Miss Reynolds, silent for a moment, softly said, "I don't know for sure, but I think he became one of the children of the street." He did leave and he never came back. For the last six years of Agnes' life she never saw him again, though she would occasionally hear from friends about him and once or twice he may have tried to contact Agnes for money, but she had washed her hands of him.

Agnes later told a reporter, "All I can do is pray that he'll follow the principles I've taught him and make his way independently and successfully."

What became of Sean? Nobody really knows. It is one of the mysteries of Agnes' life. Once he left, it was as if all traces of him vanished. There was speculation that he finally went to Vietnam. But Larry Russell says that Sean and Russell's brother, Mark, went to Switzerland and for a while lived off the good graces of actress Paulette Goddard. Eventually Russell's brother returned, but not with Sean, and he too lost contact with him. Quint Benedetti says that Agnes would occasionally, while they were alone together driving across country to yet another one-woman show, let her guard down. She would mention Sean, wondering what became of him and questioning, though not really wanting an answer, what she had done wrong.

II

By the late 60's Quint Benedetti was accompanying Agnes across country by automobile in his role as stage manager and promoter of her one-woman shows. Benedetti maintains that his business know-how in negotiating the deal to locate her acting school at the Santa Monica Playhouse had impressed Agnes so much that he was made correspondence secretary and eventually her road manager, and in doing so greatly increased the fee she charged for her one-woman show from $1,500 per show to approximately $5,000. Quint says that when they drove across country Agnes would open up to him in a way she would never do otherwise. Often they would travel by automobile because of Agnes' dislike of airplanes with Quint driving or her chauffeur, Rochelle. What bonded her to Quint was religion; two of Quint's brothers were Catholic priests. They could spend hours speaking about theology — not that Quint was an especially religious man by this time, but he grew up in a very strict Catholic household. "She was pious but she could also be outrageous," Quint recalls. They also enjoyed playing standard car traveling games such as "what does that cloud look like" or who could identify the most license plates from different states. Agnes enjoyed stopping in small cafes just to have a hamburger "drenched with catsup." Fans recognized her and approached her, but if it got to be too much, Quint would "politely, but in a firm way, tell them that 'Miss Moorehead is trying to enjoy her meal.'" While Agnes usually made time for her fans, she didn't like being disturbed when she dined. Besides religion, Agnes would open up on other personal subjects which she rarely spoke of to anyone else — such as her failed marriages. To Quint, she described Jack Lee as "an abusive alcoholic" and said that Robert Gist "just used her to get ahead." She also let him in on her feelings about never winning the Oscar. "She said that it isn't everything, but she would have liked to have won."

When it came to paying her help, Quint maintains that Agnes was very tight and would "forget" to pay them or try to underpay them. Occasionally, Freddie and Polly would come to Benedetti and ask him to remind Agnes that they hadn't been paid. "Sometimes you had to press her about what was owed, saying you owe me X amount of dollars and be firm about it." It wasn't only her housekeepers who got shortchanged, but also himself. "I would tell her we need to sit down and discuss it and go over the figures. I had everything down, the bookings and the expenses, everything that was owed, and she would get mad because it was a business thing and I would tell her, 'you owe me this,' and she was very tight." Eventually she would pay them what was owed. But Agnes, herself, "wasn't a good business woman." She was continually, despite the large income she got from *Bewitched*, in debt — primarily because she was "pouring thousands and thousands of dollars into building her dream house" on her farm in Ohio, where Quint maintains that Agnes intended to go into semi-retirement by 1975. Yet if she saw an expensive antique, "she wouldn't pass it up." While Agnes could be very tight when it came to wages, she

With a fan in the early 1970s.

was generous in other ways with gifts or including her employees in her lavish parties. Quint has come to the conclusion that Agnes was a "very complicated lady," someone who could tell one person one story and another person a different story — whichever best suited her purposes at the time.

But, despite this, Quint was "very fond" of Agnes because "she gave me back my self-respect." When he came to work for her he had just gone through a difficult divorce and was estranged from his two daughters. He had been a gay man living a lie. When at home he was a family man, but when he was out on the road he would have one-night stands with other men. Due to his strict Catholic upbringing he often felt guilt. By the time he began working with Agnes he was an "emotional wreck." "I felt I was the worst person in the world," Quint recalls of that time, "but Agnes gave me a chance." He was able to rebuild his life. While he says, "I came out (of the closet) a little bit to myself. But not to anyone else," he accepted his sexuality and began to take part in the Hollywood gay social scene. He says that despite Agnes' strong fundamentalist beliefs she was very accepting of homosexuals. He says that a choreographer, who was gay, lived in an apartment on her property, and that at one point Agnes even asked Quint if he wanted to move in, but because he was involved with somebody at the time he declined. Many of her close friends were known to be gay in the industry, including her frequent escort and friend, Cesar Romero. Still, Quint didn't feel that he could speak freely with Agnes regarding his own homosexuality. He once told her that he was in therapy and she scoffed, "All you need is God and the Bible."

In their cross-country travels, Quint also got to know Mollie. "We would drive to Reedsburg quite regularly or she would fly out to California," recalls Quint. He remembers Mollie as "quite outspoken" and when people would come up to her and say something about Agnes, "she would say, 'I want you to know I have two daughters,' not forgetting Margaret." Mollie was the only one who could "upstage" Agnes; when Mollie was around, Agnes was "like a little girl . . . instead of the strong woman I knew. She was never short with her mother and all Mollie had to do was say 'Now Agnes — Shush' — and Agnes would obey her." Mollie made an impression on others who got to know her, including Paul Gregory. "Her mother was very sweet, but tried to convert people," Paul recalls. "Agnes was the same way and I always withdrew from her when she started with the Bible thumping; when she did that I would say, 'Time for champagne,' which was our code phrase for 'change the subject.'" Paul also says that one reason that Mollie didn't live with Agnes was because Agnes really didn't want her to. "Agnes was very religious but she also liked to have fun and liked to serve champagne and a little wine which her mother wouldn't have approved of."

(Photo by Carl Dickson)

The house in Reedsburg, Wisconsin where Mollie Moorehead lived and Agnes visited often.

Jeanne Marking, of Reedsburg, Wisconsin, would remember Mollie as a "most gracious lady" who always dressed well and wanted her clothes to "fit perfectly." She described Mollie as having a relatively small stature that required special alterations to fit her body which was "short-waisted and slightly large in girth." Mrs. Marking did a great deal of sewing and alterations for both Mollie and Mollie's companion, Grace Conklin. "They were very appreciative of the fact that I could sew for them with results that satisfied them. I remember specifically doing a pink lace outfit for Mollie," Marking recalled. "It was a particularly flattering color for her. She also liked purple and dressed a bit more ostentatiously than did Grace." Mrs. Marking describes Mollie and Grace as "devoted companions" who shared their lives together, with Mollie being a widow and Grace never marrying. She recalls that Mollie and Grace usually brought their little white poodle with them wherever they went, "the dog often had curlers in her hair, wore pink ribbons in hair, little sweaters or vests and was truly an enjoyable part of their lives." Occasionally Mollie, Grace and the little poodle went to the local pizza parlor; "they . . . would tuck the little dog into their coat or somewhere where she would not be noticed."

Mrs. Marking had the opportunity to meet Agnes once at an afternoon luncheon. She described Agnes as "a very devoted daughter and a most interesting and enchanting woman . . . I was always a fan of her's and watched her performances whenever I had the opportunity." After Agnes died, Mollie gave Mrs. Marking a pair of Agnes' earrings "which I still have."

According to family friend Gordon Emery, Agnes enjoyed coming to Reedsburg because it allowed her to "unwind and let her hair down and everyone knew her not as 'Miss Moorehead,' but as Agnes." Emery recalls Agnes as "not flamboyant in real life but she was heavily made up all the time, but then so was her mother. They both liked to wear very expensive and gaudy jewelry." Occasionally Agnes would be driven to Reedsburg by her chauffer, Rochelle. Emery recalls that Rochelle was "very protective of Agnes. When he was around, he wore a black suit, black hat and white gloves. If he drove her anywhere he would stand out by the car while she was shopping or running some errand and he would just be using a rag wiping spots — whether they were there or not — from the car."

Emery recalls Mollie as independent, well into her 90's. "I once asked her if she was afraid of living alone and she said, 'Not at all,' and she went over and opened up a drawer and showed me a revolver she kept." But as the years went on she did begin to exhibit some eccentric behavior. "One day Mollie called," Emery remembered, "and told me that her dog had been sick for a couple of days and had not gotten out of his bed. Well, I said I would come over and take a look. and when I got over there I checked out the dog and he was as stiff as could be — he had been dead for at least three days and Mollie hadn't really noticed."

Grace Conklins at piano and Agnes' mother Mollie with her cello. Circa 1966.

In the spring of 1967, with *Bewitched* on hiatus, Agnes went to visit Mollie and Grace Conkling. Like Mollie, Grace was quite elderly. The devoted roommates could often be heard in the evenings in the Music Room at their home on Walnut Street in Reedsburg making music — Mollie on cello and Miss Conkling at the piano. Agnes arrived in May when the unexpected happened and Grace suffered a heart attack. Agnes went into detail in a letter to Georgia Johnstone: "It must have been divine guidance that brought me home at this time. Mother's companion, Grace, who has lived with her for over thirty years — died Sunday morning of a heart attack — Mother called me around 2:00 A.M. and by 2:30 she had gone to her eternal house." Agnes said the "doctor stayed with us," but "details" of the funeral planning had fallen into Agnes' hands. She reported that she was "exhausted" from calling florists, mortuaries and so on. "It has helped my mother and that is what is important. I hate to leave her alone. She says she will be alright, but the loneliness will come in great gusts and she is heartsick. I have never seen anyone die before. I found myself in awe and reverence — Strange emotions — one is so helpless when it's God's will to take one of his lambs home."

Another death, early in 1967, also deeply affected Agnes; her old friend and radio colleague, Harry McNaughton passed away just shy of his 71st birthday. McNaughton's widow wrote to Agnes, and Agnes forwarded her note to Georgia requesting that she "respond very sympathetically," adding, "I liked Harry very much."

In November 1967, Agnes took offense over a newspaper profile of her printed by the *Kansas City Star*, which painted her in a somewhat unflattering light. Agnes felt so strongly she wrote to the writer: "I've read and reread the results of the interview . . . and my reaction is one of puzzlement and disbelief. I'm puzzled because, having been raised a Christian, I never 'sneer' at anyone. Since you've used this term a number of times I wonder why you can't remember one single pleasant or gentle comment I made during the entire discussion. Is it because you believe the type of article you've written is what the public wants to read. I'm certain you didn't intend the public to think of me as 'blunt and overbearing,' 'sneering,' or 'moans,' 'drawls,' 'speaks disgustedly,' 'twisting her mouth . . . down in disdain' 'with a sneer' and finally 'sneered' again. Yet this is the impression anyone reading the article will receive. How could it be otherwise? I choose to believe you wanted to show my talent for acting, and I am grateful to you for that, but in doing so you made me seem like an ugly person. I hope we shall meet when I visit Kansas City again, That meeting might provide an opportunity for us to know each other better." In an accompanying letter to Georgia Johnstone, Agnes was still venting. "How about this?" she wrote. "I never sneered at anyone in my life let alone the press, but here is a woman who loves her snide remarks and her ability to destroy you . . ."

(Courtesy of Wade Ballard)

With Mike Douglas, early 70's.

Agnes went into 1968 hard at work on *Bewitched* and by the spring would be on the road. Leaving L.A. for Chicago and a series of personal appearances from March 26–29, and then to Reedsburg to visit her mother until April 2, she was back to Chicago for a couple of days and then an appearance with her one-woman show in Rock Island, Illinois on April 6. She flew into Las Vegas for Debbie Reynolds' opening at the Tropicana on April 7, and was back home by April 8.

In May 1968, Agnes appeared as a presenter on the Emmy Awards and turned an embarrassing situation into one of the highlights of that year's program. Agnes would call the program "chaos." She had been asked to present an award with Melvyn Douglas. "Of course he (Douglas) knew I was supposed to be there," Agnes would recall, "but (host) Dick Van Dyke didn't. When I appeared Dick looked at me as though I was Sonny Tufts."

She didn't have any cue cards, as they were all written for Douglas, "and he never suggested that I read any of the nominations, so I stood there — mute. I thought of several things I wanted to say but I have Charles Laughton and Orson Welles to thank for thinking on my feet and exerting self-discipline." Finally, after realizing how ridiculous it was for Agnes to just stand there while he was reading all the nominations, Douglas turned to Agnes and asked, "Why don't you read one of the nominations?" Coolly and with poise, Agnes responded, "Oh no, it's your turn." It was one of the biggest laughs of the night. NBC sent her two dozen roses and a note of apology the next day.

In June, Agnes received an invitation from Broadway producer Alexander Cohen to appear in a musical version of *The Madwoman of Challot* with Angela Lansbury. She declined. That spring and summer of 1968, Agnes was out on the road performing her "one-woman show" almost constantly, returning to Beverly Hills by early July to begin filming *Bewitched* which was going back into production with its fifth season. In late August Agnes reported to Georgia Johnstone that she was "contemplating writing a book, after much inquiries as to publishers." The president of her fan club, a man named Roy Buchanan, was also working on a book about Agnes' career and Agnes, through Georgia, would occasionally answer his inquiries. Had she been serious about doing her own book, clearly Buchanan would have been cut off as she would not want dueling biographies. In September 1968 she wasn't sure of her future plans with *Bewitched*, writing to Georgia Johnstone, ". . . I don't know whether *Bewitched* will go on — or whether I will be on it. I have asked for more money if they take up an option — but if they don't I'll have to book a fall tour — and so I've been waiting to see what they are going to do."

III

The filming of the fifth season of *Bewitched* was going along relatively smoothly. From late June to late November 1968 the cast had completed roughly twenty episodes for the season. But in the past two years Dick York had been a man working under almost constant pain from the severe back injury he had suffered ten years earlier making *They Came to Cordura*. Despite the pain, York was a trouper and his suffering was never evident in his still-energetic performances. York was also at the top of his game in Hollywood. For the 67–68 seasons (the fourth) York had finally been recognized by his peers and nominated for an Emmy as Best Lead Actor in a comedy series. It was a long overdue honor. Time and again the Academy had nominated people like Bob Crane for *Hogan's Heroes* and Don Adams for his very funny, but strictly one-noted Maxwell Smart on *Get Smart*, while ignoring York's consistently three-dimensional performances on *Bewitched*. York not only was funny but he was also incredibly romantic and sweet in his scenes with Elizabeth Montgomery. He was, in this author's opinion, with the exception of Dick Van Dyke, the best light comedy actor on television during the 1960's. York's wife, Joey, recalls that Paul Lynde came up to her at a season wrap party and told her he felt Dick was the "funniest man" he ever met.

After the Thanksgiving holidays in 1968, the *Bewitched* company had returned to film an episode titled "Daddy Does His Thing," with guest star Maurice Evans appearing as Samantha's father Maurice. York had a prominent role in the original script of this episode. He was not feeling well and for the first time he didn't even look well on camera — in the existing footage he looks thin, drawn and tired. There was a reason for this — he was sick. He had not been able to sleep, he was suffering from chills and his chronic back pain was acting up. In the morning he shot a couple of scenes with Montgomery and Evans, feeling "confused and disoriented."

At lunch he went to his doctor, who gave him a shot of Vitamin B12 to help get him through the day. He returned to the set without eating. The next shot would be a scene with Evans on a scaffold (as if Maurice and Darrin were levitating above a room). Dick climbed up the scaffold and sat there with Evans as the scene was being lit — fifteen feet up in the air. As the time went on, and the procedure continued with a tiny light flickering in front of his eyes, York began to feel increasingly ill. He is trying to go over his lines with Evans but finally it began to be too much for him and he asked a member of the crew to help him down. As he was being helped down, York apparently suffered a seizure and the next thing he would remember was waking up lying on the floor with his friend David White, "my dearest friend . . . on the set," looking panic-stricken over him. York was rushed to the hospital. He would never return to the set.

York's wife, Joey, was contacted and William Asher, who picked her up, drove her to the hospital. Mrs. York says that she was the one who forced the issue of Dick leaving *Bewitched* with Asher prior to his visiting Dick in his room. Joey asked him not to let Dick continue with the show — it was killing him. Asher went into his room and asked him, "Do you want to quit?" Dick replied, "If it's all right with you, Billy." Asher told him, "OK, kid, I'll tell 'em." Then, for the first and last time, Dick and Asher hugged.

It wasn't as easy as that. ABC and the sponsors didn't want him to leave. He was the lead male actor in one of the biggest hits on television. According to Mrs. York, Screen Gems executives came to the York home several times to persuade him to stay — but Dick decided to put his health first. No announcement was immediately made. In all that time, from the period when Dick suffered his seizure until the official announcement that he was leaving the show, neither Elizabeth Montgomery nor Agnes called him. Mrs. York is philosophical about this. She says it is "status quo" in show business. You work with someone then it ends and people "just move on." Still, over the years she has heard that Dick was fired from *Bewitched*, and sensational rumors were made which depicted her husband as a "pill popper" — to which Mrs. York responds, "If he were (a pill popper), how could he have given such consistently fine performances?"

Agnes wrote to Georgia Johnstone on February 2, 1969. "Have been going at breakneck speed and today I have just stayed in bed all day. Dick York has *resigned* — back and mental ailments — and we, Elizabeth and I are on the treadmill — they cancelled Monaco (Agnes was to appear as a judge at a film festival in Monaco at the request of her old friend, Princess Grace)which was a disappointment to me — but we are shooting back to back and I have to be here for work. The new fellow won't go on until fall — Dick Sargent — I don't know him but Bill thinks he is very good. By the way, I got all I asked for in the contract — so here we go for another

6th year." Publicly, Agnes acknowledged that she was "sad" to see York go but, "it happens all the time in the theatre," adding, "of course it is a big adjustment for us." A family friend, Gordon Emery, recalls that Agnes was "concerned about the first Darrin" and that when he left the show, it "created quite a crisis — Agnes was very loyal to him and concerned about him and if the change would mesh. I got the impression she was very close to the original Darrin." But for whatever reason, either because she didn't want to disturb him at a time when he was recuperating or because she decided it might embarrass him or herself to do so, she never spoke to York again.

But, clearly, Agnes did not take the decision well. For a woman known for her graciousness and professionalism, her initial meeting with York's replacement, Dick Sargent, did not go well. According to Herbie J Pilato, the *Bewitched* biographer, David White told him what transpired on Sargent's first day on the set for a script reading. In front of the entire cast, including Sargent, "Agnes very slowly, though firmly stated, 'I don't like change.'" Pilato also states, "Agnes Moorehead had a very strong working relationship with Dick York for five years. And then, he

(Courtesy of Wade Ballard)

The 1969 cast of *Bewitched*: Maurice Evans, Agnes, Elizabeth Montgomery, Erin Murphy and Darren #2, Dick Sargent.

wasn't there anymore. It was like losing her left arm. And she could do nothing about it. She wasn't in a position of power to have the final casting say over the series and, in essences, she wasn't really Endora, Agnes Moorehead's power, in this regard, was limited."

Agnes did feel she was on a "treadmill" because Elizabeth was pregnant yet again and, rather than taking the traditional spring hiatus, the *Bewitched* company was kept in production to film several episodes for the series' sixth season before she would take her maternity leave. That Agnes also received a big boost in her salary wasn't unexpected either. With York gone, it was imperative that they keep Agnes and keep her happy. To have lost both York *and* Agnes would have been fatal to the show. It is also likely that Elizabeth probably would not have continued with the show had "Mother" not continued on.

In August 1969, Agnes' home in Beverly Hills was robbed while she was away. In a letter to Agnes, Johnstone expressed her concerns. "I'm in a state of despair about my country. Life in N.Y. City is rapidly becoming a hell. When one considers moving out the question arises as to where one can feel peace and safety? I have no answer." She goes on to state, "What is the story of the Tate business (The Sharon Tate murders at the hands of Charles Manson and his disciples)? Can't believe a word I read the papers these days. What about the Kennedy mess? (Edward Kennedy's accident at Chappaquiddick)."

December 30, 1969

Dearest Agnes:

First of all, I want you to know how disappointed we were that we could not make your Christmas party, but it was impossible. I hear it was a smash as always.

Thank you for the mistletoe. It is in its rightful place, but unless you get to Palm Springs during the holidays, I'm afraid you won't get your kiss from Gary.

Love,
Lucy and Gary

Lucille Ball to Agnes, 1969.

Agnes convinced her mother to join her in California for the Christmas holidays. "Christmas has come and gone for another hectic year!" she wrote to Georgia Johnstone. "What a time I had getting Mother out of her nest and bask here for the winter." She was apparently working on her book. "I have written some — but with all the work, I've just got bogged down. But it will all be straightened out one of these days — 3 more years of *Bewitched* without options! Can you believe it? Well one can't be choosy these days — so many are out of work — I'm very lucky!" In a subsequent letter written to Johnstone two weeks later, she wrote, "Mother seems to be contented but looking forward to this country house. What a time to build! — but then it could be worse. I think we are in for a recession — What does Bill (Georgia's husband) think of the stock market?"

The house which Agnes is referring to was being built on her farm in Ohio. It was Agnes' plan to go into semi-retirement at the new house by the mid-70's with her mother living with her. But she, as Quint Benedetti noted, was spending a fortune on it. In April 1970, Agnes refers to the problems she is having in a letter to Johnstone: "Now the farm is coming along. But the contractor has made so many mistakes — I can't tell you. He burned a little house down, that was in need of a great deal of repair, but I was going to fix it up for a studio. And without my permission, burned it down. The roof and outside were not finished and no heat, we nearly froze, but the handy man started making fires in the fireplace and with the help of electric heaters we managed to survive. I didn't want Mother to go through all this turmoil but she thinks it a great adventure and won't stir from the place. I fired the contractor who swore at me and threatened to spread my name all over the papers — I don't know what for — but some detrimental reason. I have paid him $85,000 in cash which he says is just 'spit' — and furnished myself — the heating, dry walls, plumbing accessories — freezers, washers, stoves, etc. — and still the outside of the house isn't finished. I have now had permission to tap the main gas line and I hope they will have it on when I get back! What a mess." She summed it up, "I can't tell you the many things that have to be done. It's quite disheartening. I fired the contractor — they have never seen a 'witch' at work — and I use the term loosely."

That spring Agnes got yet another invitation to do a prominent stage production, to replace Katharine Hepburn in the stage musical *Coco*, the story of fashion designer Coco Chanel, a part Agnes would have been ideal in. But, as with most of her offers during the *Bewitched* years, she had to decline. "I couldn't with my show going back to filming in Salem in the first week in June."

The cast went to Salem, Massachusetts to film several episodes of *Bewitched* in the early summer of 1970. They were mobbed and huge crowds gathered below their windows at their hotel and called out for Elizabeth or Agnes. Agnes would sum up the experience, "Salem was frightening. The crowds tore our clothes off and our hair out. Real Witchery."

In November 1970, Georgia Johnstone wrote Agnes once again

Out on the town, circa 1970.

complaining about contemporary morals. "The enclosed clipping reminded me of our conversation some time ago. You said that 'before long some group would try to go to the bathroom onstage.' Well that is old hat by now, having been done often and then it was followed by masturbation, the sexual act between male and female, then between males and I thought, well now they've reached the limit, there is nothing more to do and they'll get back to clean, talented writing and acting. Well how wrong can I be? Judging from the enclosed they've only scratched the surface. Did you ever read anything more disgusting in your life? It makes me want to secede from the human race." Agnes responded, "Honestly it's getting to be frightful, this stage text — it's evil. We are living in precarious times. I really think it's the last days, but of course, one is subject to mockery and laughter, but too many things are falling into place. Imagine trying to make points by this means, it will be reaped in time." I'm not sure what clipping Georgia sent to Agnes, but to cause Agnes to proclaim her belief that we were in the "last days" it must have truly offended her senses.

But Agnes wasn't keeping her opinion of contemporary morals only between herself and Georgia, she used her status in the industry and access to the media to speak out. The *Detroit Free Press* asked the question, "Will there be Brotherhood in the 70's?," to which Agnes was selected to give a response. "Unless the country and the people in it go back to some Christian principles, there will be no peace. We must really care for each other. Just being polite is caring for your fellow man, but these times call for a great deal more than that. There is nothing more inspiring or so infectious as a good example. I am a religious person and I think that the hope of the world is in the Prince of Peace whose principles, if they were followed, would bring a greater understanding between human beings."

She told the *LA Times* that the youth of 1970 needed more discipline. "Materialism has brought about confusion and decadence. The youth of today have their eyes open to what harm has been done by measuring a man by the size of his bank account, and I feel sorry that so few of them know where to turn because they have lost respect for those closest to them." And, "Permissiveness in society springs from a lack of standards. There must be a rule of behavior, an appreciation of basic values." Perhaps she was thinking of Sean when she said that.

When asked about *Oh, Calcutta,* the play where most of the cast sheds its clothes and appears nude on stage, Agnes said, "Nudity begins at home. After all who wants to see everybody flying around in their birthday suit? It takes all the magic and illusion out of the theatre."

Photoplay magazine asked "Should prostitution be legalized?" Actress Barbara McNair wrote in the affirmative. Agnes argued differently. "Legalizing prostitution wouldn't make any difference these days anyway. The whole country is loose, so what's the difference . . . I don't care what everybody else is doing. I just look at whether it's right or wrong."

This Lioness found plenty to roar about in this turbulent era of open sex, drugs, and rock n roll, protests in the streets over civil rights, women's rights, gay rights and the war in Vietnam. If only the young people would go to church and their parents would stop pampering them. Agnes had become the ultimate establishment figure. After years of publicly staying neutral in political campaigns, she embraced the conservative movement and openly supported her old friend Ronald Reagan the both times he ran for Governor. She felt that the State had to get tough with the universities and colleges where decadence was "running rampant." In 1972, when the Democrats nominated George McGovern, the antiwar candidate who was painted as pro-abortion and pro-acid, she openly came out for Richard Nixon.

In April 1970, Agnes received a great honor from Rep. Phillip Philbin (R-MA) when she was recognized as one of the "Great Living Bay Staters" from her home state of Massachusetts. Rep. Philbins' words of commendation were read into the Congressional Record: "I deemed it a special honor as well as a pleasure to present the award to the famous Miss Moorehead, a distinguished and delightful lady . . . Her entire professional career comprises one success after another in virtually every field of the performing, dramatic arts . . . She won fame as a founder, an organizer, an innovator, a charter member, and player with many of the most famous people in the theater . . . Her great talents stand out like the Washington Monument, and have won her credits and honors too numerous to mention." It was truly a great honor on behalf of her birth state and genuinely deserved.

V

In the fall of 1970, while she was filming *Bewitched*, Agnes accepted one of her few lead roles in a motion picture, an offer by producer Jack Clement to appear in the film, *Dear, Dead Delilah*. "The seven weeks we spent filming . . . had Agnes darting back and forth to the West Coast and moonlighting between *Bewitched* segments in order to be with us," production manager Fred Carmichael would recall. "She would phone me one day and say she could be on such and such a flight and would be able to stay three or four days. And she would add that if I met her at the plane, allowed a half hour to the mansion where we were shooting, she could be in makeup immediately and work through the night if necessary. What a trouper she was! Words can never capture her almost desperate desire for perfection and total dedication to her craftsmanship."

Delilah is a gothic horror film shot on the cheap in Nashville by a company called Southern Star Pictures. It tells the story of a woman who as a young girl is accused of killing her mother with an ax. All the evidence points to her. After many years in a correctional center for women she is released, now middle-aged (the character "Luddy" is played by Patricia Carmichael, wife of the production manager of the picture, Fred). While in a park sketching, she is accidentally knocked unconscious and taken to the mansion of a wheelchair-bound woman named Delilah (Agnes) who takes a liking to her and invites her to stay on as her housekeeper. While Luddy is in Delilah's home, many strange things begin to happen to her, including waking to find a bloody hatchet in bed with her. Delilah is surrounded by greedy relatives who may wish to speed up her death. They use the strange circumstances of Luddy's mother's death, and her incarceration for the crime, in their own efforts to do away with Delilah — or do they?

During production, one of the younger players came on the set wearing a cast on his broken arm. Agnes, always the professional, took the actor aside and lectured him on his unprofessional behavior in allowing such a thing to happen. Fred Carmichael would recall, "Agnes told him how silly he was to risk himself when he had signed to do a film and (that he) 'belonged to the producer and owed it to the producer to take care of himself.' Then she launched into a long speech on the meaning of craftsmanship in our business and what the actor ought to do about it and what he should bring to it." Carmichael would recall that he often wished that lecture Agnes gave the young actor had been recorded so he could "play it for each young actor whenever they came for an audition or interview. It was glorious. She had such a respect and love for the business."

The last scene that Agnes shot was her own death scene, which occurs at the end of the film. In the scene, Agnes has collapsed and is on the ground and several different takes were to be done of her position on the ground. It was a long shoot and between shots, Carmichael asked Agnes if she wanted to rest in a trailer. "No," Agnes answered. "It would waste time to have to get me back into the same position." So she spent her time, between takes, lying on the cold ground. Carmichael recalls that when on the set Agnes commanded respect, "she seemed to demand it by her very presence more than anything else." He said the grips would stop swearing when she showed up on the set. "Once when I brought her onto the set, they were ripping off four letter words, she gave a quiet 'shhh' and that was it."

Carmichael recalls Agnes' "delicious sense of humor." He remembered that they once went to a local diner for lunch and the manager, apparently not knowing who she was, asked her if anyone had ever mistaken her for Endora in *Bewitched*. To which Agnes replied, "Yes, I was, and would you like to be turned into a frog?" The manager "literally" backed out of the room "and was not seen again." He says that she would often do impressions and one which really "astounded" them was her "excellent" imitation of Hermione Gingold from the play, *A Little Night Music*.

Carmichael recalls Agnes' tender side and her love of animals. On one occasion he drove her from Nashville to her farm in Ohio, a ten-hour trip, and the entire time Agnes had a kitten on her lap — a stray she had found and would give a home to on her farm.

Though the film was shot in 1970, but was not released until 1972, and then mostly in southern and Midwestern markets. In a letter to Agnes dated January 17, 1971, Fred Carmichael wrote that he had just seen a rough-cut of the picture and wanted to let her know how things were progressing. "The film was most interesting and brought back so many memories. Had seen some of the cutting, and I must say we do have an excellent editor, and was great to see the whole thing more or less in order . . . I think you will be very pleased with the picture." He ends the chatty letter by mentioning that he "trusts the movie with Shelley went well. She is a — well, volatile person. Pat (who had recently directed her in a stage show) had her troubles but they ended up respecting each other in their respective areas which is always a good thing." Carmichael is referring to a movie which Agnes had actually shot after *Dear, Dead Delilah,* but would be released before it, another horror film, *What's the Matter With Helen?*, and Shelley was the wonderful but temperamental actress, Shelley Winters. The film was co-produced by Debbie Reynolds, who asked Agnes to appear in a cameo role as Sister Alma, an Aimee Semple McPherson-like Evangelist. Reynolds, herself, had her run-ins with Winters. "We had some of the biggest battles of my life. I loved the picture and hated the work (Thanks to Shelley)."

Agnes as Sister Alma in *What's the Matter with Helen?*, with Shelley Winters. 1971.

In February 1971, Agnes was sent a script for the film *Dutch Treat*, written by Marc Zagoren and David Meranze, whose accompanying note said that they were "most eager to show you (the script) because we think you would be so marvelous in the leading role." The film is described as a "love story about an energetic sixty-eight-year-old married woman from Philadelphia who goes to visit her daughter in Amsterdam, and while there meets a striking Portuguese gentleman a few years her senior. Much of the movie is comedy, but any emotional involvement late in life is by nature poignant, and so we have tried to make the movie's resolution touching as well as charming." The script is included in the Moorehead collection at the Wisconsin State Historical Society and it is indeed a charming project and makes one wonder why she turned down such an opportunity to do this film — certainly it gave her more to do than *Delilah* or *Helen,* but the film was never produced at all.

She was staying busy appearing in features and made-for-television movies between *Bewitched.* In the spring of 1971 she did the first of the two movies she would appear in for ABC during the 71–72 season, *Marriage: Year One.* It was actually a pilot for a TV series and starred Sally Field and Robert Pratt as a young married couple, and it explores the difficulties they encounter in their first year of marriage — the period of adjustment. Veteran actor William Windom played Sally Field's father, with Agnes appearing as her grandmother. Windom doesn't remember much of this film, but does recall his first encounter with Agnes. "My only memory of

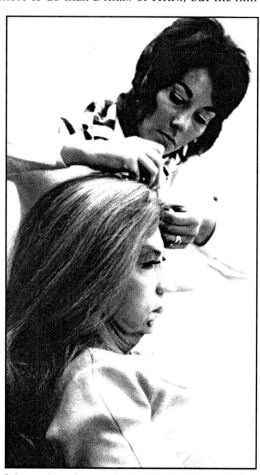

(Courtesy of Wade Ballard)

Being made up for an episode of *Night Gallery,* 1970.

Marriage: Year One was the sight of a dubious Miss Moorehead barging into my dressing room to see if I 'looked young enough to play her son.'" Windom adds, "Naturally I have enjoyed her work as has most of the civilized world, but that moment was mine alone."

Conrad Binyon stayed in touch with Agnes through the years. He had left acting and, due to his interest in aviation, he began a career in the United States Air Force. In the early 1970's he had befriended a fellow pilot, David Guerra, his wife Dora and their two young children, Judith Ann and David Andrew, known as "Tiger." Both children suffered from a rare form of paralysis called Verdnig-Hoffman Amyotonia, today known as Spinal Muscular Atrophy, a terminal form of Muscular Dystrophy. "Tiger" died a few days after his 4th birthday.

(Courtesy of Wade Ballard)

The Lioness, circa 1971.

Dora Guerra remembers, "The program, *Bewitched*, in which Ms. Agnes Moorehead played a leading role was a very popular one. The children and I watched it without fail, and Judith Ann was immediately drawn to Ms. Moorehead. She became what today would be called an 'Agnes Moorehead groupie.' She truly couldn't wait for the program to come on, so we could sit down to watch her favorite 'witch.' During one of Conrad's visits to San Antonio, *Bewitched* happened to be on and Conrad sat down to watch it with the kids while I cooked for us. Judith Ann, who at the time must have been 6, began to tell Conrad how WONDERFUL Ms. Moorehead was, and she went on and on about her. Conrad let her carry on, and then informed Judith Ann that Ms. Moorehead was a good friend of his. Judith Ann was speechless. She was absolutely transformed with awe, and began to ply Conrad with questions about Ms. Moorehead. She just couldn't hear enough about her. Conrad told Judith Ann he'd talk to Ms. Moorehead about her and suggested maybe, just maybe, Judith Ann would hear from her.

"Weeks and weeks later, an autographed picture, dedicated to Judith Ann, came in the mail. You cannot imagine the joy it brought to our home, and to that incredible child of mine. I will never forget the moment, nor Ms. Moorehead's and Conrad's kindness. Judith Ann insisted on writing to say 'thank you' and the correspondence between them began. One of the highlights of the day was to 'dictate' a letter to Ms. Moorehead."

One letter was sent to Agnes shortly after the 1971 Los Angeles earthquake, dated February 11, 1971:

Dear Aggie,

I have been very worried about you. Did the earthquake get your house? I hope not. I don't want anything to happen to you. If your house was it, you can come stay with us. We will take care of you. I still watch *Bewitched* all the time. I still think you are great. I love the way you say "Darwin" or "What's His Name." I notice you wear purple and pink a lot. They are my favorite colors too. I have them in my room. Guess what? I made a straight A report card. My teacher is giving me 2nd grade work already, and it is fun. Here are some pansies from my garden, that my mother dried for you, and some pictures I drew for you. In the mail there will be a Valentine surprise for you too. Enjoy! Please let me know how you are, and whether the earthquake stopped shaking. That's Shooo Bizzy! I love you very much.

Judith Ann Guerra

Agnes replied to Judith Ann on March 15, 1971:

Dear Judith Ann,

Your letter of February arrived during my absence from Los Angeles, hence the delay in writing you. I've been traveling the countryside again which prevents me from keeping up with my correspondence. I am ever so pleased to hear from you again. The enclosures, your drawings and those delightful pansies, pressed and ready for careful placing in my scrapbook are gifts I'll always treasure. No, the earthquake didn't "get" my house though we were shaken up thoroughly. So many houses were damaged, I feel so very lucky to have been spared the expense and trouble of having repairs made. The good Lord had his hand over me and my home. I want to thank you for your kindness in inviting me to stay with you if I needed shelter. I'll never forget that. I'm so pleased to learn you had a straight A report card and are now doing 2nd grade work. Marvelous! As you go on with your work you'll find it more and more interesting. Take care and write me again when you have the time. With every good wish.

    Cordially yours,

    Agnes Moorehead

Dora Guerra would recall the final time that little Judith Ann was hospitalized. "The other great moment between them was when Ms. Moorehead sent Judith Ann a most lovely nightie during what turned out to be Judith's last stay in the hospital. Ms. Moorehead sent it directly to Lackland Air Force Hospital. The return address carried Ms. Moorehead's name on it, written in her own hand. By the time the gift reached Judith Ann in the intensive care unit, the whole hospital floor became aware that Judith Ann Gurerra had Ms. Agnes Moorehead for a friend, and she was the most popular patient for several days. Everyone would come in to her bedside to ask her about Ms. Moorehead. You've never seen a child gleam, in spite of how ill she was. She never failed to mention how 'her good friend Conrad Binyon was a VERY SPECIAL friend of Ms. Moorehead's and brought them together.' Judith Ann died a week after Ms. Moorehead's gift arrived."

Just prior to her passing, Little Judith Ann, just shy of her 8th birthday, dictated a final letter to her favorite "star" Agnes Moorehead:

Dear Aggie,

Oh how gorgeous! I just love it! My Daddy took a picture of me in it, and I will send it to you. I feel like a Queen in it. Thank you so very very much. I love you. Judith Ann.

    p.s.

Tell what's his name hello. Uncle Arthur too.

For making a dying child's final month happy and memorable, Conrad Binyon would later say that Agnes Moorehead "has a place in heaven, in my book."

15

CURTAIN (1972–1974)

Bewitched filmed its 254th episode in December 1971, completing its slate for the 1971–72 season and preparing to take an unusually long hiatus. The cast and crew fully expected to be coming back by the late spring of 1972 for the series' ninth season. For Agnes, the eighth season had been her least active on the show — appearing in only 13 out of 26 episodes, many of those only requiring her services for not more than a day. By this time the writers were increasingly recycling ideas, scripts, and even dialogue from earlier, better episodes, and the boredom was becoming painfully evident. By now Agnes had done all she could with the Endora character — there were few new tricks, and while professional as always, the spark was missing. Even more telling were Elizabeth's performances in that final season. Given a new "hip" attitude, she seemed to have lost the sparkle and good-natured humor which she brought for seven years to the character of Samantha Stephens. There may be two explanations of why this happened. The first was due to the increasing marital problems between Elizabeth and Bill, unrelieved due to having to work together. The second, after eight years of playing one character, she had, indeed, become bored and was ready to lick her acting chops with other projects. "I think she did begin to tire of the show in the last couple of years," says Kasey Rogers. "Personal problems were also creeping in, but she did her job and never complained. But you knew something was wrong. On the set, Elizabeth and Bill were professionals."

Agnes didn't look well during this final season, appearing drawn and fragile. Quint Benedetti recalls that she had recurring bouts with the flu over the course of the season. He recalls that one day she was so ill she could barely move, and she had Benedetti call in sick for her. Minutes later, the phone rang and Benedetti gave it to Agnes. She later told him that she had been bluntly told, "either you come in or you will be put on suspension." With an iron will, Agnes got herself up from her sickbed and went to the studio. When she arrived on the set she went to the director and said, "Here I am — are you satisfied?" She worked that day but her condition worsened and she was finally granted time off. Elizabeth, always gracious and solicitous of Agnes, sent flowers with a note. "Dearest Aggie we all miss you — me especially. Much love, Elizabeth." And even Dick Sargent, whom she had finally mellowed toward, sent flowers with his regards, "Aggie stop this foolishness and get well."

With the show on a long hiatus Agnes hoped her strength would return as she turned her attentions and waning energies to planning what would turn out to be her final Christmas party at the Beverly Hills home. It was another star-studded event and a guest list which, as always, made it an A event party: Elizabeth and Bill Asher, Dick Sargent, David White, and other *Bewitched* regulars hobnobbed with friends like Debbie Reynolds and Harry Karl, Fred MacMurray and his wife June Haver, Kathryn Grayson, Jimmy and Gloria Stewart, Lucille Ball and Gary Morton, and the Karl Maldens, among others. Debbie Reynolds recalls that at these Christmas parties the champagne and wine flowed and more than a few got tipsy — but teetotaler Agnes "stood straight as a dime with an amused look on her face." According to Debbie, "nobody had more fun at the party than Paul Lynde." It was a fun evening and was written up in the society pages of the local Hollywood papers the next day — proclaiming the Hollywood Christmas party season officially open. Kay Gable, Clark's widow, wrote to Agnes the next day, "for many years now being at your beautiful parties gives me the spirit to get right on the Xmas path. You looked perfectly lovely, and I thank you and love you."

As always, the holiday party coincided with Agnes' birthday, her 71st, and her friend Mary Roebling remembered her with a touching telegram: "A star danced and you were born. All my love on your birthday."

At Christmas Agnes gave a slip to the mother of her dedicated maid, Freddie Jones. Freddie thanked her for "your thoughtfulness . . . your friendship and being the human being you are."

It was clear to Agnes that she was not getting much better. She decided she needed a thorough examination and, as expected, was off to Rochester, Minnesota and her trusted Mayo Clinic. On February 17, 1972, she was admitted to Methodist Hospital to begin a series of tests. They came back positive — Agnes had cancer. As always when confronted with adversity,

Agnes put herself in God's hands and prayed. She knew she had the best doctors and was at the best hospital and that God would take care of the rest. With the exception of a few people, including her trusted staff, Freddie, Rochelle and Polly — and her friend and frequent house guest, Jack Kelk, she told no one of the nature of her illness. Friends either thought she was on vacation or visiting her mother. She underwent surgery on February 22, and remained an in-patient until March 7. While hospitalized, she received a letter (affectionately addressed to Maude) from Kelk, who was staying at her Beverly Hills home: "Your marble halls are not ringing with the laughs we used to have. I remember when either one of us would find something funny in print, or on the tube and converge in the halls, in various states of undress, and yak until the wee small hours. We miss you. The house is running smoothly of course, due to the girls (Polly and Freddie), who love you, and think only of your best interests . . . Agnes, if you are alone, and I suspect you are, I will beg, borrow or steal to be there with you. I hope you know that . . . The phone doesn't ring much; people think you are simply on holiday. Our prayers are with you, that you know. Father Curtis wonders who I'm having all the masses said for, but he is a man of God, and does not ask questions. The 'household' worries when we don't hear from you. We want you home. The grounds look lovely and the wisteria is almost opening your bedroom window looking for you. The birds keep saying you will be here soon. Love, Jack."

Agnes remained an out-patient after being released from the hospital for a week and then went to recuperate with her mother in Reedsburg. But during her stay in Reedsburg she redeveloped the flu and was readmitted to Methodist in April. The staff adored her and she befriended many during her time at the hospital. One lady who worked in the business office received an autograph and gift of candy for her daughter. It was during this second hospitalization that Debbie wrote, "We all miss you and send gobs of love and best wishes that all is well and that you are getting a much needed rest. I have spoken with Polly a few times but she indicated you weren't up to calls yet. Thus this note." Harry Ackerman, the executive producer of *Bewitched*, wrote to her on March 16: "One of my relatives in Albany (NY) sent me today a news item from one of the papers to the effect that you have been hospitalized in Rochester . . . I had no idea you were ill . . ."

Soon Agnes, released and back in Reedsburg, heard from Ackerman again, by letter, breaking the news that *Bewitched* would be leaving the air. For the first time since 1963, Agnes — while recovering from major surgery for a life-threatening illness — once again had to worry about where and what her next job would be. It was done in a typical Hollywood way — a short letter with the news that the show was cancelled, a line about his appreciation for a job well done, and then a "call me when you're back in town and I'll take you out to lunch." A nice Hollywood kiss-off after 8 years as Endora. That Agnes was unaware that the episode she filmed in December would be her final one is a quote she gave to *Chicago Today Magazine* on 1/4/72, "I will be doing more one-woman shows . . . about five or six in April and back to filming *Bewitched*."

She also heard from her attorney, Franklin Roemer, who was apparently also in the dark about the urgency of Agnes' medical problems. "When I called Freddie on March 6th to ask what plane at what hour would be bringing you in on the 7th (which I'd heard from her earlier was the intended date, when I called to invite you to a do with us) I took her word for it that you'd simply found some spare time loose from t.v. to stay in the east until mid-April. I pooh-poohed the comment of a friend that he'd read in the papers you were at Mayo's. 'Routine check-up.' Freddie wouldn't have known — and she couldn't be that brilliant an actress to play the scene that casually. Then Elmer Rigby said yesterday that he'd heard you were seriously ill at Mayo clinic — and my heart sank. Think I didn't know how much I love you till that awful sinking feeling hit me. Today I called Freddie with terrible trepidation — and can't tell you how relieved Gladys and I both are that you're well and coming home in a couple of weeks . . . "

Gradually she began to gather strength and began to think about her career. In May she received an offer to play Mrs. St. Maugham in *The Chalk Garden* at the American Shakespeare Festival in Stratford, Connecticut. Burry Fredrik wrote in his letter offering her the part, "We feel you would be brilliant in the role." She was too weak at that point to consider a stage role.

She signed for a pair of made-for-television movies for ABC, which she quickly filmed in the early summer. The first was called *Rolling Man* and starred Dennis Weaver as a man sent to prison. Agnes was cast as his dead wife's grandmother who takes care of his sons while he is locked up, until she is too sick to care for them anymore. Her part was not large, but she received special billing and got to utilize a country-southern accent. The second film, *Night of Terror*, cast Agnes as a physical therapist named Bronsky who tries to motivate a paralyzed woman, played by Donna Mills, to fight harder to recover the use of her legs. But again, the part was relatively small, and most of the story was a standard crime drama with the Mills character hiding from killers. Still, she felt good to be back at work, and without the income from *Bewitched* she needed the money — and these made-for-tv movies seemed to utilize older stars in ways that the current film industry didn't.

An entrepreneur named Lee Orgel decided to produce a revival of *Don Juan in Hell*. Despite it being over twenty-years since she last played Dona Ana, Orgel proposed to cast Agnes in her original role. Filling the other parts would be Ricardo Montalban as Don Juan, Edward Mulhare as the Devil and Paul Henried as the Commander. Agnes was happy to accept, in part, because she loved the play but also because it would provide her with several months of work and steady income. To direct, Orgel approached Agnes' old Mercury companion, John Houseman. Houseman accepted and decided to stay as close to the Laughton-Gregory formula as possible — the simple set with the four actors seated on stools in front of music stands. Another reason for this fidelity may have been due to Agnes' presence. "Agnes sustained us with coffee and sandwiches and stimulated us with admonitions about the show she knew so well. She was mentor and queen bee, reminding us

Greeting a fan backstage at _Don Juan in Hell_. December, 1972.

of what Laughton had created so brilliantly 20 years before — why he made the choices he did and how he amended them in response to audience reaction." Agnes enjoyed working with this cast and had high praise for them, as they had for her. Mulhare would recall her "very high strict professionalism." Montalban would always credit Agnes for making it possible for him to play Juan.

The show opened, like the original, in the California Central Valley — but instead of Stockton, it was Fresno where they played before a black-tie audience. The tour wouldn't be as extensive as the original but it would still be exhausting especially for a nearly 72-year-old woman who had a recent bout with cancer. They would play for two weeks in Chicago in late September, followed by another two weeks in Boston, and then go on to the National Theater in Washington, D.C. for three weeks. This was followed by a week in Cincinnati, two weeks in Philadelphia, a week in Pittsburgh, a week in Wilmington, Delaware, two weeks in Toronto, culminating in a four-week engagement at the Palace Theater in New York. In all, 18 weeks of travel and performances.

In Fresno Agnes gave Ricardo Montalban a pen as an opening night gift. Addressing his "Dearest Agnes" letter, Montalban warmly thanked her. "I hate to write! That is I used to hate to write. Now I love it, with this beautiful pen from a beautiful lady. It's a joy and a privilege to be in hell with you."

Still, the tour seemed to revive Agnes. She was back in the spotlight and she conducted interview after interview in each city talking about any number of subjects, including her old nemesis — the modern theatre. "They don't write mature, reasoned, scintillating things involving the audience anymore. My gracious when I go to the theater now, I think maybe this time the magic will begin. Then, the curtain goes up to reveal a garbage pail on the stage . . . and I say, 'oh, not again.'" Or, "Of course, I think we're living in a mediocre age anyway, and it's like a drug. 'Give me some more because it feels so good' is the attitude. Mediocrity is poured into the brains of the people. Much of the theater is mediocre now. It isn't like the theater that I started in. This kind of mediocrity is slovenliness and garbage pails and dirty words. I'm not interested in constantly feeding people tawdriness and confusion and chaos. The world is chaotic as it is. Why feed it to them constantly?"

When Mary Roebling heard that *Don Juan in Hell* was coming to Philadelphia and New York she wrote Agnes insisting on giving a party in her honor in Philadelphia (it turned out to be a party honoring the entire cast), and allowing Agnes the use of her New York apartment, "if you would not object to my bunking with you on occasion . . ." With 14 rooms it is doubtful they would be falling all over each other.

There was one person who was distinctly not happy about this revival of *Don Juan in Hell* — Paul Gregory. "Montalban had no background for Shaw. He didn't understand the words," Gregory states. "When Agnes did (this revival) I sent her a note with one word on it — WHY? Of course, I knew why — she loved to work and needed to work and went through money like there was no tomorrow."

The reviews were generally good, but not spectacular. The *Chicago Tribune* said "Montalban verges on the hammy only occasionally . . . Mulhare is quite effective . . . Moorehead is cool, coy — quietly playing a clever obbligato . . . Henried, a firm counter point."

The Dean of Boston Critics, Eliot Norton wrote, ". . . still a triumphant theatrical experience . . . Agnes Moorehead knows the high style of Shaw, the sense of mockery and mischief and behind it a feeling of truth, as Shaw saw truth." The *Christian Science Monitor* perhaps summed it up best, "An event to be welcomed with open arms . . . though doesn't match its predecessor." The *Washington Star and News* was hard on Agnes, "Miss Moorehead, however, has become a parody of Donna Ana . . . her coquetry is flagrantly false this time."

On opening night in New York, January 15, 1973, Agnes, as was customary, received many encouraging telegrams:

FROM BETTE DAVIS: "Wish I could be in the audience tonight will be there soon much luck and love. Bette D.

FROM CESAR ROMERO: "Dear Agnes wish you and all great success tonight. Love my elephants (Romero collected elephant ceramics and received some as a gift from Aggie). Miss you. Love, Cesar.

FROM GEORGIA AND BILL JOHNSTONE: "Your stage mother and father know you can't miss our love is with you every minute."

In his book, *Final Dress,* John Houseman pays handsome tribute to Agnes as Donna Ana. "I can see her still, in both engagements, in a lilac gown of her own designing, with a small gold crown set atop the flaming red hair that made her the equal, in authority and presence, of the three tall, handsome, formally clad males with whom she was appearing on stage." (Incidentally, while rehearsing *Don Juan in Hell,* Houseman gave Agnes an autographed copy of his then-current autobiography, *Run-Through,* personally inscribed: "For Agnes with love and admiration — building and accumulating during a very long and inspiring association. Above all, with thanks for her incalculable advice and help with staging and production of 'Don Juan in Hell' in its second time around tour.")

In this same book, Houseman writes bitterly about the review the show received at the hand of the *New York Times* critic. "Against my emphatic and frequently repeated advice, an impatient backer insisted on bringing it into New York, where it ran head on into (critic) Clive Barnes's irrational detestation of Shaw and all his works. As a result I had the dubious thrill of seeing my name in lights for a week over the marquee of the Palace Theatre on Broadway and the annoyance of receiving one of the worst notices ever given to a production in which I was involved." Houseman exaggerates a bit; the show did play its intended four-week run in New York, not a week. But he is correct about Barnes's review in the *New York Times,* it's devastating from its first paragraph: "When one stands out of joint with current dramatic history, one can either fake it or admit it. I prefer to admit it. Most people who have an opinion on the matter regard George Bernard Shaw as one of the great playwrights of this century. I do not." Since he was prejudiced against Shaw to begin with, one wonders why he was allowed to review the show. His review goes on to state, "The performance, which was dull and stilted, did, I gratefully consider, strike a strong but, in retrospect, unfair blow for anti-Shavianism. The play is not so bad as it appears to be here." What must really have stuck in Houseman's craw is this line: "I did not see the Laughton version, even by envisioning the former cast, one senses that it must have been better." The cast didn't go unscathed: " . . . we have the monotonous delivery of Mr. Montalban whose rise and fall phrasing runs up and down Shaw's drearily antithetical phrases like a child on a roller coaster. Then there is Mr. Henried's world-weary commander who seems lazily cynical, and Mr. Mulhare's decent but tamed, clubbable but foolish, Devil. These are not electric performances, and though Miss Moorehead shows some excitement, it is not always sustained."

The show closed on February 4, 1973, after a run of 24 performances. But she would be back in New York before the end of the year to mount one more Broadway opening — and take one final bow.

II

Agnes stayed on for a bit after *Don Juan* closed, taking in some Broadway shows and appearing as a mystery guest on the syndicated version of the popular panel show, *What's My Line?*, which reuniting her with her old friend Arlene Francis. Then it was back to California for a short rest before hopping a jet to take her to London where she accepted a role in an NBC two-part mini-series, *Frankenstein: The True Story,* supposedly based with more fidelity to Mary Shelley's novel. The film had a stellar cast including James

(Courtesy of Wade Ballard)

As Mrs. Blair, Victor Frankenstein's curious landlady in *Frankenstein: The True Story* (1973).

Mason, Leonard Whiting, David McCallum, Jane Seymour, Michael Sarrazin, Michael Wilding, Ralph Richardson and John Gielgud. Agnes plays Mrs. Blair, Dr. Frankenstein's housekeeper. Again, it is not a huge role and part of it is played as an invalid since Mrs. Blair suffers a stroke. This project would keep Agnes occupied through the early spring of 1973. When it was shown in the United States on NBC in the fall of 1973, it did well in the ratings; in Europe it was edited down and eventually released as a feature film.

Agnes' final feature film was released early in 1973 — *Charlotte's Web*, based on the children's book by E. B. White and animated by Hanna-Barbera. Debbie Reynolds voiced the part of Charlotte, with prominent roles by Paul Lynde (Templeton the rat), Henry Gibson (the runt piglet Wilbur), Martha Scott (Mrs. Arable), and Agnes as a Goose. Composers Richard and Robert Sherman, who had scored *Mary Poppins* as well as several other Disney films, wrote some delightful songs — including a duet performed by Agnes and Lynde, "A Veritable Smorgasbord." Lynn Kear described Agnes' voice as "strong and dignified — even when stuttering." The film did well at the box office, probably due to it being family-friendly, and the reviews were decent — *Variety* called the film "heartwarming." And Agnes wanted to make sure there were plenty of family-friendly films available. Like Jerry Lewis, in the early 70's, Debbie Reynold's lent her name to develop a string of family movie theaters and, with Debbie's encouragement, Agnes supported this project. It never really got off the ground.

Now we are back to where we began — Agnes cast as Aunt Alicia in *Gigi*. Prior to its New York opening in November, Agnes had endured a long, exhausting 25-week tour with the musical. Her arthritis was worsening and she wasn't feeling well but she somehow made it through each performance. An appearance in St. Louis at an outdoor theater in pouring rain was especially trying. Quint Benedetti recalls her being so exhausted that he would literally have to carry her from her car to her motel room. Cesar Romero recalled that Agnes described *Gigi* as "her hardest show" and that she had "began to wilt from the endless rehearsals and the grueling tour." He knew something wasn't right when she complained of her intense fatigue and made the comment "I'm tired into the future," because it wasn't the Agnes he knew — who often revived from being on the road and performing before an audience. From Detroit, Agnes would write to Georgia Johnstone that the tour had so far been "Madness!" Fred Carmichael would recall *Gigi* as "an unhappy experience for her from first to last." Unhappy due to the show not living up to her expectations and unhappy too because her health was clearly declining.

In October, just prior to the Broadway opening, she did get a reprieve and was able to travel to her beloved Ohio farm where she could enjoy the cool, crisp fall weather and its beautiful colors. She often found peace, serenity and renewal at the farm. Freddie Jones would recall, "She often mentioned how serene it was at the farm . . . It replaced ships, trains and everything as a private place. Once she stopped me at what I was doing and said, 'Freddie, don't you ever listen to silence?'" She told the *Los Angeles Times* in 1970 that on her farm, "there are forests, streams, fresh air, tranquility, time for reading and reflecting. This is the source of beauty."

She liked and enjoyed Vic and Margery Stover, the couple who managed the farm and lived in the old farm house. They had a young and active family which gave her great pleasure when she visited. Margery Stover related to author Warren Sherk how the children would put up signs with streamers welcoming Agnes home whenever she came to the farm, which was at most two or three times per year. This would be her final visit to the farm. When she was in New York appearing in *Gigi*, the Stovers sent her a cyclamen plant; she wrote back thanking them for remembering "this tired, weary traveler who longs for home and fireside." For her final Christmas they remembered her with a "beautiful collection of gifts," including a lilac tote bag and soap, which Aggie told them was "almost too pretty to use," as well as the book, *The Prayers of Peter Marshall*. "I shall treasure it," she replied in gratitude.

Clearly she knew something was wrong and maybe even in the back of her mind she knew it could be a recurrence of the cancer she had so bravely fought off in 1972. But she didn't really want to acknowledge it openly — yet to many people who saw her during those last weeks prior to her leaving *Gigi*, she would acknowledge her concern. Quint Benedetti states that a young former acting student and nurse by profession was "slowly wheedling her way into Agnes' life." He says that during the run of *Gigi* the young woman began giving painkilling shots to Agnes. But it should be made clear that Benedetti is quite biased against this young woman and claims that she began spreading ugly gossip about him to Agnes in an effort to get him removed from Agnes' employ. Other people this author has spoken to, including Laurie Main and Debbie Reynolds, make it clear that this woman was devoted to Agnes and that Agnes came to value her friendship and companionship. For instance, Debbie says this young assistant began Agnes on a regiment of eating peeled grapes because the grapes were considered an excellent source of fighting off cancer.

Paul Gregory recalls Agnes as "pensive" during this time, as if she knew something was wrong but didn't really know what it was. He says he told her "to live for today — be concerned with the now — right now — live for the moment."

Agnes' final radio show for CBS Mystery Theatre. January, 1974.

For Himan Brown she recorded her final radio appearances on his *CBS Mystery Theatre* in January — "The Old Ones Are Hard to Kill," broadcast on January 6, and "Ring of Truth," broadcast on January 26, but she was already in the hospital when these were aired. Brown detected nothing in her performances or manner during the tapings of these programs to indicate she was ill — except he recalls that she complained of being more tired than usual. When I interviewed him, Brown was 92 years old, but says he vividly recalls the last time he saw Agnes. "She called and said she wanted to say 'goodbye' to me as she was planning on going back to California in two weeks. So my wife and I invited her for dinner. She couldn't have been more gracious. Out of the blue she said, 'Oh, on the way home I'm going to stop off at the Mayo Clinic for a complete physical. I just haven't been feeling myself.'"

Laurie Main recalls going backstage after a performance of *Gigi* as the last time he saw her. "She looked tired and worn. I said, 'Sweetheart, you need a rest.' She said she was going to take one and that she had given her two-week notice and she was going for a rest at the Mayo Clinic — and she did — and of course it was there that they discovered the terminal cancer."

Debbie Reynolds recalls that one day Agnes called her and said, "I have to go to the hospital. I can't stand up anymore."

She had given her notice and she did leave the show; Arlene Francis came in as her replacement but it didn't help and the show quickly closed after a few more weeks. Jerry Wunderlich took Agnes to the train station and she was on her way to Rochester where she was initially treated for pneumonia.

While at Methodist Hospital she again requested that no information be given to the press about the nature of her illness. She also kept most friends in the dark. While in the hospital only two people were constantly present — her mother and Freddie, her maid. "I don't think she thought it was her final days," Debbie Reynolds recalls. "She thought she would beat it and she put herself in God's hands." Still, even when ill and near death, her impeccable good manners never failed her. The Stovers sent her messages of hope and inspiration including a poem from daughter Kathy:

A GET WELL CARD ON A WONDERFUL DAY
WHEN THE FIELDS ARE FULL OF CLOVER AND HAY
AND EVEN THOUGH I'M FAR AWAY
I THINK OF YOU IN EVERY WAY.

Agnes responded warmly from her hospital bed, ". . . Somehow you all make me homesick telling me about the snow and the deer. I love and miss this kind of life, the good clean fresh air of the country and hope one day I, too, will be able to settle down to having my fill of it . . ." She still had hope. By January 12, Agnes had begun a course of Vincristine and Adriamycine. Vincristine is a drug which interferes with the growth of cancer cells, slowing their growth through the body, and is used as a cancer chemotherapeutic agent.

In February, Agnes was released and taken to her mother's home in Reedsburg. According to one report, Agnes' release was insisted upon by Mollie, "but this proved impractical and Moorehead was back in the hospital again." The record does indicate that Agnes returned to the hospital on April 9. Her decline over the next three weeks was rapid as the cancer viciously spread throughout her body. She began to fight the disease with chemotherapy. She began to lose her hair. Debbie Reynolds wanted to be with her, but Agnes had forbade it, just as she forbade Debbie to try and locate Sean. "I begged her to allow me to try and find Sean to have him come and see her, but she forbid it. She said, 'I don't want to talk about it — it will just upset me.'" The last time Debbie spoke with Agnes was five days before she died:

"Agnes, I'm flying in."
"Oh, no, dear, I don't want you to see me like this."
"Like what?"

"I've lost all my hair from the chemotherapy."

"What chemotherapy?"

"Well, Debbie, it's over . . . I'm dying. Pray for me."

Debbie states that these were the final words that Agnes ever spoke to her. Agnes had finally accepted her fate. She was preparing herself for her eternal house and to meet her God whom she loved and worshiped.

Georgia Johnstone, her loyal secretary for 40 years, never knew how sick she was, having "no idea" of the severity of her illness. Georgia later stated, "Agnes had a firm belief that in order to maintain her glamorous image as a star, it was essential to remain aloof. She felt there was no glamour in death, so she decided to keep her illness a secret. It was an emotional decision to keep her friends away. I was her closest friend, yet she didn't want to see even me. Only her mother was permitted to visit."

Mollie later stated that Agnes didn't give in to her illness until only three weeks before she died. "She was convinced she was going to get better and she fought with all her strength to get fit again . . . then she knew she was dying and she wasn't afraid because she had a deep religious belief. Toward the end, she was too weak to do much and I sat and read to her from the Bible . . . Agnes died beautifully. Her last word was 'Mama.'"

Agnes Robertson Moorehead died April 30, 1974 at age 73.

Her friends in the industry were surprised when they heard of her passing. James MacArthur would recall getting a phone call with the news — surprised — as he had no idea, and neither did his mother, Helen Hayes. Jane Wyman, who worked with her in five major films and considered herself a friend, was "shocked" when she heard the news — she never even knew she had been ill. Ricardo Montalban was opening in *The King and I* in Los Angeles on the night that she died. "I was apprehensive enough as it was. Just as I was to go on the stage, in the final throes of preparation, someone said to me, 'Isn't it terrible about Agnes?' 'What is terrible?' I asked. 'She died today, somewhere in the Midwest.' I couldn't believe it. I returned to my dressing room to try to recover myself. Just as I entered it another party said to me, 'Do you realize you are using the same dressing room Agnes Moorehead used in *Gigi*?' That did it. I broke down." Montalban also recalled that at his next stop in San Francisco he immediately realized that, again, he was using a dressing room which Agnes had previously occupied. How? "The lamp bulbs had all been painted lavender, her personal trademark, you know."

Many of the obituaries, as Agnes had foreseen, emphasized her role as Endora and usually the picture included was of her made up as that iconic character. This was only natural due to the success of the show and its reach. But the obituaries also reflected on her overall career as well. *Variety*, the "Bible" of show business, said that as an actress Agnes was "considered one of the most versatile in range." The *Washington Post* called her "a gifted character actress who ranged easily from being elegant, assured and arresting to being confused, cackling and comical." The *New York Daily News* called her "outstanding and versatile." The *New York Times* said that while, "Miss Moorehead was perhaps best known to modern audiences as Endora, the witch . . . she was a highly versatile actress who was equally at home on television or radio as on the stage and in the movies." *Newsweek* called her "gifted." Those are two words seen over and over in the obituaries — gifted and versatile.

Her friends and colleagues remembered her warmly:

DEBBIE REYNOLDS: "She was a brilliant actress and a brilliant teacher. She was so spiritual. We became very close friends and my fondest memory of Agnes would be of me calling her up and telling her to 'light the fire' — she had this enormous fireplace and could literally stand inside of it — and then we would just kick off our shoes and talk for hours before this roaring fire."

PAUL GREGORY: "She had a basic love of herself and the love of her craft. There was nothing retiring about Agnes. She had an enthusiasm for many subjects . . . so many actors you have to hit them over the head to get a performance out of them. You didn't have to kiss-ass with Agnes."

JANE WYATT: "She was a brilliant actress and a wonderful human being."

NORMAN CORWIN: "Aggie was a woman of great kindness, very compassionate, alert, prompt . . . She was reliable, steady and without peer as an actress in our industry."

HIMAN BROWN:	"If Agnes had been born in England, she would have been knighted. She would have been Dame Agnes Moorehead — she was as good as there was."
QUINT BENEDETTI:	"She was just bigger than life."
JANE WYMAN:	"Aggie was so versatile . . . each character she played was different from the other. I was very fond of her."
KARL MALDEN:	"She was a quiet person and quiet people don't get noticed much. Her whole thing was up there (onscreen) and when she wasn't acting she was as normal and nice and sweet as anyone I knew. It was a pleasure knowing her."
CAROL LYNLEY:	"She was quite simply always a joy."
ROSE MARIE:	"She was a wonderful lady and a tremendous actress."
BERNARD FOX:	"She was always a consummate professional."
KASEY ROGERS:	"She was bigger than life, yet down to earth."
WILLIAM ASHER:	"She was so good at everything she did. I was crazy about her."
MARY ROEBLING:	"Despite her fame there was nothing pretentious about Agnes; she displayed the same ease and grace with youngsters as she did with the elite of the world."
JOSEPH COTTEN:	"Aggie was the most disciplined actress we ever met. She was the hardest working member of our profession."
LUCILLE BALL:	"Agnes was a dear and valued friend — an elusive one — because she was forever helping someone in our business. She was one of the greatest teachers and comedy advisors in our profession. Her timing was

impeccable . . . I admired her greatly and miss her every day."

Finally, a poem by CHARLES LAUGHTON:

> TO A PURE ARTISTE
> TO A BEAUTIFUL CREATIVE SOUL
> TO A KIND, GOOD LADY
> A LAVENDER QUEEN
> BEST EVER IN FAIRY TALES
> MY ETERNAL LOVE AND ADMIRATION

AFTERWORD

Her body was flown from Rochester to Dayton, Ohio so she would be buried in the family crypt at Dayton Memorial Gardens near her beloved father and her sister. She was transferred in a 13-gauge, sealer-type casket which cost $1,035. In her will she requested that no funeral service or memorial be held for her and her wishes were respected — she also requested that the nature of her final illness not be revealed. Her estate, when her will was probated, was estimated to be in excess of $400,000. Her last will and testament was signed in Los Angeles on August 23, 1973, only eight months before she died.

Sean was not mentioned in the will. "I declare that I am single and have no children, natural or adopted, living or deceased." She was generous to the people who served her so well for so long. Her personal maid, Freddie Jones, was bequeathed $5,000. Olivia Garland, a.k.a. Polly, was bequeathed $5,000 and her sable jacket. Her friend Tanya Hills, who befriended her late in her life, was bequeathed $1,000 and her beaver coat with the sable collar. Her attorney's wife, Vanya Rohner, was left her two mink coats. The only entertainment figure remembered in the will was Elizabeth Montgomery, who would receive Agnes' diamond sunburst pin only upon the death of Aggie's mother (Mollie gave the pin to Montgomery anyway). She remembered various charities she had helped support during her lifetime: The Motion Picture Country House and Hospital received $5,000. The Pacific Garden Mission of Chicago received $5,000. The New York Gospel Mission to the Jews, Inc. in New York City also received $5,000. To the Radio Bible Class of Grand Rapids, Michigan went $2,500.

For Muskingum College, she left $25,000 with instructions to fund one or more complete or partial scholarships to be known as the "Agnes Moorehead Scholarships." She also bequeathed half of her manuscripts and theatrical library to the University of Wisconsin and the other half to Muskingum College. She left her collection of bibles and biblical research material to John Brown University of Siloam Springs, Arkansas. She left her farm including "all buildings and other structures, crops, livestock, machinery and all furnishings and other tangible property located upon or used in connection with the operation of said farm" to John Brown University; she requested that they operate the farm as a memorial to her father and mother, solely for "university, missionary and /or retreat purposes — and does not attempt to, and does not sell, lease or rent the farm or in any way suffer or permit the mining of coal thereon." In a provision, she also looked out for the Stover family who were living on the farm. "It is my strong desire that Mr. and Mrs. E.V. Stover, so long as either or both be living, be retained as caretakers of the farm, and be allowed to live in the small old house located on the farm." She also stated that it was her desire that Freddie and Polly be offered employment as domestics in connection with the maintenance of the large house located on the farm.

She left her mother all of her clothing and jewelry as well as one-half of all income received by her Executor during the administration of her estate. Furthermore, she instructed that her estate should pay for all expenses for insurance, maintenance, upkeep and repair of the farm and that if Mollie were "at any time, in need of funds for her reasonable care, maintenance and support, then my trustee may pay to or for the benefit of my mother, such part of the principal of the Trust Estate, up to the whole thereof, as the trustee shall deem necessary to provide for my mother's reasonable care, maintenance and support."

She left her Beverly Hills home to her attorney, Franklin Rohner, along with "all household furnishings and all personal property located therein." This last item was surprising to Debbie Reynolds, who was the executioner of the estate. She maintains that Agnes' original will had no such provision. According to Debbie the house was originally left to her mother and all proceeds from selling the house were to go to Mollie. Yet Paul Gregory maintains that it didn't make sense to leave the house to Mollie since she wasn't about to move to California and was comfortable living in her small two-story house in Reedsburg and would have free access to the farmhouse in Ohio during her lifetime. Why leave a house to a woman who was 88 years old and not likely to live in it? Besides, Agnes' will made sure that her mother would be comfortably taken care of for the remainder of her life.

Who would have imagined that Mollie would live on for another sixteen years, living to the great age of 106? She remained remarkably healthy, but began to lose her mental facilities by the early 1980's. Her friend, Gordon Emery, who continued to look out for Mollie and her needs, recalls he and his wife being invited to Mollie's for a dinner party. When they arrived, they were welcomed by Mollie and ushered into the dining room where the "other guests" were assembled. They were shocked when the other guests were photographs of famous stars, that Aggie had given to her mother through the years, sitting in their frames on dining room chairs. After a moment, she suddenly snapped out of it and told the Emerys, "Well, I guess they are not really real." Mollie had begun to lose some grasp with reality and soon after was admitted to the Sauk County Retirement Home where she lived comfortably for the remainder of her life.

I cannot end this narrative on the life of Agnes Moorehead without addressing a question nearly everyone has asked me — "Was Agnes Moorehead gay?" I found no smoking gun — nothing in her papers which indicates she ever had a lesbian relationship. I asked many of the people I interviewed. Paul Gregory, who knew her for almost a quarter of a century and was often blunt in his responses to my questions, said that he never saw any indication of it, adding, "Now, Claudette Colbert, oh yes, she most definitely was, but I can't make that statement regarding Agnes." Quint Benedetti, himself a gay man, who worked closely with Aggie in the last decade of her life, stated he was "quite sure that Agnes was not a lesbian." He had an interesting theory about why these rumors began. He claims that Paul Lynde, who he knew as a child growing up in Ohio, could be quite vicious especially when drunk, and that he began to spread rumors — including Lynde's famous quote, "The whole world knows Agnes was a lesbian — I mean classy as hell, but one of the all-time Hollywood dykes." Benedetti says that Lynde soon was spreading rumors regarding Agnes and Debbie Reynolds — the most enduring of the rumors.

Debbie, for her part, is quite adamant that Aggie was not a lesbian and that they had no more than a very close and loving platonic relationship. I asked her why she thought these rumors began. "Why, indeed? I was once interviewed in San Francisco and this young man comes in and asks me about a love affair I was supposed to have had with Agnes. I said, 'Why do you believe this?' He says, 'Well, everyone talks about it.' Well, I asked him if he thought that two women could be dear friends and love each other without it being sexual? He says, 'Well, I don't know.' I told him, 'Agnes wouldn't have gotten along with you because you aren't using your brains!'

But Agnes was very religious — piously religious. If it were true, I would acknowledge it — there is no reason not to. If I knew that Agnes was a lesbian I would acknowledge it, but she simply wasn't."

Yet, the rumor is spread in many books and articles without anything to back it up. For instance, in David Thomson's excellent biography of Orson Welles, Thomson states, "Welles revered Moorehead more than any actress he worked with. In a trailer made for *Kane*, he called her 'one of the best actresses in the world.' Nothing happened between them: Moorehead was not heterosexual." Where did that come from? Nobody ever insinuated that Orson or Agnes ever had anything more than a mutual admiration for one another. Other books have also argued that Agnes was a lesbian such as *The Sewing Circle*, which repeated the Paul Lynde quote as evidence. Boze Hadleigh's book *Hollywood Lesbians* included a 1972 interview that the author had with Agnes which was not published until years after Agnes' death. As was usual with Hadleigh, he began innocently enough in his questioning but gradually built up to asking the critical questions. Aggie says at one point, "A woman may love a person who is this or that, male or female. Love doesn't have a sex. It's men who always have to bring sex and activities into everything . . . Women operate on a different plane; the feelings are emotional not physical." Innocent enough, but at one point Hadleigh does get a vague acknowledgement of something. "You apparently have your own informants. I don't know what you've heard, and I don't want to hear, and some of it may even be true." Is it conceivable that Agnes, at some point in her 73 years, ever had a "Sapphic" encounter? Perhaps — and if so, what does it matter? But can this biographer say definitively that she was a lesbian or bisexual — no. There simply is no known evidence to collaborate it, with nobody willing to go on record affirming it. Yet many who willingly went on the record with me deny it as inconceivable.

It might be that because Agnes was a strong woman, who was unsuccessful in marriage in an industry with many closeted gays, she was pegged as a lesbian. Also, *Bewitched* has many gay fans who identify with a show about a witch who is "in the closet." The cast of *Bewitched*, too, had several actors associated with it who were either homosexual or allegedly homosexual, including Dick Sargent, Paul Lynde and Maurice Evans; the temptation is to include Aggie in that list. Sargent, who came out of the closet openly in 1990, discussed the rumors in *Out/Look* magazine. "I heard those rumors (regarding Aggie), but I never saw anything to back it up. In fact, the few times I was at Agnes' house, Debbie was never there, so I have no idea. That's one of those Hollywood stories you always hear, but I don't know." In 1992, even Elizabeth Montgomery commented in the *Advocate* magazine, "I've heard rumors, but I never talked with her about them. I don't know if they were true. It was never anything she felt free enough to talk to me about. I wish that Agnes had felt she could trust me. It would have been nice. She was a very closed person in many ways. We were very fond of one another but it never got personal."

The years since her death have been kind to Agnes. She is, through the wonder of television, still recognizable when many character actors from her era are long forgotten. *Bewitched* is more popular today than anytime since the first years of its original run. Endora is an integral part of why that show is still strong today. I think people relate to her character, particularly liberated women. Endora was a strong, self-reliant woman who didn't depend on a man. In some ways, I think, she is disappointed not only that her daughter married a mortal but that she decided to domesticate herself in the process. Endora enjoyed an open marriage and more than a few episodes made it clear that she was not spending her nights pining for Maurice. The series has been a staple on the nostalgia channel, TV Land, where at its peak it was shown four times a day and making many new fans in the process. The internet is full of websites devoted to the memory of this classic television series and one of the best ones is Harpie's Bizarre, which takes its title from a witch's magazine Endora was partial to. Fans on these sites enjoy an active message board and are a constant wonder in how they are able to recall the most minute details of *every* episode. But they have fun doing it and their numbers are growing and Hollywood is taking notice. In the summer of 2005, a movie version of *Bewitched* will be released in theaters and the cast for this feature film is awesome: Nicole Kidman, Will Farrell, Michael Caine and, appearing as Endora, Oscar-winning actress Shirley MacLaine. With this cast and a script by Nora Ephron (*Sleepless in Seattle*), this movie is bound to be a big box office success — and will without doubt keep interest in the series strong.

But it isn't only *Bewitched* that has kept Agnes' memory burning. Film lovers can enjoy one of many Agnes Moorehead films nearly every week — sometimes more than once a week — on such cable channels as Turner Classic Movies and American Movie Classics. One of the great benefits of having worked with people like Orson Welles, James Stewart, Bette Davis, Greer Garson, June Allyson, Humphrey Bogart, Jane Wyman, Gregory Peck, and their like, is that their movies will live on for the ages and people who start out watching the movie because it has Bette Davis or Bogey in it will also discover Agnes. Her own work is acknowledged thanks to the interest in Orson Welles and his films. In the DVD version of *Citizen Kane*, director Peter Bogdonovich does audio commentary and when it comes to that short scene of Agnes as Kane's mother he points out that many people consider her performance to be the best in the film, despite its brevity. Over the years *The Magnificent Ambersons* has also been analyzed by critics and film lovers alike and they all come away with the same conclusion that the critics of 1942 did — Agnes' performance as Aunt Fanny is a priceless performance which will live on forever. Over the years dozens of books have been published analyzing the art of Orson Welles and through her association with "the great man" Agnes lives on in print as well.

Lovers of old-time radio hold a special place in their heart for Agnes Moorehead. She was one of the busiest and definitive actresses of that medium. Collections of her work for the Mercury Theater, *The Shadow, Suspense* — especially her definitive "Sorry, Wrong Number," and many others, sell well over the internet, at conventions or in stores. It is difficult to maintain memories of something someone has done on stage, but the Gregory-Laughton version of *Don Juan in Hell* continues to be performed just as the original drama quartette performed it over fifty years ago, on a simple stage with the actors in evening clothing and sitting on stools with the scripts propped up on lecterns. It's hard to improve on something so simple, yet so effective. The bottom line is that Agnes Moorehead is one of the few actresses who succeeded in every realm of show business: stage, radio, film, and television. She was even successful in recordings with her devotional albums and soundtracks of *Don Juan in Hell* and "Sorry, Wrong Number" selling hundreds of thousands. The respect of her peers can be summed up in these statistics: Four Academy Award nominations, seven Emmy nominations — with one win, two Golden Globe nominations — with two wins, and the Best Actress award from the New York Film Critics.

Agnes was an intensely private person in a profession where everybody lives in a fish bowl. She only said what she wanted in interviews and maintained in her personal appearances the glamorous image of a star. She, herself, said it best in a *New York Times* interview in 1947: "I think an artist should be kept separated to maintain glamour and a kind of mystery. Otherwise it's like having three meals a day. Pretty dull. I don't believe in the girl-next-door image. What the actor has to sell to the public is fantasy, a magic kind of ingredient that should be analyzed." In all likelihood she would not have approved of a book written on her life — unless she was the one writing it and revealing only what she wanted revealed. A book published shortly after her death by her friend Warren Sherk was a very incomplete biography which honored her privacy by not revealing that she had a sister, no details of her marriages, not a word about Sean, avoided any career controversies she was involved in and made no mention of what killed her. It was called *A Very Private Person.* The title summed up Agnes better than anything in the text. But she was much more than a mystery — she was a flesh and blood human being who happened to be one of the most extraordinary actresses of her time. The human foibles she had made her more formidable and, in my opinion, more sympathetic. In discussing the art of acting she liked to say, "It's the illusion!" The ability to make people believe that she was someone else, without showing the acting techniques. In her private life she did the same trying to maintain an illusion even when she was not working, or as Paul Gregory said, "She was ON 23 out of 24 hours." The woman who was behind the illusion was infinitely more interesting — and even admirable.

Sources & Notes

Chapter 1
"Religion Softens the Edges"

Quint Benedetti, Laurie Main, Paul Gregory, Debbie Reynolds and Himan Brown all told me that Agnes complained of fatigue and ill health during the run of *Gigi*. Miss Reynolds also writes of it in her book, *Debbie: My Life* (with David Patrick Columbia, London: Sidgwick & Jackson, 1988).

The nursing/traveling companion who administered injections to Agnes is not identified even though I was provided a name by Quint Benedetti. Debbie Reynolds also spoke very highly of this individual, and how sympathetically she tried to help Agnes, in an interview with the author on 6/20/04.

Edwin Lester to Agnes, 2/15/73, The Papers of Agnes Moorehead, Wisconsin State Historical Society Archives, Box 138.

Agnes' quote, "I'm tired into the future," attributed to her friend, Cesar Romero, came from Warren Sherk's memoir of Agnes, *A Very Private Person* (Philadelphia: Dorrance and Company, 1976).

Agnes being unable to eat more than mashed potatoes was confirmed by Debbie Reynolds in an interview with this author, 6/20/04. She also wrote of it in *Debbie: My Life* (pg. 384).

Christmas being a favorite time of the year for Agnes is confirmed by several sources including Quint Benedetti and Debbie Reynolds, who also spoke extensively to me regarding Agnes' annual Christmas/Birthday party. The information regarding Christmas, 1973 with Mary Roebling, and the delivery of Christmas presents to her farm in Ohio, came from Warren Sherk's *A Very Private Person*.

The joint New Years party between the casts of *Gigi* and *Irene* came from Debbie Reynolds, who also spoke of it in *Debbie, My Life* (pg. 384).

Paul Gregory's last visit with Agnes at "21," and their stroll up Fifth Avenue, was related to me in an interview with Mr. Gregory, 10/22/03. He also spoke of this last encounter with Warren Sherk in *A Very Private Person,* where the quote, "Religion Softens the Edges," came from.

Debbie Reynolds learning that Agnes had left *Gigi* and was on her way to the Mayo Clinic in Rochester, Minnesota was related to me by Miss Reynolds in an interview on 6/20/04, and she also wrote of it in *Debbie, My Life* (pg. 386).

CHAPTER 2
"WHO ARE YOU TODAY, AGNES?"

"Aye, pretzel has less twists than our departed friend possessed," Peter Opp, Jr. to Georgia Johnstone, 8/26/74, The Georgia Johnstone Papers Re: Agnes Moorehead, T-Mss 2003-63 Billy Rose Theatre Collection, New York Public Library for the Performing Arts.

Gordon Emery, of Reedsburg, Wi., and his wife, were friends of Mollie Moorehead's and often helped her get around town or worked at various chores around the house. They also met Agnes occasionally and Gordon recalls picking Agnes up from the train station when she would come into town, "she hated to fly — so she often took the train." He was of valuable assistance to me, telling me stories about John and Mollie Moorehead — which were told to him by Mollie. His parents were married by Rev. Moorehead when he lived in Reedsburg in the early 1920's. Many of the anecdotes regarding John and Mollie Moorehead come from Mr. Emery's recollections. He was also kind enough to take me on a tour of Reedsburg one summer day in 2002 and showed me the house Mollie lived in and the church that Dr. Moorehead preached in. Sadly, Mr. Emery passed away in November 2003, but his contribution to this book is much appreciated.

"The family farm which had been deeded to the Moorehead family by two presidents . . ." *Alias Agnes Moorehead* (*Screen Guide,* April 1946 pg. 66).

". . . great man with a magnificent voice and very handsome . . ." *Agnes Moorehead: A Great Lady* (Kurtain Kall, July 1, 1973).

". . . an imposing lady of strong opinions . . . ," Tom Groeneweg to author.

"Dr. Moorehead always put his sermons on one 3x5 file card . . . ," Gordon Emery to author, 6/8/02.

"She was invited to give concerts away from church . . . ," Gordon Emery to author, 6/8/02.

"... She sang the hymn, 'The Lord is My Shepherd' ... ," *Chameleon of the Air* (*Radio Guide*, October 14, 1933, Hilda Cole).

"PK (Preacher's Kids)," Gordon Emery to author, 6/8/02.

"My sister and I used to come to the Sunday table filled with deviltry ... ," *Alias Agnes Moorehead* (*Screen Guide*, April 1946, Dorothy Deere, pg. 66-67).

"When it came to discipline her father's favorite method ... ," *Alias Agnes Moorehead* (*Screen Guide*, April 1946, Dorothy Deere, pg. 67)

Mollie's "tiny hand could smart," *Agnes wants more 'beauty,' 'gentility,' 'appeal to spirit'* (*Chicago Tribune*, October 1, 1972).

"Each person at the table was always required to weave a story ... ," *Agnes Moorehead* (*Radio Life*, May 12, 1946 pg. 7).

"Mollie once found Agnes huddled in a corner of her bedroom crying ... ," *Agnes Moorehead* (*Radio Life*, May 12, 1946 pg. 6).

Agnes spending a year in Colorado as a child, *Hollywood Reporter*, 3/18/70.

"Taught me everything about the house ... ," *Birmingham Post Herald*, 4/23/70.

"Agnes was close to her maternal grandfather ... ," *The Ghost That Changed Her Life* (*Screen Life*, July 1967 pg. 21).

"Well isn't that wonderful? My little girl is good enough to make the ballet ... ," *She Doesn't Need Glamour* (*Hollywood*, October 1942, Gloria Brent).

"... always interested in theatre ... it was always a goal ... ," The Papers of Agnes Moorehead, Wisconsin State Historical Society Archives, Box 60, Folder 13.

"I think my first professional appearance was in St. Louis ... ," The Papers of Agnes Moorehead, Wisconsin State Historical Society Archives, Box 60, Folder 13.

Agnes performing a "bump and grind routine ... ," *Guess Who Did Bumps in Boston? Agnes Moorehead* (*Hollywood Citizen News*, May 5, 1948).

"I never had a date by myself until I was in college ... ," *St. Louis Post*, 1/11/69.

"... nice and nice looking," *Famous Wisconsin Film Stars* (Kristin Gilpatrick, Badger Books, Inc., 1992, pg. 27).

"A smile for her students ... ," Orland Helgeson to author, 3/16/04.

"... one such play was Peter Pan ... ," *Famous Wisconsin Film Stars* (Kristin Gilpatrick, Badger Books, Inc. 1992, pg. 27).

"That was a heart-warming experience ... ," *Soldiers Grove's Agnes* (by

J.D. Spiro). Article was found in The Papers of Agnes Moorehead, Wisconsin State Historical Society Archives, Box 143 (Name of publication not known).

"I feel strong about them that to compromise . . . ," (Name of publication not known).

CHAPTER 3
"THERE GOES THE STRAIGHTEST BACK I'VE EVER SEEN"

Agnes' audition report, dated August 14, 1926, courtesy of Betty Lawson and staff of The American Academy of Dramatic Arts (AADA).

Quotes attributed to Lawrence Langner, regarding the AADA and Charles Jehlinger, came from a piece Langner wrote, *Mean More Than You Say* (*Theatre Arts*, July 1953).

Quotes attributed to Rosalind Russell, in the entire chapter, regarding the AADA, came from her autobiography, *Life is a Banquet* (with Chris Chase, Random House, 1977).

"I was more mature and I had the valid experiences of University to help me . . . ," *Hollywood Speaks: An Oral History* (Mike Steen, G.P. Putnam's Sons, New York, 1974).

Recollections of Agnes' roommate/classmate Elizabeth Council Craft came from Warren Sherk's *A Very Private Person*.

Quotes on lectures delivered by Charles Jehlinger; Agnes' paper "Analysis of a Character; and notes on plays Agnes attended and observations she made as part of a class project came from her AADA notebooks found in Box 60 folder 1-2 at the Wisconsin State Historical Society Archives, The Papers of Agnes Moorehead.

Quote, "The Straightest Back I've Ever Seen," attributed to John Griffith Lee, regarding Agnes, came from the article, *She Doesn't Need Glamour* (Gloria Brent, *Hollywood Magazine*, October 1942). Quote regarding John Griffith Lee, " . . . A handsome man who dressed well in pinstripe suits . . . ," by Elliott Reid, interview with the author, 10/3/04.

John Griffith Lee's audition report was sent to the author, courtesy of Betty Lawson and staff at the American Academy of Dramatic Arts (AADA)

Jack Lee's recollection that the AADA "didn't favor young love," as well as Agnes' follow up comments, came from *Screen Guide* (*Alias Agnes Moorehead*, April 1946).

Information and reviews of plays that Agnes and Jack Lee appeared in while at the AADA come from a scrapbook Agnes kept during that period of her life found in Box 143 at the Wisconsin State Historical Society Archives, The Papers of Agnes Moorehead, as well as from the indispensable *Agnes Moorehead: A Bio-Bibliography* (Lynn Kear, Greenwood Press, 1992).

Letter from Mollie Moorehead to Agnes regarding Margaret's condition, as well as Agnes' letter to Margaret following Margaret's death, are found in Agnes' black AADA notebook located in Box 60, folder 1, at the Wisconsin State Historical Society Archives, The Papers of Agnes Moorehead.

Articles and profiles of Jack Lee's appearance in *Subway Express* are found in a scrapbook Agnes kept from this period of her life, located in Box 143 at the Wisconsin State Historical Society Archives, The Papers of Agnes Moorehead.

Agnes' recollections of her "salad days" in New York, following her graduation from the AADA, came from the article *My Favorite Script* (*Guideposts*, August 1965).

Information on Phillips H. Lord and the *Seth Parker* radio show came from the excellent *The Encyclopedia of Old Time Radio* (John Dunning, Oxford University Press, 1998). Information on the nationwide tour that Agnes participated in with the *Seth Parker* cast, playing Lizzie Peters, came from a scrapbook that Agnes kept of articles and other memorabilia, located in Box 143 at the Wisconsin State Historical Society Archives, The Papers of Agnes Moorehead.

Quotes attributed to Himan Brown regarding his casting of Agnes in *The Gumps,* as well as other quotations directly attributed to Brown, are derived from an interview with Himan Brown by the author by phone on 6/5/03.

James MacArthur's comments regarding the relationship between his mother, Helen Hayes, and Agnes were derived from an e-mail from Mr. MacArthur to the author, 8/23/03.

CHAPTER 4
"ORSON AND THE MERCURY THEATRE"

Agnes spoke many times in interviews of her belief that she first met Orson Welles when he was a child at the Waldorf Astoria in the early 20's. This particular account is taken from an article titled *Agnes Moorehead* (*Radio Life*, May 12, 1946).

Biographical information on Welles is from several sources: *The Great*

Filmmakers: The Encyclopedia of Orson Welles (Chuck Berg & Tom Erskine, Checkmark Books, 2003), *Famous Wisconsin Film Stars* (Kristin Gilpatrick, Badger Books, 2002), *Citizen Welles* (Frank Brady, Anchor Books, 1989), *Orson Welles: The Road to Xanadu* (Simon Callow, Vintage, 1996), *Rosebud* (David Thomson, Vintage Books, 1997). Jane Wyatt was interviewed by the author on 9/27/02.

Elliott Reid was interviewed by the author on 10/3/04.

Information on *The Shadow* came from two primary sources: *The Encyclopedia of Old Time Radio* (John Dunning, Oxford University Press, 1998) and *The Shadow: An In-Depth Look at Radio's Foremost Man of Mystery* (Anthony Tolin, Radio Spirits Inc., 2002).

Simon Callow's comments on *Les Miserables* come from his book *Orson Welles: The Road to Xanadu* (Vintage Books, 1996).

Arthur Anderson was interviewed by the author on 9/26/04.

Orson Welles' comments that *First Person Singular* was "experimental . . . It may prove a failure" come from the *New York Times,* August 14, 1938, in the article, *The Shadow Talks* by Richard O'Brien.

Frank Brady's *Citizen Welles* (Anchor Books, 1989) is the primary source of information regarding the radio adaptation of "Dracula."

Elliott Reid provided wonderful thumbnail sketches of other Mercury alumni: Joseph Cotten, Ray Collins, Everett Sloane, Karl Swenson and Martin Gabel, 10/3/04.

Primary information on "The War of The Worlds" came from these sources: *The Encyclopedia of Old Time Radio* (John Dunning, Oxford University Press, 1998), *Citizen Welles* (Frank Brady, Anchor Books, 1989) and *This is Orson Welles* (Orson Welles & Peter Bogdanovich, edited by Jonathan Rosenberg, Da Capo Press, 1998).

Infighting with the sponsors of *The Campbell Playhouse* over using Irene Dunne and "blue-penciling" scripts came from *The Encyclopedia of Orson Welles* (Chuck Berg & Tom Erskine, Checkmark Books, 2003) and also Frank Brady's *Citizen Welles.*

"Welles could produce, direct, write and star in his projects . . . ," *Orson Welles Citizen Kane: The Fiftieth Anniversary Album* (Harlan Lebo, DoubleDay, 1990).

"Mercury had a group of bungalows . . . ," *Rosebud* (David Thomson, Vintage Books, 1997).

The argument between Welles and Houseman at Chasen's over Mercury players being cut off monertarily by RKO until Welles had submitted a completed script is repeated in several books on Welles but this account came from *Rosebud* (David Thomson, pg. 134-135).

Welles' account that he and Herman Mankiewicz "started searching for the man it was going to be about . . . ," came from *This is Orson Welles* (Orson Welles & Peter Bogdanovich, Edited by Jonathan Rosenberg, Da Capo Press, 1998).

David Thomson's quote that Mrs. Kane was "among the most mysterious mothers in film" appears in *Rosebud* (pg. 185).

Thomson's quote that Agnes appears in "two of the most indelibly humane" moments in *Citizen Kane* appears in his profile of Moorehead in his essential reference book *A Biographical Dictionary of Film* (Alfred A. Knopf, New York, 1996). Thompson's description of Agnes appearing to look "like a Madonna . . . " appears in *Rosebud* (pg. 184).

Frank Brady's quote, "Although Agnes Moorehead had appeared on the screen for only a few moments . . . , " came from *Citizen Welles* (pg. 316).

The charming story of Agnes at a cocktail party in the 1970's "cackling" over the teenager who asserted, "It's not like she was in *Citizen Kane!*" was related to me by Francine McAsey as told to her by a friend who was present at that encounter.

CHAPTER 5
"FANNY"

Agnes going back to New York and doing "a lot of little things . . . ," came from The Papers of Agnes Moorehead, The Wisconsin State Historical Society Archives, Box 60, folder 13.

Orson Welles "allowing himself" to sign a new contract with RKO, which allowed the studio to get the right of the final cut, and then writing much of *The Magnificent Ambersons* on King Vidor's yacht came from Citizen Welles (Frank Brady, Anchor Books, 1989).

That there was "never any doubt" that Agnes would play Fanny Minafer is from *This is Orson Welles* (Orson Welles & Peter Bogdanovich, edited by Jonathan Rosenberg, Da Capo Press, 1998).

Agnes' 12/3/45 lecture at the Actor's Lab, which gives much detail about the rehearsal process and Welles' direction of *The Magnificent Ambersons,* is found in Box 60, Folder 3 at the Wisconsin State Historical Society Archives, The Papers of Agnes Moorehead.

The use of the prerecorded soundtrack on the first day (10/28/41) of

The Magnificent Ambersons' shooting comes from *Citizen Welles* (pg. 318-319).

Welles' relationship with cinematographer Stanley Cortez is drawn from *Citizen Welles* (pg. 319-320).

Agnes' comments on the famous boiler scene come from her lecture at the Actor's Lab, 12/3/45, found in Box 60, Folder 3 at the Wisconsin State Historical Society Archives, The Papers of Agnes Moorehead and from *TV Guide* (July 17, 1965, pg. 25).

Peter Bogdanovich's question to Welles about rehearsing Agnes so much that she became "hysterical," and Welles' response, came from *This is Orson Welles* (pg. 129).

Welles' belief that the original ending of *The Magnificent Ambersons* was the best scene in the picture, and the description of that scene, is from *This is Orson Welles* (pg. 130).

Frank Brady writes of Orson painting a mustache on Agnes in *Citizen Welles* (pg. 320).

Telegram from George J. Schaefer to Orson Welles praising *The Magnificent Ambersons* and specifically Agnes' performance came from *Citizen Welles* (pg. 324). Follow up special-delivery letter to Welles from Schaefer regarding the disastrous first preview also came from *Citizen Welles* (pg. 324-325). The "heartfelt" letter to Welles from Joseph Cotten appears in *This Is Orson Welles* (pg. 121-122).

Welles' suggestion for an alternate "upbeat ending" to *The Magnificent Ambersons* came from *This Is Orson Welles* (pg. 123).

James Naremore's comments on Agnes' performance as Fanny comes from his book, *The Magic World of Orson Welles* (Oxford University Press, 1978). Pauline Kael's review of Agnes "as the nervous, bitter, hysterical old maid aunt . . ." came from her book, *Kiss Kiss Bang Bang* (Bantam Books, 1968). Kenneth Tynan's comments on Agnes' performance being "the best performance of its kind . . ." came from his book *Focus on Orson Welles* (Englewood Cliffs, New Jersey: Prentice-Hall, Inc. 1976).

Kenneth Tynan's letter to his friend, dated 4/11/43, about Agnes' performance, is from *Kenneth Tynan-Letters* (Edited by Kathleen Tynan, Random House, 1994).

Background on the balloting for the NY Film Critics Award came from *Movie Awards, The Ultimate Unofficial Guide to the Oscars, Golden Globes, Critics, Guild and Indie Honors* (Tom O'Neil, Berkley Publishing Group, 2001).

Agnes' acceptance speech before the NY Film Critics, The Papers of

Agnes Moorehead, Wisconsin State Historical Society Archives, Box 60.

David Selznick to Agnes (congratulations on NY film critics award), 12/30/42, The Papers of Agnes Moorehead, Wisconsin State Historical Society Archives, Box 141.

Background on the 1942 Academy Award ceremony came from *Movie Awards, The Ultimate Unofficial Guide to the Oscars, Golden Globes, Critics, Guild and Indie Honors* (Tom O'Neil, Berkley Publishing Group, 2001), *Inside Oscar: The Unofficial History of the Academy Awards* (Mason Wiley & Damien Bona, Ballantine Books, 1986) and *Behind the Oscar: The Secret History of the Academy Awards* (Anthony Holden, Plume, 1994).

Agnes' comments about Welles being her "Svengali," The Papers of Agnes Moorehead, The Wisconsin State Historical Society Archives, Box 60, folder 13.

"The only piece of advice . . .," *LA Herald Examiner*, 8/10/70.

CHAPTER 6
"THE FIRST LADY OF SUSPENSE"

Agnes' "tongue in cheek" complaint about working with Welles, "I think Orson is determined to make me the ugliest girl in pictures . . . ," *Hollywood* magazine (*She Doesn't Need Glamour,* October 1942).

Agnes' account of Orson Welles talking her out of signing with 20th Century-Fox for $650/week came from The Papers of Agnes Moorehead, The Wisconsin State Historical Society Archives, Box 60, folder 13.

Background material on *The Mayor of the Town* came from *The Encyclopedia of Old Time Radio* (John Dunning, Oxford University Press, 1998).

The author exchanged several e-mails with Conrad Binyon, who played "Butch" on *The Mayor of the Town.* Mr. Binyon shared his memories of working with Agnes and Lionel Barrymore and some background on the show itself which appears in this chapter.

The *Radio Life* profile of Lionel Barrymore, *We Heard Lionel in His Den,* Shirley Gordon.

That Welles privately coached Agnes to pattern Mrs. Reed "along the lines" of Aunt Fanny is found in *The Great Filmmakers: The Encyclopedia of Orson Welles* (pg. 273). The relationship between Welles and Joan Fontaine during the filming of *Jane Eyre* comes from Fontaine's autobiography *No Bed of Roses* (William Morrow & Company, 1978).

Welles wanted Agnes for the Edward G. Robinson role in *The Stranger,* from *This Is Orson Welles* (pg. 187).

Agnes' campaign for the role of Aspaira Conti in *Mrs. Parkington* comes largely from the article that Agnes clipped titled *The Role I Liked Best . . .* by Agnes Moorehead, *Saturday Evening Post,* May 7, 1949.

Letter from Leon Gordon, dated 7/2/45, regarding his decision not to cast Agnes in *The Green Years,* is found in The Papers of Agnes Moorehead, Wisconsin State Historical Society Archives, Madison, Wi, Box 143.

Background information on the classic radio series *Suspense* came from *Suspense: Twenty Years of Thrills and Chills* (Martin Gram, Jr., Morris Publishing, 1997), a very comprehensive history of that program which includes logs of every episode. Additional information came from *The Encyclopedia of Old Time Radio,* which discusses *Suspense* and "Sorry, Wrong Number" at length.

Elliott Reid appeared several times on *Suspense* and generously offered his considerable insight on the man behind the show, William Spier, to the author in an interview, 10/3/04.

Lucille Fletcher's recollections of how she came up with the idea of "Sorry. Wrong Number" and Agnes' comments regarding her initial reluctance to the episode, *Suspense: Twenty Years of Thrills and Chills* (both on pg. 22). Articles in *TV Radio-Life* (9/12/52) and *World of Yesterday,* Linda Downey (12/79), also includes background on "Sorry, Wrong Number."

Agnes' comments about not being "bitter" about not getting the movie version of *Sorry, Wrong Number* appear in *The New York Sun,* 9/1/48, in an article by Eileen Creelman.

CHAPTER 7
"HOLLYWOOD'S LEADING CHARACTER ACTRESS"

Bette Davis to Agnes, 10/24/44, The Papers of Agnes Moorehead, Wisconsin State Historical Society Archives, Box 141.

". . . It was like a circus . . . ," *This Is Orson Welles* (pg. 177).

". . . red circus wagons . . . , " *Citizen Welles* (pg. 363).

"Your flowers were truly beautiful . . . ," Susan Peters to Agnes, The Papers of Agnes Moorehead, Wisconsin State Historical Society Archives, Box 142.

"I always liked Jack . . . ," Conrad Binyon to author, 2/5/03.

"We ran the rough cut on *Dark Passage* . . . ," Jerry Wald to Agnes, 2/5/47,

The Papers of Agnes Moorehead, Wisconsin State Historical Society Archives, Box 144.

Telegram from Jane Broder to Agnes, 11/17/45, The Papers of Agnes Moorehead, Wisconsin State Historical Society Archives, Box 142. (Agnes' response is written on the back of this telegram.)

". . . after the opening of *Around the World* . . . ," Orson Welles to Agnes, 3/22/46, The Papers of Agnes Moorehead, Wisconsin State Historical Society Archives, Box 144.

". . . are you free and willing to be the greatest Emelia in the history of *Othello* . . . ," Orson Welles to Agnes, 2/3/49, The Papers of Agnes Moorehead, Wisconsin State Historical Society Archives, Box 146.

Background material including contracts, salaries, casting decisions and preview audience reaction to *The Lost Moment* come from The Papers of Walter Wanger, Wisconsin State Historical Society Archives, Mss 136AN, materials dealing with *The Lost Moment* are held in Box.

"Do you ever think before you say a line, hatchet face?," *Dark City Dames, The Wicked Women of Film Noir* (Eddie Muller, Regan Books/HarperCollins, 2001, pg. 23).

Miss Jane Wyman spoke to the author by phone regarding Agnes and their experiences working together on *Johnny Belinda*.

"I listened to you on the *Theatre Guild* . . . ," Helen Hayes to Agnes, 1/19/48, The Papers of Agnes Moorehead, Wisconsin State Historical Society Archives, Box 145.

"You wuz Wonderful . . . ," Peter Opp, Jr. to Agnes, 1/5/48, The Papers of Agnes Moorehead, Wisconsin State Historical Society Archives, Box 142.

". . . otherwise you would have heard from me before this . . . ," Robert Whitehead to Agnes, 4/7/48, The Papers of Agnes Moorehead, Wisconsin State Historical Society Archives, Box 146.

Agnes unable to attain film rights to Jessamyn West's novel *Friendly Persuasion,* letter from Henry Volkening to Agnes, 12/27/48, Wisconsin State Historical Society Archives, Box 145.

"Well, I am trying again . . . ," Robert N. Montgomery to Agnes, 12/17/48, The Papers of Agnes Moorehead, Wisconsin State Historical Society Archives, Box 145.

"Happy New Year and Thanks for your nice letter . . . ," Ronald Reagan to Agnes, 1/1/49, The Papers of Agnes Moorehead, Wisconsin State Historical Society Archives, Box 146.

"All my love, darling . . . ," Jack Lee to Agnes, 12/6/48, The Papers of Agnes Moorehead, Wisconsin State Historical Society Archives, Box 145.

". . . Your fan mail is indicative of the great popularity you enjoy among your audiences . . . ," G.A. Bunting to Agnes, 6/29/48, The Papers of Agnes Moorehead, Wisconsin State Historical Society Archives, Box 145.

Robert Montgomery acting like the "host of a bachelor party . . . ," *Inside Oscar* (pg. 187).

Instructions to nominees to the 21st Academy Awards, The Papers of Agnes Moorehead, Wisconsin State Historical Society Archives, Box 147.

". . . win, lose or draw . . . ," Jerry Wald to Agnes, 3/23/49, The Papers of Agnes Moorehead, Wisconsin State Historical Society Archives, Box 147.

"Did I or didn't I put on my girdle tonight? . . . ," *Inside Oscar* (pg. 189).

CHAPTER 8
"THE HIGHLIGHT OF MY CAREER"

Agnes' comment that Hollywood "was a place to earn enough money to be able to do . . . ," came from *The Sunday Pictorial* (*The Bright Lights* by Dick Richards, 6/10/51).

Agnes' comments regarding *Caged* are made to author Boze Hadleigh in his book *Hollywood Lesbians* (Barricade Books, 1994, pg. 189-190).

Letter of recommendation for Agnes from The LA Sheriff's office to Miss Alma Holzchuh, Superintendent, California Instituion of Women, Tehachapi, California, dated 6/23/49, found in The Papers of Agnes Moorehead, Wisconsin State Historical Society Archives, Madison, Wisconsin, Box 146.

Hedda Hopper's story about Agnes asking for divorce (*Film Actress Moorehead Asks Divorce, LA Times*, 5/16/50).

Information on Agnes' 1950 appearances on *Cavalcade of America* and *Suspense* come from Martin Grams, Jr. books, *The History of The Cavalcade of America* and *Suspense: Twenty Years of Thrills and Chills*.

Agnes becoming foster mother to Sean, interview with Debbie Reynolds by author, 6/20/04, and additional quotes are from *Debbie, My Life* (pg. 279).

Comments by Vincent Price regarding *The Adventures of Captain Fabian, Vincent Price: A Daughter's Biography* (Victoria Price, St. Martin's Griffin, 1999, pg. 195-196).

Paul Gregory stopping at a bar and watching Charles Laughton on *The Toast of The Town* appears in Simon Callow's excellent biography *Charles*

Laughton: A Difficult Actor (First Fromm International Paperback, 1997), which was corroborated by the author in an interview with Paul Gregory on 10/22/03.

Charles Laughton telling Elsa Lanchester ". . . don't be deceived by Paul's looks . . . ," appears in *Elsa Lanchester Herself* (Elsa Lanchester, St Martin's Press, 1983, pg. 202).

Simon Cowell's comments that in Elsa, Laughton had found, "a friend; a companion . . . ," (*Charles Laughton: A Difficult Actor*, pg. 22).

Elsa Lanchester's statement that "Paul Gregory came along just when Charles needed him most," *Elsa Lanchester Herself* (pg. 201).

Charles Laughton's assertion about wanting "not necessarily the best actors, but the best voices . . ." for *Don Juan in Hell* appears in *The Laughton Story: An Intimate Story of Charles Laughton* (Kurt Singer, The John C. Winston Company, 1954, pg. 257).

Elsa Lanchester's assertion that Madeline Carroll was the first choice for Donna Ana appears in *Elsa Lanchester Herself* (pg. 213).

Paul Gregory explained to the author that Miss Carroll was eliminated because "she didn't possess the sense of drama . . . ," interview on 10/22/03. Beulah Bondi as a possibility for Donna Ana appears in *Charles Laughton: An Intimate Biography* (Charles Higham, Doubleday & Co., Inc. 1976).

Paul Gregory's assertion that Charles originally wanted Elsa Lanchester for Donna Ana was told to the author in an interview, 10/22/03.

Charles Laughton on Agnes, "She is with us because Donna Ana has to change . . . " appears in the Manchester Daily Dispatch, 6/16/51. Paul Gregory's comments to Hedda Hopper appear in an article titled "Modest Miss Moorehead" from the *Chicago Sunday Tribune,* April 13, 1952.

Laughton's comment that Boyer is "the master of the tirade," *The Laughton Story: An Intimate Story of Charles Laughton* (pg. 258). Paul Gregory's comments on Boyer, ". . . great facility for the written language," interview with author on 10/22/03.

Laughton's comments regarding Hardwicke's ability to "speak an author's lines as if they were fresh . . . ," *The Laughton Story: An Intimate Story of Charles Laughton* (pg. 257). Paul Gregory's recollection of Hardwicke as a man of "humor and warmth," interview with author, 10/22/03.

Agnes' insistence on Robert Gist as stage manager was told to the author by Paul Gregory in an interview on 10/22/03.

Agnes' calling Laughton "a big bear with a big pink plush heart," *The Laughton Story: An Intimate Story of Charles Laughton* (pg. 101).

Charles Laughton working for "weeks" to make Agnes "emotionally involved" rather than relying on "phony tricks" was told to the author by Paul Gregory in an interview on 10/22/03.

Background on *Show Boat* is from MGM's *Greatest Musicals: The Arthur Freed Unit* (Hugh Fordin, Da Capo Press, NY, 1996).

Laughton's nerves and his belief that he "fucked up" the careers of the *Don Juan* actors prior to the play's opening in Claremont, *Elsa Lanchester Herself* (pg. 213). Laughton's reply to Boyer regarding "why rest?" is told in *The Laughton Story: An Intimate Story of Charles Laughton* (pg. 259).

Elsa Lanchester's assertion that "it was his (Gregory's) sheer invention to book tours . . . ," appears in *Elsa Lanchester Herself* (pg. 257).

The February travel itinerary for *Don Juan in Hell* was found in The Papers of Agnes Moorehead, Wisconsin State Historical Society Archives, Madison, Wisconsin.

Agnes' comments about the two farmers from Sacramento appear in *Modest Miss Moorehead* by Hedda Hopper, April 13, 1952.

Hardwicke coining the phrase "The Cranberry Juice circuit" appears in *Elsa Lanchester Herself* (pg. 214). Hardwicke's comment that ". . . one woman is vastly more clever than three men" appears in *The Laughton Story: An Intimate Story of Charles Laughton* (pg. 264).

Paul Gregory's comment that travel was "a nightmare" was made to author in an interview on 10/22/03. Boyer's nervousness when traveling is found in Charles Higham's *Charles Laughton: An Intimate Biography.*

Charges and countercharges made in the divorce proceedings of Agnes and Jack Lee were found in several newspaper clippings which Agnes kept in The Papers of Agnes Moorehead, The Wisconsin State Historical Society Archives, Box 149.

Paul Gregory's comments that Agnes was " . . . a tough, tough, tough woman . . . ," made to author in an interview on 10/22/03.

Telegram from Jack Kelk to Agnes, dated 5/19/51. The Papers of Agnes Moorehead, The Wisconsin State Historical Society Archives, Box 149.

Cedric Hardwicke's tax problems, and the temporary announcement of Boris Karloff as his replacement in the England tour, found in the *Daily Graphic,* 6/1/51, and *Daily Telegram,* 6/2/51, as well as in an interview by the author with Paul Gregory on 10/22/03.

John Clement not allowing anyone to present "any part" of *Man and Superman* in London while his play was booked appears in the *Birmingham Gazette,* 4/27/51.

Laurence Olivier's role as executive officer of the Festival of Britain is referred to in Simon Callow's *Charles Laughton: A Difficult Actor* (pg. 213)

That, for Laughton, the British tour of *Don Juan in Hell* was "bittersweet" due to he and Elsa not returning to Britain during the war and for receiving American citizenship is found in *Charles Laughton: A Difficult Actor* (pg. 213) and *Elsa Lanchester Herself* (pg. 216)

Various quotes by Agnes regarding the tour of *Don Juan in Hell* in Britain are found in newspaper clippings she kept in a scrapbook devoted to this tour in The Papers of Agnes Moorehead, Wisconsin State Historical Society Archives, Box 63.

Moorehead's Donna Ana, ". . . was perhaps the most inspired portrayal" (*Manchester Daily Dispatch's* article, *Triumph of the Don Juan Quartette,* by Ernest Lewis, 6/19/51). ". . . She is magnificence itself" (The *Birmingham Evening Dispatch,* Norman Holbrook, 6/26/51).

Note from Vivien Leigh to Agnes, The Papers of Agnes Moorehead, Wisconsin State Historical Society Archives, Box 148.

". . . The highlight of my career" (*The Role Agnes Moorehead Loves Most* from The *Cincinnati Post,* 11/29/72).

Additional background on *Don Juan in Hell* appears from a lecture which Agnes presented at the Fresno Convention of the Western Speech Association titled, "Staging *Don Juan in Hell,*" May 1954, The Papers of Agnes Moorehead, The Wisconsin State Historical Society Archives, Box 60.

CHAPTER 9
"THE FABULOUS REDHEAD"

James Robert Parish's comments regarding Agnes being an actress who "no longer was the striving actress seeking to reach a higher plateau . . . ," comes from his book *Good Dames* (A.S. Barnes and Company, 1974).

Letter to Agnes inviting her to participate in the "April in Paris" Ball, dated 4/2/52, The Papers of Agnes Moorehead, Wisconsin State Historical Society Archives, Box 150.

Telegram from Hume Cronyn to Agnes, dated May 7, 1952 and delivered to the Plymouth Theatre where Agnes was appearing in *Don Juan in Hell,* The Papers of Agnes Moorehead, Wisconsin State Historical Society Archives, Box 150. Letter from Hume Cronyn to Agnes Moorehead, dated May 24, 1952, The Papers of Agnes Moorehead, Wisconsin State Historical Society Archives, Box 150. Letter from Hume Cronyn to Agnes

Moorehead, dated May 30, 1952, The Papers of Agnes Moorehead, Wisconsin State Historical Society Archives, Box 150.

Background on Sylvia Richards, *Naming Names* (Victor Navasky, Viking Press, 1980). Letter from Robert Richards to Agnes, dated 10/9/51, The Papers of Agnes Moorehead, Wisconsin State Historical Society Archives, Box 150. Norman Corwin's comments that Agnes was "the most apolitical person I ever knew . . . ," came from an interview the author had with Mr. Corwin on 9/30/03.

Comments by Paul Gregory regarding the relationship between Agnes and Robert Gist, "she could keep him on a short leash . . . ," and Gist dyeing his hair to match Agnes', were made by Mr. Gregory to the author in an interview dated 10/22/03. Helen Hayes' note to Agnes, congratulating her on her marriage to Gist, dated 8/27/54, The Papers of Agnes Moorehead, Wisconsin State Historical Society Archives, Box 73. Details on Agnes buying the "old Sigmund Romberg house" in Beverly Hills came from Jill's Hollywood, *Transit Riders' Digest,* dated 8/24/53.

Agnes saying, "I'm as big a star as Greer Garson" to Paul Gregory and his response was told to the author by Mr. Gregory in an interview, 11/5/03.

The sections regarding Vincent Price replacing Charles Laughton in *Don Juan in Hell* are drawn from Victoria Prices' *Vincent Price, A Daughter's Biography* (pg. 204-205).

"Actors go through dry spells . . . ," Paul Gregory to the author, 11/5/03.

"I am almighty serious about this reading thing . . . ," Charles Laughton to Agnes, 6/5/49, The Papers of Agnes Moorehead, Wisconsin State Historical Society Archives, Box 145.

"I hope to goodness you persist with the reading thing . . . ," Charles Laughton to Agnes, 7/11/49, The Papers of Agnes Moorehead, Wisconsin State Historical Society Archives, Box 145.

Comments by James Thurber thanking her for helping him sell more books through her "popular readings," came from Warren Sherk's *A Very Private Person.* Agnes reading Queen Elizabeth's letter to the Bishop of Pike ("Prrroud Prrrelate . . . "), from James Robert Parish's *Good Dames.* Selections which Agnes used in her one-woman show are included in Warren Sherk's *A Very Private Person* (pg. 67).

Paul Gregory overhearing an audience member refer to Agnes as "The Fabulous Redhead," Paul Gregory to author, 11/5/03.

Charles Laughton's directorial advice to Agnes prior to her Salt Lake City show, The Papers of Agnes Moorehead, The Wisconsin State Historical

Society Archives, Box 150. Paul Gregory's comments that "all Agnes wanted him (Laughton) to do was view the show and say, 'you were wonderful, darling . . . ,'" to author on 11/5/03.

Paul Gregory's assertion that Agnes "threw a fit" when he offered Robert Gist a part in *The Caine Mutiny Court-Martial,* interview with author on 11/5/03.

Jane Wyman's comments regarding the film *Magnificent Obsession* were made in a phone interview with the author. Otto Kruger's comments regarding the same film came from *Jane Wyman: The Actress and the Woman* (Lawrence Quirk, December Books, 1986). Agnes' comment that there was "something starry-eyed, something out of balance . . ." about the film *Magnificent Obsession* were also from the book, *Jane Wyman: The Actress and the Woman* (pg. 160).

Paul Gregory's comment that Agnes was "a shit" for directing an independent version of *Don Juan in Hell* in 1955, was said in an interview by Mr. Gregory to the author, 10/22/03. Mary Astor's regard for Agnes as a director and her lack of comfort on the road touring in *Don Juan in Hell* come from Miss Astor's autobiography, *A Life on Film* (Dell Books, 1967, pg. 209).

Mary Astor's letter to Agnes regarding her complaints about *Don Juan in Hell,* The Papers of Agnes Moorehead, Wisconsin State Historical Society Archives, Box 150. "Mary was not steeped in the classics," Agnes quoted in *Role Agnes Moorehead Loves Most,* from *Cincinnati Post,* 11/29/72.

Synopses of Agnes' appearances on *Suspense* during the 50's, from Martin Grams, Jr's book, *Suspense: Twenty Years of Thrills and Chills.*

Agnes not getting the TV version of *Sorry, Wrong Number,* produced by John Houseman, came from *Front and Center.*

The synopses and reviews of Moorehead films released in 1956 come from *Agnes Moorehead: A Bio-Bibliography* (Lynn Kear, Greenwood Press, 1992).

"Wouldn't you?," Debbie Reynolds to author, 6/20/04.

CHAPTER 10
"RIVALRY, TEMPEST & GINGER"

Sources of information regarding the film *The True Story of Jesse James* come from *Nicholas Ray* (John Francis Kreidl, Twayne Publishers, 1977) and *Nicholas Ray, An American Journey* (Bernard Eisenschitz, London;

Boston, Faber & Faber, 1993).

Paul Gregory to Harold Williams ("you and I had better get together . . ."), The Paul Gregory Papers, American Heritage Center, University of Wyoming, Laramie.

Paul Gregory to St. John's Military Academy, The Paul Gregory Papers, American Heritage Center, University of Wyoming, Laramie.

Sean was a "very dear and very sweet-natured boy . . . ," Paul Gregory to the author, 10/22/03.

Norman Corwin's comments regarding Agnes and *The Rivalry* were made to the author in an interview on 9/30/03.

Letter from Paul Gregory to *The Rivalry* actors ("as you know . . . is based on a very controversial subject . . ."), dated 9/17/57, The Agnes Moorehead Papers, Wisconsin State Historical Society Archives, Box 151.

Telegram from Arlene Francis Gabel to Agnes, 9/22/57, The Papers of Agnes Moorehead, Wisconsin State Historic Society Archives, Box 151. Telegram from Paul Gregory to Agnes, The Papers of Agnes Moorehead, Wisconsin State Historical Society Archives, Box 151.

Agnes' comments that there are "3 stars and not one or two . . . ," and Paul Gregory's observations that "If Ray Massey had an interview, she had to have one too," Paul Gregory to author, 10/22/03.

That Agnes had an "absolute fit" when he cast Robert Gist in *The Naked and the Dead*, Paul Gregory to author, 11/5/03.

Gregory's letter that Gist had been cast "completely against my wishes," The Paul Gregory Papers, American Heritage Center, University of Wyoming, Laramie. Agnes response that Gist is "the malaria kid in every sense of the word . . . ," The Paul Gregory Papers, American Heritage Center, University of Wyoming, Laramie.

Agnes comments on *Tale of Two Cities* to Kay Gardella, 3/27/57, Paul Gregory's congratulations on her performance as Madam DeFarge, The Paul Gregory Papers, American Heritage Center, University of Wyoming, Laramie.

"The part of the mother in Ben-Hur isn't so great — it's only long," Agnes to Paul Gregory, The Paul Gregory Papers, American Heritage Center, University of Wyoming, Laramie. Gregory also confirmed that Agnes had been offered this part in an interview with the author.

Details on *The Scourge of the Sun,* from correspondence between Paul Gregory and Agnes, The Paul Gregory Papers, American Heritage Center, University of Wyoming, Laramie.

"Darling, don't worry about making a living . . . ," Paul Gregory to Agnes, The Paul Gregory Papers, American Heritage Center, University of Wyoming, Laramie.

New York Times review of *The Psalms of David,* 7/6/58.

Lynn Kear's comment about *Night of the Quarter Moon* being "hilariously dated" is from her book, *Agnes Moorehead, A Bio-Bibliography.*

Comments made by Carol Lynley regarding working with Agnes, from an interview with author, 4/10/03.

"In view of the approach of Halloween . . . ," The *New York Times,* 10/28/58.

Announcement of Agnes and Viveca Lindfors appearing in *Mary Stuart* appears in The *Vancouver Sun,* March 7, 1959. Information regarding Agnes' demand for a maid and apartment at the expense of the Vancouver International Festival, in addition to $8,000 salary, is confirmed by Paul Gregory in an interview with the author on 10/22/03, who added, "Agnes was always making outlandish demands."

Paul Gregory spoke extensively with the author in interviews on 10/22 & 11/3/04 regarding problems with Ginger Rogers and the interference of Ginger's mother, Lela, on *The Pink Jungle.* Paul Gregory's quote from Fred Astaire about "Gin" requesting a "dance-in" were also made to the author on 11/3/04. Additional sources include, *Variety,* 10/16/59, Hedda Hopper, *Los Angeles Times,* 10/30/59, *Boston Daily Globe,* December 3, 1959, and the *New York Post,* December 9, 1959 (where Ginger is quoted as saying, "it needs more than a face-lift. They better bury it." Also consulted was a letter from Paul Gregory to Ginger Rogers, dated 1/19/60, which outlined to Ginger his view that she was "laboring under a delusion" as to why the show closed as well as the interference of her mother, The Paul Gregory Papers, American Heritage Center, University of Wyoming, Laramie. Ginger Rogers comments regarding *The Pink Jungle* appear in her autobiography, *Ginger: My Story* (HarperCollins, 1991). Vernon Duke's comment to Agnes regarding Paul Gregory's intention to "reopen the show minus G," was written on a postcard Duke sent to Agnes, dated 1/3/60, The Papers of Agnes Moorehead, Wisconsin State Historical Society Archives, Box 153.

CHAPTER 11
"DEBBIE, COLUMBO & PENGO"

"The Disney studios was one of the best studios to work at . . . ," Karl

Malden to author, 10/1/02.

"We were like a family . . . ," Malden to author, 10/1/02.

"Aggie was a strong, solid person . . . ," Malden to author, 10/1/02.

Richard Anderson was interviewed by the author on 5/27/03.

"The reason I suggested her," and other background information on "The Invaders," from *The Twilight Zone Companion* (Marc Scott Zicree, Silman-James Press, 1992).

Detailed proposal of *Agnes Moorehead Presents* found in The Papers of Agnes Moorehead, Wisconsin State Historical Society Archives.

The information that Agnes auditioned for the role of *Hazel*, provided by Ted Key, the creator of the comic strip which appeared for many years in *The Saturday Evening Post,* in a letter to the author dated 3/25/04.

"Screaming Howard . . . but I loved him," Karl Malden to the author, 10/1/02.

"Jim was a professional . . . ," Karl Malden to author, 10/1/02.

"In one scene our movie family was required to witness a trading post burn . . . ," *Baby Doll* (Carroll Baker, Arbor House, 1983).

". . . but I also discovered that she had a very dry inside type of humor . . . ," Debbie Reynolds to author, 6/20/04.

"You know, it's rare to form a lasting friendship . . . ," Agnes in *Photoplay,* October 1966, *My Son Owes His Life to Debbie.*

"I thought she was quite brilliant . . . ," Debbie Reynolds to author, 6/20/04.

"I tried setting her up a few times . . . ," Debbie Reynolds to author, 6/20/04.

"The logs of the raft were slippery . . . ," *Baby Doll* (pg. 217)

"Theater is the best ambassador of peace I know of . . . ," *Dayton Journal Herald* (*Actress Sees Theater as Peace Instrument,* 10/26/61).

Letter from James Clavell to Agnes, 2/19/62, Wisconsin State Historical Society Archives, Box 64.

Letter to Agnes from Anthony Lyons, 2/6/62, The Papers of Agnes Moorehead, Wisconsin State Historical Society Archives, Box 128.

Details on how much actors made and their billing are found in financial information/contracts found in *Prescription: Murder* files in the Paul Gregory Papers, American Heritage Center, University of Wyoming, Laramie.

"It never bothered Aggie that she was only in the first act . . . ," Paul Gregory to author, 11/5/03.

". . . made us feel welcome to the Golden Gate . . . ," *Vanity Will Get You*

Somewhere (Joseph Cotten, toExcel Press, 1998, pg. 148).

". . . justifiably earned her the title Queen of the Road . . . ," *Vanity Will Get You Somewhere* (Cotten, pg. 147)

Story about Agnes describing the pains of labor she experienced delivering Sean was told by Paul Gregory to the author, 11/5/03.

"Jo murdered Aggie just before my entrance . . . ," *Laid Back in Hollywood* (Patricia Medina Cotten, Belle Publishing, 1998, pg. 126).

"I was slowly pulling on my gloves . . . , " *Vanity Will Get You Somewhere* (Cotten, pg.148-149)

Letter from William Barrett to Agnes, 1/31/62, The Papers of Agnes Moorehead, Wisconsin State Historical Society Archives, Box 128.

Wierum was "able and professional . . . ," *Vanity Will Get You Somewhere* (Cotten, pg.149)

Letter from Gavin Lambert to Agnes, The Papers of Agnes Moorehead, Wisconsin State Historical Society Archives, Box 65.

"A very satisfying show . . . ," Paul Gregory to author, 11/5/03.

"Boyer wouldn't let her . . . ," Paul Gregory to author, 11/5/03.

"By no means is it all I hoped for from the stand point of Miss Swanson . . . ," Paul Gregory to Agnes, 7/10/62, Paul Gregory Papers, American Heritage Center, The University of Wyoming, Laramie.

". . . she didn't push herself on you . . . ," Laurie Main to author, 4/21/04.

Good luck telegrams to Agnes on the opening night of *Lord Pengo* from the Papers of Agnes Moorehead, Wisconsin State Historical Society Archives, Box 66.

Basil Rathbone to Agnes, 11/25/62, The Papers of Agnes Moorehead, Wisconsin State Historical Society Archives, Box 66.

Mrs. Kennedy being presented to the cast of *Lord Pengo* in the "only secure room deemed by the secret service," was told to the author by Laurie Main, 4/21/04.

"Not that I want to crowd J. Edgar Hoover out of a job . . . ," Agnes to Vincent Price, *Vincent Price: A Daughter's Biography* (pg. 288)

". . . it is good to know he has been freed . . . ," Remsen Dubois Bird to Agnes, 2/4/63, The Papers of Agnes Moorehead, Wisconsin State Historical Society Archives, Box 68. (Bird was an educator and President of Occidental College).

". . . you are so clever . . . ," telegram from Paul Gregory to Agnes, 12/6/62, The Papers of Agnes Moorehead, Wisconsin State Historical Society Archives, Box 66.

CHAPTER 12
"THE WITCH OF ENDOR"

"I consider it a privilege to work with such a fine actress . . . , " Jerry Lewis to Agnes, 4/11/63, The Papers of Agnes Moorehead, Wisconsin State Historical Society Archives, Box 67.

"The picture is getting along beautifully . . . ," Agnes to Georgia Johnstone, 4/21/63, The Georgia Johnstone Papers re: Agnes Moorehead, T-Mss 2003-039, Billy Rose Theatre Collection, The New York Public Library for the Performing Arts, Box 1, folder 2.

"It was quite a pressure . . . ," Agnes to Georgia Johnstone, 5/7/63, The Georgia Johnstone Papers re: Agnes Moorehead, T-Mss 2003-039, Billy Rose Theatre Collection, The New York Public Library for the Performing Arts, Box 1, folder 2.

". . . Most teenagers are alike . . . ," Agnes in *The Cleveland Daily Banner*, Cleveland Tn., 3/21/63.

Paul Gregory preparing *One of My Lovers is Missing for Agnes*, from the Paul Gregory Papers, American Heritage Center, University of Wyoming, Laramie.

"2 large stones were found and removed . . . I only hope and pray that she will have some good normal years ahead of her," Agnes to Georgia Johnstone, 6/12 & 6/13/63, The Georgia Johnstone Papers re: Agnes Moorehead, T-Mss 2003-039, Billy Rose Theatre Collection, The New York Public Library for the Performing Arts, Box 1, folder 2.

Agnes' comments from the *Flashbacks* program found in clippings of an article titled *Moorehead about Virginia, Unrealistic and Sick* by Helen McNamra, found in The Papers of Agnes Moorehead, Wisconsin State Historical Society Archives, Box 154.

Letters in support of Agnes' comments in *Flashbacks* also found in The Papers of Agnes Moorehead, Wisconsin State Historical Society Archives, Box 154.

The backstage story on the development of *Bewitched* comes courtesy of *Bewitched Forever* (Herbie J Pilato, The Summit Publishing Group, 1996), an excellent biography of the show and its cast and crew A must for any serious fan of the show.

Elizabeth Montgomery was "a lot of fun . . . ," Laurie Main to the author, 4/21/04.

"He was from Chicago and was in New York . . . ," Karl Malden to author, 10/1/02.

Account of York injuring his back on *They Came to Cordura* from *The Seesaw Girl and Me* (Dick York, New Path Press, 2004).

"Dick, she isn't as ugly as you said she was . . . ," told to the author by Joey York, 6/30/02, and also recounted in *The Seesaw Girl and Me* (pg.86)

"He was just too perfect for the part . . . ," William Asher to author, 3/28/02.

Story of how Elizabeth Montgomery approached Agnes at Bloomingdales about playing "Mother" was told by William Asher to author, and is also included in *Bewitched Forever* (pg.18)

Paul Gregory's belief that he was "instrumental" in getting *Bewitched* for Agnes, Paul Gregory to author, 11/5/03.

"The script sent to me by Dozier was titled, *Bewitched* and they want me to play a witch . . . ," Agnes to Georgia Johnstone, 10/24/63, The Georgia Johnstone Papers re: Agnes Moorehead, T-Mss 2003-039, Billy Rose Theatre Collection, The New York Public Library for the Performing Arts, Box 1, folder 2.

"I thought people would rather watch an operation or something," Agnes in the *Dallas Times Herald*, 6/7/65.

"I'm not at all wicked . . . ," Agnes quoted by Sally Hammond in the *LA Citizen News*, 8/1/64.

"The Ultimate mother-in-law," William Asher to author, 3/28/02.

". . . Please don't worry about preliminary indications of wild ghost outfits . . . ," William Dozier to Agnes, 11/7/63, The Papers of Agnes Moorehead, Wisconsin State Historical Society Archives, Box 73.

"The whole thing was very strange . . . ," Elizabeth Montgomery to Herbie J Pilato, *Bewitched Forever* (pg. 4)

Agnes stating she was "trapped" when pilot of *Bewitched* was picked up, *TV Guide*, July 17-25, 1965.

"I found my series was sold . . . ," Agnes to Georgia Johnstone, 2/20/64, The Georgia Johnstone Papers re: Agnes Moorehead, T-Mss 2003-039, Billy Rose Theatre Collection, The New York Public Library for the Performing Arts, Box 1, folder 3.

"*Barefoot* was offered to me . . . ," Agnes to Georgia Johnstone, 4/1/64, The Georgia Johnstone Papers re: Agnes Moorehead, T-Mss 2003-039, Billy Rose Theatre Collection, The New York Public Library for the Performing Arts, Box 1 folder 3.

". . . she's not hateful but mischievous . . . ," *The Detroit News*, 11/11/71.

". . . very easy to work with and such a professional . . . ," Karl Malden to author, 10/1/02.

Background on the filming of *Hush . . . Hush, Sweet Charlotte* comes from the following sources: *Fasten Your Seatbelts: The Passionate Life of Bette Davis* (Lawrence J. Quirk, William Morrow & Company, 1990) and *Joan Crawford, A Biography* (Bob Thomas, Simon and Schuster, 1978).

". . . bless you my dear friend . . . ," Joan Crawford to Agnes, The Papers of Agnes Moorehead, Wisconsin State Historical Society Archives, Box 72.

"I will be in the middle of this series . . . ," Agnes to Georgia Johnstone, 7/28/64, The Georgia Johnstone Papers re: Agnes Moorehead, T-Mss 2003-039, Billy Rose Theatre Collection, The New York Public Library for the Performing Arts, Box 1, folder 3.

"Thank you so much for being so nice to me . . . ," Joan Crawford to Agnes, 9/4/64, The Papers of Agnes Moorehead, Wisconsin State Historical Society Archives, Box 72.

"When it came to the actual shoot . . . ," *Debbie: My Life* (pg. 277-278).

"I am in a literal merry-go-round . . . ," Agnes to Georgia Johnstone, 8/3/64, The Georgia Johnstone Papers re: Agnes Moorehead, T-Mss 2003-039, Billy Rose Theatre Collection, The New York Public Library for the Performing Arts, Box 1 folder 3.

"The chief charms of *Bewitched* are . . . ," The *New York Telegram,* Harriett Van Horne, 9/18/64.

"Playing her mischief brewing mother . . . ," The *New York Daily News,* Kay Gardella, 9/18/64.

"Between you and me and Halloween . . . ," *TV Guide,* Cleveland Amory.

Chapter 13
"A Star is Born"

Fan mail sited found in The Papers of Agnes Moorehead, Wisconsin State Historical Society Archives, Box 73.

"I am so tired, I can't tell you they can take these series and go some place far away . . . ," Agnes Moorehead (AM) to Georgia Johnstone (GJ), The Georgia Johnstone Papers re: Agnes Moorehead, T-Mss 2003-039, Billy Rose Theatre collection, The New York Public Library for the Performing Arts, Box 1, folder 3.

"Aggie's big debate . . . ," Dick York to Herbie J Pilato, *Bewitched Forever* (pg. 58).

"She took direction better . . . ," *Bewitched Forever* (pg. 58-59).

"A luxury shoot," Kasey Rogers to author, 1/11/04.

Montgomery was "every man's idea of the ideal wife . . . ," and York, "was a hell of a comedian . . . ," Kasey Rogers to author, 1/11/04.

Sam's twitch . . . "Do Something!," Bill Asher quoted in the *New York Times,* 11/22/64.

"She has quality, charm, warmth intelligence. Of course you know she plays herself . . . ," Agnes re: Elizabeth Montgomery, *TV Guide* article, *Agnes Moorehead's Recipe for TV Success,* July 17, 1965.

Telegram from Elizabeth Montgomery to Agnes re: TV-Radio Mirror Award, 2/19/65, The Papers of Agnes Moorehead, The Wisconsin State Historical Society Archives, Box 78.

Comments by *Bewitched Forever* author, Herbie J Pilato, from an e-mail interview, 1/17/04.

TV Guide's profile of Dick York, which includes York's comments on being "open to any and all ideas and thoughts . . ." re: religion, and Agnes's comment that "I probably understand him better than the others . . . ," published in *TV Guide,* May 29, 1965.

"Dick York absolutely loved Agnes . . . ," Herbie J Pilato to author, e-mail interview, 1/17/04.

"Dick admired and enjoyed working with Aggie . . . ," Joey York to author, interview, 6/30/02.

Robert Palmer's comment that Agnes believed that York was the one "who really held the show together . . . ," from *Dreaming of Jeannie, TV's Prime Time in a Bottle* (Steve Cox with Howard Frank, St. Martin's Press, 2000).

Background on the Golden Globe awards telecast 2/8/65 from Tom O' Neil's *A Variety Book Movie Awards: The Ultimate, Unofficial Guide to the Oscars, Golden Globes, Critics, Guild & Indie Honors* (pg. 273-274).

Background on the Academy Award ceremony on 4/5/64 come from the following sources: Tom O'Neil's *A Variety Book Movie Awards: The Ultimate Guide to the Oscars, Golden Globes, Critics, Guild & Indie Honors* and Mason Wiley & Damien Bona's *Inside Oscar: The Unofficial History of the Academy Awards.*

Information on Agnes' run in *High Spirits* came from a folder that Agnes kept of clippings and other information on the show, The Papers of Agnes Moorehead, Wisconsin State Historical Society Archives, Box 79.

Agnes' comment on Marlon Brando while visiting the set of *The Chase,* AM to GJ, The Georgia Johnstone Papers Re: Agnes Moorehead, T-Mss

2003-039, Billy Rose Theatre Collection, The New York Public Library for the Performing Arts, Box 1, folder 3, dated 7/11/65.

"I am not of the mumbling school . . . ," *LA Herald Examiner,* 8/10/70.

Agnes' comments regarding the death of Everett Sloane and the "fair" script of *The Singing Nun,* AM to GJ, The Georgia Johnstone Papers Re: Agnes Moorehead, T-Mss 2003-039, Billy Rose Theatre Collection, The New York Public Library for the Performing Arts, Box 1 folder 3, dated 8/23/65.

Agnes' comments regarding "the star treatment" she got at MGM from The Georgia Johnstone Papers Re: Agnes Moorehead, T-Mss 2003-039, Billy Rose Theatre Collection, The New York Public Library for the Performing Arts, Box 1, folder 3, dated 9/30/65 & 10/13/65.

Paul Gregory preparing a film for Agnes, Tallulah Bankhead and Janet Gaynor, *Tallulah! The Life and Times of Tallulah Bankhead* (Joel Lobenthal, Regan Books, 2004, pg. 524); Tallulah calling Agnes regarding a play on suffragettes, from same book, pg. 524-525.

Letter from Shirley Temple Black to Agnes, dated 10/7/65, The Papers of Agnes Moorehead, Wisconsin State Historical Society Archives, Box 81.

Cesar Romero's comments on "the annual party" and Freddie Jones' comments on Agnes' routine prior to the Christmas party, both in Warren Sherk's *A Very Private Person*; Kasey Rogers comments on the Christmas party, interview with author on 1/11/04; Laurie Main's comments, "grand fun — everyone who was anyone in Hollywood . . . ," made to author in an interview dated 4/21/04.

Letter to Agnes inviting her to sit on the member nominating committee for foreign language films from the Academy of Motion Pictures Arts and Sciences, 12/30/65, The Papers of Agnes Moorehead, Wisconsin State Historical Society Archives, Box 87.

Karl Malden's story of his purchasing a Chevy from Agnes, interview with author, 10/1/02.

Barron Polan to Agnes, 5/2/66: "Now, I am relieved to have had a call from Georgia the Johnstone, telling me that you've already had the knife . . . ," The Papers of Agnes Moorehead, Wisconsin State Historical Society Archives, Box 88.

"My lumpy buddy," Debbie Reynolds to Agnes, The Papers of Agnes Moorehead, Wisconsin State Historical Society Archives, Box 88.

Interview with Rose Marie, 8/1/02.

"Sweet Agnes — I know you were pleased for Alice . . . ," Debbie

Reynolds and Harry Karl to Agnes, 5/23/66, The Papers of Agnes Moorehead, Wisconsin State Historical Society Archives.

Background on Agnes' acting school by Quint Benedetti in interviews with author, 7/22/03 & 7/23/03.

Bernard Fox generously wrote the author of his relationship with Agnes and his experiences working for her acting school in letters dated 3/19/04 & 3/29/04.

Laurie Main's experiences at the acting school, interview with author on 4/21/04.

"Their relationship was the kind where they were great friends . . . ," James MacArthur, regarding Helen Hayes and Agnes, from an e-mail interview on 8/23/03.

Helen Hayes to Agnes, 9/22/66, The Papers of Agnes Moorehead, Wisconsin State Historical Society Archives, Box 91.

James MacArthur on Paul Gregory, e-mail interview, 8/23/03.

Agnes' use of her spare time, "she even used to climb a very high ladder to wash windows . . . ," came from Warren Sherk's *A Very Private Person*.

Agnes assembling her household help on Sundays to recite the Bible was told to author by Bernard Fox in a letter dated 3/29/04.

Telegram from Rock Hudson to Agnes inviting her to an informal party for Lauren Bacall, dated 10/14/66, The Papers of Agnes Moorehead, The Wisconsin State Historical Society Archives, Box 90.

Lucille Ball's story about urging Agnes to see *How the West Was Won* from *Lucy in the Afternoon* (Jim Brochu, Simon and Schuster, 1990 pg. 78).

Agnes' relationship with Polly Garland and Freddie Jones is told in Warren Sherk's *A Very Private Person*.

"Agnes . . . absolutely loved Ronald Reagan," Quint Benedetti to author, 7/22/03.

Ronald Reagan to Agnes, 12/7/66, The Papers of Agnes Moorehead, Wisconsin State Historical Society Archives, Box 93.

The background story of the making of *Alice Through the Looking Glass* came from an interview by the author with Nanette Fabray, 9/26/04.

Quint Benedetti's comment to author of his belief that Orson Welles "kept making excuses," to avoid seeing Agnes, were made in an interview dated 7/22/03.

Beatrice Welles letter to Agnes, April 25, 1967, The Papers of Agnes Moorehead, The Wisconsin State Historical Society Archives, Box 99.

Congratulations by Joan Crawford on Agnes' Emmy win, 6/16/67, The

Papers of Agnes Moorehead, The Wisconsin State Historical Society Archives, Box 99.

Conrad Binyon to Agnes, 7/17/67, The Papers of Agnes Moorehead, The Wisconsin State Historical Society Archives, Box 99.

Agnes taking lessons in sign language, *Tampa Tribune & Times,* 11/12/67.

CHAPTER 14
"THE LIONESS IN WINTER"

"I wouldn't say she was hard . . . ," Quint Benedetti to the author, 7/22/03.

Larry Russell and the author e-mailed back and forth on the subject of Agnes and Sean — Mr. Russell lives in Canada. Most of the information printed in this chapter are from e-mails dated 3/29/04, 3/30/04, 4/2/04, 4/5/04, & 4/6/04. He provided me with a great deal about his family history, which he gave me as a way of establishing his credibility, but has asked that I not put his family background in print — l can say it is a very prominent and wealthy family.

". . . I told her that she didn't allow him any breathing space . . . ," Debbie Reynolds to author, 6/20/04.

"I didn't find Sean to be unusual . . . ," Debbie Reynolds to author, 6/20/04.

"He wanted to be on his own, with his own friends . . . ," Agnes in *TV Radio Show,* December 1970, *Bewitched Star's Son Vanishes.* (Agnes also kept a copy of this article, written by Clarke Hall, in a scrapbook, Box 129, The Papers of Agnes Moorehead, Wisconsin State Historical Society Archives — which is where I discovered it).

Agnes finding empty beer cans in Sean's room, *Debbie: My Story* (pg. 280).

"He wouldn't listen . . . he is so bright . . . ," Agnes in *TV Radio Show,* December 1970, *Bewitched Star's Son Vanishes.*

"Sean is nowhere to be found . . . ," Agnes to Georgia Johnstone, 9/11/67, The Georgia Johnstone Papers re: Agnes Moorehead, T-Mss 2003-039, Billy Rose Theatre Collection, The New York Public Library for the Performing Arts, Box 1, folder 6.

"Barron . . . about the latest difficulty with Sean . . . ," Georgia Johnstone to Agnes, 9/20/67, The Georgia Johnstone Papers re: Agnes Moorehead, T-Mss 2003-039, Billy Rose Theatre Collection, The New York Public Library for the Performing Arts, Box 1, folder 6.

"She knew he was very angry at her and finding a gun . . . ," Debbie Reynolds, *Debbie: My Story* (pg. 280).

". . . I think he became one of the children of the street," Debbie Reynolds to author, 6/20/04.

Sean and Mark Russell going to Switzerland and living off "the good graces of Paulette Goddard," Larry Russell to author, 3/30/04.

"All I can do is pray . . . ," *Pasadena Star News Independent,* August 10, 1970.

Quint Benedetti's recollections of traveling cross-country with Agnes, his observations that Agnes "had a convenient way of forgetting to pay her employees" and his assertion that Agnes "gave me back my self-respect" come from interviews with Mr. Benedetti on 7/22 & 7/23/03.

Quint Benedetti on Mollie Moorehead, " . . . she didn't want Margaret to be forgotten . . . ," Quint Benedetti to author, 7/22/03.

"Her mother was very sweet, but tried to convert people . . . ," Paul Gregory to author, 10/22/03.

Jeanne Marking, of Reedsburg, Wisconsin, spoke of Mollie and Grace Conkling in a letter to the author, 4/25/02.

Gordon Emery's recollections of Agnes and Mollie Moorehead are from an interview with author, 6/8/02.

"It must have been devine guidance that brought me home at this time . . . ," Agnes to Georgia Johnstone, 5/15/67, The Georgia Johnstone Papers re: Agnes Moorehead, T-Mss 2003-039, Billy Rose Theatre Collection, The New York Public Library for the Performing Arts, Box 1, folder 6.

Agnes' response to what she felt was an unfair newspaper profile of her is dated 11/11/67, The Georgia Johnstone Papers re: Agnes Moorehead, T-Mss 2003-039, Billy Rose Theatre Collection, The New York Public Library for the Performing Arts, Box 1, folder 6.

Agnes' account of the 1968 Emmy Award snafu appears in *The Boston Herald Traveler*, 6/18/68.

Agnes reporting to Georgia Johnstone that she is "contemplating writing a book . . . ," (letter dated 8/27/68) and her comments ". . . I don't know whether *Bewitched* will go on or whether I will be on it . . . ," (letter dated 9/28/68), The Georgia Johnstone Papers re: Agnes Moorehead, T-Mss 2003-039, Billy Rose Theatre Collection, The New York Public Library for the Performing Arts, Box 1, folder 7.

Joey York told author of Paul Lynde's comment to her that he felt that Dick was "the funniest man" he ever worked with, 6/30/02.

Background on the circumstances which led to Dick York leaving

Bewitched appear in Dick York's excellent and very original autobiography, *The Seesaw Girl and Me* (New Path Press, New Jersey, 2004).

"Mrs. York is philosophical about this . . . ," Joey York to author, 6/30/02.

Gordon Emery's comments regarding Agnes and Dick York are from an interview on 6/8/02.

"Have been going at breakneck speed . . . ," Agnes to Georgia Johnstone, 2/2/69, The Georgia Johnstone Papers re: Agnes Moorehead, T-Mss 2003-039, Billy Rose Theatre Collection, The New York Public Library for the Performing Arts, Box 1, folder 7.

Agnes comment "I don't like change" and "Agnes Moorehead had a very strong working relationship with Dick York," from Herbie J Pilato in an e-mail interview dated, 1/17/04.

"What a time I had getting mother out of her nest and bask her for the winter . . . ," Agnes to Georgia Johnstone, postmarked 1/16/70, The Georgia Johnstone Papers re: Agnes Moorehead, T-Mss 2003-039, Billy Rose Theatre Collection, The New York Public Library for the Performing Arts, Box 1, folder 8.

"Now the farm is coming along . . . ," Agnes to Georgia Johnstone, 4/10/70, Georgia Johnstone Papers re: Agnes Moorehead, T-Mss 2003-039. Billy Rose Theatre Collection, The New York Public Library for the Performing Arts, Box 1, folder 8.

". . . I couldn't with my show going back to filming in Salem in June" (AM to GJ, 4/10/70), "Salem was frightening . . ." (AM to GJ, 6/26/70). The Georgia Johnstone Papers re: Agnes Moorehead, T-Mss 2003-039, Billy Rose Theatre Collection, The New York Public Library for the Performing Arts, Box 1, folder 8.

"Materialism has brought about confusion . . . ," *Los Angeles Times,* 4/19/70.

"Will there be brotherhood in the 70's?" *Detroit Free Press,* 12/28/69. "Should prostitution be legalized?" *Photoplay,* December 1971.

Much of the background on the filming of *Dear, Dead Delilah* comes from Warren Sherk's *A Very Private Person* (pg. 10-15), which included most of the quotes provided by production manager Fred Carmichael.

"The film was most interesting and brought back so many memories . . . ," Fred Carmichael to Agnes, 1/17/71, The Papers of Agnes Moorehead, The Wisconsin State Historical Society Archives, Box 129.

"My only memory of *Marriage: Year One* . . . ," William Windom to author in a note in response to a letter sent to Mr. Windom, dated 9/15/03.

Conrad Binyon kindly put me in touch with Dora Guerra, the mother of Judith Ann Guerra, and she was most helpful in telling me the story of how Judith Ann and Agnes became pen pals. She also sent me copies of the letters Agnes sent to Judith Ann. The Agnes Moorehead Papers at the Wisconsin State Historical Society archives holds the letters which Judith Ann sent to Miss Moorehead.

CHAPTER 15
"CURTAIN"

"I do think she did begin to tire of the show . . . ," Kasey Rogers to author, 1/11/04.

"Either you come in or you will be put on suspension . . . ," Quint Benedetti to author, 7/23/03.

Agnes "stood straight as a dime . . . " & "nobody had more fun at the party than Paul Lynde," Debbie Reynolds to author, 6/20/04.

Kay Gable to Agnes, 12/7/71, The Papers of Agnes Moorehead, Wisconsin State Historical Society Archives, Box 131.

Freddie Jones to Agnes, 1/7/72, The Papers of Agnes Moorehead, Wisconsin State Historical Society Archives, Box 131.

"A star danced and you were born . . . ," Mary Roebling to Agnes, 12/6/71, The Papers of Agnes Moorehead, The Wisconsin State Historical Society Archives, Box 129.

"Your marble halls are not ringing with the laughs we used to have . . . ," Jack Kelk to Agnes, The Papers of Agnes Moorehead, The Wisconsin State Historical Society Archives, Box 132.

"We all miss you and send gobs of love . . . ," Debbie Reynolds to Agnes, The Papers of Agnes Moorehead, The Wisconsin State Historical Society Archives, Box 132.

"One of my relatives . . . ," Harry Ackerman to Agnes, 3/16/72.

"Call me when your back in town . . . ," Harry Ackerman to Agnes 4/12/72, The Papers of Agnes Moorehead, The Wisconsin State Historical Society Archives, Box 132.

"I will be doing more one-woman shows . . . ," *Chicago Today,* 1/4/72.

"When I called Freddie on March 6th . . . ," Franklin Roemer to Agnes, 4/2/72, The Papers of Agnes Moorehead, The Wisconsin State Historical Society Archives, Box 132.

Burry Fredrik to Agnes, 5/24/72, The Papers of Agnes Moorehead,

Wisconsin State Historical Society Archives, Box 132.

Background on the second tour of *Don Juan in Hell* came from *Final Dress* (John Houseman, pg. 475-476).

"As to your stay in New York . . . ," Mary Roebling to Agnes, The Papers of Agnes Moorehead, Wisconsin State Historical Society Archives, Box 132.

"My Dearest Agnes . . . ," Ricardo Montalban to Agnes, The Papers of Agnes Moorehead, Wisconsin State Historical Society Archives, Box 132.

"Montalban had no background . . . When Agnes did this . . . ," Paul Gregory to author, 10/22/03.

Telegrams to Agnes on opening night of *Don Juan in Hell,* The Papers of Agnes Moorehead, Wisconsin State Historical Society Archives, Box 137.

"I can see her still . . . ," John Houseman in *Final Dress* (pg. 475).

Clive Barnes' *New York Times* review which Houseman spoke of appeared in the *Times* on 1/16/73, *Stage: Shaw's 'Don Juan in Hell' at 70.*

Lynn Kear's description of Agnes' voice being "strong and dignified," *Agnes Moorehead: A Bio-Bibliography* (pg. 144).

Agnes being so exhausted that she would have to be carried to her motel room, Quint Benedetti to author, 7/23/03.

Cesar Romero's comment that *Gigi* was Agnes' "hardest show" and Fred Carmichael's comment about it being "an unhappy experience for her from first to last," Warren Sherk's *A Very Private Person.*

Recollections of Freddie Jones ("she often mentioned how serene it was at the farm . . . ") and those of Margery Stover come from Warren Sherk's *A Very Private Person.*

". . . slowly wheedling her way into Agnes' life," Quint Benedetti to author, 7/23/03.

Debbie Reynolds and Laurie Main expressed to me their admiration for this young nurse, and how Agnes came to value her friendship and companionship, in their interviews with me.

Agnes being "pensive," Paul Gregory to author, 10/22/03.

"She called and said she wanted to say goodbye . . . ," Himan Brown to author, 6/6/03.

"She looked tired and worn . . . ," Laurie Main to author, 4/21/04.

"I have to go to the hospital . . . ," Debbie Reynolds to author, 6/20/04

". . . somehow you all make me homesick telling me about the snow and the deer . . . ," *A Very Private Person.*

"I begged her to allow me to try and find Sean . . . ," Debbie Reynolds to author, 6/20/04.

"Well, Debbie, it's over . . . I'm dying . . . ," *Debbie, My Story* (pg. 387).

"Agnes had a firm belief that in order to maintain her glamourous image as a star . . ." and ". . . her last word was 'mama,'" *The Lonely Courage of Agnes Moorehead* from *New York Daily News*, 6/30/74.

Ricardo Montalban finding out of Agnes' death, *A Very Private Person*.

"She was a brilliant actress and a brilliant teacher . . . ," Debbie Reynolds to author, 6/20/04.

"She had a basic love of herself and the love of her craft . . . ," Paul Gregory to author, 11/5/03.

"Aggie was a woman of great kindness . . . ," Norman Corwin to author, 9/30/03.

"If Agnes had been born in England . . . ," Himan Brown to author, 6/6/03

"She was just bigger than life," Quint Benedetti to author, 7/28/03.

"She was a quiet person . . . ," Karl Malden to author, 10/1/03.

"She was quite simply always a joy," Carol Lynley to author, 4/10/03

"She was a wonderful lady . . . ," Rose Marie to author, 8/1/02.

"She was always a consummate professional," Bernard Fox to author, 3/19/04.

"She was bigger than life . . . ," Kasey Rogers to author, 1/11/04.

"She was so good at everything . . . ," William Asher to author, 3/28/02.

"Despite her fame . . . ," Mary Roebling to Warren Sherk, *A Very Private Person*.

"Aggie was the most disciplined actress . . . ," Joseph Cotten, *Vanity Will Get you Somewhere,*

"Agnes was a dear and valued friend . . . , " Lucille Ball to Warren Sherk, *A Very Private Person*.

"To a pure artiste . . . ," Charles Laughton, *A Very Private Person*.

AFTERWORD

The specifics about who got what came from the last will and testament of Agnes Moorehead.

"Now Claudette Colbert, oh, yes . . . ," Paul Gregory to author, 11/5/03.

". . . quite sure that Agnes was not a lesbian," Quint Benedetti to author, 7/28/03.

Benedetti also told the author that he believed that these stories were spread around Hollywood by Paul Lynde, who he said could be "quite vicious."

"Why, indeed? . . . ," Debbie Reynolds to author, 6/20/04.

"Nothing happened between them: Moorehead was not heterosexual," *Rosebud* (pg. 184)

"A woman may love a person who is this or that . . . " (pg. 191) and "You apparently have your own informants . . . " (pg. 192), both from *Hollywood Lesbians.*

"I heard those rumors . . . ," Dick Sargent in *Southern Voices,* December 19–January 1 (pg. 7).

"I've heard rumors . . . ," Elizabeth Montgomery in *The Advocate* (1992).

"She was on 23 out of 24 hours," Paul Gregory to author, 11/5/03.

Appendix

THE FILMS OF AGNES MOOREHEAD

(MAJOR OR SIGNIFICANT FILMS IN THE MOOREHEAD CANON ARE HIGHLIGHTED)

1. ***Citizen Kane*** (1941 – RKO) Director: Orson Welles
    Cast: Orson Welles, Joseph Cotten, Everett Sloane, Agnes Moorehead, Dorothy Comingore, Ray Collins, George Coulouris, Ruth Warrick, William Alland, Paul Stewart, Erskine Sanford. 119 minutes. Black and White. AM's five-minute performance as Kane's mother is considered by some critics to be the best performance in the film. Leonard Maltin, the film historian and critic, gave *Citizen Kane* a four-star rating in his book, *Leonard Maltin's Movie and Video Guide* (Plume, 1992), calling it, "a film that broke all the rules and invented some new ones."

2. ***The Magnificent Ambersons*** (1942 – RKO) Director: Orson Welles.

Cast: Tim Holt, Joseph Cotten, Dolores Costello, Anne Baxter, Agnes Moorehead, Ray Collins, Richard Bennett, Erskine Sanford, Orson Welles (narrator). 88 minutes. Black and White. AM's performance as Aunt Fanny is justifiably considered her best screen performance. Agnes received her first Academy Award nomination for Best Supporting Actress and won the New York Film Critic's award as Best Actress of the year. Maltin, in his four-star rating, wrote, "Welles' follow-up to *Citizen Kane* is equally exciting in its own way."

3. *The Big Street* (1942 – RKO) Director: Irving Reis.

Cast: Henry Fonda, Lucille Ball, Barton MacLane, Eugene Pallette, Agnes Moorehead, Sam Levene, Ray Collins, Hans Conried, Ozzie Nelson and his Orchestra. 88 minutes. Black and White. AM's first comedy, based on the Damon Runyon story "Little Pinks." Her first non-Welles film.

4. *Journey Into Fear* (1942 – RKO) Director: Norman Foster (and, uncredited, Orson Welles).

Cast: Orson Welles, Joseph Cotten, Dolores Del Rio, Ruth Warrick, Agnes Moorehead, Everett Sloane, Jack Moss, Hans Conried. 69 minutes. Black and White. AM's final Welles/Mercury production is not up to the level of the others, but is passable entertainment.

5. *The Youngest Profession* (1943 – MGM) Director: Edward Buzzell

Cast: Virginia Weidler, Jean Porter, Edward Arnold, John Carroll, Agnes Moorehead, Scotty Beckett. Guest appearances: Lana Turner, William Powell, Robert Taylor, Greer Garson, Walter Pidgeon. 82 minutes. Black and White. AM's first MGM film under the terms of a seven-year contract.

6. *Government Girl* (1943 – RKO) Director: Dudley Nichols. Cast: Olivia de Havilland, Sonny Tufts, Anne Shirley, Jess Barker, James Dunn, Paul Stewart, Agnes Moorehead. 94 minutes. Black and White. Director Nichols was a noted screenwriter, having penned such John Ford films as *The Informer* and *Stagecoach.*

7. ***Jane Eyre*** (1944 – Twentieth Century-Fox) Director: Robert Stevenson. Cast: Orson Welles, Joan Fontaine, Margaret O'Brien, Henry Daniell, John Sutton, Agnes Moorehead, Elizabeth Taylor, Peggy Ann Garner, Sara Allgood, Aubrey Mather, Hillary Brooke. 96 minutes. Black and White. AM's final film with Orson Welles. Director Stevenson later helmed such Disney films as *Old Yeller* and *Mary Poppins.*

8. *Dragon Seed* (1944 – MGM) Director: Jack Conway, Harold S. Bucquet.

Cast: Katharine Hepburn, Walter Huston, Aline MacMahon, Turhan Bey, Hurd Hatfield, Agnes Moorehead, Frances Rafferty, J. Carrol Naish, Akim Tamiroff, Henry Travers. 145 minutes. Black and White. The longest film AM had appeared in, up to this time. Based on the Pearl Buck novel.

9. ***Since You Went Away*** (1944 – Selznick International) Director: John Cromwell.

    Cast: Claudette Colbert, Jennifer Jones, Joseph Cotten, Shirley Temple, Monty Woolley, Hattie McDaniel, Agnes Moorehead, Craig Stevens, Keenan Wynn, Robert Walker, Lionel Barrymore. 172 minutes. Black and White. AM's only film for producer David O. Selznick (*Gone With the Wind*), who also wrote the screenplay. At nearly three hours, this film beats out *Dragon Seed* in the length department but is much more enjoyable. Leonard Maltin calls it a "tearjerker supreme."

10. *The Seventh Cross* (1944 – MGM) Director: Fred Zinnemann.

    Cast: Spencer Tracy, Signe Hasso, Hume Cronyn, Jessica Tandy, Herbert Rudley, Felix Bressart, Ray Collins, Alexander Granach, Agnes Moorehead, George Macready, Steven Geray, George Zucco. 110 minutes. Black and White. With the exception of Orson Welles, Zinnemann may be the best director (*High Noon, From Here to Eternity, Oklahoma!, A Hatful of Rain, The Nun's Story, A Man for All Seasons, Julia*) that Agnes ever worked with; unfortunately this would be their only collaboration.

11. ***Mrs. Parkington*** (1944 – MGM) Director: Tay Gannett.

    Cast: Greer Garson, Walter Pidgeon, Edward Arnold, Gladys Cooper, Agnes Moorehead, Peter Leftward, Dan Duryea, Lee Patrick. 124 minutes. Black and White. Aggie's first film with Greer Garson (not counting Garson's cameo in *The Youngest Profession*), and they would become lifelong friends. Agnes won her second Academy Award nomination for this film, as well as a Golden Globe. Agnes often said that her role in this film was her favorite.

12. ***Tomorrow, the World!*** (1944 – United Artists) Director: Leslie Fenton.

    Cast: Fredric March, Betty Field, Agnes Moorehead, Skippy Homeier, Joan Carroll, Boots Brown. 86 minutes. Black and White. One of Aggie's least known, but better, films. It tells the intriguing story of a couple who adopts a German boy, trying to undo Nazi influences inside of him. Interestingly, Agnes and Betty Field would later compete with Shirley Booth for the lead in the TV series, *Hazel*.

13. *Keep Your Powder Dry* (1945 – MGM) Director: Edward Buzzell.

    Cast: Lana Turner, Laraine Day, Susan Peters, Agnes Moorehead, Bill Johnson, Natalie Schafer, Lee Patrick. 93 minutes. Black and White. Leonard Maltin said it best in his capsule review: "glossy on the outside, empty on the inside." Still, it featured two future television legends: Agnes (*Bewitched*) and Schafer (Lovey Howell on *Gilligan's Island*).

14. ***Our Vines Have Tender Grapes*** (1945 – MGM) Director: Roy Rowland.

    Cast: Edward G. Robinson, Margaret O'Brien, Agnes Moorehead, James Craig, Frances Gifford, Morris Carnovsky, Butch Jenkins. 105 minutes. Black and White. One of Aggie's all-time best. This gentle and heartwarming film cast her as the Norwegian mother of little Margaret O'Brien. The premiere of this film was held in Baraboo, Wisconsin, near Reedsburg where Agnes' mother lived and where Aggie often visited. Leonard Maltin praised it as an "excellent view of American life."

15. *Her Highness and the Bellboy* (1945 – MGM) Director: Richard Thorpe.

    Cast: Hedy Lamarr, Robert Walker, June Allyson, Carl Esmond, Agnes Moorehead, Rags Ragland. 112

minutes. Black and White. Agnes' first film with Allyson, who would also become a good personal friend. Not much to say about this film except it had the typical MGM gloss, and little more.

16. **Dark Passage** (1947 – Warner Bros.)
     Director: Delmer Daves.
     Cast: Humphrey Bogart, Lauren Bacall, Bruce
     Bennett, Agnes Moorehead. 106 minutes. Black and
     White. Agnes' first film under a Warner Brothers
     contract. This *film noir* contains one of Aggie's great-
     est shrews and she makes quite an exit near the end
     of the film. A must-see for Moorehead fans.

17. **The Lost Moment** (1947 – Universal)
     Director: Martin Gabel.
     Cast: Robert Cummings, Susan Hayward, Agnes
     Moorehead, Joan Lorring, Eduardo Ciannelli, John
     Archer, Minerva Urecal. 89 minutes. Black and White. One of Agnes' proudest roles and one of her
     most unrecognizable, as she plays a 105-year-old woman, in this adaptation of Henry James' *The
     Aspern Papers*. Directed by her longtime radio, and later stage, colleague, Martin Gabel. Hayward
     dubbed this film "The Lost Hour and a Half."

18. *Summer Holiday* (1948 – MGM) Director: Rouben Mamoulian.
     Cast: Mickey Rooney, Walter Huston, Frank Morgan, Agnes Moorehead, Butch Jenkins, Selena Royle,
     Marilyn Maxwell, Gloria DeHaven, Anne Francis. 92 minutes. Color. Agnes' first color film, a lavish
     musical remake of *Ah! Wilderness*. Aggie and Frank (The Wizard of Oz) Morgan work well together.
     Filmed in 1946.

19. *The Woman in White* (1948 – Warner Bros.) Director: Peter Godfrey
     Cast: Eleanor Parker, Alexis Smith, Sydney Greenstreet, Gig Young, Agnes Moorehead, John Emery,
     John Abbott. 109 minutes. Black and White. A good thriller, with a strong Warner Brothers cast.
     Agnes' first film with Parker.

20. *Station West* (1948 – RKO) Director: Sidney Lanfield.
     Cast: Dick Powell, Jane Greer, Tom Powers, Raymond Burr, Agnes Moorehead, Burl Ives, Steve Brodie,
     Gordon Oliver. 92 minutes. Black and White. Agnes' first western, one with elements of *film noir*. An
     interesting little film.

21. **Johnny Belinda** (1948 – Warner Bros.) Director: Jean Negulesco.
     Cast: Jane Wyman, Lew Ayres, Charles Bickford, Agnes Moorehead, Stephen McNally, Jan Sterling,
     Rosalind Ivan, Alan Napier. 101 minutes. Black and White. The first (and best) of five films that
     Agnes worked in with Wyman. Both Wyman and Agnes were nominated for Academy Awards. The
     film itself was nominated for twelve nominations, including Best Picture, but the only award it won
     was for Wyman.

22. *The Stratton Story* (1949 – MGM) Director: Sam Wood.

Cast: James Stewart, June Allyson, Frank Morgan, Agnes Moorehead, Bill Williams, Eugene Bearden, Bill Dickey, Jimmy Dykes, Robert Gist. 106 minutes. Black and White. Originally, Van Johnson and Donna Reed were cast in this film, but when Stewart expressed interest he got the part; he reportedly vetoed his *It's a Wonderful Life* co-star, Donna Reed, because that film had not done well at the box office. Agnes, still married to Jack Lee, met her future husband, Robert Gist, on this film.

23. *The Great Sinner* (1949 – MGM) Director: Gottfried Reinhardt.

Cast: Gregory Peck, Ava Gardner, Melvyn Douglas, Walter Huston, Ethel Barrymore, Frank Morgan, Agnes Moorehead, Ludwig Stossel, Ludwig Donath, Erno Verebes, Curt Bois. 110 minutes. Black and White. Good cast, so-so film.

24. *Without Honor* (1949 – United Artists) Director: Irving Pichel

Cast: Laraine Day, Dane Clark, Franchot Tone, Agnes Moorehead, Bruce Bennett, Harry Lauter, Peter Virgo, Margie Stapp. 68 minutes. Black and White. A good B+ film with a strong cast.

25. *Caged* (1950 – Warner Brothers) Director: John Cromwell.

Cast: Eleanor Parker, Agnes Moorehead, Ellen Corby, Hope Emerson, Betty Garde, Jan Sterling, Lee Patrick, Jane Darwell, Sandra Gould. 96 minutes. Black and White. One of the last really outstanding films of Aggie's career, boasting a strong cast and a compelling story. Featured in a small role is the future second Gladys Kravitz, Sandra Gould. Agnes reportedly expected that she would be nominated for an Academy Award for her crusading prison superintendent, but she wasn't.

26. *Fourteen Hours* (1951 – Twentieth Century-Fox) Director: Henry Hathaway.

Cast: Paul Douglas, Richard Basehart, Barbara Bel Geddes, Debra Paget, Agnes Moorehead, Robert Keith, Howard da Silva, Jeffrey Hunter, Martin Gabel, Grace Kelly. 92 minutes. Black and White. A good film. Agnes' first with Hathaway, Kelly and Hunter, all of whom she would work with again.

27. *Show Boat* (1951 – MGM) Director: George Sidney.

Cast: Kathryn Grayson, Ava Gardner, Howard Keel, Joe E. Brown, Marge Champion, Gower Champion, Robert Sterling, Agnes Moorehead, William Warfield, Leif Erickson. 108 minutes. Color. Agnes' second color film — her previous one, *Summer Holiday*, was also a musical. The film is good, but many do not feel it stacks up to the 1936 Universal version.

28. *The Blue Veil* (1951 – RKO) Director: Curtis Bernhardt.

Cast: Jane Wyman, Charles Laughton, Joan Blondell, Richard Carlson, Agnes Moorehead, Don Taylor, Audrey Totter, Everett Sloane, Natalie Wood, Vivian Vance, Alan Napier. 113 minutes. Black and White. Filmed just prior to Laughton and Agnes embarking on their tour of *Don Juan in Hell*. Written by her friend Norman Corwin, who would later pen the play *The Rivalry* which Agnes co-starred in.

29. *The Adventures of Captain Fabian* (1951 – Republic) Director: William Marshall.

Cast: Errol Flynn, Micheline Prelle, Vincent Price, Agnes Moorehead, Victor Francen, Jim Gerald, Howard Vernon. 100 minutes. Black and White. Agnes was on location filming this movie when she got the telegram from Charles Laughton inviting her to join them in *Don Juan in Hell*.

30. *Captain Black Jack* (1952 – Classic) Director: Julien Duvivier.

Cast: George Sanders, Herbert Marshall, Patricia Roc, Agnes Moorehead, Marcel Dalio, Howard Vernon. 90 minutes. Black and White. Good cast is generally wasted.

31. *The Blazing Forest* (1952 – Paramount) Director: Edward Ludwig.

Cast: John Payne, William Demarest, Agnes Moorehead, Richard Arlen, Susan Morrow, Roscoe Ates, Lynne Roberts, Walter Reed. 90 minutes. Color. Agnes' third mediocre film in a row during 1951–52, all done when she had some off time from her tours of *Don Juan in Hell*. Her first for Paramount.

32. *The Story of Three Loves* (1953 – MGM) Director: Gottfried Reinhardt.

Cast: Moira Shearer, James Mason, Agnes Moorehead, Jacob Gimpel, Milos Rozsa, John Lupton, Jack Raine. 122 minutes. Color. Three separate stories are told. Agnes', "The Jealous Lover," is set on an ocean liner.

33. *Scandal at Scourie* (1953 – MGM) Director: Jean Negulesco.

Cast: Greer Garson, Walter Pidgeon, Donna Corcoran, Agnes Moorehead, Arthur Shields, Philip Ober, Rhys Williams, John Lupton. 89 minutes. Color. The second Garson-Pidgeon film to feature Agnes. They are all past their prime in this one, which didn't copy the box-office success of their previous pairings. Agnes plays a nun for the first time.

34. *Those Redheads from Seattle* (1953 – Paramount) Director: Lewis R. Foster.
Cast: Rhonda Fleming, Gene Barry, Agnes Moorehead, Teresa Brewer, Guy Mitchell, Cynthia Bell, Kay Bell, Jean Parker. 90 minutes. Color. Aggie's third musical is pleasing, but not much more. Agnes' first teaming with Gene Barry, who she would later work with on his television series, *Burke's Law.*

35. *Main Street to Broadway* (1953 – MGM) Director: Tay Garnett.
Cast: Tom Morton, Mary Murphy, Agnes Moorehead, Herb Shriner, Rosemary DeCamp, Clinton Sundberg, Florence Bates, Tallulah Bankhead, Ethel Barrymore, Lionel Barrymore, Gertrude Berg, Shirley Booth, Faye Emerson, Mary Martin, Rex Harrison. 97 minutes. Black and White. Interesting film, especially seeing Agnes interacting with Bankhead, who plays herself. Agnes plays Bankhead's agent.

36. **Magnificent Obsession** (1954 – Universal) Director: Douglas Sirk.
Cast: Jane Wyman, Rock Hudson, Agnes Moorehead, Barbara Rush, Gregg Palmer, Otto Kruger, Paul Cavanagh, Sara Shane. 108 minutes.Color. Not really a very good film, but it became very, very popular, especially with female moviegoers. Rock Hudson became a major star with this Ross Hunter-produced film. Wyman was nominated for an Academy Award. Leonard Maltin gives this film *** and writes, "Sirk pulls out all the stops in this baroque, melodramatic remake."

37. *Untamed* (1955 – Twentieth Century-Fox) Director: Henry King.
Cast: Tyrone Power, Susan Hayward, Richard Egan, Agnes Moorehead, Rita Moreno, John Justin, Hope Emerson, Brad Dexter. 111 minutes. Black and White. So-so action film aided by a strong cast. This film was shot on location in South Africa in CinemaScope. Robert Mitchum was originally slated for the lead with Lana Turner; Eleanor Parker and Jane Wyman were both considered for the Hayward part, according to author Lynn Kear.

38. *The Left Hand of God* (1955 – Twentieth Century-Fox) Director: Edward Dmytryk.
Cast: Humphrey Bogart, Gene Tierney, Lee J. Cobb, Agnes Moorehead, E.G. Marshall, Jean Porter, Victor Sen Yung, Benson Fong. 87 minutes. Color. Agnes' second and final film with Bogart. Tierney barely made it through production of this film due to her delicate mental state. She credits Bogart with helping her finish the film. Author William Barrett, who wrote the novel, greatly admired Agnes' performance as Beryl.

39. **All That Heaven Allows** (1956 – Universal) Director: Douglas Sirk.
Cast: Jane Wyman, Rock Hudson, Agnes Moorehead, Conrad Nagel, Gloria Talbott, William Reynolds, Virginia Grey, Charles Drake, Hayden Rorke. 89 minutes. Color. Follow-up to *Magnificent Obsession* is actually the better film. Beautiful color photography. Hudson's performance is much more assured.

40. *Meet Me in Las Vegas* (1956 – MGM) Director: Roy Rowland.
Cast: Dan Dailey, Cyd Charisse, Agnes Moorehead, Lili Darvas, Jim Backus, Oscar Karlweis, Cara Williams, George Chakiris, Betty Lynn. 112 minutes. Color. This is Agnes' fourth musical. Choreography was by Fred Astaire's longtime collaborator, Hermes Pan.

41.   *The Conqueror* (1956 – RKO) Director: Dick Powell.

Cast: John Wayne, Susan Hayward, Pedro Armendariz, Agnes Moorehead, Thomas Gomez, John Hoyt, William Conrad, Ted de Corsia, Leslie Bradley, Lee Van Cleef. 111 minutes. Color. Probably the nadir of Agnes' film career. *Time* summed up John Wayne's performance: "He portrays the great conqueror as a sort of cross between a square-shootin' sheriff and a Mongolian idiot." What a waste of a fine cast. Many people believe that location shooting in the radiation-filled sands of the Utah desert led to the untimely cancer deaths of a remarkably large percentage of actors and crew members connected with this film. Leonard Maltin writes, "Expensive epic has camp dialogue to spare."

42.   *The Revolt of Mamie Stover* (1956 – Twentieth Century-Fox) Director: Raoul Walsh.
Cast: Jane Russell, Richard Egan, Joan Leslie, Agnes Moorehead, Jorja Curtright, Michael Pate, Richard Coogan, Alan Reed, Eddie Firestone, Jean Willes. 92 minutes. Color. Aggie runs the "dance hall" that Mamie Stover works at. Of course, in the novel by William Bradford Huie, the dance hall is a brothel and Agnes' character is a madam. Russell was cast as Mamie Stover when Marilyn Monroe proved unavailable.

43.   *The Swan* (1956 – MGM) Director: Charles Vidor.

Cast: Grace Kelly, Alec Guiness, Louis Jourdan, Agnes Moorehead, Jessie Royce Landis, Brian Aherne, Leo G. Carroll, Estelle Winwood, Van Dyke Parks. 107 minutes. Color. A wonderfully cast film, based on a play, which still seems awfully stagy. Aggie's second and final film with Grace Kelly who shortly left Hollywood for the principality of Monaco(interestingly Kelly is cast as a princess in this film), but over the years they remained friends. Agnes is cast as a Queen and has some good lines: "Boys, behave yourselves. This is not a republic . . . I am your sovereign and also your aunt once removed. You should respect them both."

44.   *Pardners* (1956 – Paramount) Director: Norman Taurog.

Cast: Dean Martin, Jerry Lewis, Lori Nelson, Agnes Moorehead, Jeff Morrow, Jackie Loughery, John Baragrey, Lon Chaney, Jr., Milton Frome, Richard Aherne, Lee Van Cleef, Jack Elam. 82 minutes. Color. Dean and Jerry in their next to final film together. Agnes plays the New York society mother of meek and timid Lewis. He decides to escape from an arranged marriage and pursue his dreams of being a cowboy out west with buddy Dino. Agnes enjoyed working with Lewis and this was the first of two Lewis films she would appear in.

45.   *The Opposite Sex* (1956 – MGM) Director: David Miller.

Cast: June Allyson, Joan Collins, Dolores Gray, Ann Sheridan, Ann Miller, Leslie Nielsen, Charlotte Greenwood, Agnes Moorehead, Jeff Richards, Joan Blondell, Alice Pearce, Carolyn Jones, Jim Backus, Dick Shawn. 117 minutes. Color. Effective remake of the 1939 film, *The Women*, with a good cast that was not as stellar as the original. This remake also includes men, where the original had an all-female cast. Alice Pearce, who later worked with Agnes as the first (and best) Gladys Kravitz on *Bewitched*, is a standout here as Olga. This was Agnes' seventh and final film release for 1956.

46. ***The True Story of Jesse James*** (1957 – Twentieth Century-Fox) Director: Nicholas Ray.
Cast: Robert Wagner, Jeffrey Hunter, Hope Lange, Agnes Moorehead, Alan Hale, Alan Baxter, John Carradine, Rachel Stephens, Barney Phillips, Biff Elliott, Frank Overton. 92 minutes. Color. Director Ray wanted Elvis Presley as Jesse James but had to settle for Wagner — who is effective nevertheless. Aggie plays Jesse and Frank's mother. This was Agnes' second film with Hunter, but she would be his unofficial dialogue coach when he played Jesus in director Ray's film, *King of Kings* a few years later.

47. *Jeanne Eagels* (1957 – Columbia) Director: George Sidney.
Cast: Kim Novak, Jeff Chandler, Agnes Moorehead, Charles Drake, Larry Gates, Virginia Grey, Gene Lockhart, Joe de Santis, Murray Hamilton. 108 minutes. Black and White. Aggie's first and only film for Columbia, but she would spend eight years playing "Endora" on *Bewitched* at Screen Gems, the television arm of Columbia pictures. Noted drama teacher Agnes actually plays a drama teacher in this bio-pic — clad in a garish blonde wig

48. *Raintree County* (1957 – MGM) Director: Edward Dmytryk.
Cast: Montgomery Clift, Elizabeth Taylor, Eva Marie Saint, Nigel Patrick, Lee Marvin, Rod Taylor, Agnes Moorehead, Walter Abel, Jarma Lewis, Tom Drake, DeForest Kelley. 187 minutes. Color. The longest running film of Agnes' career (beating *Since You Went Away* by 15 minutes). Aggie plays Montgomery Clift's mother in this Civil War drama which aspired to be another *Gone With the Wind*. It was during the production of this film that Clift suffered a near fatal car accident which left his face seriously impaired, causing even greater mental anguish that lead to a decade-long decline culminating with his tragic death in 1966 at age 46.

49. *The Story of Mankind* (1957 – Warner Brothers) Director: Irwin Allen.
Cast: Ronald Colman, Hedy Lamarr, Groucho Marx, Harpo Marx, Chico Marx, Virginia Mayo, Agnes Moorehead, Vincent Price, Peter Lorre, Charles Coburn, Cedric Hardwicke, Cesar Romero, John Carradine, Dennis Hopper, Marie Wilson, Edward Everett Horton, Francis X. Bushman. An all-star cast in a interesting story about a court meeting between the Devil (Price) and the spirit of man (Colman) to discuss whether the human species is worth saving. A good premise, but the finished product is muddled. Aggie does get a chance to play Queen Elizabeth opposite her longtime friend and constant escort in the 60's and 70's, Cesar Romero. All three Marx Brothers appear, but work separate from one another.

50. *Night of the Quarter Moon* (1959 – MGM) Director: Hugo Haas.
Cast: Julie London, John Drew Barrymore, Nat "King" Cole, Anna Kashfi, Dean Jones, James Edwards, Agnes Moorehead, Arthur Shields, Cathy Crosby, Edward Andrews, Ray Anthony, Jackie Coogan, Charles Chaplin, Jr. 95 minutes. Black and White. Not a very good film but, for its day, it did bring up relevant social issues. Diverse cast, with Agnes cast as the racially intolerant mother of Barrymore. Cole sings the title song, probably the best thing about the film.

51. *The Tempest* (1959 – Paramount) Director: Alberto Lattuada.

Cast: Silvana Mangano, Van Heflin, Viveca Lindfors, Geoffrey Horne, Oscar Homolka, Robert Keith, Agnes Moorehead, Helmut Dantine, Finlay Currie, Vittorio Gassman, Laurence Naismith. 121 minutes. Color. Set in 1770 Russia, Agnes is the pipe smoking wife of a Captain holed up at an isolated fort. The producer is the prolific Dino De Laurentiis.

52. **The Bat** (1959 – Allied Artists) Director: Crane Wilbur.

Cast: Agnes Moorehead, Vincent Price, Gavin Gordon, John Sutton, Lenita Lane, Elaine Edwards, Darla Hood, John Bryant. 80 minutes. Black and White. This film is significant for being one of only two films where Agnes is the lead actress. This is an adaptation of the play by Mary Roberts Rinehart and Avery Hopwood. It is a horror/suspense film which has every stereotype of that genre, but is a fun popcorn movie to watch on a stormy night.

53. *Pollyanna* (1960 – Buena Vista) Director: David Swift.

Cast: Hayley Mills, Jane Wyman, Richard Egan, Karl Malden, Nancy Olson, Adolphe Menjou, Agnes Moorehead, Donald Crisp, Kevin Corcoran, James Drury, Reta Shaw, Edward Platt. 133 minutes. Color. Aggie's first and only Disney feature film is good family fun. Agnes is a hoot as the crotchety hypochondriac who is mellowed by the always positive Pollyanna. Agnes' fifth and final film with Wyman.

54. *Twenty Plus Two* (1961 – Allied Artists) Director: Joseph M. Newman.

Cast: David Janssen, Jeanne Crain, Dina Merrill, Agnes Moorehead, William Demarest, Brad Dexter, Jacques Aubuchon, Robert Strauss. 102 minutes. Black and White. Author Lynn Kear (*Agnes Moorehead: A Bio-Bio-Bibliography*) believes that even though Agnes only appears in one scene in this film "it represents one of her better film performances of the 1960s. Her portrayal of Mrs. Delaney is well-drawn, encompassing great complexity. The character is first seen as arrogant, angry and impatient. Slowly the character becomes more vulnerable, warmer."

55. *Bachelor in Paradise* (1961 – MGM) Director: Jack Arnold.

Cast: Bob Hope, Lana Turner, Janis Paige, Jim Hutton, Paula Prentiss, Don Porter, Virginia Grey, Agnes Moorehead, Florence Sundstrom, Reta Shaw. 109 minutes. Color. This early 60's Bob Hope sex comedy features Aggie as a divorce judge. *Time* called the film "tripe." However, Henry Mancini and Mack David received an Oscar nomination for the title song.

56. *Jessica* (1962 – United Artists)
Director: Jean Negulesco.
Cast: Angie Dickinson, Maurice Chevalier, Noel-Noel, Agnes Moorehead, Gabriele Ferzetti, Sylva Koscina, Marcel Dalio, Danielle DeMetz. 105 minutes. Color. Angie is a sexy American midwife in an Italian village who attracts the attentions of the men much to the chagrin of their wives — including Aggie. Agnes' third film with director Negulesco, one of her favorites, but it is a far cry from *Johnny Belinda*.

57.   *How the West Was Won* (1962 – MGM) Directors: Henry Hathaway, John Ford, George Marshall. Cast: Debbie Reynolds, Carroll Baker, James Stewart, Karl Malden, Agnes Moorehead, George Peppard, Gregory Peck, Carolyn Jones, Robert Preston, John Wayne, Henry Fonda, Richard Widmark, Walter Brennan, Andy Devine, Raymond Massey, Thelma Ritter, Lee Van Cleef, Jay C. Flippen. 165 minutes. Color. Mammoth film, filmed in Cinerama, with an all-star cast. Agnes plays the mother of Reynolds and Baker in episodes directed by Hathaway. Agnes and Debbie formed a lifelong friendship on the set of this film.

58.   *Who's Minding the Store?* (1963 – Paramount) Director: Frank Tashlin. Cast: Jerry Lewis, Jill St. John, Ray Walston, Agnes Moorehead, John McGiver, Nancy Kulp, John Abbott, Kathleen Freeman, Richard Deacon. 90 minutes. Color. Pretty funny comedy with Agnes, as the mother of St. John, who tries to break up her daughter's romance with an uncouth idiot, played by, guess who?

59.   ***Hush . . . Hush, Sweet Charlotte*** (1964 – Twentieth Century-Fox) Director: Robert Aldrich. Cast: Bette Davis, Olivia de Havilland, Joseph Cotten, Agnes Moorehead, Cecil Kellaway, Victor Buono, Mary Astor, Bruce Dern, George Kennedy. 133 minutes. Black and White. Agnes, who was nominated for her fourth Academy Award for Best Supporting Actress and won a Golden Globe award, plays the slovenly maid of Bette Davis' Charlotte who tries to protect her longtime employer from the evil doings of her cousin, played by de Havilland (who replaced Joan Crawford). Agnes' fifth and final film with her longtime friend Joseph Cotten.

60.   *The Singing Nun* (1966 – MGM) Director: Henry Koster. Cast: Debbie Reynolds, Ricardo Montalban, Greer Garson, Agnes Moorehead, Chad Everett, Katharine Ross, Ed Sullivan, Juanita Moore, Tom Drake. 98 minutes. Color. Agnes was surrounded by many of her closest real life friends in this film (Reynolds, Garson, Montalban). Debbie is a guitar-strumming nun who initially arouses displeasure from Sister Cluny (Aggie). Based on the true story of the real life Singing Nun, Soeur Sourie.

61.   *What's the Matter with Helen?* (1971 – United Artists) Director: Curtis Harrington. Cast: Debbie Reynolds, Shelley Winters, Dennis Weaver, Agnes Moorehead, Michael MacLiammoir, Sammee Lee Jones, Robbi Morgan, Helene Winston, Swen Swenson. Agnes plays an Aimee Semple McPherson-like evangelist. Behind the scenes, Debbie and Shelley had a heated feud.

62.   ***Dear, Dead Delilah*** (1972 – Southern Star) Director: John Farris. Cast: Agnes Moorehead, Will Geer, Michael Ansara, Dennis Patrick, Patricia Carmichael, Anne Meacham, Robert Gentry. 90 minutes. Color. Significant only as the second of two films in which Agnes had the lead role (*The Bat*, 13 years earlier, was the first). Like Davis and Crawford, Agnes was cast in a tawdry-type of shock horror film with decapitated heads and plenty of blood.

63.   *Charlotte's Web* (1973 – Paramount) Directors Charles Nichols, Iwao Takamoto. Cast: The voices of Debbie Reynolds, Paul Lynde, Henry Gibson, Rex Allen, Martha Scott, Agnes Moorehead, Dave Madden, Danny Bonaduce. 93 minutes. Color. Animated cartoon of the E.B. White book, scripted by Earl Hamner, Jr., of *The Waltons* fame. Agnes plays the Goose.

II

1. *Revlon Mirror Theatre*. October 3, 1953. CBS
   "Lullaby." Cast: Tom Drake, Agnes Moorehead, Betty Lynn.

2. *Colgate Comedy Hour*. April 10, 1953. NBC
   "Roberta." An adaptation of the stage musical, and starring Bob Hope (who was also in the original Broadway production in 1933).

3. *Matinee Theatre*. May 1, 1956. NBC.
   "Greybeards and Witches." Cast: Agnes Moorehead, Cathy O'Donnell, Judy Nugent, Louis Letteiri. Agnes portrays a woman trying to keep a dangerous secret.

4. *Climax*. August 2, 1956. CBS.
   "Child of the Wind." Cast: Agnes Moorehead, Susan Kohner, Marshall Thompson.

5. *Studio 57*. October 28, 1956. DuMont.
   "The Teacher." Cast: Agnes Moorehead in the title role.

6. *Schlitz Playhouse of Stars*. March 1, 1957. CBS.
   "The Life you Save." Cast: Gene Kelly, Janice Rule, Agnes Moorehead. Kelly made his television debut as a one-armed man who falls in love with a deaf mute.

7. *Climax!* July 4, 1957. CBS.
   "False Witness." Cast: Eddie Bracken, Agnes Moorehead, Dean Harens, Gloria Talbot, John Baragrey.

8. *Wagon Train*. November 20, 1957. NBC.
   "The Mary Halstead Story." Cast: Agnes Moorehead (title role), Ward Bond, Robert Horton, Terry Wilson, Frank McGrath, Tom Laughlin.

9. *DuPont Show of the Month*. March 27, 1958. CBS.
   "A Tale of Two Cities." Cast: Eric Portman, Agnes Moorehead, James Donald, Gracie Fields, Denholm Elliott, Fritz Weaver, Rosemary Harris, George C. Scott. Aggie reportedly beat out Elsa Lanchester for the part of Madame DeFarge — to Elsa's considerable annoyance. Elsa reportedly said, "They felt that she was a bigger name — imagine?" Robert Mulligan, who later directed *To Kill a Mockingbird*, helmed this production.

10. *Playhouse 90*. April 10, 1958. CBS.
    "The Dungeon." Cast: Paul Douglas, Agnes Moorehead, Julie Adams, Dennis Weaver, Patty McCormick. Aggie's second 90-minute anthology tv appearance within two weeks.

11. *Suspicion.* May 12, 1958. NBC.

"Protegee." Cast: Agnes Moorehead, Phyllis Love, William Shatner, Jack Klugman. An *All About Eve*-type story which features future television legends Shatner and Klugman.

12. *Shirley Temple's Storybook.* October 27, 1958. NBC.

"Rapunzel." Cast: Carol Lynley, Agnes Moorehead, Don Dubbins. In a foretelling of things to come, Aggie is cast as the witch in this childhood classic.

13. *General Electric Theater.* March 1, 1959. NBC.

"Deed of Mercy." Cast: Carol Lynley, Agnes Moorehead, Ronald Reagan. Reagan was the longtime host of this anthology series and occasionally, as in this episode, acted in a play.

14. *Alcoa/Goodyear Theatre.* March 9, 1959. NBC.

"Man of His House." Cast: Agnes Moorehead, Brandon De Wilde, John Anderson, Helen Conrad, Read Morgan, Eve McVeagh, William Fawcette, Don Grady. Brandon De Wilde (*Shane*) plays a teenager who runs the family ranch following his father's death making him the "Man of the House." However, his mother (played by Aggie) still believes she has a right to discipline him and was going to give him a "whipping." However, he considers him too much of an adult to be submitted to such a childish punishment.

15. *The Rebel.* December 6, 1959. ABC.

"In Memoriam." Cast: Nick Adams, Agnes Moorehead, Madlyn Rhue. Adams was the star of this Western series, with Aggie appearing in a guest shot telecast on her 59th birthday.

16. *Ford Startime.* February 16, 1960. NBC.

"Closed Set." Cast: Joan Fontaine, John Ireland, Agnes Moorehead. Gavin Lambert, who later wrote the novel *Inside Daisy Clover*, wrote the script to this episode.

17. *The Millionaire.* April 20, 1960. CBS.

"Millionaire Katherine Boland." Cast: Marvin Miller, Agnes Moorehead, Tuesday Weld, Jerome Cowan, Bob Newkirk. Aggie plays a woman who receives a million dollars and uses it for her niece's debutante debut.

18. *Chevy Mystery Show.* August 7. 1960. NBC.

"Trial by Fury." Cast: Agnes Moorehead, Warren Stevens, Laurie Carroll, John Alderman, Donald Foster, Vinton Hayworth, Walter Slezak (host).

19. *The Shirley Temple Show.* September 18, 1960. NBC.

"The Land of Oz." Cast: Shirley Temple, Jonathan Winters, Agnes Moorehead, Ben Blue, Gil Lamb, Serling Holloway, Arthur Treatcher, Frances Bergen. Based on the Frank Baum *Oz* stories. Aggie plays Mombi, the wicked witch, with her friend Frances Bergen (wife of Edgar Bergen and mother of Candice) as Gilda the Good Witch. William Asher is the producer, and later would be the major director and producer on *Bewitched*.

20.	*Adventures in Paradise*. October 31, 1960. ABC.

"The Irishman." Cast: Gardner McKay, Weaver Levy, Linda Lawson, Agnes Moorehead, Henry Slate, James Holden, George Tobias, Sondi Sodsai, Lani Kai. Aggie plays a Moro tribal queen. Series regular Tobias (Trader Penrose) would later work with Aggie on *Bewitched*, portraying the long-suffering husband of snoopy neighbor Gladys Kravitz.

21.	*Harrigan and Son*. December 9, 1960. ABC.

"There's No Fool Like an Old Fool." Cast: Pat O'Brien, Roger Perry, Georgine Darcy, Helen Kleeb, Agnes Moorehead.

22.	*Rawhide*. December 9, 1960. CBS.

"Incident at Poco Tiempo." Cast: Clint Eastwood, Eric Fleming, Sheb Wooley, Gigi Perreau, Agnes Moorehead. Busy character actress Aggie appears in two different shows on the same night (see above for the first).

23.	*The Shirley Temple Show*. December 11, 1960. NBC.

"The House of the Seven Gables." Cast: Shirley Temple, Agnes Moorehead, Robert Culp, Martin Landeau, Jonathan Harris, John Abbott. Aggie's second appearance of the season on the *Temple* show, and her third of the series, with a cast full of familiar TV names.

24.	*The Rifleman*. December 27, 1960. ABC.

"Miss Bertie." Cast: Chuck Connors, Johnny Crawford, Paul Fix, Joan Taylor, Agnes Moorehead, Richard Anderson, Bill Quinn, Glenn Strange. Miss Bertie travels from Philadelphia out west where she tries to apprehend an outlaw (played by Anderson) for the reward money.

25.	*Twilight Zone*. January 27, 1961. CBS.

"The Invaders." Cast: Agnes Moorehead. Rod Serling (host). With the exception of *Bewitched*, this is probably the most famous television appearance by Aggie due to the continued popularity of Serling's science-fiction anthology series and Aggie's tour-de-force performance, done without dialogue.

26.	*My Sister Eileen*. March 1, 1961. CBS.

"Aunt Harriet's Way." Cast: Elaine Stritch, Shirley Bonne, Agnes Moorehead, Jack Weston, Rose Marie, Raymond Bailey, Stubby Kaye. Aggie guest stars as Aunt Harriet in this short-lived sitcom which also features the future Sally Rogers from *The Dick Van Dyke Show*, Rose Marie, and the future Mr. Drysdale from *The Beverly Hillbillies*, Raymond Bailey.

27.	*My Sister Eileen*. March 29, 1961. CBS.

"The Protectors." Cast: Elaine Stritch, Shirley Bonne, Agnes Moorehead, Leon Belasco, Jack Weston, Rose Marie, Raymond Bailey, Stubby Kaye, Roy Roberts. Aunt Harriet (Aggie) shows up for a second guest appearance.

28.	*Poor Mr. Campbell*. August 7, 1962. CBS.

Cast: Agnes Moorehead, Edward Andrews, Ruta Lee, Mary Grace Canfield, Harry Landers, Barbara

Pepper. This is a pilot which didn't sell. Aggie is the nagging wife of "Poor Mr. Campbell" played by veteran character actor, Edward Andrews.

29. *Camera Three.* March 17, 1963. CBS.
"The Reminiscences of Wanda Landowska." Cast: Agnes Moorehead. Aggie was justly proud of her appearance in this cultural show in which she did readings by the harpsichordist and musical scholar.

30. *The Shari Lewis Show.* June 29, 1963.
Agnes appears with the popular puppeteer.

31. *Burke's Law.* December 27, 1963. ABC.
"Who Killed Beau Sparrow." Cast: Gene Barry, Gary Conway, Regis Toomey, Leon Lontoc, Agnes Moorehead, Dan Tobin, Ken Murray, June Allyson, Yvonne De Carlo. Aggie made the first of three guest appearances in this police mystery series about a wealthy police Captain.

32. *Channing.* March 4, 1964. ABC.
"Freedom is a Lovesome Thing, God Wot!" Cast: Henry Jones, Jason Evers, Agnes Moorehead, James Earl Jones. Aggie guest stars in this college-based drama.

33. *Greatest Show on Earth.* April 14, 1964. ABC.
"This Train Doesn't Stop Till It Gets There." Cast: Jack Palance, Stu Erwin, Andrew Duggan, Spring Byington, Rory Calhoun, Agnes Moorehead, J. Pat O'Malley, Sheree North, Sally Kellerman, Deborah Walley. Aggie makes a guest shot on this circus-based drama produced by Desilu.

34. *Burke'sLaw.* May 1, 1964. ABC.
"Who Killed Don Pablo?" Cast: Gene Barry, Gary Conway, Regis Toomey, Leon Lontoc, John Cassavetes, Patricia Medina, Agnes Moorehead, Cesar Romero, Forrest Tucker, Cecil Kellaway. Among the guest stars is Medina, the wife of Aggie's longtime friend and colleague Joseph Cotten, and who also worked with Aggie in the play, *Prescription Murder.*

35. *You Don't Say.* July 6, 1964. NBC.
Game show hosted by veteran game show host Tom Kennedy.

36. *Bewitched.* September 17, 1964 – July 1, 1972. ABC.
Cast: Elizabeth Montgomery, Dick York (1964–1969), Dick Sargent (1969–1972), Agnes Moorehead, David White, Maurice Evans, Irene Vernon (1964–1966), Kasey Rogers (1966–1972), Alice Pearce (1964–1966), Sandra Gould (1966–1971), George Tobias, Marion Lorne (1964–1968), Mabel Albertson, Bernard Fox (1965–1972), Paul Lynde (1965–1971), Alice Ghostley (1969–1972). Classic series about a beautiful young witch (charmingly played by Montgomery) who falls in love with a mortal (the superb Dick York for the first five years) and marries him, much to the chagrin of her grande dame mother, Endora, played by Aggie. The young marrieds, Samantha and Darrin Stephens, try to live an ordinary mortal lifestyle but inevitably something comes up which needs to be resolved

Appendix 373

by witchcraft — in many instances due to the
instigation of Endora and Samantha's other relatives.
254 episodes were telecast, but Aggie, due to a clause
in her contract, performed in only 151 so she could
have time for other outside projects. The following is
a listing of those episodes featuring Endora:

"I Darrin, Take This Witch Samantha." September 17, 1964
The pilot episode, filmed in December 1963, where
Samantha and Darrin meet, fall in love, and marry
— and then Darrin discovers his wife is a witch.
Nancy Kovack makes her first appearance as Darrin's
ex-girlfriend, Sheila Sommers. Aggie doesn't have
much to do in this episode except zap her amorous
son-in-law from his hotel room to the hotel lobby —
to which Samantha tells her mother, "Even witchcraft
can't keep him out there all night. It's our honeymoon." Jose Ferrer narrates the opening of the first
four episodes of the series, only after Robert
Montgomery turned it down.

"Be It Ever So Mortgaged." September 24, 1964.
Darrin buys a new house in the suburbs (1164 Morning Glory Circle), and Samantha and Endora go
to look it over and exchange decorating ideas. The wonderful character comedienne, Alice Pearce,
makes her first appearance as the snoopy but likeable Gladys Kravitz. One of the highlights of this
episode is Endora reciting, for the first time, the following poem: "We are quicksilver, a fleeting
shadow, a distant sound. Our home has no boundaries beyond which we cannot pass. We live in
music, in a flash of color. We live on the wind and in a sparkle of a star."

"It Shouldn't Happen to a Dog." October 1, 1964.
The Stephens hold their first dinner party in their new home to impress a client who becomes a bit too
amorous regarding Samantha, who changes him into the "dog" he is.

"Mother Meets What's His Name." October 8, 1964.
It had to happen sooner or later, but Endora finally meets her Darrin. The moment they meet is
charming. Endora actually arrives ringing the front door bell and when Darrin opens the door, they
both share hesitant smiles with Samantha in the background grinning broadly. From there, things go
down hill — with Endora getting to the heart of why she objects to this marriage by asking, "Why do
you object to my daughter being herself, young man?" While that is certainly a highlight, so is the
comic brilliance of Alice Pearce especially when she discovers that the phone she is using over at the
Stephens' is not hooked up — the look on her face is priceless.

Another high point:

LITTLE BOY: Are you a good witch or a bad witch?

ENDORA: Comme ci, comme ca.

"Help, Help, Don't Save Me." October 15, 1964.

Samantha and Darrin have their first real fight, and nobody did it better than Montgomery and York. No matter how ferocious their fights could be, their chemistry reveals just how much they truly loved each other. Samantha goes home to mother and Endora couldn't be happier, but love conquers all — even Endora.

"Witch or Wife." November 12, 1964.

One of my all-time favorite episodes, with Endora taking Samantha out to lunch — to Paris, to be exact — and a fashion show where they run into Darrin's boss, Larry Tate (the superb David White) and his wife, who proceed to call Darrin, to let him know they are looking after "Sam" while she is in Paris. This is a good episode which focuses on the Samantha-Endora relationship, with Endora at one point wistfully asking her daughter, "what was once between us is no longer?"

"Just One Happy Family." November 19, 1964.

This episode introduces us to Samantha's father, Maurice, played by Maurice Evans who comes to finally meet his son-in-law, "Duncan" — he is as good at remembering Darrin's real name as Endora — though with her you get the idea it is intentional. It sounds like Maurice's family didn't approve of Endora, who at one point says, "his mother was a real witch."

"It Takes One to Know One." November 26, 1964.

Darrin creates a "Miss Jasmine" for a perfume account. In the first of many dirty tricks by Endora, she employs a beautiful witch to tempt Darrin, to test his fidelity and the strength of the Stephens' marriage.

"A Is for Aardvark." January 14, 1965.

Many fans consider this the definitive *Bewitched* episode — certainly producer/director William Asher does. Darrin sprains his ankle and Samantha finally gets tired of running up and down the stairs running errands for him. She gives him the ability to perform magic himself and becomes so accustomed that he forgets everything about the two of them living as normal mortal man and wife. But Samantha hasn't and in an emotional scene (played beautifully by Montgomery) she reminds him that his love is more important to her than anything conjured up by witchcraft. Ida Lupino directs.

"The Cat's Meow." January 21, 1965.

Darrin thinks Samantha has changed herself into a cat to spy on him when he meets an amorous client (Martha Hyer) on her yacht.

"A Nice Little Dinner Party." January 28, 1965.

Darrin's parents and Endora finally meet at a dinner party where Endora openly flirts with the father, Frank, much to the mother's, Phyllis, annoyance. The mother-in-laws would have a stormy relationship from this time forward.

"Your Witch is Showing." February 4, 1965.

Trouble brews when Darrin forbids Samantha to accompany Endora to a relative's wedding in Egypt. When things start to go wrong at work, Darrin assumes Endora is behind it only to discover she isn't. Endora gets the last laugh on the mortal who blames all his trouble on something other than himself.

"Eye of the Beholder." February 25, 1965.

Endora is up to it again when she conjures up a painting showing Samantha as she was centuries earlier — causing Darrin to wonder how he will age while Samantha will remain youthful looking.

"Red Light, Green Light." March 4, 1965.

Samantha wants a new traffic light on their street and convinces Darrin to come up with an advertising campaign to sell the idea.

"Which Witch is Which." March 11, 1965.

Endora does a favor for Samantha, who needs to be in two places at once, by turning herself into Samantha's double — but as could be expected she flirts with an attractive author who turns out to be a friend of Darrin's and just happens to be coming over to the Stephens' for dinner.

"Driving is the Only Way to Fly." March 25, 1965.

This episode is the first appearance by Paul Lynde; not as his wacky Uncle Arthur persona, but as neurotic driving instructor Harold Harold. While out on a driving instruction with Samantha, Endora causes mischief nearly causing Harold a nervous breakdown.

"Open the Door, Witchcraft." April 8, 1965.

Samantha uses witchcraft to create an electric garage door opener. Darrin revolts and buys the mortal kind and eventually they get locked in the garage where Samantha refuses to use magic to release them — a most unusual episode.

"George the Warlock." April 22, 1965.

Endora takes the opportunity of Darrin's seeming infatuation with sexy neighbor "Danger" O'Reilly, to convince a handsome playboy warlock to woo Samantha. Actually it doesn't take much convincing.

"A Change of Face." May 13, 1965.

When Darrin is asleep, Endora and a reluctant Samantha use witchcraft to rearrange his face — adding a different nose, a mustache and new hairdo. Darrin awakens and discovers what they have done and loses his self-confidence, which Samantha must restore.

"Remember the Main." May 20, 1965.

Sam and Darrin get involved in politics again by trying to help a crusading challenger for city council; Endora gets involved by causing a water main to burst. There is a good "in-joke" when Endora mentions that she was at the Lincoln/Douglas debate. Aggie played Mrs. Stephen A. Douglas in the play, *The Rivalry*, which dealt with the Lincoln/Douglas debates.

"Eat at Mario's." May 27, 1965.

Mario's is a small Italian pizzeria and Samantha and Endora use witchcraft to plug his business while Darrin is working for a client who is a competitor.

"Cousin Edgar." June 3, 1965.

Endora summons Cousin Edgar, who is highly protective of Samantha, to make trouble for Darrin. Will she ever give up? Nah. The last episode of the first season.

"Alias Darrin Stephens." September 16, 1965.

The first episode of the second season. Aunt Clara turns Darrin into a chimpanzee — by mistake! Remember, Clara is the one relative of Samantha's who is accepting of Darrin.

"A Very Special Delivery." September 23, 1965.

Samantha (as well as Elizabeth Montgomery) is pregnant, and Endora thinks that Darrin needs to be taught the lesson that pregnancy is no piece of cake and puts a morning sickness spell on him.

"My Grandson, the Warlock." October 7, 1965.

Granddaddy Maurice, not exactly in the loop as much as Endora, mistakenly thinks that his grandchild has already been born and thinks baby Jonathan Tate (son of Larry and Louise) is his grandchild. He takes the baby out when he is in the care of Samantha and Darrin — and where would he take that baby? Why, to the London Warlock's Club, of course.

"The Joker is a Card." October 14, 1965.

This is a classic. The first episode to feature Paul Lynde as Uncle Arthur, Endora's practical joking younger brother. As it turns out, Arthur has his own problems with Endora and is willing to help Darrin out by teaching him a spell to counteract Endora's witchcraft. Can you say "yaga . . . yagazoo . . . yaga?" Well, watch it, and you'll know what I mean.

"Trick or Treat." October 28, 1965.

Endora turns Darrin into a werewolf at Halloween. Have you ever wondered what Endora looked like as a child? She looks suspiciously like a young Marcia Brady dressed up like a gypsy.

"And Then I Wrote." November 11, 1965.

Samantha writes a play about the Civil War and, to help her better visualize the characters, she brings them to life and whenever she thinks of them they come popping out of her subconscious at the most inopportune times. What would Darrin say? Well, can't you guess? By the way, even with her magical powers, Endora is still a lousy typist.

"Junior Executive." November 18, 1965.

Endora is at it again, this time turning Darrin into an eight-year-old boy. Darrin, the advertising genius, takes advantage of the situation to explain, from a child's perspective, what is wrong with a product. Once again, Endora inadvertently helps Darrin's career. I don't think she ever got enough credit for that.

"Aunt Clara's Old Flame." November 25, 1965.

Aunt Clara fears what her youthful ex-flame, Hedley Partridge, will think of her (to be charitable) declining magical power. Sam decides to help her out, magic-wise. It appears, too, that Clara and Endora are not blood relatives, so is she related to Maurice? Hmm.

"My Boss, The Teddy Bear." December 9, 1965.

Sam and Darrin (well, mostly Darrin) overreact and think Endora turned Larry Tate into a teddy bear. In actuality, Endora charmingly had asked Larry, while running into him at a toy store, if he could arrange to give Darrin some time off to attend a wedding. She never gets any respect for the nice things she tried to do for Dobbins.

"Speak the Truth." December 16, 1965.

Endora gives Darrin a statue which has a "truth spell" attached to it, and anybody who comes near it can't lie his way out of a bag.

"And Then There Were Three." January 13, 1966.

Get out your hankies! This is the episode where, briefly, oh so briefly, Darrin and Endora bond over the birth of baby Tabatha (not yet spelled Tabitha). They hug and share tears together over this miracle of life. By the way, Endora is the one who came up with the baby's name. Eve Arden guest stars as Samantha's protective nurse.

"Samantha Meets the Folks." January 27, 1966.

Director William Asher uses a device he used after Lucille Ball delivered "Little Ricky" — he recut the episode from the first season where Samantha nervously first meets Darrin's folks, and added a new introduction.

"The Dancing Bear." February 10, 1966.

Those dueling grandmas, Endora and Phyllis, try and outdo each other with gifts of teddy bears for little Tabatha. Of course, Phyllis is at a disadvantage because of her lack of magic powers. Ugh, could you imagine Phyllis with magic powers?

"Double Tate." February 17, 1966.

Endora gives Darrin three wishes without telling him and this leads to trouble between him and Samantha.

"Samantha the Dressmaker." February 24, 1966.

Again, recycling from *I Love Lucy*, Samantha decides to design and sew her own dress. Of course, Lucy didn't have Sam's magical know-how. Once again, Sam and Endora take off for Paris. It must have been Endora's favorite city.

"Baby's First Paragraph." March 10, 1966.

Endora uses her hocus pocus to enable Tabitha to talk. The final episode featuring the great Alice Pearce as Gladys Kravitz, and it is depressing to see her physical appearance, but her performance itself is perfection; a great trouper.

"Disappearing Samantha." April 7, 1966.

Bernard Fox makes his first appearance not as "Dr. Bombay" but as Osgood Righmire, who exposes fraudulent witches. He recites an incantation which causes Samantha to disappear and then reappear. Endora and Sam decide they must get to the bottom of how he is able to do this.

"Follow that Witch" (Part 2) April 21, 1966.

Charlie Leach is a detective hired by a firm to investigate Darrin and Sam; he discovers that Sam is a witch and intends to blackmail her. Sorry, Charlie — you should never attempt to blackmail a real witch.

"A Bum Raps." April 28, 1966.

Samantha mistakenly takes a kindly confidence trickster for Darrin's Uncle Albert and invites him to stay. Mary Grace Canfield guests as Abner's sister Harriet Kravitz, who is "keeping house" for Abner while Gladys is away.

"Divided He Falls." May 5, 1966.

For many Bewitched fans, according to a Nick at Night poll, this is their favorite episode. It is excellent. When Darrin cancels plans for a much-needed vacation with Samantha, Endora creates two Darrins — the hard worker and the fun-loving party guy. Dick York is at his comedic best. Why wasn't he nominated more than once for an Emmy?

"The Catnapper." May 19, 1966.

Detective Charlie Leach returns and in the course of this episode he gets turned into a mouse by Sam while an attractive and flirtatious client of Darrin's is turned into a cat by Endora — hmm . . . is this the last (gulp) of Charlie Leach??

"What Every Young Man Should Know." May 26, 1966.

This is a wonderful episode and one of my all-time favorites. Sam and Darrin have a fight, and she wonders if Darrin would have still proposed to her had he known she was a witch. Endora bets not, and sends the two back in time. Once again, the overwhelming theme of this series is "love conquers all."

"The Girl with the Golden Nose." June 2, 1966.

When Larry gives Darrin an account that he initially refused to, he believes that Samantha's witchery is behind it. In the course of this episode, Endora mentions an "Aunt Agnes" who was burned at the stake in Salem. Agnes' final episode of the second season.

"Nobody's Perfect." September 15, 1966.

The series is back for season three and in color. Samantha discovers that Tabiatha is a witch and, of course, Endora is ecstatic, but how will Darrin take the news? Erin Murphy makes her debut (along with her sis, Diane) as the cutest little witch ever to grace television.

"Witches and Warlocks Are My Favorite Things." September 29, 1966.

Aunt Hagatha, Aunt Enchantra, Aunt Clara and Endora arrive to see a demonstration of Tabatha's powers. So impressed, that the coven, minus Aunt Clara, insists that Tabatha be enrolled at Hagatha's

School for little witches, and they will take her no matter what Sam or Darrin say — or chirp. It is Maurice to the rescue.

"A Most Unusual Wood Nymph." October 13, 1966.
Darrin's cousin from Ireland may not be as nice as he seems, but a witch-hating wood nymph. Endora sees through him. To reverse a Stephens' family curse, Endora sends Samantha back to 15th-century Ireland where she meets the amorous "Darrin the Bold."

"Endora Moves in for a Spell." October 20, 1966.
This and the following episode are a kind of companion piece. Both feature Endora with Uncle Arthur, continuing their rivalry. Both want to live across the street from the Stephens, which is a vacant lot which they keep zapping and then unzapping a house in. Sandra Gould is the recast Mrs. Kravitz, a very different character from the original as played by Alice Pearce, but one thing remains the same: she still can't convince Abner that she sees strange things across the street.
Funny line alert:

ENDORA:	You call yourself a brother?
ARTHUR:	Only when I'm forced to.

"Twitch or Treat." October 27, 1966.
Endora throws a cosmic Halloween party at the Stephens — even Darrin appears to be enjoying himself. Endora recites her famous "Night Before Halloween," interrupted by Uncle Arthur. She gets her revenge. Oh, did you know that Willie Mays is a warlock?

"Dangerous Diaper Dan." November 3, 1966.
The diaper service man is hired by a rival advertising firm to plant a microphone in a baby rattle in hopes of discovering Darrin's firm's trade secrets. When Sam and Endora discover this, Dangerous Diaper Dan may need a diaper of his own.

"I'd Rather Twitch than Fight." November 17, 1966.
Sam and Darrin have a fight and Endora brings in Dr. Sigmund Freud to settle their dispute.

"Oedipus Hex." November 24, 1966.
Endora puts a spell on a bowl of popcorn which causes anybody who eats from it to become lazy. Naturally, Darrin takes a handful and, rather than rushing off to work, decides to loaf around the house.

"Sam's Spooky Chair." December 1, 1966.
Clyde Farnsworth is a warlock who transformed himself into an antique chair when Samantha rejected him — a chair that Samantha purchases and which continually kicks Darrin in the shin with its leg.

"Sam in the Moon." January 5, 1967.
Darrin thinks some tea that Sam and Endora brought back from Japan is actually moon dust and has NASA come in to analyze it. Where does he get these ideas?

"Hoho the Clown." January 12, 1967.

Endora interferes again when she accompanies Samantha and Tabatha to a kiddie's show, sponsored by McMann and Tate, and "arranges" for Tabatha to win prizes, a no-no since her daddy is connected with the show.

"Super Car." January 19, 1967.

To try and mend fences with Darrin, Endora conjures up a "Super Car" for him. Initially, Darrin is excited about it until he learns it's an experimental model zapped out of its workshop in Detroit.

"Trial and Error of Aunt Clara." February 2, 1967.

A charming episode with Aunt Clara, her powers ever declining, put on trial by a jury of witches to decide if Clara should be "earthbound." Endora, Enchatra and Hagatha are the jury. Samantha defends her favorite aunt.

"Three Wishes." February 9, 1967.

This may sound familiar, but Endora grants Darrin three wishes, without his knowledge, to prove his love for Sam. Sam is sure he will, but seemingly his wishes are to spend the night in Boston with a beautiful model. How will he get out of this one?

"I Remember you . . . Sometimes." February 16, 1967.

Endora puts a spell on Darrin which gives him total recall, leading to disaster.

"Art for Sam's Sake." February 23, 1967.

Sam takes up painting, and her first effort is good for an amateur, so it isn't good enough for Endora, who zaps a masterpiece from a New York Gallery and puts Sam's name on it. Naturally, Darrin has a client who comes to the showing and wants that picture.

"Charlie Harper, Winner." March 2, 1967.

Charlie Harper, Darrin's old college roommate, has really gone places and has a snooty wife who continually rubs it into Sam's face all the luxuries he has given her. Well, Sam conjures up a mink coat to prove that Darrin is no slouch. Unfortunately, it only causes Darrin to believe that he has been a failure since he hasn't been able to give Sam everything she may want. Eventually, Sam convinces Darrin that with him and Tabatha she has everything she wants. At the end, Samantha tells Darrin, "I could never conjure up another Darrin Stephens." Well . . .

"The Crone of Cawdor." March 16, 1967.

The Crone of Cawdor transforms herself into a beautiful client of Darrin's, Terry Warbell, and if she succeeds in kissing Darrin she will steal his youth to preserve her own. Agnes does a delicious parody of famed wardrobe designer Edith Head in this episode.

"No More, Mr. Nice Guy." March 23, 1967.

Endora puts a spell on Darrin which causes everyone who comes in contact with him to hate him.

"It's Witchcraft." March 30, 1967.

Once again a confrontation between Endora and Phyllis Stephens. Darrin and Sam try to prevent Darrin's parents from learning the truth about Tabatha's parents and Endora is called in by Sam to help. Big mistake.

"How to Fail in Business with All Kinds of Help." April 6, 1967.

Through a series of misunderstandings Darrin comes to believe that a new client, Madame Maruska (Marooshkaa), is Endora in disguise and ends up insulting her and throwing away a million-dollar contract. Larry is ready to throw Darrin away (again) unless he can get the account back.

"There's Gold in Them Thar Pills." May 4, 1967.

The third season ends with the first appearance of Bernard Fox as Dr. Bombay, the "quack" witch doctor that Sam's family has gone to for years. Darrin catches a cold and Endora calls in Bombay, who gives him a pill which magically cures the cold within seconds. Darrin, and then Tate, decide to market the pills and make a fortune in the meantime.

"Long Live the Queen." September 7, 1967.

Samantha is named Queen of the Witches and Endora beams while Darrin scowls as the fourth season is launched.

"Toys in Babeland." September 14, 1967.

Endora is babysitting but is expected at a party, so she brings one of Tabatha's toys to life which Tab later copies.

"Business, Italian Style." September 21, 1967.

Darrin tries to learn Italian to impress a client; Endora decides to help him along except that now he can speak Italian but not English.

"Double, Double, Toil and Trouble." September 28, 1967.

Also known as the "pie throwing episode," due to the climactic pie throwing scene, this is a "Serena" episode. Endora calls on Serena to once again impersonate Samantha and cause mischief in the Stephens' marriage.

"Cheap, Cheap." October 5, 1967.

Endora puts a stingy spell on Darrin. How many spells has she cast on him so far?

"No Zip in my Zap." October 12, 1967.

Samantha loses her powers, and Dr. Bombay's diagnosis is because she doesn't use them enough. *Doesn't use them enough??*

"Birdies, Bogeys and Baxter." October 19, 1967.

Client Joe Baxter is an excellent golfer so Larry arranges a golf game between himself, Darrin and Baxter. Of course, Larry expects that Darrin must impress the client with his own skill as a golfer, so Endora puts a spell on Darrin — who doesn't impress the client so much as embarrasses him on the links.

"Allergic to Macedonian Dodo Birds." November 16, 1967.

Perhaps the funniest of all *Bewitched* episodes, many fans — including *Bewitched* historian Herbie J Pilato — consider this Agnes Moorehead's best episode. Endora loses her powers and becomes earthbound, staying with the Stephens and driving Durwood crazy. The scene on the patio between Darrin and the helpless Endora is a classic. Consider this: not only is this classic Endora, but an Aunt Clara and Dr. Bombay episode to boot.

"Solid Gold Mother-in-Law." November 30, 1967.

When Endora pops a picture of herself onto Darrin's desk at work, and is seen by client, Mr. Gregson, who is much taken with Darrin's dedication to his "mother-in-law," he insists on meeting this lovely lady and ends up asking Darrin to open his own ad firm, which causes a breach between Darrin and Tate.

"My What Big Ears You Have." December 7, 1967.

Endora thinks that Darrin is having an affair, and to find out she puts a spell on him causing his ears to grow each time he tells a lie. Pretty soon he is able to start flapping around like Dumbo, but he is, nevertheless, innocent of any hanky-panky.

"I Get Your Nanny, You Get My Goat." December 14, 1967.

Endora hires a nanny, named Elsbeth, for Tabitha, who also looked after Samantha as a child. However, she is taken away from a warlock employer who blames Darrin of stealing away his housekeeper.

"Once in a Vial." January 4, 1968.

Another strong "Endora" episode. Endora summons Rollo, who once dated Samantha, in her latest bid to cause disharmony in the Stephens' marriage. Rollo prepares a love potion meant for Sam, but Endora accidentally downs it and ends up falling in love and almost marrying a client of Darrin's.

"Snob in the Grass." January 11, 1968.

Sheila Sommers, Darrin's ex-flame, returns. Larry wants to land her rich daddy's account and he arranges a dinner party, where Sam can take only so much of Sheila before an overwhelming desire to twitch overcomes her sensibilities — and well-deserved too.

"If They Never Met." January 25, 1968.

One of the most romantic of the *Bewitched* episodes. Endora once again allows Sam to go back in time to see what would have happened if "they never met." It seems that Darrin would have ended up marrying Sheila, and would even have become a full partner at McMann and Tate . . . but, something is missing . . . could it be . . . true love??

"A Prince for a Day." February 8, 1968.

Tabitha brings Prince Charming to life out of her storybook and Darrin's cousin, Helen, falls in love.

"To Twitch or Not to Twitch." March 14, 1968.

>Another terrific episode, from a strong fourth season. Sam and Darrin argue over Sam's use of witchcraft. In a rainstorm, as they are traveling to the Tates' for a party in honor of a client, they experience a flat tire and Darrin asks Sam to repair the tire (via magic); she refuses and he gets angry and wet. Eventually, Sam and Tabitha leave Darrin and go home to Mother (on Cloud 8), only to come back when Darrin makes a sincere apology.

"Tabitha's Cranky Spell." March 28, 1968.

>A babysitter, Louise's Aunt Harriet, thinks that Tab can communicate with the spirit world.

"Man of the Year." April 25, 1968.

>The final appearance of Endora for the fourth season. Endora puts a spell on Darrin which causes everyone who comes in contact with him to be impressed beyond belief. Darrin, naturally, gets a big head.

"Samantha's Wedding Present." September 26, 1968.

>The first episode of the fifth season has Endora putting a spell on Darrin which causes him to slowly shrink until he is as big as a thumbnail.

"Samantha on the Keyboard." October 10, 1968.

>Darrin challenges Samantha to learn how to play the piano the "mortal way." She takes the bait, but that doesn't stop Endora from giving a booster to Tabitha which causes their piano teacher to believe that he has found a child prodigy.

"Darrin Gone! And Forgotten?" October 17, 1968.

>Carlotta (Mercedes McCambridge) comes to collect Samantha whom Endora promised years earlier would marry her son, Juke.

"It's Nice to Have a Spouse Around the House." October 24, 1968.

>Endora once again employs Serena to cause mischief in the Stephens' marriage. What they didn't expect was that Darrin has arranged a second honeymoon for Sam and himself in this slightly risque episode.

"Mirror, Mirror on the Wall." November 7, 1968.

>Endora puts a spell on Darrin which causes him to become self-centered. Another very funny Dick York performance.

"Instant Courtesy." December 26, 1968.

>When Darrin is rude to Endora, she puts a

courtesy spell on him. Of course, he is so courteous now that he drives everybody crazy.

"One Touch of Midas." January 23, 1969.

Endora puts a spell on an ugly little doll called "The Fuzz Doll" so that everybody falls in love with it and wants to buy it. Of course, Darrin wants to market it and make millions so that Sam can have everything she wants.

"Samantha the Bard." January 30, 1969.

Sam comes down with a virus which causes her to say everything in rhyme. Endora seeks Dr. Bombay for help — and, of course, he isn't much help.

"Samantha the Sculptress." February 6, 1969.

Sam takes up sculpture and molds a likeness of Darrin, which Endora brings to life.

"Going Ape." February 27, 1969.

Tabitha turns a chimp into a man, who gets involved in an advertising campaign.

"Tabitha's Weekend." March 6, 1969.

An excellent non-Darrin episode. Phyllis doesn't get enough time with Tabitha, and in her opinion, believes that Sam is overly protective, so she arranges to take Tab for the weekend, but doesn't bargain with having Sam and Endora in tow.

"The Battle of Burning Oak." March 13, 1969.

Darrin is up for membership in an "exclusive" country club, so Endora puts a spell on him, one which turns him into a terrible snob.

"Samantha's Power Failure." March 20, 1969.

The witches' council expects that Sam will sever ties with Darrin and when she refuses, her powers are taken away.

"Samantha Twitches for UNICEF." March 27, 1969.

Sam and Endora work together to get a stingy millionaire to make good in his pledge to UNICEF.

"Daddy Does His Thing." April 3, 1969.

Dick York began this episode but then suffered a seizure on the set which led to his departure from the series. It is Darrin's birthday and Sam has a surprise for him, but Maurice appears with a magical gift for Darrin which he turns down, leading Maurice to turn him into a stubborn mule. This is the final episode York filmed but not the final one he appears in chronologically.

"Samantha's Good News." April 10, 1969.

While Endora and Maurice appear to have an open relationship, it infuriates her when he openly begins to date a younger woman. Samantha manages to bring harmony when she announces that she is expecting.

"Samantha's Shopping Spree." April 17, 1969.

Samantha, Tabitha, Endora and Cousin Henry go shopping in a department store. Henry takes offense at a clerk and turns him into a mannequin.

"Samantha and Darrin in Mexico City." April 24, 1969.

The final episode of the fifth season is also the final episode to feature Dick York as Darrin Stephens. Darrin must learn Spanish to help him sell his ad ideas in a visit to Mexico. Endora casts a spell which causes him to speak Spanish flawlessly but with the side effect of disappearing every time he utters a word of Spanish. Ey, yi-yi.

"Sam and the Beanstalk." September 18, 1969.

The sixth season begins with a new Darrin, played by Dick Sargent. Sargent lacked York's rubber face and romantic quality, but he did develop a deadpan style of his own. As for Agnes, she will be increasingly absent from the series in these last three seasons, appearing in only 46 episodes, and when she does appear (with rare exception) it is usually to place a spell at the beginning, disappear from the body of the show, and then show up again to remove the spell at the end. This episode has Tabitha (who would increasingly have more storylines as she gets older) sending herself into a Jack and the Beanstalk story, with Sam to the rescue.

"Samantha's Yoo Hoo Maid." September 25, 1969

Endora believes that pregnant Samantha needs a maid. The one she has in mind is a nervous wall-flower named Esmerelda, who disappears when flustered — which happens quite a lot, especially with Darrin around. Alice Ghostley is introduced as Esmerelda.

"Samantha's Curious Cravings." October 9, 1969.

Samantha begins having cravings and the food magically appears before her, "Calling Dr. Bombay," who as usual is no help at all. His treatment reverses things and instead of food coming to Sam, Sam goes to the food. A funny episode.

"And Something Makes Four." October 16, 1969.

Sam delivers baby Adam and proud grandpapa Maurice casts a spell which causes everyone who comes in contact with Adam to fall in love with him.

"Naming Samantha's New Baby." October 23, 1969.

Maurice is upset when he learns that Sam and Darrin intend to name the new baby after Darrin's father rather than after Maurice. When Maurice is angry — look out.

"To Trick or Treat or Not to Trick or Treat." October 30, 1969.

Darrin and Endora argue about Halloween, and its stereotypes of witches. Endora turns Darrin into a stereotypical witch with a big nose, wart and lantern jaw. Believe me, Darrin makes one homely witch.

"Samantha's Secret Spell." November 13, 1969.

Darrin and Endora have yet another argument and if Dum-Dum doesn't apologize this time he will be turned into a mouse by midnight.

"You're So Agreeable." December 11, 1969.

At first, Darrin is *too* agreeable and gets on everybody's nerves, then Endora makes him disagreeable to everyone. How can a mortal ever win?

"Samantha's Better Halves." January 1, 1970.

This was actually the first episode Dick Sargent filmed, but it was held back because no one was too happy with it. It is impossible to take Dick York's finest performance and refashion it for another actor, but that is what they tried to do with this weak remake of "Divided He Falls."

"The Phrase is Familiar." January 15, 1970.

Endora casts a spell which causes Darrin to talk in clichés.

"Samantha's Secret is Discovered." January 22, 1970.

When Phyllis sees Samantha and Endora magically moving furniture, Sam decides it's time to come clean with her in-laws and admit she's a witch.

"What Makes Darrin Run." February 12, 1970.

Endora once again thinks that Samantha should be living better and puts a spell on Darrin which makes him ruthlessly ambitious and out to take Larry's place at the firm.

"The Generation Zap." March 5, 1970.

I'm partial to this episode because it was telecast on my sixth birthday, and I'm sure I must have been watching at the time. Anyhow, Endora and Serena once again team up to cause disharmony in the Stephens' marriage by making a client's daughter fall in love with Darrin.

"Ok, Who's the Wise Witch?" March 12, 1970.

The Stephens' house becomes sealed up so no one can enter or leave. Imagine Sam, Darrin, Endora, Esmerelda and Dr. Bombay all stuck together.

"If the Shoe Pinches." March 26, 1970.

Endora outsources her attempts to break Darrin and Sam up to a leprechaun.

"Mona Sammy." April 2, 1970.

My pick for the best episode of the sixth season. Endora conjures up a painting of Sam which makes her look like the Mona Lisa. Larry and Louise come for dinner and discover the painting (thanks again to Endora) and to cover up, Sam says that Darrin is the painter. Louise is so taken with the painting that she insists that he paint her — with hilarious results.

"Turn on the Old Charm." April 9, 1970.

Another standout episode. Samantha gives Darrin an amulet which makes Endora loving and courteous to him. But, "hell hath no fury like a bugged witch" when Endora discovers the truth.

"To Go or Not to Go, That is the Question." September 24, 1970.

Samantha will not attend a witches' convention in Salem if Darrin is not allowed to attend. Hepzibah (Jane Connell), the High Priestess of all witches, decides to dissolve this "mixed marriage." But when her fairness is called into question, she decides to move into the Stephens' home to observe before making a final judgment. Even Endora has to admit to Hepzibah that the paramount reason why she has not been able to dissolve the marriage after all these years is because "He loves my daughter."

"Salem Saga." October 8, 1970.

Sam, Darrin, and Endora arrive in Salem for the big convention. Exteriors were filmed on location at popular tourist attractions including the House of the Seven Gables. In this story, a "bewitched" bed warmer begins to follow Sam around.

"Samantha's Hot Bed Warmer." October 15, 1970.

Part two. The spooked bed warmer turns out to be a warlock who once had a thing for Serena who, when she tired of his advances, turned him into a bed warmer. Sam tries to get her kooky cousin to reverse the spell.

"Samantha's Bad Day in Salem." November 5, 1970.

A warlock named Waldo, who has loved Samantha since she was a child, zaps up a duplicate Samantha for himself, but Larry runs into this machine-like recreation and thinks that Darrin and Sam are having marital problems.

"Samantha's Old Salem Trip." November 12, 1970.

Esmerelda accidentally sends Samantha back to 17th-century Salem, time of the actual Salem Witch trials. Endora sends Darrin back in time to rescue her.

"Samantha's Pet Warlock." November 19, 1970.

Another ex-warlock boyfriend of Sam's, Ashley (how many have there been?), makes a pest of himself trying to get Sam back. When she rejects him (again), he turns himself into a stray dog who moves in with the Stephens.

"Samantha's Old Man." December 3, 1970.

Endora turns Darrin into a 73-year-old version of himself. When Larry and Louise come over, Darrin is introduced as Darrin's grandfather, Grover. Louise has a brainstorm; Grover would be a perfect mate/companion for her Aunt Millicent.

"The Corsican Cousins." December 10, 1970.

Endora is up to her mischief again, but this time casts a spell not on Darrin but on Sam and Serena, which causes Sam to experience the same feelings that her fun-loving, wacky cousin does.

"Samantha's Magic Potion." December 17, 1970.

After a run of bad luck at work, Samantha gives Darrin a magic potion meant to bolster his confidence.

"Mother-In-Law of the Year." January 14, 1971.

This may be the final episode that Agnes has a prominent role throughout. The last few seasons, and in the episodes to come, Endora increasingly appears sparingly usually casting a spell and then disappearing until the end when she removes the spell. Not in this wonderful episode. John McGiver plays Mr. Bobbins of Bobbins Candy who believes that Endora is the perfect representative for a new ad campaign for his product. Toward the end, Sam turns herself into Endora and Endora turns herself into Sam.

"The Return of Darrin the Bold." February 4, 1971.

Endora and Serena conjure up a plan to make Darrin a warlock (and thus more desirable to them?), by sending Serena back to 14th-century Ireland to begin the transformation, beginning with his ancestor, Darrin the Bold. Only thing: wouldn't Darrin's father also become a warlock? How would they have explained that? Would it cause Phyllis yet another "sick headache?"

"This Little Piggie." February 25, 1971.

When Endora thinks that Darrin is being "pig headed," she goes all the way and zaps a pig's head on him.

"Mixed Doubles." March 4, 1971.

Sam and Louise magically switch places. Sam now looks like Louise and Louise now looks like Sam — Sam as Louise sees through it, but not Louise as Sam. Who says blondes are dumb?

"Money Happy Returns." March 18, 1971.

When Darrin finds $1,000 in a taxi, he thinks it is Endora once again trying to interfere. Hey Darrin, I wouldn't mind that kind of interference.

"Out of the Mouth of Babes." March 25, 1971.

A remake of "Junior Executive," with Darrin turned into a ten-year-old version of himself by Endora.

"Laugh, Clown, Laugh." April 15, 1971.

Endora zaps a spell onto Darrin which makes him think he is funny when he is actually obnoxious.

"How Not to Lose Your Head to Henry VIII (Part 1)." September 15, 1971.

In Jolly old England, Sam notices a nobleman who is trapped in a portrait in an art museum. She frees him, causing the wrath of the witch who placed him there. She sends Sam back to the court of Henry VIII. First episode of the eighth and final season.

"How Not to Lose Your Head to Henry VIII (Part 2)." September 22, 1971.

Endora sends Darrin back in time to rescue Samantha. The problem: he has to convince her to kiss him, and she won't know who he is.

"Bewitched, Bothered and Baldoni." October 13, 1971.

Endora brings the Statue of Venus to life and, as she is played by Francine York, it is hard for any of the men to control themselves in her presence.

"Paris, Witch's Style." October 20, 1971.

Maurice decides to punish Darrin because he thinks he is the one who caused his beloved daughter to travel through Europe without telling him. Even Endora tries to protect Darrin in this one.

"A Plague on Maurice and Samantha." November 10, 1971.

Samantha loses her magical powers due to her constant contact in the mortal world. Maurice visits and falls "plague" to the same thing.

"Hansel and Gretel in Samanthaland." November 17, 1971.

Tabitha zaps herself into her "Hansel and Gretel" storybook, while zapping Hansel and Gretel to the modern day. Sam searches for Tabitha while Darrin roams the neighborhood searching for Hansel and Gretel.

"The Warlock in the Gray Flannel Suit." December 1, 1971.

When Darrin won't allow Samantha to attend her cousin's wedding (is this a power trip with him?), Endora decides to get even by trying to get him fired from his job.

"The Eight-Year Itch Witch." December 8, 1971.

Endora once again sets out to test Darrin's fidelity to Samantha, this time with Julie Newmar as the bait.

"3 Men and a Witch on a Horse." December 15, 1971.

Endora puts a spell on Darrin, turning him into a compulsive gambler who gets his hot tips from Tabitha's rocking horse.

"Adam, Warlock or Washout." December 29, 1971.

Adam's magic powers are tested by the Witch's Council. Maurice decides to give him a booster shot.

"Samantha on Thin Ice." January 29, 1972.

Darrin challenges Samantha to learn ice skating the "mortal way" along with Tabitha.

"School Days, School Daze." March 4, 1972.

Endora casts a spell which makes Tabitha a genius.

"A Good Turn Never Goes Unpunished." March 11, 1972.

Darrin thinks that Sam used witchcraft when she comes up with a winning slogan for a client. This leads to a fight, and Sam (with the kids) running home to Mama on cloud nine.

"The Truth, Nothing but the Truth, So Help Me, Sam." March 25, 1972.

The final episode of *Bewitched*. Endora casts a truth-telling spell which leads to a less than harmonious dinner party at the Stephens.

37. *Jonathan Winter's and the Movies.* March 6, 1965. ABC.
     Agnes guest stars in this special hosted by comedian Jonathan Winters, who became a good friend of AM's.

38. *Burke's Law.* April 7, 1965. ABC.
     "Who Killed Hamlet?" Cast: Gene Barry, Gary Conway, Regis Toomey, Leon Lontoc, John Cassavetes, Eddie Foy, Jr., Agnes Moorehead, Susan Bay.

39. *Girl Talk.* September 6, 1965. Syndicated.
     Agnes appears on the pioneering talk program hosted by Virginia Graham.

40. *Art Linkletter's Talent Scouts.* April 4, 1966. CBS
     Established performers introduce new talent. Agnes introduces singer Kelly Garrett.

41. *Mr. Blackwell Presents.* July 5, 1966. ABC.
     Agnes guests on a special hosted by the stuffy fashion designer.

42. *Hollywood Squares.* October 17, 1966. NBC.
     Agnes appeared on the first episode of this long-running game show. Her fellow "Squares": Charley Weaver, Pamela Mason, Wally Cox, Rose Marie, Morey Amsterdam, Abby Dalton and Ernest Borgnine. Peter Marshall hosts

43. *Alice Through the Looking Glass.* November 6, 1966. NBC.
     Agnes plays the Red Queen in this musical adaptation of Lewis Carroll's famous story. The other cast members include Judi Rolin as Alice, Jimmy Durante as Humpty Dumpty, Nanette Fabray as the White Queen, Ricardo Montalban as the White King, Robert Coote as the Red King and the Smothers Brothers as Tweedledum and Tweedledee. Agnes replaced Bette Davis who, according to Nanette Fabray, got a case of "the nerves."

44. *The Hollywood Palace.* November 26, 1966. ABC.
     Eddie Fisher hosted this episode of the long-running variety show, which features Agnes as a guest star. She does a parody of *Don Juan in Hell.*

45. *The Wild, Wild West.* February 10, 1967. CBS.
     "Night of the Vicious Valentine." Cast: Robert Conrad, Ross Martin, Agnes Moorehead, Diane McBain, Henry Beckman, Sherry Jackson, J. Edward McKinley. When powerful and wealthy men are being killed, the investigation leads to Washington, D.C. socialite Emma Valentine (played by Agnes) who has a nefarious plan to gain control of the government. Agnes won her only Emmy Award for her performance in this episode.

46. *Password.* April 1967. NBC.
     Agnes appears with Barry Newman on the popular game show hosted by Allen Ludden. A few weeks after Agnes appeared, Elizabeth Montgomery played the game and Ludden referred to Agnes as her "grandmother" on Bewitched to which the quick-witted Liz replied, "She won't like you for saying that."

47. *The Mike Douglas Show*. May 1–5, 1967. Syndicated.
Agnes acted as co-host for a week full of appearances on this famous talk show taped in Philadelphia and broadcast nationally.

48. *Mr. Blackwell Presents*. May 8, 1967. ABC.
Agnes does a second guest stint on Blackwell's second ABC variety special. Also appearing was Eartha Kitt.

49. *The Red Skelton Show*. November 1967. CBS.
Agnes was Red's special guest star and performed with him in a "Sheriff Dead-eye" sketch. In a letter to Georgia Johnstone, Agnes referred to the experience as "Corn! But it does pay."

50. *The Smothers Brothers Comedy Hour*. December 10, 1967. CBS.
Agnes guest stars in this popular and topical comedy series.

51. *Custer*. December 13, 1967. ABC.
"Spirit Woman." Cast: Wayne Maunder, Slim Pickens, Peter Palmer, Robert F. Simon, Grant Woods, Agnes Moorehead, James Whitmore, Read Morgan, Christopher Milo. Agnes continually sought parts which went against the grain and in these days that meant away from Endora. In this hour-long Western she plays Watoma, an Indian woman who seeks peace.

52. *The Mike Douglas Show*. May 20, 1968. Syndicated.
Agnes appears as a guest on the popular talk show.

53. *The Steve Allen Show*. August 13, 1968. Syndicated
Another talk show appearance, this time with the multi-talented Steve Allen.

54. *The John Gary Show*. October 20, 1968. Syndicated.
Agnes guest stars on this variety show.

55. *The Don Rickles Show*. December 20, 1968. ABC.
This is a variety/game show hosted by Mr. Warmth himself. Agnes makes a guest appearance.

56. *The Mike Douglas Show*. January 9, 1969. Syndicated.
I'm getting to think this was Agnes' favorite talk show.

57. *That's Life*. January 21, 1969. ABC.
Agnes guest stars on this variety hour hosted by Robert Morse. Among the other guests are Phil Harris and Rodney Dangerfield. Agnes appears as Morse's mother and sings, "You're Grown Up Now."

58. *Lancer*. November 25, 1969. CBS.
"A Person Unknown." Cast: James Stacy, Wayne Maunder, Andrew Duggan, Elizabeth Baur, Agnes Moorehead, Bruce Dern. Agnes plays a woman whose daughter finds a wounded Lancer and, rather than nurse him back to health, wants to turn him in for the bounty. Another Western for Agnes.

59. *The Red Skelton Show.* December 9, 1969. CBS.
Agnes makes a second guest appearance with Red.

60. *Oral Roberts Easter Special.* March 27, 1970. Syndicated.
Agnes and puppeteer Shari Lewis join Oral for an Easter inspiration special. Agnes reads "The Resurrection."

61. *Barefoot in the Park.* September 24, 1970. ABC.
Pilot for a proposed new series. Cast: Scoey Mitchell, Tracy Reed, Nipsey Russell, Thelma Carpenter, Harry Holcombe, Agnes Moorehead, Herbert Rudley, Patsy Kelly. Agnes guest stars in this pilot to a new series featuring African-American leads in the Neil Simon story of a young married couple.

62. *Men From Shiloah.* October 21, 1970. NBC.
"Gun Quest." Cast: James Drury, Doug McClure, Tim Matheson, Stewart Granger, Lee Majors, Agnes Moorehead, Anne Francis, Neville Brand, Joseph Cotten, Brandon de Wilde. In its final season, *The Virginian* got a title change to *Men From Shiloah.* Agnes and a stellar cast appear in a story about the Virginian (Drury) being accused of a murder he didn't commit.

63. *Night Gallery.* December 30, 1970. NBC.
"Certain Shadows on the Walls." Cast: Agnes Moorehead, Rachel Roberts, Louis Hayward, Grayson Hall, Rod Serling (host). Since Agnes appeared in one of the most famous *Twilight Zone* episodes, it makes sense that she appeared in Rod Serling's new series. Unfortunately, it's not the classic the first series was, perhaps because Serling didn't have the artistic control he had in the earlier series. Agnes plays Emma, a woman who dies, but her shadow keeps appearing on the wall.

64. *The Scoey Mitchell Show.* March 5, 1971. ABC.
Guest Star: Agnes Moorehead.

65. *It Was a Very Good Year.* July 26, 1971. ABC.
"The Year, 1941." Hosted by Mel Torme, this series focused on events of different years. In this segment Agnes discusses *Citizen Kane* and Orson Welles.

66. *The Smith Family.* September 15, 1971. ABC.
"The Anniversary." Cast: Henry Fonda, Janet Blair, Darleen Carr, Ronny Howard, Agnes Moorehead, Greg Mullavey, Vince Howard. This short-lived series dealt with the professional and family life of Det. Chad Smith (Fonda).

67. *Night Gallery.* September 22, 1971. NBC.
"Witches' Feast." Cast: Agnes Moorehead, Ruth Buzzi, Frank Ryan, Allison McKay, Rod Serling (host). Agnes plays a witch — but the resemblance to Endora ends there.

68. *The Wonderful World of Disney.* October 31, 1971 (Part 1) November 7, 1971 (Part 2). NBC.
"The Strange Monster of Strawberry Cove." Cast: Burgess Meredith, Agnes Moorehead, Annie

McEveety, Jimmy Bracken, Patrick Creamer, Parley Baer, Skip Homeier, Erin Moran. A school field trip to Strawberry Cove becomes the talk of the town when their teacher (Meredith) claims to have seen a sea monster. The head of the local bird watcher's club (Agnes) doesn't believe it and seeks his dismissal.

69. *Rowan and Martin's Laugh-In.* November 29, 1971. NBC.
Agnes has a cameo on the popular comedy-variety series.

70. *Love, American Style.* December 17, 1971. ABC.
"Love and the Particular Girl." Cast: Stephanie Powers, Agnes Moorehead, Dennis Allen. Agnes plays Stephanie's mother who hopes that she will settle down and get married.

71. *Marcus Welby, M.D.* October 17, 1972. ABC.
"He Could Sell Iceboxes to Eskimos." Cast: Robert Young, James Brolin, Elena Verdugo, Jack Haley, Agnes Moorehead, Sharon Farrell, Marion Ross. Jack Haley plays a stroke victim, with Agnes as his wife.

72. *The Mike Douglas Show.* December 13, 1972. Syndicated.
Yet another Moorehead appearance with Mike. Agnes was appearing in *Don Juan in Hell* when she appeared on this show taped in Philadelphia.

73. *What's My Line?* February 8, 1973. Syndicated.
Agnes was in New York appearing in *Don Juan in Hell* when she appeared on this panel show as the "mystery guest."

74. *The Midnight Special.* July 14, 1973. ABC.
Agnes makes a cameo appearance on the popular late night contemporary variety show.

75. *Rex Harrison's Short Stories of Love.* May 1, 1974. NBC.
"The Fortune Painter." Cast: Lorne Greene, Agnes Moorehead, Lloyd Bochner, Alan Hale, Jr. Jess Walton, Rex Harrison (host). Harrison hosted this pilot for an anthology series. Agnes once again plays a mother who doesn't think her daughter (*The Young and The Restless* star Jess Walton) is making a good choice in a mate. This episode was first shown the day after Agnes' death and was her last acting role in television.

III

TELEVISION MOVIES OF AGNES MOOREHEAD

The Ballad of Andy Crocker. November 18, 1969. ABC.

Cast: Lee Majors, Joey Heatherton, Jimmy Dean, Bobby Hatfield, Marvin Gaye, Agnes Moorehead, Pat Hingle, Jill Haworth. This was a pilot for a television series and produced by Aaron Spelling and Danny Thomas. Majors is a war hero who comes home from Vietnam and discovers that his girlfriend (Heatherton) had married while he was gone. Apparently, it was her mother (Agnes) who played a big hand in breaking them up. Hmm, Agnes certainly did get typed in this kind of part.

Marriage: Year One. October 15, 1971. ABC.

Cast: Sally Field, Robert Pratt, William Windom, Agnes Moorehead, Neville Brand, Bob Balban, Lonny Chapman, Cicely Tyson, Randolph Mantooth. Another pilot for a prospective series. Field and Pratt play young marrieds going through the trials and tribulations of the first year of marriage. Agnes plays Field's liberal (!) grandmother, and utters this line (so contrary to the real Agnes), "Hippies look . . . well, *sexy.*"

Suddenly Single. October 19, 1971. ABC.

Cast: Hal Holbrook, Barbara Rush, Margot Kidder, Agnes Moorehead, Michael Constantine, Harvey Korman, Cloris Leachman, David Huddleston. Holbrook plays a man who is suddenly single after a divorce. He is middle-aged and ready for new experiences. He works in a pharmacy where a drug sales-man (Korman) offers to help him become a "swinger" — another co-worker (Agnes) suggests caution.

Rolling Man. October 4, 1972. ABC.

Cast: Dennis Weaver, Don Stroud, Donna Mills, Jimmy Dean, Agnes Moorehead, Sheree North, Slim Pickens. Produced by Aaron Spelling, this story involves a man just released from prison (Weaver) who returns to find that his kids are in the care of his wife's mother (Agnes) who is sick and bedridden and can't care for them.

Night of Terror. October 10, 1972.

Cast: Martin Balsam, Cathy Burns, Chuck Connors, Donna Mills, Agnes Moorehead, Mary Grace Canfield. Mills plays a woman pursued by a killer (Connors). When she is paralyzed by Connors and loses her will to live, her therapist (Agnes) turns her attitude around.

Frankenstein: The True Story. November 30, 1973 & December 1, 1973. NBC.

Cast: James Mason, Leonard Whiting, David McCallum, Jane Seymour, Agnes Moorehead, Michael Sarrazin, Michael Wilding, Margaret Leighton, Ralph Richardson, John Gielgud. A faithful adaptation of Mary Shelley's classic novel, with Whiting as Dr. Victor Frankenstein and Sarrazin as the monster. Agnes plays Mrs. Blair, Dr. Frankenstein's housekeeper.

IV

RADIO APPEARANCES OF AGNES MOOREHEAD

IT IS IMPOSSIBLE TO FIND AND LIST EVERY SINGLE RADIO APPEARANCE THAT AGNES DID, SO THIS IS BY NO MEANS A COMPLETE LISTING.

1. Local Radio Stations KSD and KMOX in St. Louis (1926). During her summer vacation from teaching in Soldiers Grove, Agnes worked on radio in the city she considered her hometown, St. Louis, as a female baritone. This summer she also auditioned for the American Academy of Dramatic Arts.

2. *Believe it or Not.* circa, 1929–1930. Hosted by Robert L. Ripley, Agnes was a member of the ensemble which re-enacted record-breaking events.

3. *Sherlock Holmes.* circa, 1930–1933. NBC-Blue. Agnes was an ensemble player on this series based on the characters and stories of Sir Arthur Conan Doyle.

4. *Ben Bernie Show.* circa, 1931. Agnes appeared on the popular bandleader's program as a "stooge" and/or commercial actress.

5. *Mysteries in Paris.* 1932–1933. CBS. Agnes appears as Nana, the maid who joins her employer in solving weekly mysteries. The character of Nana became so popular with listeners that the role was expanded and represents Agnes' first big break in radio. Written and produced by Edith Meiser, one of AM's first big boosters in the business. Cast: Elsie Hitz, Agnes Moorehead, John McGovern, Alfred Shirley.
     #1: "The Octopus Appears or The Lady and the Pearls" 9/12/32.
     #2: "Death at the Eiffel Tower" 9/19/32.
     #3: "The Haunted Abbey" 9/26/32.
     #4: "The Cat Strikes" 10/3/32.
     #5: "The Fire Escape from Hotel," 10/17/32.
     #6: "The Adventure of the Poisonous Snakes" 10/24/32.
     #7: "The Adventure of the Eye of Buddha" 10/31/32.
     #8: "The Missing Mona Lisa of the Ancient Vault" 11/14/32.
     #9: "Julie of the Waxworks" 11/21/32.
     #10: "The Funeral of Three Brothers" 11/28/32.
     #11: "The Catacombs and the Piper" 12/5/32.
     #12: "The Disappearing Gold from the Underground Vaults" 12/12/32.
     #13: "Unveiling of the Monument" 12/19/32.
     #14: "Murder on the Train" 12/26/32.
     #15: "The Secret of the Avalanche" 1/2/33.
     #16: "The Ghosts of Thunder Castle" 1/9/33.
     #17: "The Great Black Loup-Garou" 1/16/33.
     #18: "The Haunted Asylum" 1/23/33.

#19: "The Mystery of the White Sister" 1/30/33.

#20: "The Curse of the Toquevilles" 2/6/33.

6. *Evenings in Paris.* 1933–1934. CBS. This was a revamped Mysteries in Paris with Agnes appearing not as Nana but as Cousin Anna.

7. *The Armour Hour.* 1933–1936. CBS. Also known as *The Phil Baker Show.* Agnes became known as Baker's comic stooge and created the character of "Miss Sarah Heartburn" an advice to the lonely columnist. In addition to the radio show, Agnes went on several tours with Baker and his sidekick "Bottle" — the English comedian Harry McNaughton, who she began a lifelong friendship with. Baker was a vaudeville headliner, who first became known as an accordionist and then comedian. *Bewitched* regular Mabel Albertson (Darrin's mother) also was a regular on the Baker show.

8. *The Gumps.* 1934. CBS. Produced and Directed by Himan Brown this was a serialization of a then-popular comic strip by Sidney Smith, with Wilmer Walter as Andy Gump and Agnes cast as his wife, Min. Brown later described these characters as "the Archie and Edith of their day." Jackie Kelk was cast as their son and became a lifelong friend and confidante of Agnes. Ralph Edwards, later of *This is Your Life*, was the announcer

9. *Heartthrobs of the Hills.* 1934–1935. NBC. Agnes was a semi-regular on this program which featured folk music and dramatizations. Ray Collins, Brian Donlevy and Billy Halop also appeared.

10. *Dot and Will.* 1935–1937. NBC-Blue. This was a daily serial which resolved around the life of a young married couple, Dot and Will Horton. Agnes played their friend Rosie. The show also featured Rosemary DeCamp as Madge.

11. *The New Penny.* October 1, 1935–March 24, 1936. NBC.
    Stage legend Helen Hayes plays Penny, an independent and self-reliant career woman, in this half-hour weekly drama. Agnes plays her adversary, with a supporting cast which included Walter Wilmer, Adele Dumas, Arlene Francis, Ned Weaver, Madeline Piere and Joe Bell. The show was produced and directed by Edith Meiser, who also helmed *Sherlock Holmes* and *Mysteries in Paris*, both of which featured Agnes. (Note: it was around this time that Helen Hayes arranged for Agnes to get a screen test for motion pictures — the screen test where the director told her to give up on any plans of a screen career).

    #1: "Lost a Husband, found Two Dozen Babies" 10/1/35

    #2: "Penelope Goes Off the Deep End" 10/8/35

    #3: "Penelope's Busy Day" 10/15/35.

    #4: "Penny Puts Her Foot Down" 10/22/35.

    #5: "Penny Starts a Fight" 10/29/35.

    #6: "Preparation for the Prize Fight" 11/5/35.

    #7: "Football Pickaninny and the Gay Divorcee" 11/12/35.

    #8: "Nurse MacDumphrey's Night Off" 11/19/35.

    #9: "Arrival of an Unwanted Baby" 11/26/35.

    #10: "Danger Threatens St. Vincent's" 12/3/35.

#11: "The Siege of St. Vincent's" 12/10/35.

#12: "Penny Plots a Romance" 12/17/35.

#13: "There is a Santa Claus" 12/24/35.

#14: "New Year's Eve" 12/31/35.

#15: "A Visit to the Hunter Farm" 1/7/36.

#16: "Sugar Plum, Gee Gee and John" 1/14/36.

#17: "The Return of John" 1/21/36.

#18: "Boodles Arrives" 1/28/36.

#19: "Penny Meets John in the 'Minuet'." 2/4/36.

#20: "The Kidnapping of Penny" 2/11/36.

#21: "The Belligerents" 2/18/36.

#22: "Nelly's Secret" 2/25/36.

#23: "John's Engagement and Mr. Crowder's Visit" 3/3/36

#24: "The Adoption of Mickey" 3/10/36.

#25: "The Fire" 3/17/36.

#26: "The Dawn" 3/24/36.

12. *The Edwards of England.* February 3, 1936. The story of various Edwards, from the I to the VII. Agnes plays a nurse and various other "voices."

13. *City Desk.* May 17, 1936. "Adventures in Painless Dentistry." Agnes has a guest role playing a nurse.

14. *Way Down East.* 1936. Syndicated. A daily 15-minute serial based on the play and movie of the same name, set in New England. Agnes and Van Heflin play the leads in this Himan Brown produced and directed program.

15. *The March of Time.* 1936–1938. CBS. This program re-enacted news events with radio actors portraying the newsmakers of the day. Agnes specialized in Eleanor Roosevelt, among many others. Mrs. Roosevelt once told Agnes that she preferred her impersonation to any other. Among the other actors who appeared on the program: Jeanette Nolan, John McIntyre, Orson Welles, Art Carney, Ray Collins, Nancy Kelly, William Johnstone, and Paul Stewart.

16. *Terry and the Pirates.* 1937. NBC-Blue. An adventure series based on the popular comic strip by Milton Caniff, with Agnes as the evil "Dragon Lady." Jackie Kelk starred as Terry Lee, young boy in the Orient who gets involved in weekly adventures versus the dragon lady.

17. *The Shadow*. 1937–1939. CBS. The show had been on several years when it was revamped with Orson Welles cast as Lamont Cranston, "The Shadow," with "The Lovely" Margo Lane, played by Agnes, accompanying him in their weekly adventures. The opening of this program is among the best known in old-time radio, "Who knows what evil lurks in the hearts of men? . . . The Shadow Knows." William Johnstone replaced Welles in 1938, with Agnes playing another season as Margo.

18. *Les Miserables*. 1937. Mutual. This seven-part series, based on the Victor Hugo book, led to the *Mercury Theatre of the Air* the following year. The stars were Orson Welles, Martin Gabel, Agnes Moorehead, Ray Collins, Frank Readick, Everett Sloane, William Johnstone, Adelaide Klein, Estelle Levy, and Virginia Welles (then-wife of Orson). This was a seven-week adaptation.

19. *Life Can Be Beautiful*. 1938. CBS. Daily serial about the trials and tribulations of the Solomon family. The opening catch phrase was, "Come in, come in. The door is open." Agnes played the part of Nellie Conrad. Also appearing: Alice Reinhart, John Holbrook, Paul Stewart, Dick Nelson, Clayton "Bud" Collyer, Ed Begley.

20. *The Columbia Workshop*. December 23, 1937. CBS. "Alice's Adventures Through the Looking Glass, Part One." An adaptation of the Lewis Carroll story, which experimented with musical sound effects, and was presented as a special holiday presentation. Helen Claire, Agnes Moorehead, Lurene Tuttle star.

21. *The Columbia Workshop*. December 30, 1937. CBS. "Alice's Adventures Through the Looking Glass, Part Two."

22. *The Mercury Theatre of the Air*. 1938. CBS. This landmark one-hour radio series dramatized literary stories and presented them in the first-person singular, as the show was originally titled. While Agnes was certainly a part of Orson Welles' Mercury Theatre of the air ensemble cast, she didn't appear in every episode. What follows are the shows she participated in.

    "Dracula" 7/11/38. Cast: Orson Welles (Dracula), Martin Gabel (Van Helsing) Agnes Moorehead (Mina), Ray Collins (The Russian Captain), Karl Swenson (The Mate), Elizabeth Farrell (Lucy). This was the debut episode.

    "Treasure Island" 7/18/38. Based on Robert Louis Stevenson's book, with Orson Welles, Arthur Anderson (as young Jimmy Hawkins), Agnes Moorehead (as Jimmy's mother), Ray Collins, George Coulouris, Alfred Shirley, and William Alland.

    "Abraham Lincoln" 8/15/38. The story of Lincoln's life as president during the Civil War. Cast: Orson Welles, Ray Collins, Agnes Moorehead (as Mary Todd Lincoln), George Coulouris, Karl Swenson.

    "The War of the Worlds" 10/30/38. The program which scared America half to death, based on the H.G. Well story about martians landing on earth. This generated so much publicity that it led to a sponsor for the Mercury Theatre, Campbell Soup, and a new name for the program: *The Campbell Playhouse*. Agnes had no dialogue but was one of the background screamers.

23. *The Columbia Workshop*. November 24, 1938. CBS. "Beauty and the Beast." Agnes narrated this operetta, which featured the Columbia Symphony Orchestra.

24. *The Campbell Playhouse.* December 9, 1938. CBS. "Rebecca." The Mercury Theatre now had a sponsor, Campbell Soup, and a bigger budget and could afford big name guest stars. In this adaptation of the Daphne du Maurier novel, Orson Welles is cast as Maxim de Winter with guest star Margaret Sullavan as the protagonist, "I." The Mercury regulars are in supporting roles. Agnes portrays the vengeful maid, Mrs. Danvers, who still idolizes the original Mrs. De Winter, Rebecca. Other episodes featuring Agnes:

"Call it a Day" 12/9/38. Story of Dorothy Gladys Smith. Special guests: Beatrice Lillie and Jane Wyatt.

"A Farewell to Arms" 12/30/38. Guest star: Helen Hayes.

"Mutiny on the Bounty" 1/13/39.

"Chicken Wagon Family" 1/20/39.

"I Lost My Girlish Laughter" 1/27/39. Allegedly inspired by David O. Selznick.

"Wickford Point" 5/5/39.

"Our Town" 5/12/39. First radio adaptation of the famous Thorton Wilder play.

"The Things We Have" 5/26/39. Written by Orson Welles, tells of an immigrant's perceptions of America.

"Victoria Regina" 6/2/39. Guest Star: Helen Hayes, recreating her famous stage role of Queen Victoria.

"Peter Ibbetson" 9/10/39. Guest Star: Helen Hayes.

"Ah, Wilderness" 9/17/39.

"What Every Woman Should Know" 9/24/39. Guest Star: Helen Hayes.

"The Count of Monte Cristo" 10/1/39.

"Liliom" 10/22/39. Guest Star: Helen Hayes.

"Vanity Fair" 1/7/40. Guest Star: Helen Hayes.

"Mr. Deeds Goes to Town" 2/11/40. Guest Star: Gertrude Lawrence.

25. *The Cavalcade of America,* 1938–1941. CBS.

Agnes was a member of *Cavalcade's* ensemble cast, alternating between starring and supporting roles on a weekly basis. This series specialized in Americana with plays about historical figures and events, and proved to be very popular, running for 15 seasons beginning in 1935. Agnes joined the cast in its fourth season. The sponsor was DuPont. Agnes appeared in the following:

"Peter Stuyvesant" 12/12/38

"Will Rogers" 12/19/38

"John Honeyman" 1/2/39

"Stephen Foster" 1/16/39. AM plays two roles, Foster's mother and Mrs. Pentland.

"Alexander Graham Bell" 1/23/39. AM plays three roles including Mrs. Bell and a female operator.

"Mark Twain" 1/30/39. AM plays Mrs. Twain.

"Nathan Hale" 2/6/39

"Allan Pinkerton" 2/13/39

"Kit Carson" 2/20/39

"George Gershwin" 2/27/39. AM plays Mrs. Gershwin.

"The Texas Rangers" 3/6/39

"Marie Dressler" 3/13/39. AM plays the world-famous actress.

"The American Clipper" 3/20/39

"The League of the Long House" 3/27/39

"The Pioneer Mother" 4/3/39. AM plays Eliza Ann Brooks.

"John Howard Payne" 4/10/39

"Patrick Henry" 4/17/39. AM plays Patrick's mother.

"Washington and the Crown" 5/1/39

"Mr. Justice Holmes" 5/15/39. AM plays Mrs. Holmes – Fanny.

"Dolly Madison" 5/22/39. AM as the First Lady.

"Sam Houston" 1/9/40

"Thomas Jefferson" 1/30/40. AM as Martha Jefferson, wife of the president.

"Stolen General" 3/5/40

"The Raven Wins Texas" 3/12/40

"Jordan's Banks" 3/19/40

"The Story of John Fitch" 3/26/40

"Benedict Arnold" 4/2/40

"America Sings: The Songs of Stephen Foster" 4/9/40

"Daniel Boone" 4/16/40. AM as Rebecca Boone.

"Thomas Paine" 4/30/40

"Nancy Hanks" 5/7/40. AM has the title role as Abe Lincoln's mother.

"Roger Williams" 5/14/40

"John Sutter" 6/4/40

"Susan B. Anthony" 6/18/40

"Walter Reed" 6/25/40

"Ann Rutledge and Lincoln" 1/23/40. AM again as Lincoln's mother.

"The Red Death" 10/30/40

"Wild Bill Hickock" 11/6/40

"Dr. Franklin Goes to Court" 11/20/40

"The Farmer Takes a Wife" 11/20/40

"Light in the Hills" 11/27/40. AM as educator Martha Berry.

"John Brown" 12/11/40

"Will Rogers" 1/1/41

"Mightier Than the Sword" 1/8/41. AM as the wife of cartoonist Thomas Nast.

"As a Man Thinketh" 1/15/41

"Dr. Franklin Take It Easy" 1/29/41

"Henry Clay" 2/5/41

"Abraham Lincoln: The War Years" 2/12/41. AM as Mary Lincoln.

"Plain Mr. President" 2/19/41

"Edgar Allan Poe" 2/26/41

"Voice in the Wilderness" 3/5/41

"Black Rust" 3/12/41

"I Sing a New World" 3/19/41

"Down to Sea" 3/26/41

"Edwin Booth" 3/31/41

"Ode to a Nightingale" 4/7/41

"A Passage to Georgia" 4/14/41

"Henry Bergh, Founder of the A.S.P.C.A." 4/21/41

"The Heart and the Fountain" 4/28/41

"The Trials and Triumphs of Horatio Alger" 5/5/41

"Theodosia Burr" 5/12/41

"David Crockett" 5/19/41

"John Hopkins" 5/26/41

"The Woman in Lincoln's Cabinet" 6/2/41

"Young Andrew Jackson" 6/9/41. AM as Rachel Jackson.

"Annie Oakley" 6/16/41. AM in the title role.

"Joel Chandler Harris" 6/23/41

"Jean Pierre Blanchard" 6/30/41

"The Mystery of the Spotted Death" 7/7/41

"Anne Hutchinson" 7/14/41. AM in the title role.

"O. Henry" 7/21/41

"Clifford Holland" 7/28/41

"Josephine Baker" 8/4/41. AM in the title role.

"Red Laterns on St. Michaels" 8/11/41

"Stephen Arnold Douglas" 8/18/41. AM as Mrs. Douglas, a role she would play on stage in *The Rivalry.*

"Leif Ericsson" 9/1/41

"City of Illusion" 9/15/41

"Native Land, Part 2" 9/29/41

"Waters of the Wilderness" 10/13/41

26. *Brenda Curtiss.* 1939–1940. CBS. Daily serial. Program tells the story of Brenda Curtiss, a famous actress who relinquishes the stage to devote time to her husband, Jim, an attorney, and her home in New York City. Vicki Viola plays Brenda, Michael Fitzmaurice is Jim, and Agnes plays the role of Brenda's mother.

27. *The Aldrich Family.* 1939–1940. NBC. Situation comedy about the life of Henry Aldrich, an overeager teenager who has a penchant for trouble. Agnes played the mother of his best friend, Homer Brown. Homer was played by her good friend, Jackie Kelk.

28. *The Mighty Show.* 1939. Agnes as Ma Hutchinson who runs a circus. Also starring is Elliott Reid.

29. *Great Plays.* April 2, 1939. Blue Network.
    "The Blue Bird." The story of two children and their search for the Blue Bird. Cast: Kingsley Colton, Pattee Chapman, Agnes Moorehead, Barbara Weeks, Eric Dressler, Donald MacDonald, John McGovern, Catherine Anderson, Harry Neveille, Arthur Hughes, Alan Reed. Host: Burns Mantel.

30. *The Fred Allen Show.* October 11, 1939. NBC.
    Host: Fred Allen. Guest Star: Agnes Moorehead. Agnes plays in a sketch as a telephone survey taker who takes surveys for her boss (played by Fred).

31. *The Columbia Workshop.* 5/1/39. CBS. "Wet Saturday." A comedy about a family staying home on a rainy Saturday. Bernard Herrmann was the composer and conductor.

32. *Life Begins.* 1940–1941. CBS. Another serial drama. All about the life and loves of Martha Webster, and her experiences with the wealthy Craig Family. Agnes plays the role of Mrs. Riley. Also appearing were Ray Collins, Donald Cook, Jeanette Nolan and Everett Sloane.

33. *Superman.* February 12, 1940. NBC.
    Agnes played Superman's mother from Krypton, Lara, with Ned Wever as Jor-El, on the premiere broadcast and in a few subsequent episodes. Radio and later game-show veteran, Bud (*To Tell the Truth*) Collyer, played the man of steel. Rollie Bester, a radio actress and wife of writer Alfred (*The Green Lantern*) Bester, played Lois Lane. Agnes' good friend and frequent co-star, Jackie Kelk, was the most memorable Jimmy Olson, cub reporter.

34. *Luncheon at the Waldorf With Ilka Chase.* February 24, 1940.
    Hostess: Ilka Chase. Agnes Moorehead is interviewed on this talk program.

35. *Bob Crosby's Music Shop.* March 2, 1940. CBS
    Host: Bob Crosby and his orchestra and The Bobcats. Guest Star: Agnes Moorehead.

36. *Radio Guild.* April 6, 1940. Blue network. "The Withering Glare of Amelia Peck." Agnes plays a spinster who becomes known for her stare.

37. *The Columbia Workshop.* May 5, 1940. CBS.
    "The Honest Captain." The story of a man who is willing to think for himself, in a community where he is surrounded by "God fearing" people. Cast: Parker Fennelly, Agnes Moorehead, Orth Bell, Vincent Donohue, Gene Leonard, Arthur Anderson.

38. *Gangbusters.* June 15, 1940. NBC.
    Agnes plays two roles in this episode of the landmark radio crime drama: a worried mother and a waitress.

Phillips H. Lord, who played "Seth Parker" on radio and gave Agnes one of her earliest breaks when she did a cross-country tour with the *Seth Parker* cast, was the creator/producer/director of this show.

39. *The Jerry Lester Show.* August 27, 1940. CBS
    Host: Jerry Lester. Guest: Agnes Moorehead. Comedy/variety program.
    An excerpt from a sketch performed by Jerry and Agnes:
    AM : (*speaking fast/nervously*) I want to send my poor dear husband Frank to your health camp. He's very nervous, he must rest, relax and get lots of rest.
    JL: Your husband Frank's nervous? Maybe he associates with nervous people!
    AM: That's not possible — I'm the only one he sees. I'm not nervous — nervous!!
    JL: If you're not nervous, why are you twitching so?
    AM: I'm not twitching, I just have good rhythm!

40. *The Helen Hayes Theatre.* November 3, 1940.
    "Alice Adams." Miss Hayes plays Alice, with Agnes cast as her mother, Mrs. Adams. Based on the Booth Tarkington novel of the same name.

41. *Bringing Up Father.* 1941–1942. NBC. Situation comedy based on the comic strip by George McManus. Agnes plays Maggie, a society matron who keeps a tight rein on her husband, Jiggs. Typical episodes dealt with Maggie forcing Jiggs to go on a diet or forcing Jiggs to join a political committee made up of the most prominent people in town.

42. *Bulldog Drummond.* 1941–1942. WOR. A weekly mystery-drama, which featured Agnes with fellow Mercury players, George Coulouris, Everett Sloane, Paul Stewart and Ray Collins. The series was produced and directed by Himan Brown.

43. *The Helen Hayes Theatre.* January 5, 1941.
    "Strange Interlude." Agnes plays Paige.

44. *Charlie and Jessie.* January 8, 1941.
    Short-lived sitcom starring Florence Lake and Donald Cook as "America's daffiest couple." Agnes has a guest role, playing Henrietta Croty.

45. *The Columbia Workshop.* January 25, 1941. "This is from David." Agnes plays a mother who ignores her son.

46. *The Columbia Workshop.* February 16, 1941. "A Crop of Beans." The story of a farm family during the Depression.

47. *Lincoln Highway.* March 15, 1941. NBC.
    A dramatic anthology series about the people who travel the 3,000-mile length of U.S. Route 30, known as "The Lincoln Highway." John McIntire was the host and Agnes guest-starred in this week's episode.

48. *The Free Company*. April 6, 1941. CBS. "His Honor, The Mayor." The program dealt with American ideals and basic freedoms. This episode, written and narrated by Orson Welles, deals with a small town mayor who allows "white crusaders," a KKK-like group, to assemble over the violent opposition of many towngoers. Ray Collins plays the Mayor and Agnes is his wife.

49. *Great Moments from Great Plays*. May 9, 1941. CBS. "Ceiling Zero."

50. *Inner Sanctum Mysteries*. June 20, 1941. CBS
   "The Eye of Shiva." A woman dies because someone told the truth. Agnes plays Ellen Kohler, the town's richest woman — the untruthful woman. Paul Lukas plays Dr. Max Thoma.

51. *The Columbia Workshop*. July 13, 1941. CBS. "Ann Was an Ordinary Girl." Agnes as Ann Rutledge, the first love of Abraham Lincoln (played by John McIntyre). Norman Corwin wrote and directed.

52. *Philip Morris Playhouse*. August 15, 1941. CBS. "Dark Victory." An adaptation of the play and famous film about a woman who is slowly dying of a brain tumor. Sylvia Sidney stars, with Agnes as her best friend.

53. *Manhattan at Midnight*. August 20, 1941. Blue Network.
   Agnes had a guest appearance on this romantic drama which starred Jeanette Nolan, Teddy Bergman and Ted de Corsia. Agnes plays Miss Marble — is she innocent or not?

54. *Mayor of the Town*. 1942–1949. CBS. A family-oriented comedy-drama, about a small town mayor and his everyday dealings with townspeople. Agnes plays Marilly, his tart-tongued maid. The mayor is played by Lionel Barrymore with Conrad Binyon as his young ward, Butch.

55. *The Cavalcade of America*. April 20, 1942. NBC. "In This Crisis." Agnes guest-stars as Mme. Bonneville.

56. *Armstrong Theatre of the Air*. July 11, 1942. CBS. "By Appointment." When her husband tells her that she is in a "middle-aged rut," Helen (Agnes) begins to get busy, volunteering with the USO, Air Raid Central and Red Cross. She is so busy her husband now thinks he can only see her "by appointment."

57. *The Abbott and Costello Show*. October 22, 1942. NBC.
   Hosts: Bud Abbott and Lou Costello. Guest Star: Agnes Moorehead. Agnes appears in a sketch as "Aunt Ruby."
   A portion of the sketch:
   AM: (to A & C) Ah, good evening boys. How are you tonight? Having the same old fun,

in the same old way, with the same old jokes?

COSTELLO: Why you old —

ABBOTT: Ah, Ah, Ah! Costello! I said to be nice.

AM: After all, Mr. Costello, remember — I'm a woman of parts!

COSTELLO: Well, go back to Lockheed, they forgot to assemble you.

58.   *Hello Americans.* November 22, 1942. CBS.
"Pizarro: El Conquistador." The story of the conquerors and liberators in South America. Orson Welles (host), Agnes Moorehead, Ray Collins, Hans Conried, Pedro De Cordoba.

59.   *Uncle Sam Presents.* December 4, 1942.
Agnes appeared on this patriotic broadcast in support of the war effort.

60.   *Hello Americans.* December 6, 1942. CBS.
"The Alphabet of the Islands." Caribbean Islands, that is. Cast: Orson Welles (host), Agnes Moorehead, Ray Collins, Miguelito Valdez, Ted Reid, Gerald Mohr. Part one of two.

61.   *Hello Americans.* December 13, 1942. CBS.
"The Alphabet of the Islands." Part two of Welles' look at the Caribbean Islands. Cast: Orson Welles (host), Agnes Moorehead, Hans Conried, Gerald Mohr, Lou Merrill.

62.   *The Cavalcade of America.* December 14, 1942. NBC. "The Man Who Wouldn't Be President." Edward Arnold plays Daniel Webster, with Agnes cast as his devoted wife.

63.   *Suspense* (1942–1960) CBS. Agnes Moorehead guest-starred so many times on this suspense anthology series that she became known as "The First Lady of Suspense." The introduction is still famous today: "The CBS radio network brings you tales well calculated to keep you in . . . *Suspense!*"

"The Diary of Sophronia Winters" 4/27/43. Agnes makes her debut in this episode about a woman who marries a psychopath. Lucille Fletcher wrote the script and Ray Collins co-stars as the husband.

"Sorry, Wrong Number" 5/25/43. This radio play is one of the most famous of all time. Agnes plays Mrs. Elbert Stevenson, an invalid who overhears a murder plot on a party line and slowly discovers that it is she who is the intended victim. Lucille Fletcher wrote the script.

"Uncle Henry's Rosebush" 6/29/43

"Sorry, Wrong Number" 8/21/43. The first rebroadcast of the famous play.

"The Sisters" 2/3/44

"Sorry, Wrong Number" 2/24/44

"The Diary of Sophronia Winters" 8/17/44

"To Find Help" 1/18/45. Frank Sinatra and Agnes in a play about a psychopath who terrorizes a woman in her home. Based on the play, *The Man*, and made into the movie *Beware, My Lovely*.

"Sorry Wrong Number" 9/6/45

"Post Mortem" 4/4/46. A winning lottery ticket is buried with a dead man.

"The Thirteenth Sound" 2/13/47. Agnes plays a woman who murders her husband (played by William Johnstone) and then begins to hear strange sounds.

"The Yellow Wallpaper" 7/29/48. Agnes plays a woman who begins to see strange pattens jumping out at her on her wallpaper.

"Sorry, Wrong Number" 11/18/48

"The Screaming Woman" 11/25/48. Agnes was so well known for her scream that she was employed to do just that in this story which starred Margaret O'Brien.

"The Trap" 6/16/49

"The Chain Letter" 4/27/50. Agnes as a woman who sends a chain letter, one which may have caused the death of a woman.

"The Death Parade" 2/15/51

"The Evil of Adelaide Winters" 9/10/51

"The Fall River Tragedy" 1/14/52. Agnes plays Lizzie Borden.

"Sorry, Wrong Number" 9/15/52

"Death and Miss Turner" 11/17/52

"The Signalman" 3/23/53

"The Empty Chair" 9/21/53

"The Wreck of The Maid of Athens" 11/30/53. The story of a shipwreck.

"Weekend Special: Death" 5/24/54. Agnes as a woman trapped in a supermarket, hiding from two killers.

"Death and Miss Turner" 5/19/57

"The Yellow Wallpaper" 6/30/57

"Sorry, Wrong Number" 10/20/57

"The Chain" 3/9/58

"The Whole Town's Sleeping" 8/31/58. Ray Bradbury wrote this story about a serial killer on the loose.

"Don't Call Me Mother" 1/4/59

"Sorry, Wrong Number" 1/14/60. It is fitting that Agnes' last appearance on *Suspense* is appearing in yet another airing of her most famous radio play.

64. *Hello Americans.* January 10, 1943. CBS.

A portrait of Cortez and Montezuma, Juarez, Zapata in old Mexico. Cast: Orson Welles (host), Hans Conried, Lou Merrill, Agnes Moorehead, Ray Collins.

65. *The Lady Esther Screen Guild Theatre.* May 31, 1943. CBS.

"Rebecca." Cast: Joan Fontaine, Brian Aherne, Agnes Moorehead. Agnes takes on the role of Mrs. Danvers once again, with Fontaine recreating her screen role as "I" and Fontaine's then-husband Aherne as Maxim De Winter.

66. *Hollywood Theatre of the Air.* August 2 & 5, 1943.

"Magnificent Ambersons." Agnes starred in this two-part adaptation of Booth Tarkington's bestseller and recreation of her own acclaimed film performance as Fanny Minafer.

67. *The Adventures of Leonides Witherall.* September 7, 1943. CBS. Leonides Witherall, a British criminology professor at the Meredith School for Boys in the town of Dalton, and his housekeeper, Mrs. Mollet, who also heads a ladies' literary group, team up together to solve mysteries. This was the one-hour pilot to a short-lived mystery series, but Agnes, who plays Mrs. Mollet only participated in this initial episode.

68. *Ceiling Unlimited.* December 19, 1943. CBS.

This series was, in the words of radio historian John Dunning, "aggressively patriotic." The theme of the week is Christmas. Joseph Cotten writes "a letter to an unborn son." Cast: Joseph Cotten, Agnes Moorehead, Pedro De Cordoba, Lou Merrill, Hans Conried.

69. *The Jack Carson Show.* January 19, 1944–September 27, 1944. NBC.

Host: Jack Carson. Agnes had a recurring role as "Mrs. Freddy Martin," wife of Carson's bandleader, who thinks that Freddy is the real talent and Jack is a nothing.

Typical sketch:

> AM: (*to Freddy Martin*): Oh, hello, Frederick dear.
> JC: Oh, Mrs. Martin! Well, let's not beat around the bush — what d'ya know that's nasty!
> AM: Mr. Carson, you shouldn't talk to me like that after I just came from seeing one of your pictures — *The Hard Way!* And when you finished that big death scene, I cried, and cried, and cried!
> JC: Really?
> AM: Yes — but they wouldn't give me my money back!

70. *Orson Welles Almanac.* January 26, 1944–July 19, 1944. CBS. Host: Orson Welles. Regulars: Agnes Moorehead, Hans Conried, Ray Collins. Welles and many of his Mercury players appeared on this variety show which featured songs, skits and dramatic interludes such as dramatizations of short stories. Agnes had a recurring character as the head of the "Orson Welles Fan Club" and referred to the host as "Wellesy." Due to a running dispute with sponsor Mobil Oil, the show was short-lived.

71. *Ceiling Zero.* April 5, 1944. CBS.

The theme of the week is Easter. Cast: Joseph Cotten, Agnes Moorehead, Constance Moore.

72. *Fifth War Loan Drive.* June 12, 1944. CBS. Agnes, Orson Welles, Keenan Wynn, Walter Huston and President Roosevelt participate in this war bond drive, sponsored by the U.S. Treasury Dept.

73.   *Goodyear Theatre.* July 9, 1944.
      "Thief is an Ugly Word." Cast: Walter Pidgeon, Agnes Moorehead.

74.   *This is My Best.* April 10, 1945. CBS.
      "The Master of Ballantrae." Cast: Orson Welles, Ray Collins, Agnes Moorehead, Alan Napier. An
      adaptation of Robert Louis Stevenson's classic, produced and directed by Orson Welles.

75.   *Cavalcade of America.* June 18, 1945. NBC. "Party Line"

76.   *Cavalcade of America.* September 17, 1945. NBC.
      "Nellie Was a Lady." Agnes was cast as that cunning female reporter of the 19th century,
      Nellie Bly.

77.   *This is My Best.* September 17, 1945. CBS.
      "Colonel Paxton and the Haunted Horse." Agnes guest stars in this Orson Welles-produced and
      -directed program.

78.   *Hallmark Charlotte Greenwood Show.*
      October 14, 1945. NBC.
      Agnes guest-starred on this short-lived situation comedy
      as Dema Parker, Charlotte's secretary and friend.
      Conrad Binyon also had a part in this episode.

79.   *Calamity Jane.* March 1946. CBS.
      Agnes starred in this short-lived (three episodes) drama,
      not based on the Western heroine, but on a contemporary
      female reporter who works to expose racketeers and
      other bad guys. Dan Wolfe plays her grandfather, also
      the publisher of the newspaper she works at. Also starring
      William Johnstone and Cathy Lewis.

80.   *Radio Hall of Fame.* March 24, 1946. ABC.
      Agnes does a portion of her famous "Sorry, Wrong Number" on this program.

81.   *The Lady Esther Screen Guild Theatre.* April 1, 1946. CBS.
      "On Borrowed Time." Cast: Lionel Barrymore, Agnes Moorehead, Vincent Price. Barrymore and
      Agnes work together outside of the popular *Mayor of the Town* in this story about a man (Barrymore)
      who stalls death (Price). Agnes plays Demetria.

82.   *Philco Radio Hall of Fame.* March 24, 1946.
      Agnes again performs a portion of "Sorry, Wrong Number."

83.   *Cavalcade of America.* March 25, 1946. NBC. "The General's Wife."

84. *Amazing Mrs. Danbury.* April 2, 1946–June 16, 1946. CBS.

Agnes begins another short-lived series, this time a comedy about Mrs. Jonathan Danbury (Agnes), a sharp-tongued old woman and owner of the Danbury Department Store, and her domestic life with her daughter (Cathy Lewis) and son (Dan Wolfe).

85. *The Mercury Summer Theatre.* September 13, 1946. CBS.

"King Lear." Cast: Orson Welles, Agnes Moorehead, Edgar Barrier, Elliott Reid, Lurene Tuttle, Norman Field. A 30-minute adaptation of the Shakespeare classic.

86. *Stars in the Afternoon.* September 29, 1946. CBS.

Ozzie and Harriet host this preview of the new CBS 1946–47 radio season. Agnes and Lionel Barrymore preview the fifth season of *The Mayor of the Town.*

87. *Cavalcade of America.* October 14, 1946. NBC.

"The Hickory Tree." Agnes plays the role of Andrew Jackson's wife, Elizabeth.

88. *Armstrong Theatre of Today.* October 19, 1946. CBS.

"The Great Burden." Agnes plays Helen Seaton in a story of a woman who helps her husband find a new life. Two years earlier, Ralph Seaton had been convicted of bank theft, a crime he didn't commit, and was sent to prison. New evidence clears him but he must readjust to the outside world.

89. *Barbed Wire Sky.* May 6, 1947. ABC.

"ABC in cooperation with the United Jewish Appeal in a special program dedicated to 170,000 children who survived the Nazi concentration camps." John Garfield, Agnes Moorehead, Paul Muni, Edward G. Robinson and Sylvia Sidney each tell a story. Agnes explains why and how United Jewish Appeal was dedicated.

90. *Armstrong Theatre of Today.* June 28, 1947.

"Mama Love." Agnes plays Mary Bronson, a mother who learns a lesson while teaching her son the meaning of responsibility. She spoils her youngest son who later causes a hit-and-run accident. She tries to cover for him. Eventually, she convinces him to turn himself into the police.

91. *The Sunny Side of the Atom.* June 30, 1947. CBS.

Agnes plays a reporter who does research on the benefits to mankind of the atom.

92. *Mystery in the Air.* August 14, 1947. CBS.

"The Lodger." Peter Lorre hosts and stars in this episode about a serial killer in London. Agnes guest stars.

93. *Theatre Guild on The Air.* January 1, 1948. ABC.
"The Little Foxes." Agnes stars as Regina Gibbens in this adaptation of Lillian Hellman's famous play. Thomas Mitchell and Zachary Scott co-star.

94. *The Camel Screen Guild Theatre.* February 9, 1948. CBS.
"Johnny Come Lately." Cast: James Cagney, Agnes Moorehead. The story of a reporter who takes on corruption in a small town.

95. *The Academy Awards.* March 20, 1948.
Dick Powell and Agnes co-host. Agnes also presents the award for color cinematography.

96. *In Your Name.* March 22, 1948. Syndicated.
Question and Answer. Agnes participates in this drama on behalf of the Red Cross fund campaign.

97. *Ellery Queen.* March 25, 1948. ABC.
"The Farmer's Daughter." Agnes guest stars as the week's "Guest Armchair Detective" who tries to guess the identity of the killer.

98. *Betty Crocker Magazine of the Air.* August 31, 1948. Syndicated.
Agnes guest stars on this cooking, recipe and interview program.

99. *Lynn Looks at Hollywood.* November 12, 1948.
Agnes Moorehead guests on this interview program.

100. *One Great Hour.* March 26, 1949. CBS.
"World Retreat." Agnes joins Gregory Peck, Ida Lupino, Glenn Ford, Roddy McDowall, and President Truman in this fund-raiser to aid displaced persons in Asia and Europe.

101. *Operation Dawn.* May 22, 1949.
Himan Brown produced this program on behalf of United Jewish Appeal. Hosted by Al Jolson, with Agnes making a guest appearance.

102. *Anacin Hollywood Star Theatre.* June 4, 1949
"Return from Nowhere." Agnes introduces, but doesn't act in, this play and later has a short interview with Leo Penn, the young actor who was highlighted in the episode. Leo Penn is the father of actor Sean Penn. In the conclusion, Leo impersonates Lionel Barrymore as the "Mayor" to Agnes' "Marilly."

103. *Armstrong Theatre of Today.* February 25, 1950. CBS.
"Doctor's Wife." Tells the story of Dr. Homer Williams, MD, who, 25 years earlier, hung out his shingle in Gainesville, TX and, with the help of his devoted wife, Martha (Agnes), has taken care of his neighbors ever since. As the town's population doubles, Homer takes fewer and shorter vacations and works harder than ever, finally another doctor arrives in town, but old Doc Williams continues to be as busy as ever.

104. *Edgar Bergen with Charlie McCarthy*. November 26, 1950. CBS.
    Hosts: Edgar Bergen and Charlie McCarthy. Guest Star: Agnes Moorehead.
    Agnes appears in a sketch featuring Charlie as Rip Van Winkle and Agnes as his wife.

105. *Hedda Hopper Show*. April 1, 1951. Syndicated.
    Host: Hedda Hopper. The Hollywood columnist interviews Agnes.

106. *Hallmark Playhouse*. January 17, 1952. CBS.
    "Madam Claire." Agnes plays Lady Claire Gregory.

107. *This is Your FBI*. February 15, 1952. ABC.
    Cast: Stacy Harris, Michael Ann Barrett, William Conrad, Bea Benaderet, Georgia Ellis, J.C. Flippen.
    Guest Star: Agnes Moorehead.

108. *Inner Sanctum*. June 29, 1952. CBS.
    "Terror by Night." Agnes stars in this suspense drama about a woman being pursued by a
    killer. Produced and directed by Himan Brown. Cast: Agnes Moorehead, Karl Swenson, Everett
    Sloane.

109. *Inner Sanctum*. July 27, 1952. CBS.
    "Murder Prophet." Agnes plays a woman whose first and second husbands have been killed.
    Cast: Agnes Moorehead, Arnold Moss, Everett Sloane.

110. *Best Plays*. August 10, 1952. NBC.
    "Uncle Harry." This series adapted famous plays for the radio. Uncle Harry was one of Broadway's
    biggest hits in the early 40's. Uncle Harry hates being called "uncle" and is far from jolly. Joseph
    Schildleraut, who played "Uncle Harry" in the Broadway production, recreates his role, with Agnes as
    his wife Lettie.

111. *Stagestruck*. April 4, 1954. CBS.
    "The Story of Spring on Broadway." Mike Wallace hosts this look at the spring season on Broadway
    with guests Agnes Moorehead, Danny Kaye, and Shirley Booth.

112. *Hallmark Hall of Fame*. November 21, 1954. NBC.
    A tribute to the late Lionel Barrymore, who died on November 15, 1954. Agnes appears to pay tribute
    to her longtime *Mayor of the Town* colleague.

113. *NBC Radio Theatre*. January 8, 1956. NBC.
    "The Snake Pit." Cast: Agnes Moorehead, Lawrence Dobkin, Alice Reinhart, Vincent Price (host).
    Agnes stars as a woman wrongly committed to an insane asylum.

114. Easter Sunrise Service. April 1, 1956. Syndicated.
    Agnes Moorehead participates in a sunrise service on Easter Sunday from the Hollywood Bowl. Agnes

recited "The Salutation of the Dawn":

> ". . . Listen to the Salutation of the Dawn. Look to this day for it is life, the very life of life. In it, brief course lie all the realities and vanities of our existence . . . "

115. *Special Delivery: Vietnam.* August 24, 1969. Syndicated.

A radio-thon with Agnes Moorehead, Ann-Margret, Cesar Romero, Cliff Arquette, Eva Gabor, George Jessel, Jack Carter, Jack Webb, Lucille Ball, Raymond Burr, Nanette Fabray, Pat Boone, Phyllis Diller, Shirley Jones, Sonny and Cher.

116. *The CBS Radio Mystery Theatre.* January 6, 1974. CBS.

"The Old Ones Are Hard to Kill." Himan Brown produced and directed this anthology series of mystery stories. Cast: Agnes Moorehead, Leon Janney, Roger DeKoven, E.G. Marshall (host).

117. *The CBS Radio Mystery Theatre.* January 26, 1974. CBS.

"The Ring of Truth." Cast: Agnes Moorehead, Ian Martin, Mandel Kramer, Santos Ortega, E.G. Marshall (host). Agnes' final radio performance.

V

Stage Appearances of Agnes Moorehead

Gloria Mundi.

A one-act drama. Presented by the American Academy of Dramatic Arts, NY. Agnes played Mrs. Farnsworth.

Chinese Love.

A one-act drama. Presented by the American Academy of Dramatic Arts, NY. Agnes played Ah Mee.

The First Year.

A one-act drama. Presented by the American Academy of Dramatic Arts, NY. Agnes played Hattie.

The Last of Mrs. Cheney.

A three-act play. Presented by the Academy of Dramatic Arts, NY. Agnes played Mrs. Wynton. This play starred fellow student Rosalind Russell, with Jack Lee in a featured part.

Captain Applejack.

A three-act play. Presented by the Academy of Dramatic Arts, NY. Agnes had the leading female role of Anna Veleska.

The Springboard.

A three-act play. Presented by the Academy of Dramatic Arts, NY. Agnes played Rhoda Brice.

The Best People.

A three-act drama. Presented by the Academy of Dramatic Arts, NY. Agnes played Mrs. Lenox.

Courage.

    Opened October 8, 1928. Ritz Theatre. Agnes was an understudy and may have played a bit part in this play about a widow who struggles to raise seven children. (283 performances)

Soldiers and Women.

    Opened January 2, 1929. Ritz Theatre. Agnes was understudy to Sarat Lahiri and actually got to replace her for a few performances in this play which takes place at a military outpost in India. (64 performances)

Scarlet Pages.

    Opened September 9, 1929. Morosco Theatre. Agnes had a small part in this play about a woman attorney defending another woman of a murder charge. Elsie Ferguson and Claire Luce starred. (78 performances)

Candle Light.

    Opened September 30, 1929. Empire Theatre. Agnes had a small part in this comedy starring Leslie Howard and Gertrude Lawrence about a maid and valet who pretend to be royalty. (129 performances)

All the King's Horses.

    Opened January 30, 1934. Shubert Theatre. Agnes has a small part in this story of a king and film actor who look alike and decide to switch places. (120 performances)

Don Juan in Hell.

    Opened January 27, 1951, Stockton, California. This is the show that really launched Agnes's theatre career. Starring with Charles Boyer, Charles Laughton and Sir Cedric Hardwicke, the four actors became known as "The First Drama Quartette." Agnes plays Dona Ana, a 77-year-old woman who dies and, to her disbelief, winds up in Hell along with her ex-suitor Don Juan (Boyer), her father, the Statue (Hardwicke) who Juan killed in a duel over her honor, and, of course, Satan (Laughton). In the course of the play, the 77-year-old Donna Ana suddenly changes into the 27-year-old girl she was when she first met and fell in love with Don Juan. The four actors conduct a philosophical discourse on the meaning of life, death, chivalry and honor. The "First Drama Quartette" conducted six major tours of the United States, Canada and Britain between 1951–1954, with major Broadway appearances:

        OCTOBER 21, 1951: CARNEGIE HALL (1 PERFORMANCE), SOLD OUT IN 8 HOURS.
        NOVEMBER 29, 1951: CENTURY THEATRE (39 PERFORMANCES)
        APRIL 6, 1952: PLYMOUTH THEATRE (64 PERFORMANCES)

An Evening with Agnes Moorehead.

    Opened March 13, 1954, Academy of Music, Brooklyn, New York. This was the New York debut of Agnes' acclaimed one-woman show, better known as "The Fabulous Redhead." A two-hour collection of dramatic and comic readings, it was a Moorehead perennial for the next twenty years with hundreds of engagements across the country and around the world. In the mid-sixties it became known as *Come Closer, I'll Give You an Earful.*

The Rivalry.

Agnes, Raymond Massey and Martin Gabel toured cross-country and in Canada, with this Norman Corwin-written play on the Lincoln-Douglas debates, between September 1957–January 1958. Agnes and Massey dropped out of the play before its New York opening, which closed after only eight performances. Agnes played Mrs. Stephen A. Douglas, with Gabel as her husband and Massey as Lincoln.

The Pink Jungle.

Opened October 14, 1959 in San Francisco and closed December 12, 1959 in Boston. Trouble-plagued production, with Agnes cast as the deceased head of a cosmetic company whose spirit returns to watch over her company and her sons. Ginger Rogers co-starred in the musical-comedy and felt overshadowed by Agnes' performance. Ginger's mother suggested to producer Paul Gregory that Ginger would improve if he would cut Agnes' performance. The play closed before its scheduled Broadway opening.

Prescription Murder.

Opened: January 15, 1962 (San Francisco), closed: May 26, 1962 (Boston). Mystery about a doctor (Joseph Cotten) who murders his wife (Agnes) so he can marry his mistress (Patricia Medina). The doctor believes he has committed the perfect murder only to have it unravel when a dogged police detective named Columbo (Thomas Mitchell) is assigned to the case. Agnes has the distinction of playing the first murder victim Lt. Columbo investigates.

Lord Pengo.

Opened November 19, 1962, Royale Theatre, New York City. Agnes is reunited with Charles Boyer in this story of an art dealer who tries to get his son to follow in his footsteps. Agnes plays his loyal secretary, Miss Swanson. The cast made a cross-country tour before beginning a five-month run on Broadway.

High Spirits.

Opened June 7, 1965, Dallas, Texas. Agnes played medium Madame Arcanti in this summer stock musical which played two weeks at the state fair grounds in Dallas, Texas as part of the Dallas Summer Musical Theatre.

Don Juan in Hell.

Opened January 15, 1973, Palace Theatre, NYC. Agnes, Ricardo Montalban (Don Juan), Edward Mulhare (The Devil) and Paul Henreid (Commander) star in this revival of Agnes' most famous stage role, directed by John Houseman. Prior to the New York opening, the play played dates in Philadelphia, Pittsburgh, Wilmington, Washington, D.C., Cincinnati and Toronto.

Gigi.

Opened November 13, 1973, Uris Theatre, NYC. Agnes played Aunt Alicia in this stage production of the famous movie musical. Agnes was in poor health when she began the cross-country tour and ended up leaving the play in early January 1974, after its opening on Broadway, due to her poor health. Arlene Francis replaced her and the play closed a month later.

EPILOGUE

It's nearly impossible to pen a foreword to this revised, eloquent and complete biography of Agnes Moorehead. Whatever I write here about the award-winning actress will pale in comparison to what author Charles Tranberg has already so thoroughly relayed within the contents of this book. As I said when I read the first edition, and repeat to anyone who asks, *I Love The Illusion: The Life and Career of Agnes Moorehead* is ONE OF THE MOST COMPREHENSIVE AND INTELLIGENTLY-WRITTEN BIOGRAPHIES EVER PUBLISHED, BEWITCHED-RELATED, OR OTHERWISE. THIS BOOK NEEDS TO BE READ; PLAIN AND SIMPLE, WITHOUT QUESTION; BAR-NONE. And that's not faint praise; nor is it delusion or fantasy. It's real; as legitimate as the manifold talents that imbued the physical, psychological, spiritual and theatrical nature of Agnes Moorehead.

Whether portraying Endora, the feisty magical mother to Elizabeth Montgomery's saintly Samantha Stephens on TV's classic sitcom *Bewitched*, singing neurotic with her Oscar-nominated performance as Fanny Minafer in *The Magnificent Ambersons*, voicing control and graceful munificence and posture as Sister Cluny in *The Singing Nun*, or even grunting herself into silence as a farm woman battling tiny aliens in her classic *Invaders* episode of TV's *The Twilight Zone*, Moorehead's creative spark ignited any big or small stage and screen that was fortunate enough to host her presence. She was *old school*, personally and professionally, but retained and embraced an open mind-set that helped to catapult her status as a respected actress and human being; a co-existence that remains timeless and accessible to her multitude of adoring fans via massive body of work. Each one of her performances was different from the next. Though she created personas that stemmed from every walk of life, low or high, not one of her characters lacked spine or courage; those traits — those *gifts* — belonged solely to Moorehead. In suit, *I Love The Illusion* doesn't cater to those gifts; it christens them, itself becoming a gift to the reader in the process.

In this new Internet age of quick answers to thoughtless questions and illiterate treks on the information highway, *I Love The Illusion* offers a patient, steady and sturdy study of insight into one of the great theatrical minds of all time. Agnes Moorehead commanded any stage, motion picture or TV show, special and movie on which she appeared. Charles Tranberg now does the same with the written word in this detailed true-to-life tale of an amazing and gutsy actress who paved and sustained the path for anyone whose interest is great in any creative or technical skill, craft or art of fancy. Whatever your delight, doctrine or purpose is with reading this book, you'll walk away with not only a complete understanding of the personal and professional existence of a fine actress, but a fine understanding of how to have a complete life and career.

In short, anyone with a goal is indebted to Agnes Moorehead for displaying how to have and make a successful and honest living. Fortunately, that hefty price has been paid in full by Charles Tranberg, whose painstaking research, prose and revelations into the glorious days of Agnes Moorehead has transformed *I Love The Illusion* into an engrossing and provocative reality.

HERBIE J PILATO
AUTHOR, *BEWITCHED FOREVER*
JUNE 23, 2006

LECTURE

Thank you for coming this evening.

I thought to begin with how this book came about and some of the research that went into it and then I'll be very happy to take your questions.

About three and a half years ago I was doing research at the Wisconsin State Historical Society here in Madison. It's a wonderful place and I could spend hours there just going through many of those historical documents. After I had finished with the research I had gone there to do — I felt I had time on my hands and was interested in looking at some other material — Just for fun.

So I'm strolling through there list of collections and something suddenly caught my eyes—The Papers of Agnes Moorehead spanning the years 1928-1974. In fact, 159 boxes of papers. Well, this intrigued me. I obviously knew who Agnes Moorehead was having been a fan of "Bewitched" and also a fan of classic films. So I decided to order a few boxes and see what the collection held.

I wasn't disappointed.

Probably three hours later, and it's a Saturday, I remember that because that's the only day due to work that I can get to the archives. It's time to close and it was very tough to stop reading. I was hooked and wanted to see more.

I think then and there I determined that I wanted to try and write a book about Agnes. There had never been a comprehensive biography of her life and I felt that these 159 boxes of papers was a great place to start.

The papers consist of:

1)   Scrapbooks.

Agnes kept scrapbooks containing all kinds of treasures. Reviews, including reviews of most of her films, many of her television appearances and all of her stage appearances, even the stage work she did at the American Academy of Dramatic Art in New York City in the late 1920's. She was incredibly fair to future biographers too, she didn't only keep the good reviews but she also kept bad reviews.

These scrapbooks also contained many newspaper and magazine articles on her life and career.

The Scrapbooks included party and dinner invitations, requests for personal appearances, offers of acting jobs, letters from fans, co-workers and friends alike. Christmas and Birthday cards. Itineraries for her stage tours. Even an occasional bill she had to pay or had paid. There are telegrams from people like Orson Welles, Bette Davis, Joan Crawford, Helen Hayes, Hume Cronyn, Charles Laughton, Joan Fontaine, Rosalind Russell, among many others.

In addition to Scrapbooks, the papers included papers and note books dealing with her education with the American Academy of Dramatic Arts — the different types of classes she took such as Shakespeare, Dance, Speech, and even Fencing.

There were lectures she delivered over the years — with scribbled notes in her own handwriting.

There was her much scribbled on Acceptance speech to the New York Film Critics who had voted her the Best Actress of 1942 for her performance in "The Magnficent Ambersons."

The collection also includes many of her film, stage, radio and television scripts — again with her handwritten notes on characterization and emphasize. You get into the mind of how she would interpret a part. Many of the scripts include scenes you never saw before because they also included drafts which were later discarded along with the eventual shooting script — *The Bewitched* scripts in particular.

Once in a while I found notes on scripts such as a grocery list, a Christmas list, people she wanted to invite to a party and even in one script a half worked crossword puzzle — discarded after the shooting had been completed and forgotten.

Going through these papers and scripts was fun — the sense of discovery truly kept me interested and told me a great deal about Agnes Moorehead as both an actress and an individual.

While still researching nearly every Saturday and whenever else possible at the Archives of the State Historical Society, I also knew I had to branch out and actually talk to people who knew and worked with her.

It was a slow process at first. I would send out a bunch of letters and get no response or if I got any response at all it was "Return to Sender."

Finally, a break through. I spoke to an actress named Kasey Rogers who played the second Mrs. Larry Tate on *Bewitched*. She also gave me the title of the book, "I Love the Illusion" because she recalled, when asked why she became an actress, Agnes would dramatically extend her arms and say, "I Love the Illusion!"

From Kasey I was able to get contact information for Bill Asher, the director of Bewitched and one-time husband of Elizabeth Montgomery. And on and on.

It was always a thrill to come home and find a message on my machine from people like Jane Wyman, Karl Malden, Rose Marie, Jane Wyatt, Himan Brown, Norman Corwin and many others. I kept those messages sometimes for weeks without erasing them.

The hardest interview to get was one I felt I needed more than any other and that was with Debbie Reynolds. Debbie was Agnes' closest confidant and friend for the last 12 years or so of her life. They had a mother/daughter and teacher/pupil type of relationship and some people believe it went beyond that. For over two years I sent several letters requesting an interview with Miss Reynolds. Finally one day, a message from her secretary stating that she felt she could arrange something. Three months passed and finally a message from a hesitant Debbie Reynolds who said, "I've been trying to answer (by pen) these questions you sent me but maybe we should talk."

I could go for that.

She was incredibly giving and we spoke in two interviews totaling well over three hours. She answered every question I asked and she shed light on some mysteries in Agnes' life such as Agnes' relationship with her foster son Sean.

I could still hear the tenderness in her voice when she spoke of Agnes — some thirty years after her death.

I also had very helpful and revealing conversations with two important people in Agnes' life her long time theatrical producer, Paul Gregory, who produced *Don Juan in Hell* and Agnes' acclaimed one-woman shows and he didn't pull punches. He admired her but he didn't put her on a pedestal — he saw her as the flesh and blood person she was and his remembrances were very vivid.

Another quite helpful series of interviews was with a gentleman named Quint Benedecci, who spent several years as Agnes correspondence secretary and later her road manager. He gave some wonderful insights in the private woman behind the acclaimed actress.

Then there was interviews with many folks from Reedsburg, WI—the community where Agnes father, Dr. John Moorehead, was for five years Pastor of the Presbyterian Church and later after he died, Agnes' mother, Mollie moved back to and spent the final 52 years of her long life (she died at age 106 in 1990 — outliving her daughter by 16 years). Agnes visited her mother many times over those years and thanks to these folks I got to know something about her father and especially her mother Mollie — as well as Agnes. I'm especially indebted to a gentleman named Gordon Emery who was kind of a caregiver for Mollie for an extended interview and also for taking me to different sites around Reedsburg which figured in the Agnes Moorehead story.

So in the end I interviewed nearly forty people. I am indebted to everyone who gave me their time and recollections. It added great color and a good deal of truth to the manuscript I wrote.

Between these interviews and the archives at the Wisconsin State Historical Society, I also was able to get valuable material from the Billy Rose Library in New York City which holds a series of letters exchanged between Agnes and her long time secretary Georgia Johnstone. Some great insights into Agnes' thinking came from those letters.

Then there was the Orson Welles Papers at the Lily Library in Bloomington, Indiana. Of course Orson Welles figures very large in the career of Agnes Moorehead since she was a charter member of his acclaimed radio group, The Mercury Theatre and later went to Hollywood with Welles to appear in his productions of *Citizen Kane* and *The Magnificent Ambersons* — her two greatest films and probably his two greatest films as well.

And the Paul Gregory Papers at the University of Wyoming in Laramie — which included a blistering letter from Mr. Gregory to Ginger Rogers who he believed had sabotaged his stage production of a musical-comedy play *The Pink Jungle* because he believed that Ginger was jealous of Agnes, who was her co-star.

It took three years of research and writing and the result is the book, *I Love the Illusion: The Life and Career of Agnes Moorehead*. Over that time I knew I would finish a manuscript but I didn't know if I, somebody who never wrote professionally before, could sell a book on Agnes Moorehead. Luckily, I found BearManor Media, which specializes in books on old time radio and films of the golden age and the publisher was enthusiastic about the idea of a book on Moorehead and he asked me to send a few sample chapters. And lucky again because he liked it, and sent out a contract.

I came away from this project with an enhanced admiration for the private Agnes Moorehead. She was a woman who was very driven, but she had to be. She was married twice, her first marriage to a man who turned to alcohol when her career eclipsed his and then to a man who she felt later used her to get ahead. She had great values and a unshakeable belief system. She could be rigid, but she was always true to herself. She was the consummate professional and in the words of virtually every colleague I interviewed, one of the finest actresses of her time. I think my admiration for her is the most deeply felt in the last two years of her life, when slowly dying of cancer, she never gave up, not for an instant. She kept the pain to herself and kept working, because she knew that without the work she would probably die and die quickly. In those last two years she appeared on cross country tours of two big productions: *Don Juan in Hell* in 1972 and *Gigi* in 1973. She appeared in three television movies and a mini-series and made a number of guest appearances on episodic television. Finally, in January, 1974 after she had completed two final radio dramas, she suddenly quit "Gigi" which was appearing on Broadway because as she would later say, "I just can't stand up any more." She quietly went to the Mayo Clinic in Rochester, Mn and died on April 30, 1974. With the exception of Debbie Reynolds, not one of the people I spoke too, had any idea just how ill she was — and that is just the way she wanted it.

I'll be happy to take some questions.

Finally I think this letter that Agnes wrote to a sixteen year old fan sums up her philosophy of life:

Dear Miss Patton,

In regards to your question: What was the most important thing I learned in High School? I have always, even at a tender age, looked for cultural things in my life; my interests leaning towards dancing, art, English literature, etc. I imagine they were very important to me because they were what I could do most successfully. Never have I regretted discovering at an early age what my interests were and following through with my ambitions, regardless of discouragements and difficult times. Ballet, in particular, taught me precise discipline. I learned that I could not take enjoyment from dance without giving something in return — hard work and discipline, not only of body, but of mind . . . I hope the above will be some help to you.

Sincerely,
Agnes Moorehead

INDEX

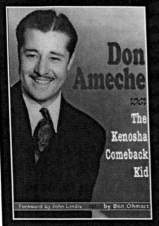